a treasury of TRIVIA

a treasury of TRIVIA

Frankly, dear Eve, I don't give a damn!

donner & eve paige spencer

cover design & illustrations; bryan stahmer

DONEVE DESIGNS, INC.
SARATOGA, CALIFORNIA

Our special thanks
to Jeff and Cybele Gold
and the I.D.H.H.B. staff.

First Edition

ISBN: 0-89715-000-7
Library of Congress Catalog Number: 78-56366

Introduction

Early universities bunched the first three of the seven liberal arts — Grammar, Logic and Rhetoric — and called it the *trivium*. Obviously things haven't changed much. (By the way, the remaining liberal arts today are Football, Dwindling, Preparing for Anonymity and Uncontrolled Weeping.) But we digress.

What you've got in this book, Buster and Busteresses, is a disoriented view of our world as seen through the bottoms of rose-colored highball glasses...in short, it reads with the same precise good sense one finds in a government press release. For instance, you will discover, as we did, that the Index has been lost. It's of little consequence: people who need an index to trivia have picked their last nit as far as we're concerned. You'll also notice there are no cross-references. We're just too good-natured for that sort of thing.

For those who must continually verify that the book they purchased has some content, we have thoughtfully supplied an entire table just full of content.

If you find the type we have selected strangely large and uncomfortably legible, put it down to a quirk we have about books being printed for the purpose of being read. However, should you be addicted to eyestrain, send us $12,500 in unmarked bills of small denomination and we'll have the usual miniscule *squinter's edition* made up just for you.

One pre-publication reviewer predicted "...and no one will be safe as long as these authors are free to walk our streets." To her we say, "Fudge!" Furthermore, the moment some demented soul buys copy number one, we're having ourselves committed.

Other reviewers have been exceedingly kind. One chap named Homer (no last name given) said, "*A Treasury of Trivia* is the best thing I've read since the *Iliad.*" A rural type wrote us: "Your book scared away the crows alright, but it killed the corn, too." It apparently appeals to the young, as well, since one innocent miss said, "I intended to read your book with Alarm, but she was picked up again." And what authors wouldn't feel exhilirated by this note: "The Horde loved it!" signed Kub. and G. Khan.

We respectfully call your attention to the final pages, on which you'll find the ANNUAL TRIVIA AWARDS. Here you will discover an opportunity for putting you own tiny minds to work, for which we can promise an equally tiny remuneration. Of course, when it comes to trivia, money's not the object. As Chalmers Piskitfowler often said,

"Throughout my life I have learned, nonetheless, that it's the little I know of much that enhances my overall." We couldn't have said it better, if at all.

On the matter of reference sources, we point with pride to the backs of toothpaste tubes, instruction manuals for assembling children's toys, *Fungicide Annual*, Anthony Jugular's *Annotated Syllogisms for Asthmatics* and the telephone directory of Fid, Kansas.

Mark Twain was to have written this Introduction, but his literary agent claims Mr. Twain has come down with a rather serious case of the deads. We had a feeling he'd weasel out of it some way.

D.S. and E.P.S.
Chortling-On-Smirk,
Lower Blather, Bankmill — 1978 or
thereabouts.

TABLE OF CONTENTS

CHAPTER ONE

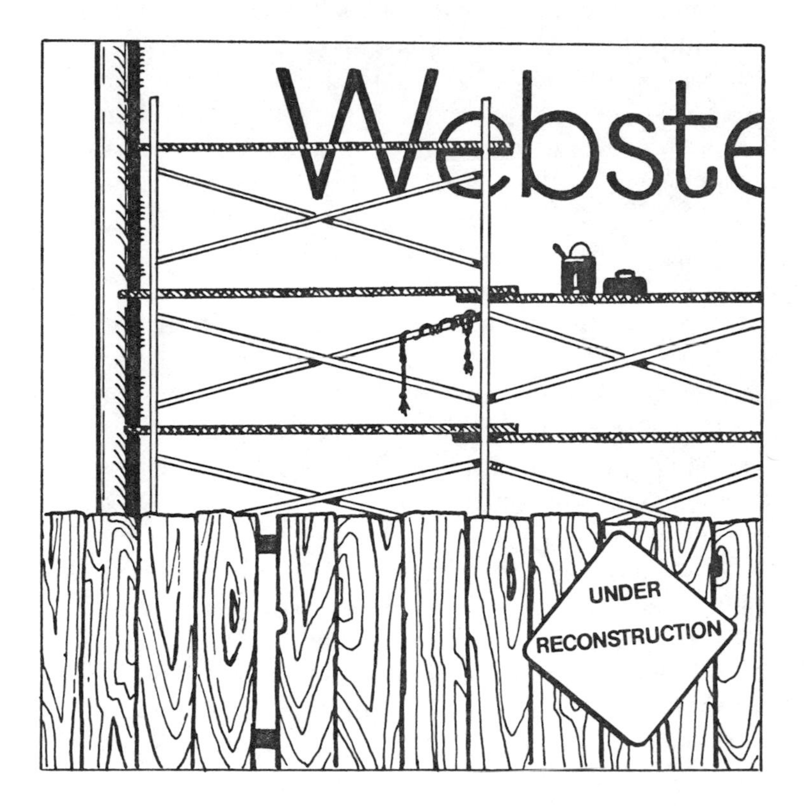

Yeah, Like, You Know, Man...Like Language

Bite your tongue, S.I. Hayakawa! Anti-semanticism is on the loose in our land!

Things were just dandy when our speech was midway between a slurred mumble and a hiccup, but now it appears we are to be treated to a generation or more of the genuinely inarticulate. We thrilled to a recent example of this laryngeal paralysis. A TV interviewer, in a doomed effort to extract something intelligible from a rising young folk-rock singer, asked, "How did you first get into music?"

"Like, you know, man...I was like, you know...maybe in my, oh, teens, man, you know, like, oh...wow, like fifteen — yeah, like fifteen, you know..." and he squirmed about in a charming imitation of a drunk sprawled in a vat of wet noodles, clawing for support.

He rambled on, displaying the ingenious manner in which his vocal apparatus, although obviously disconnected from his brain, functioned on sheer grit. He rolled his eyes, put his hands out palms up and then ran them through his lank hair...perhaps seeking the *on button* somewhere in the tangled strands. The longer we pulled for him, actually praying that at least one coherent analogy might follow the torrent of *like* and *you know*, the more we came to realize the kid was figuratively eating broth with a fork.

At last, scrooching down in his chair, he waved one hand as if removing a network of cobwebs and spat out, "Guitar, like, you know, man...and I played...wow...like."

His revelation so stunned us, we fell into a low-grade stupor and never did find out what he did with the guitar...although we suspected he may have eaten it, thus accounting for his remarkable skill at gibberish.

Obviously language has risen to the top of the trivia heap. And we're ready for it, with an ashcan full of dislocated facts and mangled phrases guaranteed to rekindle your disinterest.

We're certain you will learn as much of language as did the father who asked his teenage daughter how she did on her English exam.

"Like, not bad, Daddy. You know, first they asked...like my name...you know. I got fifty percent on that," she said with understandable pride.

The Loom of Language: He said, "You made that up out of whole cloth." She replied, "I don't believe in material things."

LANGUAGE, FOR REAL!

It is said there are some 1,500 different languages being spoken in the world today. The history of some is totally obscure. For instance, no one has figured out the evolution of the Basque language. Maltese, on the other hand, is a product of many conquests of the Mediterranean island of Malta — its origin is Arabic, but it's written in the Latin alphabet. Any Celtic tongue is difficult to master. For one thing, there aren't many active verbs. To express the idea of *hearing* will come out something like *a sound in my ears.*

The first peoples using alphabetic writing went about it any way they pleased, going from left to right and from top to bottom if that were their mood at the time. Didn't really matter much, because so few people could read. Those who could read figured out the pattern.

It is a very sad thing that nowadays there is so little useless information. *Oscar Wilde*

WE UNDERSTAND THE WHOLE. NOW FOR THE PARTS!

Many idiomatic expressions, such as *through thick and thin* for enduring good times and bad, hold their original concept intact. However, many times the individual words are now quite mysterious. For instance, in the expression above, does *thick* apply to the good times or the bad? In pre-Chaucer England, horsemen found the going tough through *thickets* and easy through *thin* woods.

Forlorn hope is a brain-bender although the implication of practically no hope is correct, the words literally don't mean that. The Dutch, when assigning soldiers an extremely risky task, called the band a *verloren* (wasted) *hoop* (troop). The English added their own spelling and lost the original words altogether while maintaining the concept.

Fishermen know that a *gaff* is a pole with a hook at its end, so the expression to *stand the gaff* must mean to take punishment. Yes...and no. In a certain English dialect, *gaff* was intended to be insulting. So, it's more likely that the term came from the latter...or maybe both.

At first blush is hard to figure out until one learns that *blush* meant glimpse a few centuries ago.

How about *dyed in the wool* for unalterable opinion. As early as the biblical days, cloth-makers knew that wool dyed *before* it was made into yarn maintained its color without alteration for a longer time.

Oddly enough, wool has much to do with the expression to *beat the tar out of* something, or someone. Scotch shepherds accidentally let the shears slip once in a while, cutting the sheep. To prevent infection, they smeared the cut with tar. The next time that sheep was to be sheared, they had to beat the tar out of the wool first.

Not dry behind the ears yet for naive also comes from the rural life. This one got started in America and referred to the fact that a small indentation in the back of the ears of newborn animals was the last section of hide to dry.

Two common, but apparently disparate expressions, stem from one age-old practice...bringing pigs to market. The first — *to buy a pig in a poke* —makes good sense knowing that farmers brought their pigs to market in a *poke* (or sack). Not wishing the pig to escape, they kept the sack tightly closed. Thus, the buyer often made a purchase sight unseen. This led a few crafty pig breeders to substitute a cat for a

RIDDLE: The capitalized letter *gamma* repeated four times is a symbol called a *gammadion*. What else is it called?

ANSWER: Swastika! For some convoluted reason, *swastika* comes from a Sanskrit word for *well being*.

pig now and then. However, if the cat got loose, in truth the farmer had *let the cat out of the bag.*

THE FARMER'S WIFE!
1st farmer's wife: You ain't got no eggs, is you?
2nd farmer's wife: I ain't said I ain't.
1st farmer's wife: Well, I ain't asked
you ain't you ain't, I asked you
ain't you is. You ain't is you?
2nd farmer's wife: I ain't.

CAENFETISH!

Herbert Caen, while roasting a scarlet-crested citizen over an open typewriter, was struck by three dots...squarely in the middle of his afterthought...and has been a hopeless trivialitic ever since.

We like to think Paul Anka's family name comes from the Egyptian ***ankh****, symbol of life. What do you like to think?*

WE CAUGHT SHIELDS SPEAKING TO YARNELL!

Just because Shields and Yarnell are known as *mimes*, doesn't mean they can't speak lines. After all, in ancient Greece a drama that made a travesty of life was called a *mime*...and so were its actors...and to add confusion, the dialogue was called *mime,* also. *Mime, all mime!*

We never saw the end of ***The Trail of the Lonesome Pine****. Did Henry Fonda catch the tree?*

VERNACULAR OF THE TWENTIES...

America in the 1920's saw the era of *flaming youth*. Original description, eh? Not exactly. The old Bard of Avon in Hamlet wrote, "To flaming youth let virtue be as wax and melt in her own fire."

A darb of a lounge lizard, while spifflicated, was filling a sheba with banana oil — telling her how she was the bee's knees and asking her if it was copacetic to get ossified with him in his struggle buggy which, even without cheaters, she could see was the cat't meow.

In case you didn't grow up in the 1920's, the above translates as follows: An elegant habitue of speakeasies, while drunk, was telling a girl with sex appeal that she was wonderful and asking her if it was okay to get drunk with him in his car which, even without glasses, she could see was an utter marvel.

Also keep in mind that the *rumble seat* is a lot older than the Model A Ford. It was an uncomfortable contraption attached to the rear of horse-drawn carriages where the servants were privileged to ride.

Apparently polite conversation has entered the realm of prostitution. A lady of the evening recently remarked to a gentleman, "It's been a business doing pleasure with you."

THE LADY OR THE FOX!

What is the *foxy lady* of the 1970's really like? One college boy readily admitted that *foxy* was the new word for *sexy*. Another said, "Built, you know!" Built like a fox? What a horrid thought! A third claimed that a *foxy* lady was a girl who knew her way around. And a fourth, giving it all he had, mumbled, "Aw, man, you know...I mean... *foxy*." A definition beyond words.

A dictionary definition of *foxy* ranges from *foxlike in disposition or looks* to *defective in some way* as from decay. If either of those apply, *foxy* ladies must not be in great demand.

Dictionaries also refer to a definition of *sour*...unpleasant tasting, especially wine or beer. As early as 1772, a certain Robert Beverly described some of the grapes of Virginia as "of rank taste when ripe, resembling the smell of a fox, from when they are called fox-grapes." That definition is enough to make a man give up wine *and* women, leaving him only *song* for solace in his lonely hours.

Among expressions we don't miss is "Quick, Herman, the Flit." (To the post-Flit generations: Flit was an evil-smelling insect spray.)

THAT'S THE TICKET!

Many people would feel linguistically naked if they lacked a current expression of affirmation. *Right on! I dig it!*

Remember *you ain't just whistlin' Dixie? Yeah man,* it's *hunky-dory* with me.

This need to agree verbally isn't new or even recent. Around the 1800's they were saying, "That's etiquette." Through mispronunciation or plain sloppy diction, it became *that's the ticket.*

*People who are **into** music or **into** sports or **into** anything should hop **into** a tub of boiling oil without delay!*

RIDDLE: On formal occasions is it more proper to refer to Dan Cupid as Daniel Cupid?

ANSWER: Only if you want to appear foolish. *Dan* is an old title of respect, much like *sir*.

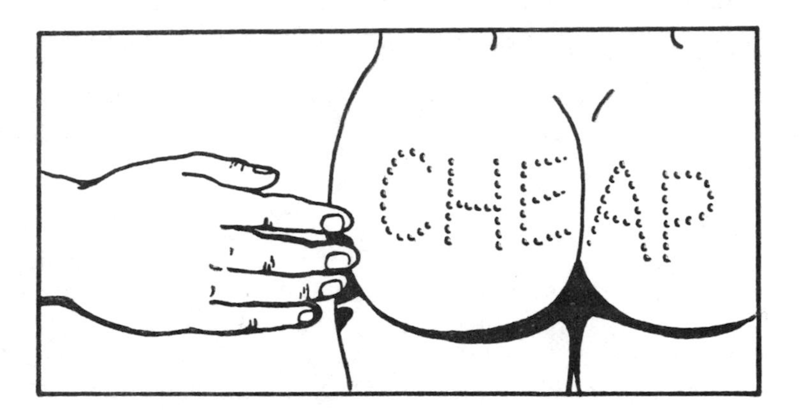

A giddy young trollop at Yale
Was tattooed with her prices for tail:
And on her behind,
For the sake of the blind,
A duplicate version in Braille.

REVIVAL TIME!

We weary of current slang and long for the old West when some of the phrases *had hair on 'em.*

Can you think of an expression today to compare with a cowboy's description of sudden wealth as: *I had enough money to burn a wet mule?*

Or what about the man who was inept: *He couldn't drive nails in a snow bank.*

Evidently, most people couldn't make coffee any better then than they do now, since it was depicted as *too thick to drink and too thin to plow.*

The loser in a gunfight was said to have *a bad case of slow.* And in that case they *put him to bed with a pick and shovel.*

Religion came in for its share of descriptive terms, such as calling preachers *sin busters* and describing a person with a religious upbringing as *raised on prunes and proverbs.*

A ticklish situation was when there was *hair in the butter.* And if further explanation were needed, the cowboy *cut the deck deeper.* But when it became hopeless, it was like *barkin' at a knot.*

So, the next time you're hungry, put a little zing into it. Sidle up to the cook and announce, "I'm feelin' a mite narrow at the equator." If the cook replies, "You're a pistol," rear back and deny that you're an inexperienced cowhand with, "Why, I've been hell with the hide off since I was no higher'n a door knob."

I have never let my schooling interfere with my education.
Mark Twain

HOW THEY SAID IT!

A buck nun poke, half full of rookus juice and madder than a rooster snatched bald, was on the prod, ready to crawl the hump of the first churn-twister who gave him any bushwa.

Translation: A bachelor cowboy, partly drunk and angry, was looking for trouble and was prepared to start a fight with the first farmer who told him a tale. It's doubtful that cowboys of the old West spoke that way in daily conversation, but they probably did use colorful language when telling stories to one another.

A cowboy's life was a hard, monotonous grind. Quite naturally the most imaginative slang terms stemmed from his life off the range and related to liquor, fighting, fleeing the law, and dying.

Nose paint, brave-maker, red-eye, and *forty-rod lightning* are a few slang terms for frontier whisky. An old-timer recalls that "A colt that new couldn't of stood up by hisself!"

I cleaned his plow or *I sharpened his hoe for him* are two expressions the winner of a fist fight used.

And, there were guns — a *black-eyed susan* or a *talking iron* or an *equalizer*. To kill another man might have been *to send him to the bone orchard, to put him over the jump, to blow out his lamp* or, one that later became gangster talk, *to rub him out.*

Killing led to flight on horseback. Cowboys must have done a lot of fleeing, too, for here are just a few of the ways they expressed it: *pull freight for the tules; dust; hit the breeze; break down timber; jump some dust; flag your ass; burn the breeze; hightail it; light out and hump your tail.*

Necktie party is still used for a hanging, and two more descriptive terms for the unhappy ending were *stretch rope* and *catch hemp fever.*

EPITAPH
Here lies Lester Moor.
Four slugs from a .44 —
No less, no more.

THE HIJACK!

There's a quaint story that would have us believe the word

RIDDLE: What were the two things cowboys used to fear most?

ANSWER: A decent woman and being left on foot.

hijack evolved years before gunmen started stealing truckloads of bootleg liquor. At one time in the old West, there supposedly were groups of tramps who followed harvest crews. On pay days, one of the tramps would accost a lone field hand and say, "Hi, Jack, got the time?" As the harvester fumbled for his watch, the tramp's partner came up behind him and gave him a whack on the head. Then they hijacked his wallet.

A beast with a belly full of bedsprings was another way of saying "bucking bronco."

TAKE YOUR PICK. LEAVE YOUR SHOVEL AND MUSKET!

You can't imagine how the arguments have raged over the origin of *flash in the pan.* Even if you can imagine, we're going to tell you.

One school has it the old flintlock musket is responsible. This clumsy weapon functioned as follows: on trigger pull, the hammer struck a flint. The spark from the flint was supposed to ignite powder in a pan which, in turn, acted as a primer to explode the charge. If the powder simply flashed and didn't ignite the charge, no shot was fired. So, a *flash in the pan* became anything showy that failed to produce results. Of course, it sounds as if the flintlock musket operated so slowly, your target may have left the country even if it did fire.

Then, there's that other school claiming the expression started with the gold-seeking hordes known as the forty-niners. Picture a prayerful miner panning for gold. Suddenly a flash of gold! On closer examination, it turns out to be iron pyrite...*fools gold.* Now, that, too, was a true *flash in the pan.*

Do you know a better way to describe confusion than "he didn't know if he were afoot or on horseback?"

In adventure films, the Marines or the cowboys or someone is always arriving in *the nick of time.* Long ago, sticks were notched to mark the passage of time. A *nick* came to be a precise time.

Come home, George. A miniature schnauzer stole the Buick and robbed a liquor store!

Someone who refuses to conform is often called a *maverick.* It all began with a Texas cattle baron, Sam Maverick. His ranch was on an island, so he didn't see any need to brand his calves. If you don't have someone's brand on you, you're a *maverick,* among other things.

He went through it with a five-toothed comb.

Geysers abound in Iceland, so it should come as no surprise that the word is from an Icelandic term *to burst forth with violence.*

It's said Okeefenokee (as in great Florida swamp) means trembling waters. Why didn't they say that in the first place?

READ THIS FROM SODA TO HOCK!

Cowpokes, back in the days when the west was wild and woolly, were suckers for a gambling game they called *the tiger* or *faro.* A deck of cards was placed in a box by the faro dealer. The first card to be exposed, before any bets were placed, was called the *soda.* The last card in the box was said to be *in hock* (so were most of the cowpokes by that time). So, *from soda to hock* was a faro player's way of saying from beginning to end.

Sign of inflation: a baker's dozen is now down to nine!

SEVEN, COME ELEVEN!

The Greek mathematician, Pythagoras, male to the core, let it be known that *even* numbers were feminine and unlucky and *odd* numbers were masculine and lucky. By the way, we got dice from the Arabs. A single die was called *al zahr,* which became *hasard* in French. Then *hazard*...and that's dice!

Parents, fight back! Wire your son or daughter for money today!

GIN! YOU'RE BLITZED!

To be *left in the lurch* has never been profitable. 16th Century Frenchmen played a dice game similar to backgammon called *lourche;* the player who dropped far behind was *left in the lurch.* Still exists in cribbage.

In the 17th Century, there was a card game with a twist we like: if one player was holding particularly bad cards, he could *turn the table* so that his opponent then had the weak hand.

If you thought *to call a spade a spade* came from cards, you're wrong. Plutarch said it in the 1st Century. Then, as now, it meant to

RIDDLE: What do *vara, hand, arpen, rod, verst* and *link* have in common?

ANSWER: They're all measures: *vara* is a Spanish length amounting to 33.39 inches; *hand*, equal to 4 inches — for gauging a horse's height; *arpen*, about an acre in France in bygone days; *rod*, five and a half yards; *verst*, a Russian way of expressing two-thirds of a mile; and *link*, 7.92 inches to a surveyor. Dreadfully useless, eh?

come to the point and stop walking like a cat...or *pussyfooting about.*

And *blitz*? That's as recent as World War II when the Nazi armies carried out lightning attacks or blitzkriegs.

Wrath is the last thing in a man to grow old.

Having been an inveterate poker player, it was natural for Harry Truman to have been the one to say, "The buck stops here." For years, a marker called a buck was placed in front of the dealer. After each hand had been completed, the buck was passed to the next player to indicate he was to deal. So *passing the buck* came to mean shifting the responsibility to someone else.

Speaking of poker, the term *kitty* came from *kist* or money chest. This changed to *kit* and eventually *kitty*.

By the way, a poker hand featuring three 5's is called a Washington Monument by players who know the height of that structure.

*We may as well add that **four-flusher** — a flash in the pan in his own right — was a poker player who sought to bluff when he had but four cards to a flush.*

STAG PARTY!

Olympics weren't the only games the ancient Greeks played. For instance, a bunch of the good old boys loved to get together for drunken revelry — a *komos* — and trade dirty songs and poems — *oide*. If you had seen some of them at the end of one of these affairs, you would have agreed — a *comedy!*

Gymnasium: what the Greeks had in mind was a place for physical training in the nude.

If you don't see any connection between *bonfire* and *kick the bucket*, you haven't been paying attention. Long ago a fellow stood on a bucket and adjusted a rope around his neck. To complete his suicide, he simply kicked the bucket out from under himself. *Bonfire* might have occurred right after the suicide, because it was originally bone fire, or a funeral pyre.

Avoid bakers who offer to bet you a dollar to a doughnut.

GOLDWYNISMS?

England has had its William Spooner and his *spoonerisms* — such as "Mardon me, padam, but you're occupewing my pie," when he found a strange lady in his church pew.

And America has had Sam Goldwyn and the *Goldwynism*. It's obvious Mr. Goldwyn could not have uttered all the statements attributed to him — he would not have had any time left over for producing movies. Suffice it to say that what we print here under the broad heading of 'Goldwynisms' are of indeterminate origin, but they are a hell of a lot of fun.

"It seems every Tom, Dick and Harry is named Sam."

"Include me out."

"A verbal contract isn't worth the paper it's written on."

"Motion pictures in color? I won't believe it until I see it in black and white."

"You've got to take the bull between your teeth."

"Our comedies are not to be laughed at."

"What a wonderful day to spend Sunday."

"It rolls off my back like a duck."

"I had a monumental idea this morning, but I didn't like it."

"That's the trouble with directors. Always biting the hand that lays the golden egg."

"Motion pictures are for entertainment. Messages should be delivered by Western Union."

"We need Indians in the picture? Don't worry, we can get them right from the reservoir."

"Tomorrow we shoot this movie, whether it rains, whether it snows, whether it stinks."

"There is a statue of limitations."

"I want to make a picture about the Russian secret police — the GOP." (If Goldwyn did actually make that statement, it must have haunted him later, since he was a staunch Republican.)

Some of the prized garblings supposedly arose because of specific circumstances. Again, they may be imaginary, but enjoyable.

Purportedly Goldwyn had given an embryonic writer an appointment. The young man leaped into his opus which he hoped would become a smash movie. All at once, he noticed Goldwyn was asleep. He awakened the producer and complained that all he asked for was an opinion of the fruits of his hard labor.

Allegedly Goldwyn replied, "*Sleeping* isn't an opinion?"

Movie folk also tell of Goldwyn introducing British war hero, Field

Marshal Montgomery, something like this: "I'd like to present my good friend, Marshal Field Montgomery."

It was another Hollywood story of long standing which claims Goldwyn voiced a refusal as "I can tell you in two words: Im Possible." This apparently led to a statement attributed to James Thurber. Goldwyn was making a movie of Thurber's *The Secret Life of Walter Mitty* with Danny Kaye, but the writer thought it too violent. Goldwyn is said to have apologized with, "I am very sorry you felt it was too blood-thirsty." Thurber allegedly replied, "Not only did I think so, but I was *horror* and *struck*."

Upon denying that one of his directors was a sadist on the set, Goldwyn supposedly said, "That isn't true. He's just a very mean fellow."

Sam Goldwyn usually gets credit, too, for two fascinating statements of optimism: "The war's all over but the shooting" and "How do you love my picture?"

Then there are the philosophical Goldwynisms. "Didn't you hear me keeping still?" he's said to have asked. Or on honesty, "If I promise, I promise on paper." Who could disagree with: "A hospital is no place to be in when you're sick." Goldwyn is supposedly the source of: "You just don't realize what life is all about until you have found yourself lying on the brink of a great abscess."

You name the subject and someone will quote you a Goldwynism. We'll never be sure if he really was the one who said, "I never put on a pair of shoes until I've worn them at least five years." Or, "I can take it with a dose of salts."

Then there's the one about Goldwyn becoming interested in acquiring the movie rights to a hit Broadway play. Apparently, one of his associates warned Goldwyn that the play was all about lesbians, to which he is said to have replied, "Don't worry about that. We'll make them all Americans."

Another tale had Goldwyn describing a particular piece of music: "The beat is two-by-four time."

An old-time director claims that Goldwyn, pleased when someone admired his wife's hands, commented, "Someday I'm going to have a bust made of them."

It's been said that Goldwyn was not familiar with the sundial. Upon seeing one for the first time and being informed of its function, he supposedly said, "My, my, what won't they think of next."

Imagine the confusion in the mind of the bookkeeper who is reported to have asked if he could reduce the mammoth proportions of the company's files by destroying the records prior to a certain year. "Certainly," the great man is said to have replied, "just be sure to keep a copy of everything."

It's better to have an antidote than an uncle who hates you.

Etymologists (don't look it up, Fred; it means an expert on word origins) will not agree on this, or little else: the word *slang* comes from a Norwegian word, *sleng*, meaning an invention or device.

He thought he had a figment, but it was only his imagination.

VAGUELY SAID!

Oh, the inaccuracies of language as we use it. Don't bother staring at your watch because someone says, "Be back in a *couple* of minutes." He didn't mean *two* at all. When a hostess asks if a guest would like more brandy, and he replies, "Just a *drop*," she won't attempt to fulfill his request accurately (unless it's 80-year old stuff). For years (that's somewhere between 1 and 1,000) farmers sold wheat, corn and other grains by the bushel. But different grains are different in size — there are a lot fewer grains of corn to a bushel than of wheat. So now the measure is X pounds of a commodity to a bushel.

But, for the ultimate in vague estimates, go out into the countryside and ask a few questions like these:

"How far is it to Millerville?"

"Just down the road apiece."

About the time you run out of gas, you'll begin to ask yourself how long a piece is.

Or "How do I get to the old Bushman place?"

"It's just over yonder," might be the average reply.

"Yes, but which direction is yonder?"

With some disgust, "Down by the creek only a mite southish."

RIDDLE: The names of three states have the word "red" in them. Which three?

ANSWER: Rhode Island stems from the Dutch words for red island. Oklahoma is made up of two Choctaw words — *Okla* (people) plus *homa* (red). Colorado comes from Spanish *color rojo* — color red. And, of course, we have one 'green' state — Vermont, from the two French words meaning green mountain.

Fifteen to one you'll never find it. Perhaps you've even tried, "Look, I'm a stranger here. Could you tell me a place where we can get cold beer and sandwiches?"

"You don't look stranger than most folks hereabouts, sonny. I don't hold with beer, myself, but I used to send folks along to Barton's on the old country road."

"Could you tell me how to find the old country road, then?"

"Same way I do, sonny."

Knowing all the answers is not too gratifying, since you never get asked all the questions.

DEFINITELY INDEFINITE!

We don't know if people are being intentionally vague when they use the word *about*, as in 'it's about a mile down the road.' However, it is an accurate inaccuracy, stemming from three Old English words for *on, by* and *outside*...or on, or at least nearby the outside of, maybe.

A couple of other indefinites made definite are willy-nilly from *will he* or *will he not* and shilly-shally from *shall he* or *shall he not*. Sorry, but *dilly-dally* and *fiddle-faddle* didn't come about in the same way. Neither did Walla Walla.

A little inaccuracy sometimes saves tons of explanation.
H.H. Munro

FROM THE REDUNDANT TO THE SUPINE!

People will think you stutter, if you persist in using terms such as *reduce down* and *young colt*.

It's all right in a song, but being *alone together* is damn well impossible in real life.

When you're lying down, can you be both *prone* and *supine* simultaneously? Not unless you're the world's greatest contortionist! In the *prone* position, your face is down and when you're *supine*, it's up. Your face is also down when you're *prostrate*. (Maybe you should remain standing.)

Santa Claus is redundant when he speaks of his *reindeer*. Dancer and Prancer and that whole crew come from Lapland where the word for deer is *rein*. In Pago Pago, we'll make an exception.

If you need
to know,
you need
Information
Please
INFORMATION
PLEASE
ALMANAC
1979
THE ANSWER BOOK
1979 Information
Please Almanac

10
35
90
30
80
25
7
20
6
15
Celsius
5
10
5
0
-5
-10
-15
The Answ

When we use the words *tree trunk*, we're repeating ourselves. *Trunk* comes from the Latin word for tree. So how did *trunk* also come to mean that heavy, awkward piece of baggage? Easy! The first *trunks* were made from the hollowed sections of a tree.

Heard on a Palm Springs, California radio station in August: "It was another sorcher today with the thermometer hitting a skizzling 105 degrees." Almost hot enough to braddle one's ains.

FAMOUS FASCINATING PHRASES!

Not only poets, but us common folk, too, enjoy alliteration, and it has had its effect on many popular expressions.

Take *spick and span* as an example. 14th Century spoons, made from a chip of wood, were called *spans. Span new* was a new spoon, then it became anything new. Almost three centuries later, someone added *spick* (a splinter or spike of wood) and the expression also picked up the connotation of neatness along with newness. *Spanking* new, by the way, simply means *very* new.

Another alliterative expression is essentially American in origin — *the whole kit and caboodle.* At first it was *the whole kit and bilin'*. *Kit* was one's whole outfit, or equipment. *Bilin'* was a slangy metaphor, as in 'the crowd of people, boiling and seething.' At that stage, then, the expression described a whole group plus their equipment — all. But it wasn't good enough. Someone substituted the Dutch word *boodle* for *bilin'*. The substitution should have been for *kit*, since *boodle* already meant all one's property...but go figure. At last, strictly for alliteration, *ca* was stuck on the front of *boodle.* Exhausting, isn't it?

When asked why she was moving, Eugenie Hines uttered these immortal words: ***Because the house next door is a sore-eye.***

PASS THE PAIL! WE'RE PUTTING PALE PAINT ON OUR PALES!

A *pale* has been a fence stake or picket for centuries. Then it grew to mean the whole fence or any enclosure. As it often seems to happen, the English government got into the act: they began referring to sections of Ireland and Scotland as being 'within their pale' or jurisdiction.

Therefore, when someone is beyond our control and beyond reason, its perfectly correct to describe him as *beyond the pale.*

She went after him with hammock and thongs.

RIDDLE: Is putting the cart before the horse preposterous?

ANSWER: Exactly! *Pre* indicates before, while *post* means after. So, putting before that which should go after is *preposterous*...and stops traffic.

IT'S GOD-SPELL!

Language is the means by which we make our thoughts explicit, right? As in the case of the young writer we know who announced he had just finished a new novel. (We thought *novel* meant new.) Then he asked if we'd like to read his *manuscript*. We informed him we never read anything written by hand. He replied that his manuscript was typed.

Sometimes language can be too accurate. Example: most children ride *dirigibles* to school! That's because a dirigible is literally any craft whose direction can be controlled.

Another word with undetected accuracy is *sophomore*. It relates to the second year in college in a descriptive sense, since it grew out of two Greek words meaning wise and foolish...as in philo*soph*er and *mor*on.

And, if we told you that all the above is *gospel*, you would have a right to believe we mean that it is infallible. Wrong! We meant *gospel* as it was originally...*god-spell* or good tidings.

The power of words is such that they have prevented our learning some of the most important events in the world's history.

Sir Norman Angell

When a building contractor in Mexico City selects the exterior material for an authentic hacienda, he speaks ancient Egyptian. Well, not quite. *Adobe* has been traced back to Egyptian hieroglyphics from which came an Arabic word *at-tob* from which came a Spanish word meaning to daub or plaster — *adobar*; and finally, sun-dried bricks — *adobe*. Exhausted?

There was a time when the French thought that a child who was ***puis****(later)* ***nee*** *(born) would not be strong. In fact,* ***puny****.*

STORY-TIME!

"To be frugal means to save," the teacher explained to her young class. "Now I want each of you to write a story using the word frugal." This was one of the stories:

"The beautiful princess went into the forest to pick berries. She went further and further until she got lost. She got scared and she ran back and forth crying, "Frugal me! Frugal me! Someone please *frugal* me!"

Prince Charming heard her, and he rode up on his white horse and he *frugaled* her and they lived happily ever after."

School Daze: If a reformatory improves children, are they doing what we think they are doing in regular schools?

George Tizmus knew very well what his daughter meant when she spoke of her boyfriend giving her *hickies*. He looked it up anyway, much to his confusion. A *hickey* is either a threaded connection joining an electrical device to an outlet box or it's a contraption for bending pipe. He intends to speak to the boyfriend about it.

Some school! One solid week they've been testing Wilbur for I.Q. and they haven't come up with one yet.

As any child will tell you, there is an insidious adult conspiracy designed to torture the young. It exhibits itself in such phrases as *Brush your teeth* and *Take out the garbage* and *Time for bed* and *Don't touch your food until your father says grace*. Oh how the children of some of our pioneer forefathers must have loved it when Dad said, "Bless the meat and damn the skin, throw back your ears and all pitch in!"

*Monster and **prodigy** both meant an omen of approaching disaster at one time. Remember that, parents. But be consoled that **precocious** meant pre-cooked.*

RIDDLE: Are we alone in confusing *pictographs* and *petroglyphs?*

ANSWER: Yes! Everyone else knows that petroglyphs are carved symbols, while pictographs are *painted* representations. Now eat your mush.

HOW CHILDREN TELL IT!

"When America started out, there were two kinds of people — the *columnists* and the Indians."

"Our *four* fathers came here on a boat and jumped off on a chicken which they called a Plymouth Rock."

"Benjamin Franklin was the *envy* George Washington sent to France."

"The first *trader* in America was Ben Dick Arnold."

"There is no pole at the North Pole but there are *bears*."

"There are two *topics* running around the Earth — the *topic of Kansas* and the *topic of Captain Horn*."

"The world has an equator so things will be *even on both sides*."

"The Alps stick up *higher* than all the other parts of Europe."

"Julius Caesar was elected *umpire* by the Romans."

"I like the words to the Star Spangled Banner but the *malady* makes it hard for me to sing it."

"Jesus Christ wrote down most of the bible himself except for *ten parts* he let Moses do."

"My father works hard but they only pay him a *celery* every week."

"If you are chasing a rabbit and he disappears, look for his *burro*."

On classroom deportment: "If I smile and be helpful to others and let them have their way, I will be the most *populous* girl in school."

"My mother says I can't stay up late to watch TV because it will make me too *wary* to go to school."

A ten-year-old boy was asked to use 'vanish' in a sentence. "My father parked his van on the street. Next morning the van had ished."

Out Of The Mouths Of Babes: It was the winter of his disconnect.

PUT THOSE TODDLERS ON KP!

An infant is one too young to talk, right? *Infans* in Latin was 'not able to speak.' They referred to a group of young soldiers as *infantry*, because they were not allowed to speak unless spoken to first. Ask any infantryman if things have changed much.

Now that you've asked: ***Snooping*** *is what the children of Dutch colonists in America were doing when they were eating sweets while no one was looking.*

What caused the postal service in America?

The color of clothing foisted on the American GI is aptly named. In the winter, it's olive *drab* from a word for dull or monotonous. In summer, it's *khaki* from a Hindustani word for dust or ashes.

In many countries, the appearance of a ***cham, margrave, wazir, hetman,*** *or* ***bey*** *caused people to snap to attention. They are all titles of authority.*

THE AMAZING MILITARY!

A *corporal* draws that name from the Latin word for head or chief; and *captain* comes from the same source. This will aid in understanding that a *corporal* ranks beneath a *sergeant*, which meant serving man.

Then there's *lieutenant*...holding the place of an officer — followed by *captain*, who, in turn is outranked by *major* (greater)...than captain. This should make it crystal clear why a *Lieutenant General* is a grade above a *Major General.*

Warning! There's a lot of hollyhocking going on!

IF YOU CAN'T OUT-FIGHT 'EM, OUT-YELL 'EM!

During the Civil War, the rebel cry was intended to strike fear in the hearts of the Union troops. And there was an ancient Scottish clan that did the same. Quite logically, they called their battle cry a *slaugh gairn*, meaning army yell. Today we pronounce it *slogan*, and politicians use it to strike fear in the hearts of voters.

Don't forget that when soldiers in the Revolutionary War said, "Lock, stock and barrel," they meant the whole gun. Today, we mean everything.

SADDLE UP OR BE CHAGRINED!

Great horsemen that they were, the Turks still had feelings. They called the rough hide of a horse's back *saghri*. The French borrowed it and eventually it became *chagrin*...an emotional rather than a physical vexation, although bareback riders claim they suffer both ways.

America's foreign policy is written in ancient gibberish!

RIDDLE: Can dictionaries be serious in saying *colonel* is pronounced kur'nel?

ANSWER: The Italians began calling a little column of infantry a *colonello*; then it also became the column's officer. The French first borrowed it as *colonelle*, but, later in some fit of Gallic pique, they made it *coronel*. The English, not to be outdone in the game of wordsmanship, borrowed the later French pronunciation and the earlier French spelling. Dictionaries threw in the sponge in 1780.

SHADES OF WATERGATE!

The Byzantine Emperor Justinian was a busy man back in the 6th Century. His armies retook northern Africa from the Vandals and drove the Ostrogoths back out of Italy. On the home front, things were humming, too...court intrigues, compromising situations...many items the emperor didn't want publicized. But the court historian was taking everything down. Realizing what hot stuff he had collected and knowing how the emperor would react if they got out, he used two Greek words to describe his manuscript. They meant 'not to be given out.' Today the two words are one — *anecdote.* Most *anecdotes* these days aren't such hot stuff.

Of all the ***nincoms*** *in this world,* ***poop*** *is the worst!*

When a Britisher refers to England as *old blighty*, it isn't derogatory at all. British troops stationed in India learned the Indian word for Europe — *Bilayati* — and mangled it in the accepted fashion.

It didn't pay to argue with Julius Caesar. He closed his speeches with, "Dictator!" Translation: "I have spoken!"

OUTCLASSING THEM ALL!

Don't look down your noses just because the ancient Irish kings practiced *tanistry*. They had to. It was the law. While an Irish king was still alive, the law said his successor was to be chosen from among his male relatives. The man elected was then called the king's *tanist*, or second in rank.

Finally, to end the controversy, ***paynim*** *is another word for pagan.*

The Parthians were a warlike people who conquered many nations in the First Century B.C., spreading their domain from the Caspian Sea to India. They were daring horsemen and fine archers. Their favorite ploy in battle was to race away from an enemy, as if defeated. But, as they fled, they turned and shot arrows into the ranks of their pursuers. The stunt was known as the 'Parthian shot.' Today's *parting shot* — a final verbal maneuver — comes from the Parthians' trick.

Anatomical impossibility: ***to cry one's eyes out.*** *We tried. Red was all we got.*

Not all the gladiatorial combats the ancient Romans loved so well took place in the Colosseum. For a little variety, they would fill two ships with gladiators and stage a naval battle. This lovely exercise was called a *naumachia* from the Greek words for ship and battle.

If the Romans had been obliged to learn Latin, they never would have found time to conquer the world. *Heinrich Heine*

OH DAMN! THE HUE'S BUSTED!

In the Middle Ages, when a citizen was attacked or robbed, he let out a *hue* — a whistle or blast on a horn. Then he let out a *cry*, such as "Stop, thief!" It's still noisy today, when someone sets up a great *hue and cry.*

Operatic Soap Opera: Siegfried, by magic, wins Brunhild for Gunther. Sieg's wife, Kriemhild, spills the beans to Brunhild, who talks Hagen into knocking off Siegfried.

PULL IN YOUR HORNS!

Several hundred years ago someone observed that snails pulled in their horn-like antennae when they sensed danger approaching. Now humans do the same.

In 16th Century England, they had a cute practice that would certainly make one *pull in his horns:* suspected heretics were literally *raked over the coals* — hot coals — to induce them to renounce their false beliefs. Fortunately, the expression implies a milder form of punishment today.

A martyr is a person who would rather die for a cause then admit it isn't worth it.

THE INQUISITION WAS AN IMPOSITION!

Perhaps it would be callous to give thanks to the days of the *boot and the iron maiden* for certain expressions that have survived.

One nasty device was the *rack*. Except for those who died before

RIDDLE: Is there any connection between *pioneer* and the chess piece referred to as a *pawn*?

ANSWER: Absolutely! Both come from a French word for a foot soldier who went ahead of the army clearing the forest. And a pawn cleared the way for the knights, king and queen.

giving in, the *rack* almost always brought a victim to the torturer's terms. From that, it evolved to *rack*, in the sense of any insupportable pain. For instance, when a landlord raised rents to an insupportable level, tenants complained they were being brought to *rack and ruin*.

The *thumbscrew* was another effective means of bringing another around to your way of thinking. Even today, undue pressure is described as *putting the screws on*.

When an Eskimo wants to get his sled team started, he yells at them in French. Yep, ***mush*** *is short for* ***mush on*** *and came from French* ***marchons*** *— let us march.*

PREPOSITIONALLY SPEAKING!

Grammar is all right, in its place. But grammarians are another matter. To put a grammarian in his place would be sublime.

Winston Churchill managed it. It seems he had sent the draft of a speech to the Foreign Office. When it came back, a grammarian had moved a preposition from the end of a sentence to its proper grammatical location.

Churchill sent the fastidious fellow this note: "This is the type of pedantic syntax up with which I will not put."

Breathless young man to maid he adored: "When will there be just twenty-five letters in the alphabet?"
Equally breathless maid: "When U and I are one."

People used to be a great deal more finicky about language. During the Renaissance, a *moment* was a fortieth of an hour. In the Seventeenth Century, it decreased to a second. Today a *moment* is precisely that lapse of time between a woman's claim of when she says she'll be ready to depart and when she is ready to depart.

When in doubt, mumble.

THERE'LL ALWAYS BE A LEXICOGRAPHER!

According to a yellowing copy of *Whiz Bang* (a naughty magazine you youngsters never heard of), Noah Webster's wife walked into the pantry one day and found her husband kissing the maid.

"I'm surprised at you, Noah!"

"No, my dear," he corrected gently. "It is I who am *surprised...* You are *astonished* and Bridget is *amazed.*"

Do not engage in any form of *ulating* without observing these rules:

Pucker up prior to ***osculating.***
Measuring your bust should precede ***formulating.***
Don't write for ***The National Geographic*** *without first* ***articulating.***
Put your glasses on before ***speculating.***

SOLIDUS!

One sees this oblique line / separating dates, as in 3/12/78, and dividing fractions. It's called the *solidus*. The British originally abbreviated *shilling* with an elongated, slanted *s*. Even that grew tiresome, so they just made the *solidus* mark /.

Hackle, saddle, coverts and hocks are all external parts of a chicken. Up until this moment, only chickens discussed such things in public.

A MISUNDERSTOOD HUSBAND!

A struggling junior executive was married to a girl who constantly corrected his speech.

One evening he reminded his wife that the annual office party would be the following day, and then he reminisced, "I'll never forget last year...what a blow-out!"

"*Celebration*," she corrected.

"That's when," he continued, "Jack..."

"Say '*John*', dear."

"One of the vice-presidents was fascinated by a little blonde with a terrific chassis, and..."

"*Torso*, never chassis," she warned.

"Yeah, well," his enthusiasm waning, "John started laughing and..."

"*Commenced*, dear," she sighed.

"But he could hardly stop," he completed.

"*Desist* is much more refined," she prompted.

"Well, he almost got fired," he ended angrily.

"I would prefer *terminated*, you know."

"Oh, hell, I'm going to put out the light," he cried. And her final remark from the darkness was "*Extinguish*."

RIDDLE: What do they call the anatomical juxtaposition of two orbularis oris muscles in a state of contraction?

ANSWER: ***They*** **call it a kiss. If you do, you won't be.**

The following night he came home quite late and a bit tipsy and she confronted him with an angry "Well?"

"You see, I was driving home and I heard this thump. And I thought 'oh, oh' a *celebration.* So I *desisted* the car, got out the *john* and *johnned* her up. None of the tires had a *celebration*, so I felt around the *torso* to see if it was hot. After all, I didn't want it to catch *terminate*. Then I got back in, pressed the *commencer* and came home."

He took a deep breath, surveying his wife's face. Then, satisfied he still had the floor, he said, "That's why I'm late. I hope you're not *extinguished.*"

But she was, either way.

This story is wonderful. In fact, it's prolific.
Sam Goldwyn

GENDER, SMENDER!

Here are four words which began their language lives as strictly masculine terms: *hoyden*, a boorish man; *virtue*, manly excellence; *bawd*, a rogue; and *harlot*, a vagabond.

What happened? All four are now strictly feminine terms.

On being put off for an appointment to a day 37 days later, the client replied, "I'm sorry, but I have a funeral that afternoon."

NOX IS A GOOD EKENAME!

The Anglo-Saxons simply couldn't let their words alone. First, they had *ekename* — added name. Since it often had the article *an* before it, they brought the *n* to the front of *ekename* to make what we now call *nickname*. They also tried the same stunt with other words — a nox, a negge, a napple — but it didn't last. And that's not a nanecdote!

If ***world*** *comes from the Old English words for* ***man*** *and* ***age*** *and meant* ***Age of Man****, what would we call the world before the Age of Man?*

PUTTING ON THE RITZ!

Imagine the following introduction at a formal gathering these days: "Field Marshall, I would like to have you meet Lord and Lady Frithing; our local constable; a visiting member of the Royal House of Scotland, Mr. Stewart; and one of our neighbors."

Go back to a distant day when these words had other meanings and the same introduction would read: "Horse-servant, I would like to have you meet Frithing the bread-keeper and his wife, the bread-kneader; our local stable boy; a Scottish pig-keeper; and our next-door farmer."

Most people can't get into a good minority anymore!

PLUMB LOCO!

If someone tells you to go *plumb to hell*, it means *straight* to hell. Same use of *plumb* shows up in *plumb* bob and *plumb* line. And you can tell your angry friend that he can go to hell in a hand-basket, *plumb* or otherwise!

The Bordello On The Prairie! Just when we thought sex and violence were on their way out as TV fare, we learned that the Italian word for little house is ***bordello.***

YOU'RE PULLING MY LEG:

Ancient Romans were so superstitious that they were accompanied by a servant whose sole job was to see that the master stepped over a threshold on the correct foot. You guessed it: he was called a *footman*.

Mansion has always meant a very grand house, right? Nope! It was simply the building you lived in. And your *residence* was the place where you sat back.

Ouija isn't a secret word a medium uses. It's simply the French *oui* and the German *ja*, adding up to yes-yes.

In another age, you'd have made a fool of yourself calling your brother's son your nephew. The original definition of *nephew* was grandson.

In olden France when a bell rang each night, the citizens were to *couvre-feu*...cover their fires and go to bed. We now say *curfew*.

It wasn't always a popular ambition to live in a penthouse. That's because *penthouse* originally stood for a slope-roofed shed built against the side of a building. In other words, a lean-to. Hardly glamorous, those early penthouses.

In Old English the ***bedstead*** *was simply where the bed stood.*

RIDDLE: Is *brothern* an Old English word from which we get brethren?

ANSWER: It's an Old English word. It meant a ruined person, and the word we get from it is *brothel*, or place of ruined persons.

If, at high gnun, a gnude gnusboy gnutered a gnubile gnu,
Could a phast-phingered phisher phinish a philter of phiphty phileted phlounders by phive o two?
If a knaive knipper of knine knitted a knosegay of kniknety knasturtiums by three,
Then resne on the gresne in the plesne of Spesne would give pesne to the lord of the demesne, you see.
If a pneumonic pneumismatist pneaded pneumerous pneumatic pneudles into pneutrient pneugats by eight,
Would the wife of Julius Caesar sqaesar twaesar in the phraesar just to pleasar mate?

WHO'S LOOSE IN THE ZOO?

Up until the 13th Century, there was a unique way of disguising one's lack of knowledge about animal nomenclature. It was perfectly acceptable to refer to all fauna as deer...including deer, dear.

Most animal names are aptly descriptive; that we use words from foreign languages tends to obscure the description. For instance, the Greek word for squirrel was *shadow tail*, and a porpoise was a *hog-fish*; even hyena, *like a hog*, fits.

Expressive words were a specialty of American Indians, too. In Algonquin, a caribou was a *scratcher* and a moose one who *strips off bark*.

What's simpler than the Greek *nose horn* for rhinoceros? Or dinosaur from *fearful lizard?* Or the Latin *pig with spines* for porcupine?

We also like the Malayan term, *man of the woods*, for orangutan.

However, there is one term that confuses: *dwarf lion*...the Greek term for the chameleon. It must stem from the ruff around the neck, but even so, *lion?*

In old England they planted a ***tun****, or hedge, around a group of houses to keep out ferocious animals. Now we say* ***town****.*

In the 19th Century, American middle westerners spoke of *freemartins, bang-boards* and *titrams.* When a cow had male and female twin calves, the female twin was almost always sterile and so was butchered...that's the unfortunate *freemartin*. Came corn-shuckin' time, they put an extra sideboard on the wagon...a *bang-board.* And the runt pig of a litter who had a rough time finding a milk spigot...was the *titram.*

A company of rabbits is not called a herd or flock. It's called a ***colony.*** *Makes one ponder: is there any connection with a nudist colony?*

Out Of His Gourd: To the Romans, a farmer who let his oxen wander *de* (out) of the *lira* (furrow) was in a *delerium*. (He'd also be on a *funny farm.*)

When the cat weighs, the mice will play with him.

Of course a *scapegoat* is someone who takes the blame for another's acts. It might have been a *scapecamel*, except that when ancient Jewish priests symbolically piled the sins of the people on an animal, a goat happened to be handy. After undergoing this rite of contrition, the goat *escaped* into the desert.

To prove that man's mind often moves in similar fashion, the early Greeks used their words for *gravel* and *lizard* to designate the *crocodile*. Much later the Spanish used their word for the lizard — *el lagarto* — to designate the American crocodile, or *alligator*.

When the ancient Greeks first saw the *giraffe*, it looked to them to be a long-necked, spotted camel; so, they called it a *camelopard. Giraffe* comes from Arabic. For camel freaks: *dromedary* (one hump) is from the Greek word for running; *Bactrian* (two humps) stems from a region of ancient Persia.

If you ever had trouble naming a cat, you can sympathize with those Greeks on their first encounter with the leopard. Having a name for the lion (*leon*) and for the tiger (*pardos*), they simply gave the new feline double-billing as leopard or lion-tiger.

To an archaic Greek, ***sarcasm*** *really had a bite. It literally meant a dog's tearing at a person's flesh.*

FLASH! GORILLAS ARE DESCENDED FROM MAN!

Hanno, a Greek explorer of the 5th Century B.C., came ashore on the west coast of Africa and encountered a tribe of wild, hairy natives. He picked up one of their words to describe these primitive men — *gorilla!* It wasn't until the 19th Century that an American missionary in Africa used *gorilla* to designate the anthropoid ape.

To get your back up is a 200-year-old way of imitating an angry cat.

RIDDLE: In the old French fables, was Reynard the Fox a coward?

ANSWER: Reynard was brave! The hare was called *Coart*, which meant to *turn tail*. So, those who turn tail and run like rabbits are cowardly!

HEY, DUMMY, THE RACCOON'S OVER HERE!

Many popular expressions originated with mistakes, with ineptitude and some resulted from great skill.

Americans have used hounds to hunt raccoons for years. A poor excuse of a dog was one that treed a raccoon and then *barked up the wrong tree.*

And the musket was not the most reliable weapon. Supposedly, it was on safety when the hammer was cocked halfway, but all too often it *went off half-cocked*...or without preparation.

Because the thundering racket of a lightning bolt reminded people of a cat-and-dog fight, they described the downpour that followed as *raining cats and dogs.*

Arctic regions are cold, so you think the word comes from another language's term for cold. Wrong again! The Greek word *arctos* meant bear, and the arctic regions simply refer to the northern constellation known as *The Great Bear.*

No wonder grizzly bears are bad tempered. Zoologists call them ***ursus horribilis.***

RIDE 'EM, EQUESTRIAN!

A *horse show* has been described as a bunch of horses showing their asses to a bunch of horses' asses showing their horses.

The expression for being calm — *not to turn a hair* — goes back to Jane Austen. She spoke of a horse who hadn't worked hard enough to ruffle his hair.

No, the ***pony express*** *was never a speedy way to ship young horses.*

Is there any sillier sight than a duckling at full tilt, flapping furiously and confident he is about to be airborne? That's where we get the word *flapper*. Then, since someone saw the resemblance, giddy young girls came to be called *flappers*.

When ***ruffs*** *mate with* ***reeves****, the* ***reeves*** *produce little sandpipers.*

We were astounded when we read about a chap who was joining pens with cobs and creating cygnets, until we learned that male swans are *cobs*, female swans are *pens* and their offspring are *cygnets*.

*The **osprey** was named for his habit of dropping his catch on the rocks to kill it. It comes from two Latin words meaning bone-breaker.*

FROM THE COLOR OF THAT ELEPHANT, YOU'VE BEEN HAD!

Is there a garage-sale devotee alive who has never squandered money on some utterly useless prize? In the hope we can cure you of these paroxysms of foolishness, we'll tell you how *white elephant* originated.

In bygone days, the kings of Siam were an overbearing bunch. For instance, if a rare albino elephant was captured, it automatically belonged to the king. He was the only person who could ride one of these white elephants, and no one could destroy them without the king's permission. Got the picture?

Now, if the king took a special dislike to a member of his court, the most fiendish thing he could do was to give the person one of his white elephants. The recipient could not ride the beast, could not use him for labor and could not have him killed. All he *could* do was to feed the ravenous animal and continue to feed him, until he was, finally, financially ruined. Now that's a *white elephant*!

*Stop worrying! It's perfectly proper to call all spider webs **cob** webs. The old Dutch word for spider was **cop**; and it became **cob**. Jiggers, the spiders!*

If someone states, "I bought two *kudus* for nine *kroons*," most of us are curious enough to ask the meaning of the strange words. When we discover that a *kudu* is an African antelope and that a *kroon* is the monetary unit of Estonia, we've learned three things...two new words and that the fellow who used them is a nut.

When an enemy has said something uncomplimentary about you, why do you first hear about it from a friend?

FINANCIAL FABLES, FOIBLES AND FRIPPERY!

It was ever thus: a 1st Century Roman, down to his last toga, visited his banker in hopes of a loan. Naturally, the banker wanted to know if he was *se cura*...without care...or possessed of some security. He and the banker both knew that if he were without care he would not be asking for a loan. New, eh? In the past, the banker had always said,

RIDDLE: Which National Park comes to mind when you think of bears?

ANSWER: Yellowstone National Park is the home of many bears, but Yosemite is an Indian word meaning *grizzly bear*.

"*Deficit*!" which simply meant, it is wanting. However, on that day, the banker had some money *re venio* — come back...which he counted as *revenue*; in fact, he thought of it as something good...a *bonus*.

So, he smiled at the loan applicant and said, "*Credo*," or I believe...I'll okay your credit.

The last thing the borrower remembered was a discussion of *interesse*, which can be translated as 'to be between.' In later days, this expression was to be expanded: 'to be between a rock and a hard place.'

And that's the way it was in *finance*...which meant ending.

Auction is from a Latin word for **increase**. *Makes sense...we've never been to an auction where the price decreased.*

JUNO AND THE PAYOFF!

It was being noised about in ancient Rome that the army was in a skimpy state supply-wise. Since this would put a crimp in their favorite occupation — making war — they put a call in to Juno. In a whimsical mood, she told the chappies in their funny short skirts not to give it another thought. Since this was what the army did best, they complied.

Well, the ensuing slaughter was a glory to behold! In a fit of delight, the army built a temple in Juno's honor, calling it the *moneta*...the advisor. A few years later, they minted their first silver coins in the very same temple. Quite naturally the coins were called *moneta*.

If you're ever short of *money* or supplies, call Juno. That's area code...

"Fortune," according to Theophile Gautier, "loves to give bedroom slippers to people with wooden legs."

NOT WORTH HIS SALT!

The ancient Roman legionaries always hoped to supplement their soldier's pay with plunder. But they weren't always in battle, so they had to subsist on their pay alone at times. Part of this money went to pay for salt. The Latin word for salt was *salarium* (from which we get our word *salary* incidentally). So, if the commander of a Roman legion described one of his soldiers as *not being worth his salt*, he meant not even worth the small portion of his pay that went for salt. In short, next to nothing, or in Latin — *zilch.*

*The **itch** is the urge: itching palms crave money; itching feet crave travel.*

Help! I'm Being Whitemailed! Very possible. And ancient Scotch word — *mail* — meant tribute or rent. A Scot paying off in black angus cattle was paying *blackmail*; and when he ponied up in silver, that was *whitemail.*

CONFUSION ON THE MONEY FRONT!

If 25 cents is two-bits, was a dollar originally an eight-bit piece? No, but it's a complex tale.

The Count of Schlick lived in the Joachim Valley near Prague. Having a nice silver mine on his estate, he started making his own money in 1518. They were described as *Joachimthalers* (from the valley of Joachim), then simply as *thalers*, and in some dialects, *dalers*. Change reels.

The *daler* became *dollar* when it came into England. Being thoroughly logical, the British used *dollar* to designate the widely used Spanish *pieces of eight*. Since *pieces of eight* were common in the American colonies, and they were also known as *dollars*, wc called our first silver coinage *dollars*. Hell, we're lost!

The optimist proclaims that this is the best of all possible worlds, and the pessimist fears this is true.

James B. Cabell

The British *pound sterling* got its name in a peculiar way. The Saxons were also called Esterlings because they came to England from the East. They introduced a coin into British trade, and so it was called an *esterling*. Since it contained about one pound of silver at that time, it soon came to be known as an *esterling pound*; then the 'e' got lost and we now have the *pound sterling*.

*Around 1720, some counterfeiters turned out a phony Irish half-penny. The bogus coin was nicknamed a **rap**. Ever since, we've used the expression that an item 'isn't worth a rap.'*

RIDDLE: What can never be found with cash, is always in debt and never out of danger?

ANSWER: The letter E.

PENNYPINCHERS!

A person could go broke if he were unable to distinguish between 'to reimburse' and 'to disburse.' Start with knowledge that *bursa* was Latin for pocket. Reimburse is *back in* the pocket; disburse is *out of* the pocket...and gone forever.

Genies are offering only two wishes this year!

I'LL TAKE THE RUG!

A *bargain* has been described as something you don't need which costs less than what you do need. A proverb goes: offer a starving Persian, shipwrecked on a barren island, his choice of a plate of food or a fine rug, and you will be short one rug.

Hemp is fiber food! Eat a rope!

The Persian word meaning Mountain of Light was applied to one of the world's most famous diamonds — the *Kohinoor.* Before it was cut up to become part of the English crown jewels, the Kohinoor was 793 carats in size. *Carat* comes from a Greek word meaning horn through Arabic for the horn-like pod of an Abyssinian tree. The seeds apparently varied in weight ever so slightly, so they came to be used for weighing gold. Nowadays, a *carat* is a weight measure for precious stones or to define the purity of gold alloys.

*Say **crinimal alunimum** thirteen times. Feel better?*

UP THE SPOUT AND DOWN THE DRAIN!

Those two expressions mean the same thing — lost resources. Perhaps there's a difference in degree of loss. *Down the drain* is certainly lost forever. A faint hope exists when your belongings go *up the spout.*

The pawnbrokers of 18th Century England usually had a second-floor warehouse for storing pawned goods. The freight elevator they used was called a *spout.* So, the poor chap who pawned his belongings knew that once they went *up the spout*, he'd probably never see them again. Eventually, the pawnshop itself was called the *spout.*

If the wheel hadn't been invented, roulette players would have nothing to do.

Breathes there a man with wallet so slim who hath not to himself said, "My God, I didn't know there was a cover charge?" It's a French ploy. *Couvert* meant everything on the table — knives, forks, spoons, salt and whatever. The French cafe owner charged for their use.

Skeezix used hair spray!

DOW JONES AND ALL THOSE CATS!

In case you're not a stock market enthusiast, a *bear* is one who makes his profit from a falling market. His favorite ploy is to *sell short*, meaning to sell a stock he doesn't yet own in hopes of being able to buy it later at a depressed price. It all came from an old saying: *to sell the bearskin before you've caught the bear.*

And the *bulls*? *Bear* came first; then, since the English of that day enjoyed two lovely sports called bull-baiting and bear-baiting, the *bulls* came to represent the opposite of the *bears.*

Considering the high cost of living and the high cost of dying, the frugal person is a bit short of options.

WINE, WOMEN AND MUNICIPAL BONDS!

A *broker* used to be the fellow who tapped a wine keg. From that he came to be known as a wine dealer. And for a time in late 17th Century England, *broker* was a polite name for *pimp*. Thank you, Paine Webber?

Richard Fields, call your broker. The top fell off your convertible debentures!

HOME IS WHERE THE ECONOMIST IS!

We do not pull thy leg, sir! An *economist* is literally the manager of a house...that sweet little thing right there beside you. Now, of course, we must unravel what a *home economist* might be...in addition to being a redundancy.

It's not difficult to imagine a linguistic connection between *budget* and *wallet*. *Budget* is from an old French word, *bougette*, meaning a leather bag for money. Then the British got in the act. When the House of Commons was ready to discuss expenditures, all papers pertaining to such matters were brought to them in a leather bag or *bougette*. The bag became the *budget*.

RIDDLE: Is there any connection between *typhoon* and *tycoon*?

ANSWER: Some. Both come from the Chinese. *Typhoon* is great wind; *tycoon*, great prince. We have met one or two *tycoons* who would qualify as *typhoons*.

If you've been wondering what happens once in a minute, twice in a moment yet not once in a thousand years, the answer is the letter M.

Let's Apply Some Algebra To That Fractured Fibula! It wasn't until the 17th Century that algebra became a mathematical term. Originally it was an Arabic term meaning to reunite that which was broken and even then very few *algebraists* made house or tent calls.

We've just discovered why the Roman Empire declined and fell! Their word for secretary meant ***one who keeps a secret.***

DON'T FORGET TO PACK YOUR PAREPHENALIA!

Legal hassles over estates are not new. In olden times, when a husband died, part of his estate was widow's dowry — that which she brought to the marriage as a dowry. But what about other items she may have brought? To describe such things, they borrowed from the Greek...*parephenalia* for *property outside the dowry.*

When good fortune cancels one's mistakes, it is called planning.

HOORAY FOR BUREAUCRACY!

Today we think of a large governmental division as *bureau*. Before that a *bureau* was an office where a writing desk stood. Prior to that, it was the writing desk itself. But, even before that, it was a wool cloth that was placed on top of a writing desk. Give a *bureau* an inch and it'll take over the entire building.

We know a pretentious lady who never says ***bureau****...always* ***chiffonier****. We're dying to tell her that chiffonier is French for* ***rag-picker****.*

What with the federal government dropping sacks of taxpayer dollars into the waiting talons of researchers, why don't they get down to the serious stuff, such as: Are there male ladybugs? If so, is he called a ladybug person of the male persuasion?

While we're on research, doesn't that mean to search again? How come they didn't make all those expensive discoveries the first time? Maybe what this country needs are *search grants*.

Some of those who work for the government are called civil servants. The rest are called taxpayers.

Former Democratic Governor of Mass., tells of a father explaining politics to his son.

Son: "Father, what's a renegade?"

Father: "A renegade is a Democrat who votes for a Republican."

Son: "Well, what is a Republican who votes for a Democrat?"

Father: "A convert, my boy, a convert."

A reactionary is a somnambulist walking backward.

Franklin D. Roosevelt

THAT PINKO RADICAL!

The term *radical* stems from a Latin word for *root*. A radical, then, was someone who wanted to get at the root of a matter. Same word pops up in our word for that pinko edible root, the radish.

A radical is a man with both feet planted firmly in the air.

Franklin D. Roosevelt

You've probably heard that *barbarian* was a Greek word for foreigner. Actually, the definition went further. A *barbarian* was a stammerer — that is, the Greeks couldn't understand his language. On the other hand, when the Greeks used the word *idiot*, it didn't refer to intelligence. An *idiot* was simply a person who lived on his own and took no interest in politics and civic affairs. Today a lot of idiots do get involved in politics.

Fact: The ability to describe others as they see themselves.

A. Lincoln

And it's only accurate if Senators are older than Congressmen, on the average, since *senator* is a Latin word meaning old man. By the way, in ancient Rome, a Senator received no pay, just respect. The opposite appears to be true quite often nowadays.

Injustice isn't so bad when you consider that justice is rendering to each of us exactly what we're due.

RIDDLE: *Amnesia* and *amnesty* look alike. Are they similar in origin?

ANSWER: You bet your sweet loss of memory they are. When you can't remember, that's *amnesia*. When a government decides not to remember an unlawful act, it grants *amnesty*. Same Greek root for both.

It's easy to see how the Latin word for oaken, *robustus*, became our *robust.* It's harder to figure *corroborate*, but it meant to harden the oak, as with testimony.

A politician is a person with whose politics you don't agree: If you agree with him, he is a statesman.

David Lloyd George

FOR THE MAN WHO HAS EVERYTHING BUT GOOD SENSE!

Charlie Mimmerling is a secret reader of toothpaste tube labels and all other manner of trivia. Recently, while perusing a pamphlet on left-handedness among Coptic camel-drivers, he ran across the word *duopsony*. Blithely referring to his dictionary, he discovered that a *duopsony* is an *oligopsony* limited to two buyers. This so dampened his curiosity, he refused to go further, so we did: an *oligopsony* is a sales ploy in which a small number of buyers control the demand from a large number of sellers. Wait 'til Charlie hears!

"The secret for being a bore is to tell everything," according to Voltaire.

SYNONYMS TO LIVE BY!
*Your **righteous indignation** is his **prudery**.*
*She **exaggerates**; you **use your imagination**.*
*They're **picky**; you're **neat**.*
*Your **firm conviction** is his **stubborn streak**.*
*Their **hunch** is your **theory**.*
*She's a **snoop**; you're **alert**.*
*He's **insanely jealous**; you're **protective**.*

If you've been dying to know how the 'editorial we' evolved, fret no more. At one juncture in the Roman Empire there were two emperors — one in Rome and one in Constantinople (Byzantium). Therefore, all decrees, in order to be official, had to be issued under their joint authority. The "I" of prior times became "we."

Only presidents, editors and people with tapeworm have the right to use the editorial "we." *Mark Twain*

TO COLOGNE OR NOT TO COLOGNE, IS THAT THE QUESTION?

While enjoying an hour of commercials on television the other evening, a break occurred as the station inserted a smidgin of program material. This gave us the opportunity to close our eyes and review the marvelous sales pitches we'd seen.

The dancing cats had been as effective as ever; some new hamburger chain had devised a meat patty that squirted; a beer company had come to the rescue of a prize fighter who was on the verge of losing his something or other; a maternal lady had saved a dyspeptic warehouse foreman's day; but then there had been a puzzling young thing who had murmured a very odd phrase — something to the effect that her men wore a particular cologne (*Old Saddle Blanket*, perhaps) or *they didn't wear anything*.

Unraveling language being a hobby of ours, we dug in. Obviously *her* men wore that specific cologne or no cologne. Yet, if *she* had no preference, why should we? Or, was she implying that if her men had neglected to use that cologne, their only alternative was to disrobe right there on her doorstep?

We are as American as the next chap, and we feel duty-bound to follow the wise instructions coming from our television. The pretty young lady of the cologne commercial was desirable, forceful and knew her men. But how are we to select the proper course of action, when there are such alternatives?

In the Middle Ages they disinfected with smoke. They called it ***perfuming.***

RIDDLE: The word *pretty* seems to be losing its meaning. Is this true?

ANSWER: ***Pretty*** **has been moving from one meaning to the next for centuries. It began as a synonym for** ***crafty;*** **moved along to merely** ***clever;*** **then made a sudden switch to** ***courageous;*** **dropped back to** ***foppish;*** **then became** ***handsome*** **in a feminine sense. Some people use it in place of** ***very*** **and** ***quite*****.**

Silly found its way into our language through the Anglo-Saxon. To them it meant happy, as in: he proposed; she accepted; he felt perfectly *silly*.

Don't burn Bridget's behind, you!

PSHAW! SHE'S A HUSSY!

Whether one should attribute it to gossips or not, obviously someone had it in for women. For example, at one time *tart* was akin to *dear*...certainly not anymore. A *courtesan* formerly denoted a female member of a royal court. How about *wench?* A *wench* was simply a child...the contempt crept in later.

Of all things, a *hussy* was a housewife...any housewife. Before it picked up its current connotation, a *hussy* was also the name for a small bag in which a housewife kept her needle, thread and thimble.

At least *woman* reversed the procedure and gained in stature. Originally it was merely *a man's wife.*

NON SEQUITUR THOUGHTS:
"Martha, that button came off my shirt again."
"Oh, Arthur, I think I forgot to sew it on."
"Well, that explains why it fell off again."

ENTER BUXOM, EXIT POUTING!

At one time, a prison of sorts was known as a *spin-house* in England. There were no *buxom* women there, since *buxom* meant obedient — only *spinsters*, or immoral women.

If that mixes you up, we'll remind you that a *debut* was the first shot taken in billiards and a *coquette* was a man who strutted around like a cock.

Not only that, but to *wed* meant to wager — as in whether a groom was taking a bride 'for better or for worse.' And, if the bride got the sulks, she was sent off to the *boudoir*...or pouting room.

Long ago in England, **nice** *meant foolish. Isn't that nice?*

As two women reached the top of the stairs of the subway station, one stuck out her hand and complained, "When we got on the train fifteen minutes ago it was nice and *sunny*. Now look at this *rain!*"

"Well," her friend said philosophically. "It's better than no weather at all."

Her evening gown defied temperature, gravity and decency!

The plot of the famous English puppet shows *Punch and Judy*, called for Punch to win out over his shrewish wife in the end, which made him *pleased as Punch*.

Fashion designers are equal opportunity employers: they hire the emaciated!

MEANWHILE, DOWN IN THE MEADOW!

It hasn't been long since divorced women were called *grass widows*. Few guessed its earlier meaning. The British of the 16th Century used the term to describe an unmarried woman...especially if she were pregnant.

The *widow* part is easy — unmarried. *Grass* was an educated guess as to the bed on which the child was conceived.

The Scandinavians had a similar term which translates as *straw widow*.

A shifty-eyed **shegetz** *is someone who thinks a* **shicksa** *is an electric razor.*

The French have a word whose definition is to tie up in a bundle. That became *trousseau*, or the bundle of items a bride took to her new home. Of course, there have been brides who were carrying a bundle of a different sort and it wasn't considered part of her *trousseau*.

A **stuffed shirt** *is a person who laughs by appointment only.*

TAKE OFF THAT MILK AND SUGAR DRESS!

If various wardrobe articles and materials had maintained their original meanings, you might own some of these remarkable items: leg garments or *pajamas* (which makes pajama *tops* strange indeed); a little body, or a *corset* (which was the effect it aimed to create); a dress woven by Polish women or a *polka-dot* dress; a pair of knee bends or *garters*; twenty-two Croatians or *cravats*; and a summer dress of milk

RIDDLE: Is it correct to say that blondes have *auburn* hair?

ANSWER: It once was correct. The word came from the Latin word for fair-haired — *albernus*. The French fiddled with it and it came out *auburne*; then, in total confusion, they got it mixed up with *broune*, their own word for brown. After all this, a girl was lucky to have any hair at all.

and sugar or *seersucker*. With that we will *do on*, or don our coat and *do off*, or doff our hat and leave by the *bread closet* or pantry.

HECKLE THAT TEASE RIGHT OUT OF YOUR HAIR!

You can, you know. In the early days of cloth manufacturing, a *hekel* was a tool for combing wool and flax; a *teazel* was another tool, used to raise the nap on a fabric. Now *heckle* and *tease* mean about the same thing.

The original sense of **disheveled** *was bald, making* **disheveled** *hair unlikely. Applied to clothing, can we presume it indicated nudity?*

IS THAT A SHOE YOU'RE WEARING AROUND YOUR NECK?

In the 16th Century, *necklace* was quite logically lace for the neck. Then some crazy started calling shoe strings *laces*. Jewelers gave in and called any cord around the neck a *necklace*. Shoemen stick to your laces to the last!

When a French workingman became uncontrollably upset with management, he took off one of his wooden shoes and tossed it into the machinery. They called it an act of *sabotage*, because the wooden shoe was a *sabot*. And 'putting a monkey wrench into the works' actually describes another act of sabotage. Equally effective.

We didn't know that you knew a scye is the armhole of a garment.

THRILL YOUR EARS AND DRILL YOUR NOSE!

Thrillen was Middle English for pierce. In their imaginative way they pictured the nose as a solid hunk of flesh with piercings or *nostrils*. Oh, yes, and to *thrill* was to pierce with emotion.

Wearing damp stocking caps causes mildewed earlobes.

FABRICATIONS!

The well-mannered woman of the 17th Century guarded against soiling her gown while *bibbing* (or sipping) wine by folding a piece of linen or lace across her breast and attaching it to the neck of her gown. This item was called a *tucker*. So, best bibbing tucker eventually became *best bib and tucker.*

Handkerchief is another word the English twisted to their own purposes. At first the French had the *couvrir chef* or cloth to cover the head. The British borrowed it, but since they used the cloth to wipe their faces, they stuck *hand* in front of the original word.

Excuses: Premeditated lies.

Mothers, before you go discarding your son's favorite corduroys, be aware of the regal background of this maligned material. Corded fabric has been with us a long time. In France, the very finest of such cloth was called *corde du roi* — cord of the king. He probably let his get filthy, too.

Chiffon has been a tricky little fabric. You may think of it as delicate and gauzy. In Germany, it was once a stout-woven linen fabric, while in Romania it was bleached cotton shirting material. And to the French it simply meant a rag. In loomed materials, it's generally thought the lengthwise threads are called the *warp,* while the cross-threads are termed the *woof.* However, lengthwise threads have also been called *organzine, twist* and *caine*; besides woof for the cross-threads, *weft, tram, shoot* and *filling* have also been used.

A canopy used to be a bed protected from mosquitos with netting...all around.

CALLED ON THE CARPET!

Carpet used to be any thick, woolly cloth. One could wear *carpet.* Then it became a bedspread or tablecloth. So, a serious matter being considered by a council was one they *put on the carpet* for discussion. Meanwhile, the poor fellow who couldn't tell a bedspread from a tablecloth...

Melancholy babies come from crossing cantaloupes with Scottish sheep dogs.

MADE TO MEASURE!

The English weavers used to measure cloth by the elbow or, as they put it, from the *eln* (forearm including the hand) to the *boga* or bending.

Many centuries before, the Greeks had a similar unit of measure (from the knuckles to the elbow) which they called a *pygmaios.* Now you also know how the word *pygmy* originated.

RIDDLE: What is always leading fashion but still always out of date?

ANSWER: The letter F.

If you can fathom the above, maybe you can fathom the *fathom*. In old England, that was the distance between your two outstretched arms or, on the average, six feet.

If you have been using the old expression *it's as broad as it is long*, you are guilty of a linguistic inaccuracy. You see, only the greater of two dimensions may be designated as length. In the case of a square object, all dimensions are of *equal length*. (Don't you hate a smart ass!)

POTPOURRI!

If you see no connection between *Brittany, klafter* and *biscuit,* consider yourself normal. *Brittany*, the northwestern portion of France, derives its name from the Britons who fled there from England in the 6th Century. Before the Britons arrived, it was called Armorica.

Klafter is an old Austrian measure, no longer used. It was a hair over two yards.

And *biscuit* originally applied to a thin, flat bread doled out to French troops. *Biscuit* meant two bakings. That consumed the moisture so the bread would keep a long time. Today *biscuit* is also known as 'the bride's revenge.'

Is it the British insistence upon calling a cracker a ***biscuit*** *that drives them* ***crackers?***

Edward VII, England's monarch from 1901 to 1910, was Queen Victoria's oldest son. That eminent lady had the longest reign in British history, so Edward had sixty years of being the Prince of Wales before attaining the throne. He whiled away his hours as a *bon vivant*. After becoming King, he had the royal chef whip up one of Edward's very own recipes — *chicken a la king*. He was also known as the father of King George V. We prefer to remember him for the latter achievement.

Bangers: British slang for breakfast sausage and for billiard balls. Hmmm!

If you mix milk or cream with wine, and whip it, you have produced an item called *sillabub*. It's to be eaten, not drunk. On the other hand, if you fry a mixture of peas, wheat flour, barley, baking soda and salt, you'll come up with a Scottish bread called *bannock*. And if you're wondering why some soups are termed *chowders*, the word came from a French word for the cauldron in which fishermen cooked fish soup.

*Since **loaf** once meant bread and **bread** stood for crumbs, is a loaf of bread crumby?*

It's true that the Indians inhabiting what is now the northeastern portion of the United States led a simple life. But their language was far from simple. *Massachusetts* and *Connecticut* are American simplifications of their words. In their language, an edible fish found in New England's coastal waters was called the *mishcuppauog*. American colonists liked the fish but couldn't swallow the name, so they dubbed it the *scup*.

The earliest 'gourmets' knew little about fine food, being stable boys.

Before digging into that tomato *aspic*, take note of the fact that this toothsome jelly got its name from being *cold as an asp*...same snake that did Cleopatra in.

Avoid all meals described as 'a potpourri'...it means rotten pot!

Luncheon, in an old English dialect, began as *lunshin*...a lump of food. It's amazing how many fast-food outlets have discovered this.

*Irv and Nora Weissman had Connie McKenzie for dinner and pronounced her **delicious**!*

Tantalus was a mythical Greek king who was punished for a crime by being sent to the underworld. There he was forced to stand in water up to his neck. Above his head were branches covered with tasty fruit. Whenever he tried to reach for the fruit, it was pulled back from him. Whenever he bent to drink the water, it receded. From poor Tantalus comes the word *tantalize*.

Tapioca pudding? Ugh! Didn't you know it means 'squeeze out the dregs?'

When the French harvested their grapes, they used a pruning hook they knew as a *grappe*. The English mistook the tool for the fruit and so we have *grape*.

RIDDLE: Does *garlic* look like an onion leaf?

ANSWER: It did to someone in England long ago, because *garlic* comes from their words for onion leaf.

FUNGUS, SPICES AND JUICE ON YOUR COTTAGE CHEESE?

Lots of people do it, we're told. It all started when the Dutch brought back from China a sauce made from fungi, spices and juices which the Chinese called *ke-tsiap.* Later on someone added tomatoes and called it ketsup, catsup and a lot of other things.

Relish, coming from the French for *leave behind*, makes sense when you think of the bite you leave until last. (Except on your hot dog.)

Claptrap: any trick to get a clap from the audience. Seriously!

ENCORE, HELL. NO CORE AT ALL!

Most audiences today are sedate, at least when measured against times when fruit and vegetable throwing were common reactions of displeasure.

A favorite way of voicing disapproval was to hiss at the players. As this simulated the sound geese make, it came to be known as *to get the goose.* Eventually it became simply *to get the bird.*

Continuing in the bird vein, a performer's farewell appearance was called a *swan song* from an ancient legend that the voiceless swan burst into glorious song just before dying.

Not being particularly adept at catching the words of foreign songs, we're not sure of how that Polish *Melody of Love* goes, but to us it sounds like *Numb-skull, Your Ankle's in the Cola.*

She was graceful and sweet — half antelope, half canteloupe!

STRIKE UP THE DANCERS!

It's easy to see how we got to the current meaning of *orchestra* since the French called that the area for musicians. But, how in the hell did the French get it, when the Roman's *orchestra* was a spot reserved for Senators; and before them, the Greek's *orchestra* designated the spot in their outdoor theaters where the dancers performed?

A 'carol' was a dance and a 'chorus' a group of dancers. Singers are pushy.

The only thing the *pibroch* and *coronach* have in common is that both are played on the bagpipe. The *pibroch* is a giddy martial air while the *coronach* is a funeral dirge.

FOLD YOUR ASS AND GET OFF THE GRASS!

Not you...that painter over there.

You see, the Dutch took one look at an artist's easel and decided it looked akin to a carpenter's sawhorse. So, they gave it their name for an ass — *ezel.*

The British, in a typical fit of euphemism, simply altered the spelling of their earthier Dutch neighbor's word.

When you steal from one author, it's plagiarism; if you steal from many, it's research.

Wilson Mizner

THE CONFUSING HUCKSTERS!

Advertising personnel must have special dictionaries unlike ours. Their use of certain words is mystifying. We are now told that a certain cigarette is composed of *virgin* tobacco. We presume such tobacco to be pure, unsullied, not used. Is it then proper to assume that all those other cigarettes are prepared with impure, sullied, used tobacco? How on earth can they use it and still be able to make a passable cigarette from it?

Heredity runs in his family.

SMOKEY SLOGANS!

Damn the Surgeon General! Well, of course he was perfectly right warning us of the ill effects of tobacco. But didn't he realize what he was doing to the vibrant prose of the cigarette hucksters?

RIDDLE: Is smoking *sea foam* hazardous to one's health?

ANSWER: We don't know anyone who has tried it. Are you confused with the German *meerschaum*, meaning sea foam, which is a white mineral used to make pipes?

There is nothing stirring about a mundane discussion of the relative merits of cigarettes based upon their tar and nicotine content. And at least one firm was honest enough to label the war of length as a *silly millimeter.*

Come on, boys, stop giving us macho types who leer at us from giant billboards and tell us they smoke some brand or other simply because they like it. Few of us are moved to emulate defiant children! And please quit with sniggering references as to *how far women have come, baby!*

Give us some of the old-time slogans, something we'll remember and perhaps even repeat without knowing why.

You want *macho* the way it was in the Thirties? How about the tobacco company that browbeat us into buying their cigarette because *Nature in the Raw is Seldom Mild.* Of course, they spoiled it by adding some drivel about toasting. Same outfit went straight for the jugular when they pitched the ladies with *Reach For a Lucky Instead of a Sweet!*

There was a simple-minded charm in the promise made for Old Golds — *Not a Cough In Carload.* And Chesterfields were the soul of brevity — *They Satisfy.*

You want product loyalty? Oh, what they did with the slogan *I'd Walk a Mile for a Camel*...including such jokes as, "Yes, and I'd walk twice as far for a girl." We knew men who got so they gagged every time they lit up, but they wouldn't show the white feather. No indeed! They had a commitment!

So, open up your typewriters and attack! Here's one for a starter: *The Surgeon General Wears Corrective Army Shoes!*

*Why must it be **bashful** and never **full of bash**?*

COUNT YOUR BLESSINGS!

Don't be embarrassed if you must use your fingers to count. That's the way the decimal system started. And Anglo-Saxon swineherds counted their hogs on their fingers. When they got past ten, they used *el lif,* meaning one left; twelve was *twa lif* or two left. Then for reasons known only to Anglo-Saxon swineherds, they jumped to *threotyne* — their words for three and ten. You didn't really expect this to make a lot of sense, did you?

The natives of Tasmania, the island lying just below Australia, counted it as *many*. Many Americans would count it as a *few*.

When you can't mend the fence, it's time to stonewall it!

THE SINISTER LEFT-HANDER!

Most prejudice is deep-rooted and, that against left-handedness is no exception. The Romans referred to the right hand as *dextra*. From that we get *dextrous*, implying adept; *ambidextrous* or both right hands, signifying adeptness with either hand as if both were right hands. And the French word for the law or the right is *droit*, from which we get another term for adeptness, *adroit*.

On the other hand, literally, the Latin *sinistra* meant left-handed. And in French, it's *gauche* — awkward. In England, *gawky* was left-handed. Even *left* is defined as the side on which muscular action is weaker...*right* as the side of more skilled motor action.

The only break given left-handers, that we can think of, is in the military...all forward marching begins *left, right, left.*

Except for being faultless, he has no faults. *Pliny the Younger*

EITHER KNUCKLE UNDER OR KNUCKLE DOWN!

Knuckles weren't necessarily a person's finger joints. For instance, the expression *to knuckle under* referred to the knee joints — to indicate submission by falling to one's knees.

But *to get one's back into a job* is akin to *knuckle down*, since the knuckles involved were the vertebrae.

Most phants are crazy. The craziest is the sychophant.

RIDDLE: You know that *cranial* pertains to your skull and *abdominal* pertains to your abdomen. See if you can match the adjectives below in the left-hand column with the parts of your body in the right-hand column:

1. gular	**A. ankle**
2. malar	**B. nostril**
3. gnathic	**C. fingers or toes**
4. tarsal	**D. cheek**
5. metopic	**E. ear**
6. patellar	**F. forehead**
7. dactylic	**G. throat**
8. otic	**H. kneecap**
9. narine	**I. jaw**

ANSWER: The proper match-ups are: 1-G; 2-D; 3-I; 4-A; 5-F; 6-H; 7-C; 8-E; and 9-B. Now you know why you can never rub your *gular* region against your *metopic* area.

In 1905, a certain Dr. Des Voeux, complaining to the Public Health Congress about London's smoke and fog, called the stuff ***smog.***

KNEE BONE CONNECTED TO THE LEG BONE!

That old song seems to cover every possible pair of connecting bones except the *cuckoo's beak connected to the sacred bone. Sacrum* is the Latin word for the end of the spinal column, where it joins the pelvis; appended to the sacrum is the Greek word for a cuckoo's beak — *coccyx* — because that's how it looks.

Spinning Dreams: To 'sleep like a top' has nothing to do with spinning. It comes from the illusion that a spinning top is immobile.

FEELING DAUNCEY? DRINK A LITTLE SWITCHEL!

In some sections of mid-America *dauncey* was a 19th Century word meaning to feel listless, and *switchel* was a tonic of molasses and water flavored with ginger.

Same area, same time: a sled with a barrel on it was called a *lizard* and it was used to haul water in the summer. A *sugan* was a heavy bedspread. And the *fraid-hole* was shelter from a cyclone.

Sixty-two percent of America's private hospitals are out of pellagra! Give!

ANOTHER HECTIC DAY AT THE HOSPITAL!

Long ago — even before Blue Cross — the Greek physician Galen noticed that a great many of his coughing patients always had flushed cheeks. Recognizing this as a symptom, he referred to all such patients as 'habitually flushed'...only he shortened it to the Greek word for habitually — *hektikos.*

Physicians in the 15th Century started calling the disease associated with flushed cheeks 'Hectic Fever.' Now we know it as *tuberculosis.* Sufferers of TB are understandably nervous and excitable...a condition described as *hectic.*

You won't be nearly so petrified the next time you get a flu shot if you think of that object in the nurse's hand as a ***hypodemic nerdle.***

Have you ever noticed that recipes and medical prescriptions begin the same way, with *take two eggs* or *take four times a day*? There's a perfectly good reason for the similarity: *recipe* is a Latin verb meaning to take, and the Rx of prescriptions is simply an abbreviation for it.

There once was a Spoctor named Dooner
Who travelled by schip, not by shooner
Had a tarvelous mime
On the Rhanube and Dine
Said he'd rather go sate than looner.

THE GREEKS HAD A WORD FOR IT!

Is *seasick* the correct word for that lovely sensation one gets aboard ship? The question is: is it the motion of the sea that sickens us, or is it the motion of the ship *on* the sea? The Greeks evidently leaned toward the latter — their word for ship was *naus* which leads directly to *nausea*.

But, perhaps, when the condition hits you, you're not too concerned with etymology.

Metrically speaking, as we are wont to do these days, twenty-eight and almost over one third grams of prevention are worth just about .453 of a kilogram of cure. Work it out!

SAIL AWAY!

Stop biting your nails! We are about to reveal to you some of the mysteries of words with a naval background.

A *gob* is a sailor for the simple reason that the Chinese word for sailor is *gob*.

Describing an object's condition as *A-1* comes straight out of Lloyd's Shipping Register and means that the hull, anchor, cables and stores are first-rate.

A ship is referred to in the feminine gender because the Ancients dedicated a new ship to a goddess to gain her protection. And, the bow was carved in the goddesses' likeness, so she could help them find the way at sea.

Even that old expression *to make ends meet* is nautical in origin. Centuries ago, the owners of some sailing ships were such cheapskates (a non-naval term meaning a worthless old horse) they wouldn't buy new rope. Instead, they forced the sailors to splice the broken ends

RIDDLE: We know a *twitch* is a sudden movement or spasm. Is there another meaning?

ANSWER: Midwesterners once called a stick with a rope loop at one end a *twitch*. The loop fitted around a horse's upper lip. An assistant held it while the blacksmith shod the horse. Given that treatment, who wouldn't twitch?

together — that is, they *made both ends meet* and saved money.

On sailing ships, a good sailor was one who *knew the ropes*.

Don't be confused that *governor* comes from the Greek to direct a ship. Even way back then, they used the metaphor *ship of state*.

In the days of piracy, a person, capturing a pirate with a price on his head, was paid what was known as *head and gun* money.

Derelictus — Latin for wholly forsaken. When everyone leaves a ship, it becomes a *derelict*. And society has forsaken the men on Skid Row.

*Put together the Latin words for **almost** and **island** and you get **peninsula**.*

THE QUIZ!

Quiz is a modern word. It has the distinction of being the only one added to dictionaries as the direct result of a bet. More surprising is the fact that when the word was first formed, it was meant to mean exactly — *nothing*.

Quiz, as a word, was born in Ireland about 1780. Its parents were the manager of a Dublin theater (a Mr. Daly) and some of his friends.

One night they discussed the gullibility of people. Daly asserted that "the mob" could be made to believe and accept well nigh anything. His friends maintained that people were not that stupid. But Daly was adamant and said he was prepared to prove his point. He claimed he could make the masses adopt a new word — a meaningless chain of letters — just overnight. He was ready to bet on this. His friends felt quite safe in agreeing to the wager, feeling secure that the odds were in their favor.

All night Daly and his helpful friends rushed through the streets of Dublin with pails of paint and brushes.

Next morning, Dubliners, wherever they went, found — on houses, pavements and fences — four mysterious letters: Q U I Z .

Everyone began asking what they meant. Before long the *quiz* spread throughout Dublin and then all over the world. Originally introduced to prove man's foolishness, it now is used to demonstrate the extent of his knowledge, which is yet another paradox of human life. (Some people have seen in *quiz* an abbreviation of the word inquisition, i.e. questioning.)

I am always ready to learn, although I do not always like being taught.
W. Churchill

FOR THE BOTANIST!

We know that shamrock is an Irish word for *little clover*. Hell, we even know that *petunia* got its name because it looked like a little tobacco plant, or as the Indians called tobacco — *petun*. That ain't all: *nasturtium* is just two Latin words meaning nose-twisting. *Crocus* and *lilac* aren't all that tough either: the Greek word for yellow is *crocus* and blue was *lilac* in Persian. Understand?

A bird in the hand is worth two brushes.

Picture a group of people with three things in common: each has a vivid imagination, a knowledge of various languages and a love of plant life. Now you've had a glimpse of the men and women responsible for the names of many flowering plants.

In England, someone admiring a *daisy* was reminded of the rays of the rising Sun, or as they called it — the day's eye. In Greek *coreopsis* meant the appearance of a bug, and that's what its seeds look like. The seed pods of the *geranium* look like a crane, or *geranos* in Greek and, since the geranium is of the *pelargonium* genus, it was natural to borrow the Greek word for stork.

In the *gladiolus* flower, another saw the Latin *gladius*, sword. The French word for thoughtful — *pensee* — inspired the name for the *pansy*; and the French tooth of the lion — *dent du lion* — led to *dandelion*.

RIDDLE: What is a *buccaneer*?

ANSWER: Either very expensive corn or the guy who sells it.

Someone who knew the Turkish word for *turban* named the *tulip*. Another saw the *heliotrope* turn toward the Sun and merely used the Greek words for this reaction. In a similar vein, *philodendron* evolved from Greek *tree-loving*. And one that requires little translation — *larkspur*, like the spur or claw of the lark.

Ronald Thigsby claims to have great difficulty in distinguishing *halophytes* from *xerophytes*, and he's almost as uncertain when faced with *epiphytes* and *hydrophytes*. If Ronald would brush up on his botany, he'd know that *halophytes* are plants loving saline soil, while *xerophytes* just love any dry soil; naturally, the *epiphyte* is a plant which takes in moisture from the air, while a *hydrophyte* is mad about water. So most plants fall into which of these *phytes*? Gotcha! None of them. Most plants are *mesophytes*, meaning they like a middling amount of water.

A creature which eats other animals is called ***carnivorous****, one which eats plants is called* ***herbivorous*** *and a child who eats his parents is called an orphan.*

If California's place names seem hard to pronounce, consider that many were Indian words which the Spanish tinkered with and then the Americans garbled a bit more. In the process, the original meanings were obscured as well. Take the California resort and artist's community of Ojai (Ō'hī). It either means *nest* or *big tree* or *moon* — take your pick.

If *parking strip* means to you the space between the sidewalk and the curb, you're not from Akron, Ohio, where it's called a *devil strip*, or from western Massachusetts where it's a *tree belt*.

Take a good look at a snapdragon flower and you'll see why it's a member of ***antirrhinum*** *genus. Antirrhinum is from the Greek meaning* ***like a nose.***

DECADE OF ACRONYM FORMATION (or DEAF)!

Human minds are forever devising new words. The 1970's has been the era when so many names for organizations have been built up from the initials. NOW, the National Organization of Women, is a current example.

While the proliferation has been greatest in recent years, World War II spawned some of the best known acronyms. For instance, *jeep* came from the Army's description of the rugged little vehicle — *G*eneral *P*urpose car. The Navy's *C*onstruction *B*attalions became, appropriately, the *seabees*.

The active role of women during the war gave birth to *WAC*s and *WAVES*. WACs were members of the *W*omens' *A*rmy *C*orps, but can you remember what WAVES signified? Here is where you see a bit of forcing to create a name associated with a function. WAVES were in the U.S. Navy, but the full title was *W*omen *A*ccepted for *V*olunteer *E*mergency *S*ervice.

Radar, too, is an acronym, and so widely used it has become a permanent part of the language. It stems from *ra*(dio) *d*(etecting) *a*(nd) *r*(anging).

Not all the acronyms of World War II were coined at the upper echelon. It was the opinion of the troops that gave rise to the famous SNAFU, which can be politely transcribed as *S*ituation *N*ormal-*A*ll *F*ouled *U*p.

In some cases, initials by themselves represented a recognized entity. *GI* (Government Issue) came to indicate anything to do with the armed forces, including the people. S.O.S. is another set of initials which is universally understood to mean a cry for help. However, S.O.S. is not the initial form of Save Our Ship, as many think, but is a message a wireless operator can send swiftly — three dots, three dashes, three dots. It was accepted as the International distress call in 1912.

A metric telephone has 8.3 numbers on the dial!

In this age of words being formed from initials we had almost forgotten that *PBX* stands for a private branch exchange telephone system.

CHAPTER TWO

Name Calling

Ever since the Neanderthal man and his playmates got sick of mucking about in the primordial ooze and starting saying things such as "Hey, for an epoch, this Pleistocene ain't half bad," we've had this urge to hang a name on everything. After all, how are we supposed to grasp anything if it has no handle?

Quicker than you can say, "I had a mastodon for lunch," man began giving *himself* names. Nothing too fancy at first — Ugh, Flump, Argh and an occasional Percival. Then, really getting into the swing of the game, they began using names to describe a man's appearance, or what he did or to describe a big event in his life. That's how we got such appellations as *Old Liver Lips*, *Hairy*, *He That Drags Women To His Cave For No Good* (an early Cenozoic zinger), *Pterodactyl Nostrils*, *Hungover*, *Droopy Loincloth* and *Donated Arm*

To Saber-Toothed Tiger Last Wednesday.

Naturally, as with any first-class frenzy, interest died down. People began taking names for granted, until, today, your average *Arthur* has no idea he's a *bear hero*...and damned few Brendas go around saying, "I'm a *sword.*"

So, awake, America! If someone introduces himself to you as Norman Sterling Wesley, get curious. Say right back at him, "What in hell does that mean?" Since the odds are he doesn't know, we'll tell you. Norman once meant *northern man;* Sterling was *eastern man;* and Wesley stood for the *west meadow.* Now, what you have is a weirdo or a guy whose parents were avowed sadists. Otherwise, why call him *Northerner Easterner of the West Meadow?* A walking road map!

Before you chuckle all over your cornflakes about poor Norman, better get a fix on your own monicker. Maybe you're Barbara Wallace. Sounds innocent enough. But, what it really means is *stranger stranger*. And, if you think that's redundant, Tamsen Thomas can give you double in spades. Her name literally comes out *twin twin*. And no wonder Parry Harrison looks glassy-eyed. How would you like to be known as *son of Harry son of Harry?*

Okay, gang...now it's on to the good stuff of which names are made.

Don't let it slip your mind that long ago if someone wanted to say 'famous healthy wolf,' they only needed two words — Rudolph Valentino.

THE THROATY POLYPHONES!

It may be just as well that we don't use the original words from which the names of several famous singers have been taken. Our house name-freak says Dinah Shore could be translated as *I'll Be Judged On the Edge. A Clerk Trying to Find Something* sounds more like an office crisis than Petula Clark. And who would interpret Julie Andrews as *A Downy-Haired Manly Person?*

And Hildegarde, settled into some swank supper club, hardly gives the impression of a *Battle Spear*. Nor does *Prosperous War of the Red Earth* suggest the delightful Edie Adams. But all Sara Vaughan

RIDDLE: Lawrence Welk had it first;
Pope Paul had it last;
Bob Hope never had it;
Clark Gable had it twice in different places; Margaret Sullivan had it twice in the same place, but after she married Henry Fonda, she never had it again. Well?

ANSWER: The letter L.

fans would agree to *Little Princess.*

Over on the virile side, Burl Ives certainly looks the part of *Shaggy Lord. Famous Son of the Wave* has a poetic lilt, so it's not surprising to learn that it's the real meaning of Bob Dylan. Deepen the color a bit and *Red Country Boy* does sound like Ray Charles.

However, it's doubtful if Fabian would have sold as many records if the translation of his name were used — *One Who Cultivates Beans.* And we're tongue-tied to discover that Glenn Campbell comes out *Crooked Mouth from the Valley.*

Leap back a few generations into the Swing Era and you'll find that Bea Wayne connotes *Blessed Wagon-Maker*, Alice Faye alludes to *Noble Fairy* and then there were *The Manly Sisters*, known to most of us as the Andrews Sisters.

And opera buffs today would have a hard time picturing Beverly Sills as *Heavenly Beaver Meadow.* Heavenly, yes.

We'll always still picture Mary Martin with a bright, happy smile, but long ago her name meant *bitter struggle of the warrior.*

Does *Little Determined Helmet* sound like a popular composer to you? It is, though. That's what Paul Williams meant once upon a time. (Hey, that's catchy.)

In one of Shakespeare's plays, one guy said, "Toby, or not Toby?" And that's the last he was ever mentioned so we didn't find out.

THE BROADCASTERS!

Little did we know the last time we saw Tony Martin on TV that his names signified *expensive warrior* (maybe the sponsor knows). We suppose it's natural that Steve Allen had been *crown of harmony*. But would you have imagined that *bear-like hero of peace* was spoken in two words...Arthur Godfrey?

Somehow or another we don't picture Lowell Thomas as a *wolf cub twin*, yet that's what the name connoted at one time. Or the popular radio program of the 1930's — Amos and Andy — would have meant *courageous and manly.*

And, in bygone days, a Barbara Walters was a ***stranger who rules people.***

RADIO BLOOPERS, People and Places Department:

"And now the President of the United States, Heebert Hover."

"From the Rump Room in Chicago's..."

"Here's Connie Boswell of the famous Soswell Bisters."
"Tonight at seven tune in to President Roosevelt's Chireside Fat."
"The old Manassa Mauler, himself, Dack Jempsey."
"It's the Andrews Sisters now with DON'T SIT UNDER THE APPLE TREE WITH ANYTHING ON BUT ME."
"Don Hutson, star end of the Bean Gray Packers."
"Labor leader John L. Lewis said today that his moal kiners would not go..."
"Dog lovers were shocked to hear today that Germany's notorious Gestapo has been training dieberman ponch...pieber...ah, the hell with it."

Telly Savalas has a gleam in his eye and one on top of his head!

IN THE SPOTLIGHT!

Long ago when someone wished to say *very wise one from Preston meadow,* they spoke two words: Elvis Presley. Or, if they used Tony Curtis, they meant *priceless courtesy.* To transform the statement: the *spear-throwing barrel-maker* met a *man following after the pigs he was guarding,* one could simply state, "Gary Cooper met Jimmy Stewart."

A *powerful bee* once was Debbie Reynolds. (How apt). Remember: *little beauty of the big town* was once spoken as Bonita Granville. And another way to say William Holden was *resolute and gracious,* while *strong fighter* came out Boris Karloff.

Would you go to a movie featuring *bird, son of Hawk of the Plain* plus a *dark-skinned clerk* and an *eastern fireman* who were all vying for the hand of a *noble champion?* If you did, you would see Darren McGavin and Dane Clark and Sterling Hayden in pursuit of Patricia Neal. A staged fight between the *wagon-maker graced by God* and *famous crooked nose* would feature John Wayne doing battle with Rod Cameron.

Old-time movie cowboy Ken Maynard knew what he was about — his name meant *handsome and strong.* On the other hand, Anthony Quinn might have suited a lawyer better because it signified *expensive counsel.*

Some actresses would have liked the dramatic ring their present names had in times past: Eva Marie Saint — *life's bitter struggle;* Bette Davis — *Oath of God, Blessed of Jehovah* (wow); Sylvia Sidney — *the wine goddess who lives in the woods.* Others might not be as pleased: Simone Signoret — *snub-nose little miss*; Ursula Andress — *manly she-bear*; Paula Prentiss — *the little apprentice*; Celeste Holm — *heavenly river island*; and Tallulah Bankhead — *running water at the top of the river's side.*

There was a time when *bright blossom* was spoken as Claire Bloom and *starry queen* as Stella Stevens. And a *watchman over eight quarts* was a Gregory Peck, while a *king of the famous spear* was Roy Rogers.

Two rather old-fashioned words are Sarah and Miles which meant ***princess beloved.***

THE LITERARY FILE!

No question about the success of playwright, Neil Simon. His name tells us something — it meant *champion who listens.*

Then we're faced with the strange case of Sherlock Holmes and his creator Sir Arthur Conan Doyle. If we were to translate their names into the words they originally represented, we would have an author named *smart, bear-like, strange hero* and his fictional detective, the *man with cropped hair who lives in the river bottom.* Apologies to the Baker Street Irregulars, but that's the way it was.

Think twice before giving an eight-year-old girl a volume of ***Rebecca of Sunnybrook Farm. Rebecca*** *implies faithful wife.*

That great sing-along *Dinah* becomes "I'll be judged, is there anyone finer." The poor guy searching for *Chloe* is calling out, "Green thumb." The well-known Aussie song out of World War II should read *Waltz Me, Mighty Battle Maiden,* but it's doubtful if that's what they had in mind.

Booth Tarkington wrote ***Seventeen.*** *We did finish the sentence. That's the title.*

So, all you prospective parents...be on guard. Bone up or you'll make a funny that your poor kid will be stuck with for a lifetime. Just like Mr. and Mrs. Simon, who thought they'd named their daughter perfectly, not realizing that *Samantha Simon* denotes the listener listening.

MILITARY DIVISION!

Douglas originally meant *dark stranger*; Mac was *son of*; Arthur was *a hero with the strength of a bear.* Pretty accurate. In civil war days, Union Cavalry General Phillip Sheridan makes sense — Phillip is *lover of horses.*

After General William Sherman's march through Georgia, southerners would have agreed that his name meant *resolute sheep shearer.* And the South's own Robert Edward Lee is a translation from *famous guardian of prosperity from the valley.*

But the name that has us undone is Clark Kent. Let's face it, gang, we're talking about Superman! So Clark Kent must convey power and adventure, right? How does **chief clerk** *strike you as a literal translation?*

AND POLITICIANS!

If we were to use the original meanings of the names of various politicians, you would not recognize some of them — such as *famous clerk and army horse-shoer* for Herbert Clark Hoover — but you'd probably recognize *farmer from the home of the people of Wassa* as George Washington.

Could anyone guess that *dweller in the house in the row by the woods and son of the resolute warrior* was the original meaning of Woodrow Wilson? But you might have predicted that the late Supreme Court Chief Justice, Earl Warren, meant *noble defender.* Long ago, if a man was called George Wallace, it meant *strange farmer.* There are probably those in the ranks of the Gay Liberation who would disagree that Anita Bryant once meant *charming strength.*

Then there was that famous Roman-Egyptian triumvirate: Marc Antony appropriately meant *warlike and expensive; bald ruler* spells Julius Caesar; and Cleopatra simply suggested she had a *famous father.*

And today there is Jimmy Carter or *following after the cart-driver.* But is the cart before the horse, that's what we need to know?

Few would argue the aptness of the late Hubert Humphrey's

RIDDLE: Did Helen Brown and Alexandre Dagmar Lawrence-Klasen have anything in common?

ANSWER: You bet! Both achieved great fame as stage actresses — namely, as Helen Hayes and Gertrude Lawrence.

name, which came from words meaning *bright mind, sweet place.*

George Bernard Shaw telegram to Winston Churchill: "Sending you two opening night tickets to my new play. Bring a friend if you have one." Winston Churchill to Shaw, "Unable to come on opening night. Will come 2nd night if you have one."

SPORTS, TOO!

In our incessant and insane search for what names once meant, we are flabbered right out of our gast to discover a *fighting, friendly farmer* would have been called a George Herman Ruth. The *Sultan of Swat* a fighting, friendly farmer?

Any of you recall Cecil Travis, fine infielder of the old *Washington Senators?* His name stands for *blind at the crossroads*. Not good for an infielder.

But Joe Louis equals *profitable fight*.

And wouldn't you say that a *wanderer with eagle power* is a good description of a touring golf pro? Well, that's what Arnold Palmer means.

Also, *one who follows wealth* is suitable for a pro footballer...Jim Otto.

But *fighting oat-grower* for Harold "Red" Grange?

And now say good-bye to Agnes Kay (*pure pure*) and Glynis Dale (*valley valley*) and Russ Adams (*red red earth*) and to Guy Wyatt MacHughson (*Guy son of Guy son of Hugh's son*).

Remember, Eulalie, your name means you're a good speaker.

THE NAME'S NOT THE SAME!

You say you don't like your name? So, change it. Actresses and actors do it all the time. For instance, there was Fernanda Maschwitz. She didn't think she could hit it big in the dramatic field with that handle. So, she changed it to Hermione Gingold.

People outside the world of the theater make legal name switches, too. We know of a certain Piegan Flitterby who is now Jean Nud.

Whether true or not, there's the case of Ida Titworth who marched into court and got herself a new name — *Martha* Titworth. Seems she had grown weary of people saying to her, "Ida sweet as apple cider."

Performers who say, "Eat your heart out," should spend three years mining bat guano.

Sometimes it's obvious why an actress adopted a professional name. For example, in the late 1940's, there was a demure actress named Vanessa Brown. Her name and appearance matched. Her real name might have run counter to the intended image, because it was Smylla Brind.

But there are times when it's difficult to fathom a name change. One of Hollywood's leading ladies in the 1930's was billed as Anne Shirley. Good name. But what was wrong with her real name, Dawn Paris? Sounds dramatic to us. Anne Shirley wasn't the only name she used, however. She had been a child star in the 1920's under the name Dawn O'Day. Mysterious!

We think we know why Christian Rudolf Ebsen prefers the nickname Buddy.

We like most of the names movie actresses have assumed. *Sylvia Sidney* had been Sophia Kosow, while *Sophia Loren* started life as Sophia Scicoloni. *Mary Pickford* beats Gladys Smith. She may have been Shirley Schrift to her family, but she'll always be *Shelley Winters* to movie fans.

Claire Wemlinger blossomed into *Claire Trevor*. Alida Maria Altenburger opted for *Alida Valli*, while Josephine Cottle substituted *Gale Storm*.

Ruby Stevens might have suited a minor actress, but not big star *Barbara Stanwyck*. Harriette Lake isn't bad, but she changed it to *Ann Sothern*. And *Simone Signoret* entered the world as Simone Kaminker.

Emma Matzo did the right thing in becoming *Lizabeth Scott*. Giovanna Scoglio saved the world a pronunciation problem by choosing *Gia Scala*. And Jill Oppenheim was well-advised to become *Jill St. John*, we think.

Donna Mullenger's pert beauty is more believable as *Donna Reed*. Paula Ragusa adapted *Paula Prentiss*. Estelle O'Brien Merle Thompson saved a lot of space when she became *Merle Oberon.* And we'd have to agree that Rosetta Jacobs lacks the pizzazz of *Piper Laurie.*

But there are some pretty famous movie names which just may not have been improvements over the real names. You choose:

RIDDLE: Barbara Bratingham Czukor, Terry Ray and Geraldine Stroock all became leading ladies in films in the forties. What are their movie names?

ANSWER: Barbara Britton, Ellen Drew and Geraldine Brooks.

Virginia McMath (Ginger Rogers); Jane Peters (Carole Lombard); Jeanette Morrison (Janet Leigh); Dawn Bethel (Sheree North); Myrna Williams (Myrna Loy); Vivien Hartley (Vivien Leigh). And then there's Vera Miles. Her name had been Vera Ralston but, ten years before she broke into movies, there had been a beautiful Czech ice-skater in films named Vera Hruba Ralston.

In 1941, a stunning Norwegian actress came to Hollywood. Fortunately, she came to be known as Karen Verne, because her real name was Ingabor Katrine Klinckerfuss.

While the Belgians have not contributed very many stars to the American motion picture scene, they did give us Edda van Heemstra. Remember her in *Breakfast at Tiffany's*? We think she was using the name Audrey Hepburn. In fact, we're sure.

It's worth mentioning that Eric Weiss was performing a trapeze act on stage when just eight years old. Oh, he was later known by the name Harry Houdini.

Nancy Carroll — there was a name that suited the pretty star of *Shopworn Angel, Broken Lullaby* and other sentimental movies of the twenties and thirties much better than her real name — Anna la Hiff. And the stage and movie star of the same era — Ina Claire — was wise to switch from Ina Fagan.

***Rin-Tin-Tin** wasn't Hollywood's first canine star. That honor goes to a pooch named **Strongheart**.*

The names of three actors — Stepin Fetchit, Slim Pickens and Rip Torn — just seem too contrived to be true. And you're right. Stepin Fetchit was born Lincoln Perry. Slim Pickens began life as Louis Bert Lindley. Mr. Torn can be excused for switching from Elmore to Rip.

Dinah Shore should be seen to be heard!

ALTERATIONS!

Selecting just the right stage name may have played a larger part in an actor or actress's success than we can imagine.

If Patti Woodward hadn't changed her name to *Jane Darwell,* she might have had difficulty projecting all that motherliness. We're certain William Pratt could never have become synonomous with monsters the way he was as *Boris Karloff.*

Remember the deep-circled eyes and aura of menace which went so well with the name *Jack La Rue*. Aren't you glad he didn't remain Gaspare Biondolillo?

Would any of us have believed that tough exterior, heart-of-gold personality projected by *Karl Malden* if he had gone on using Malden Sekulovitch?

Ask anyone who was a film nut in the 1930's and 1940's to name an actor who could transform himself in the blink of an eye from the fat, jolly businessman to the sinister, cruel manipulator of men, and you'll always get *Edward Arnold*. But what if he had gone on being Guenther Schneider?

*At the risk of revealing our age, we knew that **Ricardo Cortez** was the suave Latin lover. If we'd known he was really Jacob Kranz, well...*

It was a lucky break for movie-goers, when Anne Italiano and Shirley Beaty were cast together in a motion picture. The movie was *The Turning Point*. Oh, yes, the names you'll see on the marquee are Anne Bancroft and Shirley Maclaine. Shirley didn't make such a big change to a stage name — her middle name is Maclean.

One of my chief regrets during my years in the theater is that I couldn't sit in the audience and watch me.

John Barrymore

Bela Lugosi, Count Dracula on the screen, was born in the Hungarian town of Lugos — so that explains *Lugosi*. It's a good thing he did change his name. American audiences might have had trouble with the one he was born with — Arisztid Olt.

Item to brighten a string of screen credits: Art Direction - Van Nest Polgase.

By the way, the real name of Zasu Pitts was Zasu Pitts. *Zasu* came from the names of two aunts — Eliz*a* and *Su*san.

*Some nut told us the actress who starred in **The Solid Gold Cadillac** was Judith Tuvim. By jove, he was right. Miss Tuvim had changed her name by then to Judy Holliday.*

RIDDLE: Did John and Ethel Blythe have an older brother who was famous?

ANSWER: They did indeed! His name was Lionel. All three of the Blythes used the stage name Barrymore rather than Blythe.

Add to your list of appropriate names that of American screen actor Glenn Strange. He played the role of the monster in two Frankenstein films (not the biggie, because that was Boris Karloff's ticket to fame).

In Hollywood, the woods are full of people that learned to write but evidently can't read; if they could read their stuff, they'd stop writing.
Will Rogers

Ranking close to the top in the cumbersome name category was Gabrielle Sybille Marie Antoinette Riquetti de Mirabeau, Comtesse de Martel de Janville, who understandably preferred the pseudonym *Gyp.*

Sticks and stones will break our bones, so just call us a few names.

Of course, if you don't know what various names really mean, perhaps no one else but a trivia maniac does either. However, some kids get stuck with names that *sound* pretty ridiculous. The most obvious pitfall to avoid is the rhyming name, such as Hugh Pugh, Bryan Ryan, Kevin Levin, Boris Morris, Gordon Jordan or Wyatt Hyatt. Near rhymes aren't much better — Myra Meyer or Glynis Ennis, for examples.

When you are down and out something always turns up — it's usually the noses of your friends.
Orson Wells

Watch out for the way a given name goes with your family name. Grove is a fine family name, but we pity *Olive Grove* almost as much as we feel for *Violet Green, Carol Singer, Roland Stone, Ina Rowe, Honor Duff, Rose Thorne, Lily Bloom, Pearl Gray and Jill Blaine.*

Oh, you aren't out of the woods yet! Think of all the lists on which your child's name will appear in a lifetime — last name first! Who wants to see an ambiguous listing of *Dyer, Fanny? Black, Mark* isn't good, but *Wilde, Kitty* is worse. *Dorr, Matt* and *Logan, Barry* are in for it, too, along with *Silver, Belle* and *Day, Lee.* We'd also avoid *Golden, Ray* and *White, Noel.*

P.J. Woon! Call your mother!

And then there are pernicious initials. We don't have to spell out for you the nicknames that will be hung on Frank Albert Graham or Oliver David Draper or Samuel Aaron Pritchard. Urban Frederick Ormsby would be in for many close encounters. We can't imagine a taxpayer enjoying Ira Ralph Stafford, and the nicknaming of George Arthur Burns would be enough to make him button his lip forever.

Egyptologist Ibn Achmed named his scarabs John, George, Paul and Ringo.

Don't let it throw you if someone looks at you askance because you don't have a middle name or initial. Seventeen of our presidents found it good enough to have but two names. In fact, the first five Chiefs had no middle name or initial. John Quincy Adams, the sixth president, broke the string.

John L. Lewis wore false eyebrows!

EVER THE MOTHER!

Isn't it odd that mothers address their children with a single pet name until a disciplinary crisis arises.

"Clifford Allison Parkhurst, Junior, get back in that high chair!"

Captain Ahab jumped ship!

That brings us to the final phase of how *not* to name your child: think ahead of nicknames from a given name and how they'll sound with your family name. Some are simple to spot in advance — Pete Moss, Harry Wolf, Jimmy Locke, Tom Katz and Jack Hammer to begin. Also to be avoided are Sanford *Sandy* Beach, Christopher *Chris* Cross, Beatrice *Bea* Long, Stewart *Stew* Lamb, Hedda *Head* Hunter, Lester *Les* Small and Melvin *Mel* Lowe.

Not all interpretations of nicknames are easy to predict. William Owen sounds innocuous enough until the time *Bill Owen* applies for credit. You may like the onomatopoeic sound of Juanita Mann, but we can guarantee she'll be dubbed either *Juana Mann* or *Nita Mann.* *Went*worth West and *Just*in Fine are in for it, along with *Will*ard Ketchum, *Hy*man Stiles and *Cliff*ord Hill. And contemplate the small change jokes generated by Penelope *Penny* Nichols. And Henry *Hank* O'Hare will never stop hearing that old description of what a woman is made of.

RIDDLE: What do Thomas Edison, Richard the Lion Hearted, Audubon, Charles Dickens and Frank Sinatra have in common?

ANSWER: They all qualify for the nickname "Old Blue Eyes."

With all the admonitions we've given you, there's a good chance the kid will be voting before you're sure you've selected a safe, no-jokes name. Perhaps you should simply number your children instead.

Nelson Rockefeller is better off than he knows how!

CAPITOL NAME!

Four state capitols bear the names of U.S. Presidents — Jackson (Mississippi), Madison (Wisconsin), Jefferson City (Missouri) and Lincoln (Nebraska). But Jackson, Mississippi wasn't really named for a president. It was picked in honor of Andrew Jackson, alright, but as the hero of the War of 1812, *before* he became president. Any money you win with this one you must share with the editors.

Princess Margaret after her father George VI had succeeded his abdicated brother, "Since my poppa turned King, I don't seem to be anyone at all."

We have had three sets of commanders with the same last name — William Henry and Benjamin Harrison, Andrew and Lyndon Johnson and Theodore and Franklin Roosevelt. But we've had three vice-presidents with the same last name — the two aforementioned Johnsons plus Van Buren's vice-president, Richard Johnson. Richard Johnson had another distinction — he was the only vice-president ever named by the Senate as there was no majority vote in the electoral college in the election of 1836.

Dick Cavett drives a 1934 Syntax!

EVERY TOM, DICK AND HARRY!

Until Jimmy Carter won a White House stay, there had been a tie between *James* and *John* for most common presidential first names. Now the *James* boys are out in front, 6 to 5.

He was so old he knew Jane Withers before she turned to plumbing.

Remarkable woman, remarkable human being that Golda Meir! How else can one describe a person who said, "I've always felt sorry for people afraid...of feeling, of sentimentality, of emotion, who conceal what they feel and are unable to weep with their whole heart.

Because those who do not know how to weep with their whole heart don't know how to laugh either."

Henry Kissinger is twice as expert as he once did!

THE CLOWNS!

In 1930, Eddie Cantor starred in his first sound movie — WHOOPEE (that's the title, not a reaction). The premiere was set for the Rivoli Theater in New York City.

On the gala night, Cantor showed up in a battered old Model-T.

When the doorman asked if he could park it for him, Cantor said, "No thanks. Just sell it and keep the change."

W.C. Fields (on being realistic): "There comes a time in the affairs of men when you must take the bull by the tail and face the situation."

Originally there were four Marx Brothers — Chico, Harpo, Groucho and Gummo. Another vaudevillian gave them their nicknames: Leonard became *Chico* because he loved chicken; Arthur became *Harpo* because he played the harp; Julius was dubbed *Groucho* because of his grouchy expression; and *Gummo* was Milton's nickname because he always wore rubbers over his shoes.

Attention American 13-year-olds: From now on you have to have your own passport.

RIDDLE: There have been four well-known Fords associated with motion pictures: leading man, Glenn Ford; fine director, John Ford; character actor Paul Ford (the flustered Colonel of the TV series *Bilko*); and tousled character actor Wallace Ford. Were any of the four born with the name Ford?

ANSWER: Paul Ford was born Paul Ford. Glenn Ford had been Gwyllyn Ford. Director John Ford was originally Sean O'Fienne and Wallace Ford was Sam Grundy.

Wasn't it Roger Wills who said, "I've never seen a galvanized iron tub I didn't like?" Or something like that.

In 1927, a vaudeville comic came to Hollywood and appeared in a movie titled *Rubber Heels*. It was a turkey, so Isaiah Leopold returned to New York. But he came back to Hollywood and made it big. He also made it big on radio and TV. The name he used was his own — his middle name, Edwin, which he split into a first and last name. He had an actor son, too — Keenan.

"Jesters do often prove prophets," according to Shakespeare.

WE LOVE LUCY!

Lucille Ball comes by her comedic flair naturally. In 1933, she was selected as one of the Goldwyn Girls, a group of smashing chorines whose job it was to enhance the musical goings-on in the film *Roman Scandals*. She thought if she could get the attention of the producer, Sam Goldwyn, she might improve her prospects in Hollywood.

On the day she knew Goldwyn was holding a story conference with his writers on the second floor of the studio executive building, Lucille is said to have driven her car up to the front of the building and honked. And honked.

Finally, Goldwyn, himself, came to the balcony and glared down at the pert redhead.

She smiled up at the glowering producer and said, "Can the writers come out and play with me now?"

Darryl Zanuck said he wouldn't vacation in the Rockies as the climate might disagree with him. Alan Young — "It wouldn't dare."

ONCE A COMEDIAN ALWAYS A COMEDIAN!

If John F. Sullivan, Joseph Kubelsky, Aaron Schwatt, Iss Isskowitz, Louis Cristillo, David Kaminsky, Irving Lahrheim, Arthur Jefferson, Joseph Levitch, Lewis Offield, Joe Yule, Richard Schulefand and Dorothy McNulty are names that bring a smile, it's only natural. That was their profession under the stage names of Fred Allen, Jack Benny, Red Buttons, Eddie Cantor, Lou Costello, Danny Kaye, Bert Lahr, Stan Laurel, Jerry Lewis, Jack Oakie, Mickey Rooney, Dick Shawn and Penny Singleton.

And don't forget the old-time comedy film producer Mickall Sinott, better known as Mack Sennett.

In a TV interview, James Thurber, tongue firmly in cheek, said, "Humor is a serious thing." Especially if you make your living at it.

The co-star of one of television's most successful comedy shows was a chap named Alberto de Acha. Doesn't ring a bell? Well, we tricked you by leaving out his first and third names which were Desiderio and Arnaz in that order.

Of course the meek should inherit the earth. They deserve it.

The Eve Arden Show had a host of TV fans, but very few of them seem to recall seeing Eunice Quedons in the series. They should have, because she played Eve Arden and has ever since she changed her name from Quedons.

Rich Little's parents can't remember him!

In his later movies, comedian Harold Lloyd wore gloves. The reason is a bit gruesome. It seems Lloyd was posing for comic publicity stills when a prop boy handed him a real bomb by mistake. The thing went off in the comedian's hand, taking off his thumb and forefinger and demolishing the studio.

*Nita Naldi, one of the silent screen's prettiest **vamps** (she starred with Valentino in **Blood and Sand**, 1921), did what most of us do...she got older and fatter. When this happened, she described herself as "Dracula in drag."*

THE SILENT ERA!

Have you ever wondered how come so many of the female stars of silent films had melodious names? Simple. Their real names lacked zing, or in some cases were impossible to pronounce. Thus, the lilting, alliterative creations. After all, even if movies were silent would you have gone out of your way to see Theodosia Goodman (Theda Bara), Marianne Michaelska (Gilda Gray), Reatha Watson (Barbara La Marr), Marie Koenig (Mae Murray), Anita Donna Dooley (Nita Naldi), Appolonia Chalupek (Pola Negri), or Anjuschka Sujakevitch (Anna Sten)?

RIDDLE: Was Walter Winchell, the columnist, ever on the stage?

ANSWER: With George Jessel, Eddie Cantor and a third East-Side Manhattan boy, Walter Winchell sang tenor in a quartet in one of the earliest nickelodeon movie houses. Subsequently, they were signed up by Gus Edwards, the vaudeville impresario, and performed as part of a Newsboy's Sextet.

When Rudolph Valentino decided on an acting career, he performed two enormous favors for the owners of movie houses. First, he brought them revenue beyond their fondest dreams. Second, he saved them the expense of building huge new marquees. He accomplished this by shortening his true baptismal name — Rudolpho Alfonzo Rafaelo Pierre Filibert Guglielmi di Valentina d'Antonguolla. Now it has cost us a buck and a quarter just to put his full name in print.

Julius Ullman, that swashbuckling hero of silent adventure films, had his name legally changed to Douglas Fairbanks.

THE TWENTIES!

Name changing in the movie world took various forms. For instance, two Austrians became famous directors in the 1920's. One, Joe Stern, lengthened his name to Joseph von Sternberg. The other, Hans Erich Maria Stroheim von Nordenwall, shortened his to Erich von Stroheim.

There may be flies on you and me, but there are no flies on Jesus.
Salvation Army Song (1900)

Warner's Vitaphone cranked out a mini-musical film in 1929 starring Ruth Etting. A couple of the bit players in this forgettable epic didn't even get screen credit for their roles — Joan Blondell and Humphrey Bogart.

Wilson Mizner on Hollywood — "a trip thru a sewer in a glass-bottomed boat."

HEY, OTTO LINKENHELT! ME, ENID MARKEY!

Unlike the stars of many motion pictures, the various men who played *Tarzan* weren't given glamorous names. The first *Tarzan* of movies did change his name from Otto Elmo Linkenhelt to Elmo Lincoln, but that transition hardly comes under the heading of glamorizing.

Subsequent *Tarzans* had such handles as Gene Polar (ideal for the steaming jungle), P. Dempsey Tabler (star of *Son of Tarzan*, 1920...the son was played by an actor named Kamuela C. Searle) and Herman Brix (who later changed his name to Bruce Bennett and became a good serious actor).

Of course, Olympic aquatic stars, Johnny Weissmuller and Clarence "Buster" Crabbe, made good drawing cards under their real names.

When MGM got into the *Tarzan* act, there was a thought-provoking sequence of successive titles: *Tarzan and his Mate* followed by *Tarzan Escapes*, which in turn was followed by *Tarzan Finds a Son*.

Why *Tarzan* never met *Gidget* is still a mystery to us!

Typical of the high-blown phrases of Hollywood publicists, movies were always shown on the 'silver screen.' Of course, it was white — a material called alabastrine, which was also porous enough to allow the sound through.

The motion picture industry is not famed for its literary judgment, having paid astronomical sums for some genuine turkeys. On the other hand, they've picked up some gems for a pittance. At about the time the film studios were paying Edna Ferber $125,000 for the screen rights to her Western epic "Cimarron", they were picking up Erich Maria Remarque's "All Quiet on the Western Front" for a mere $25,000.

Author to editor: "What happened to the part where she's attacked by sex-crazed pygmies?"
Editor to author: "I started to cross it out; but I erased it instead."

In the late twenties and early thirties, quite a few movies were made in Astoria, Long Island. The producers inveigled struggling Broadway actors and actresses to come out to Astoria all day for filming. Then the tired thespians raced back to Manhattan for nightly stage assignments. The products they turned out in Astoria were not exactly memorable. A typical one of them, titled *Fast and Loose*, was reviewed as follows: "It was born in Long Island and died all over the country."

In that same era, movie actors and actresses dreaded scenes involving

RIDDLE: "Broncho Billy" Anderson probably deserves being called the first cowboy movie star. He made over four hundred one-reel oaters. Was that his real name?

ANSWER: Nope. Real name: Max Aronson, but who would have gone to see "Broncho Max" Aronson. By the way, when he retired, he did go back to his original name.

fog. To simulate fog, vaporized mineral oil was blown about the set by propeller-driven wind machines. Sticky mess.

THE THIRTIES!

We know a movie buff who is hard to fool. For instance, he knows that Jean Arthur's real name was Gladys Greene, that Mary Astor's was Lucille Langehanke, that Lauren Bacall's was Betty Pepske and Paulette Goddard's was Marian Levee. But we tripped him up on Joan Crawford. He said her name had been Lucille le Sueur. That was the first professional name she adopted. Before that she had been Billie Cassin.

Insomniacs pay heed. Late movie and stage star, Miriam Hopkins, had a simple formula: "When I can't sleep, I don't count sheep. I count lovers, and by the time I reach 38 or 39 I'm asleep."

Katharine Hepburn's first movie was the 1932 production *A Bill of Divorcement.* It wasn't until six years later that she was given her first singing role. You heard right. Katharine Hepburn...well, sang *I Can't Give You Anything But Love* in the 1938 movie comedy *Bringing Up Baby.* Her co-star was Archibald Leach, more easily recognized as Cary Grant.

Tallulah Bankhead, profane to her teeth, once said, "My heart is as pure as the driven slush."

Today's younger movie fans have probably never heard of Kay Francis. Now they will. In 1938 — heyday of such names as Jean Arthur, Ginger Rogers, Carole Lombard and Katharine Hepburn — Kay Francis's salary was $224,000, second only to Jimmy Cagney's $234,000. Yet no one ever thought she could make it as an actress. First, she was considered too tall (5'7"), too big-boned (although her shoe size was a mere 4), too wide-shouldered and she couldn't pronounce the letter *r*.

A friend, Lois Long, with whom Kay Francis shared a New York apartment in 1924, recalled that their bootlegger (Frank Costello, no less) sold them gin for $12 a case, and that Kay's breakfast consisted of a water tumbler of the stuff. When she hit it big in Hollywood, she changed her breakfast menus, slightly...adding a ham sandwich, a pickle and ice cream.

And Miss Francis didn't go the mansion-limousine route either, content to live in a modest house and drive herself around in an old Ford.

We know Claudette Colbert's real name was Claudette Chauchoin. Now you do.

GARBO!

Back in the 1930's, movie houses not only touted the feature film or films they were showing, but also proclaimed "and short subjects." One of the best known was named for its narrator and producer, Pete Smith. While most Americans knew Pete Smith for his film trivia, few knew that he was the top publicity man at MGM at one time.

One of his assignments was to arrange interviews between the press and the young Swedish actress Greta Garbo. But Garbo was so shy, Smith had a devil of a time arranging anything.

Finally, out of desperation, he decided to reverse the normal routine. He instructed Garbo to refuse interviews with a one-line excuse: "I vant to be alone." The more she refused, the more the reporters and columnists wrote. The one line Pete Smith gave her has been synonymous with The Great Garbo ever since.

Mr. Perpetual Youth, Robert Cummings, is said to have once masqueraded as a British actor named Blade Stanhope Conway.

Movie actresses of the 1930's were always confused with one another: motherly Louise Dresser and toughie Marie Dressler. Both had changed their names, and oddly enough they probably would have been just as confused with one another if they had retained their real names: *Dresser* had been Louise Kerlin; *Dressler*, Leila Kerber.

Pick up a Raquel Welch on your way home tonight!

When Robert Louis Stevenson penned *Dr. Jekyll and Mr. Hyde,* he provided future actors with one of the meatiest roles imaginable. Some of the big names in motion pictures who gave portrayals of the ill-fated split personality were John Barrymore, Conrad Veidt, Frederick March (who got an Oscar for his performance) and Spencer Tracy.

RIDDLE: In the late thirties was there a young actress who appeared in such films as *Dick Tracy's G-Men* under the name of Phyllis Isley?

ANSWER: Yep, and that was her real name. A few years later, in 1943, she won an Oscar as the star of *The Song of Bernadette*. Of course, by then she had changed her name to Jennifer Jones.

David Manners, a Canadian gift to Hollywood, played leading roles in such big films as *A Bill of Divorcement, Roman Scandals* and *The Mystery of Edwin Drood.* A practical man, Mr. Manners. He realized he might have had difficulty as an actor if he used his real name — Rauff de Ryther Duan Acklom. The same can be said for Gilbert Roland, who switched from Luis Antonio Damaso De Alonso, and Carmen Miranda, who shortened her name from Maria de Carmo Miranda de Cunha.

Helen Twelvetrees: consult your numerologist and your nurseryman!

1935 was a big year for James Stewart — both of them. Oh, you didn't know there were two well-known actors named James Stewart? The one you know for his slow, halting speech and for his roles in such famous American movies as *Mr. Smith Goes to Washington, The Philadelphia Story* and many more landed his first movie role in 1935 in *Murder Man.* The other James Stewart must have had a premonition because he changed his name to Stewart Granger when he made his London stage debut in 1935.

Yul Brynner wears a fake scalp!

WHERE?

In 1933, there was a movie titled *Rome Express.* The same basic movie was remade fifteen years later as *Sleeping Car to Trieste.*

Showing an equal disregard for direction, the 1932 movie *Shanghai Express* was remade in 1951 as *Peking Express*. A guy could get lost!

Mae West knits umbrella stands for wayward weathermen!

PICK A MORGAN!

We can think of five people named Morgan who have made it big in motion pictures. The odd part is that none of the five were born with the name Morgan. There were the two brothers who were famous character actors of the 1930's and after — Frank, the funny Morgan, and Ralph, the serious Morgan — whose real last name was Wupperman. Then there was the handsome singer and leading man, Dennis Morgan, who was born Stanley Morner. Harry Morgan, lately best known as the Captain in the TV series *M*A*S*H, came into the world as Harry Bratsburg. Finally, there was the beautiful French import, Michele Morgan, whose real name was Simone Roussel.

A chap named Frederick de Choom,
Peeping into a lady's room,
Became very distressed,
Because, as she undressed,
She also took off her bazoom.

SEX SYMBOLS!

We think movie press agents have had it too easy! What's so tough about taking a generously endowed young thing and making her a sex symbol? But think how hard they would have had to work if some of these beauties had not changed their names. Just look at this parade of cuties: *Hedy Lamarr* was really Hedwig Kiesler; *Dorothy Lamour*, Dorothy Kaumeyer; *Marilyn Monroe*, Norma Jean Mortenson; *Romy Schneider*, Rosemarie Albach-Retty; *Marie "The Body" McDonald*, Marie Frye; *Elke Sommer*, Elke Schletz; and *Mamie Van Doren*, Joan Lucille Olander. But the toughest job would have been to stimulate an eager, sex-starved world with the British 'blond bombshell' *Diana Dors*, if the press agent had been stuck with her real name, Diana Fluck.

Husbands are like fires. They go out when unattended.
Z.Z. Gabor, Newsweek 3/60

Katharine Scully Feeney and Alice Leppert have little in common except that both were movie stars who changed their names — to Sally Forrest and Alice Faye, respectively.

Silent movie we wish we'd seen: Wife of a Centaur, starring Aileen Pringle.

When asked about a *face-lift*, Adela Rogers St. Johns replied: "You may want to present to the world a blank sheet of paper, proving that you've written nothing on it in the years you've lived. I would much rather they could see on *my* face that I *have* lived, loved and had one hell of a time, bad and good."

RIDDLE: What is it that screen stars Mae Murray, Gloria Swanson, Grace Kelly, Constance Bennett and Rita Hayworth did once, but that Pola Negri did twice?

ANSWER: The first five married into royalty once; Miss Negri, at different stages in her married career was a countess and a princess. If you just can't stand the suspense, her husbands were Count Dombski and Prince Serge Mdivani.

When it was discovered that Marilyn Monroe had posed in the nude for a calendar, a reporter asked her, "Didn't you have *anything* on?" Her reply was, "Oh, yes, I had the radio on."

Another time she was asked, "Is it true you wear falsies?" Her reply was, "Those who know me better know better."

For years Maria Magdalene Von Losch had the greatest legs in the world. Perhaps you know her by her stage name — Marlene Dietrich.

Constance Keane wouldn't make a bad name for a movie star. The real Constance Keane didn't think so...she changed it to *Veronica Lake*.

One of Elizabeth Taylor's husbands was Avrom Goldenborgen and another was Richard Jenkins. The first would be ***Mike Todd*** *and the other,* ***Richard Burton****.*

Sometimes I think women want to be treated better than they rate, merely because they're women. And they grow hostile when that doesn't happen. It's sort of like demanding special privileges for age, when you have done nothing but survive to get there.

Adela Rogers St. Johns

Remember when Eddie Fisher was married to...oh, yes, Concetta Ingolia? Would you believe, Connie Stevens?

Sari was her name and she was beautiful enough to be selected Miss Hungary of 1936. Now you know her as Zsa Zsa Gabor.

It's doubtful if very many fictional heroes or heroines have not been drawn, at least in part, from real-life people. But it is unusual when the author used the actual name of the person who inspired his fictional character. Such was the case, however, with French dramatist Edmond Rostand. His *Cyrano de Bergerac* did live and did fight over a thousand duels, most of them brought about because of unkind descriptions of his mammoth nose.

Don't knock Louis XVI! Look what he did for drag!

THE GLAMOUR BOYS!

Even the wiliest movie moguls could not guarantee box office success for up and coming actors simply by blessing them with resounding names. On the other hand, it might have been impossible to make Spangler Arlington Brough a national by-word, so they dubbed him *Robert Taylor*. *William Holden*, talented as he is, might have had problems as William Beedle. Would *Tony Curtis's* impish good looks have come across as well if he'd remained Bernard Schwarz? *Rex Harrison* might have made it as Reginald Carey. Ditto for *Fredric March* if he had stayed Frederick McIntyre Bickel. But *Ray Milland* must do more for that urbane star's image than Reginald Truscott-Jones could have.

Paul Muni hung on to his real first name, which was Muni, but dropped his last name — Weisenfreund. We think Hugh Krampke made a smart move when he became *Hugh O'Brian*. *Rory Calhoun* might sound a little high-flown to some, but look what it replaced — Francis Timothy Durgin! And Ira Grossel, wavy gray hair and all, could not have packed the punch of *Jeff Chandler*.

Don't you agree *John Saxon* fits that fine actor much better than Carmen Orrico? Would you have become a fan of the TV detective series *Peter Gunn* if its star had remained Gail Shekles rather than *Craig Stevens?*

We doubt if cows or cowboys would have leaped into action if Marion Michael Morrison had hollered, "Head 'em on out!" But they jump for *John Wayne.*

Remember Mr. Smooth, *Warren William?* As Warren Krech, he might not have seemed as suave. And Byron Barr couldn't leave

RIDDLE: Did those three one-name actresses — Annabella, Belita and Margo — simply drop their last names for dramatic purposes?

ANSWER: Nope. Those weren't even their original first names. Annabella's real name was Suzanne Charpentier. Belita had been Gladys Jepson-Turner. And Margo had been christened Maria Marguerita Guadelupe Boldao y Castilla in her native Spain.

us with the same sense of belief as *Gig Young* does.

And remember *Sonny Tufts* from the thirties and forties? He was born Tufts, but Sonny replaced Bowen Charleton.

What's in a name? Could be millions, eh, Marion!

THE FROWNER'S CLUB!

From the moment the first movie camera rolled there developed a school of male dramatic acting best described as "the scowl." And all the great scowlers have macho names, on screen. But would we have been as impressed with their virility and stern presence if they had continued using their real names?

Bruce Cabot and *Richard Arlen* were two classic examples. What if we'd known they were really Jacques de Bujac and Richard Van Mattimore? We would have seen right through Julius Garfinkle's frowns if he hadn't switched to *John Garfield*. How tough would *Edward G. Robinson* have seemed as Emanuel Goldenberg? Ernest Brimmer didn't scowl effectively until he became *Richard Dix*.

One of your really big scowlers, *Kirk Douglas*, must have practiced for years, clear back to when he was known as Issur Danielovitch Demsky. And the other *Douglas, (Melvyn)*, was probably a pussy-cat until he dropped Hesselberg for Douglas. A Bernard Zanville couldn't have carried off a scowl the way he did as *Dane Clark*.

We have a new breed of scowlers, too — *Charles Bronson, Earl Holliman* and *Alex Cord*, for example. In their pre-scowling days, they were known as Charles Buchinsky, Anthony Numkena and Alexander Viespi.

Then there are James Baumgarner (James Garner to you) and Eugene Klass (Gene Barry). We've never been able to determine if they are true scowlers or simply have permanently furrowed brows.

Finally, The Scowl of Filmdom award goes to David Meyer, known as *David Janssen.*

Merv Griffin, return home! Your tennis ball's on fire!

Wong Tung Jim came to Hollywood when he was eighteen, and stayed around to become known as a superb cinematographer by the name of James Wong Howe. While we're on Wongs, that beautiful Chinese-American actress of the thirties, Anna May Wong, was born Wong Liu Tsong.

Mike Douglas lives in a guest house!

SWITCHEROO!

Walter Fleischmann not only had acting experience on the stage, but he looked a great deal like Rudolph Valentino. Hollywood's big hoopla about him was over his starring role in the 1951 film *Valentino.* By the way, his stage name was Anthony Dexter.

And don't forget Walter Palanuik. Oh, you already have? Maybe your memory will click, if we tell you he uses the name *Jack Palance.*

Herbert Lom is a damned considerate guy. When he adopted the name Lom — one of the shortest and simplest in the whole profession — he saved us all from attempting his real name: Herbert Charles Kuchacevich ze Schluderpacheru. As S.J. Perelman would say, "Hats, shoes and gloves off to Herbert Lom!"

We're not quite so certain of our premise when we come to *Jose Ferrer.* After all, this accomplished gentleman has portrayed such a variety of heroes and villains. But we are glad he simplified his name at least. We wouldn't want to try to remember Jose Vicente Ferrer Otero y Cintron.

Howard Cosell will continue to occur in most areas!

While many people in the dramatic field have changed their names, some of the alterations are subtle. Lew Ayres is an example, barely ruffling his real name — Lewis Ayer. By deleting a final *y*, Lee Jacoby became Lee J. Cobb. Quite a few axed their last names only, such as *Eddie Albert* Heimberger, *Deborah Kerr*-Trimmer, *George Montgomery* Letz and *Vera-Ellen* Westmeyr Rohe. Others made minor

RIDDLE: What do Michael Orowitz, Alan d'Abruzza and Robert Jnr have in common?

ANSWER: They have all starred in TV series as Michael Landon, Alan Alda and Brian Keith.

changes: Aldo daRe became Aldo Ray; Anna-Margaret Olson snipped away an *a* or two and her last name to become Ann-Margret; director Elia Kazan simply shortened Kazanjoglous, for which we're thankful; Phyllis Kirk was another shortener from Kirkegaard. Terry-Thomas did a few contortions going from Thomas Terry Hoar-Stevens. And W.C. Fields used his real initials and hacked off the front of his last name: William Claude Dunkinfield.

Johnny Carson eats money!

THE MUSICAL SCENE!

Actors and actresses aren't the only ones who have changed their names. Singers and musicians have switched from their true names for years. *Al Jolson* was Asa Yoelson. For some reason, *Julie Andrews* saw fit to discard Julia Vernon. Only one of The Beatles altered his monicker — Richard Starkey going to *Ringo Star*. Few blamed *Judy Garland* for dropping Frances Gumm. Did you know *Sophie Tucker* was originally Sophia Abuza? Composer *Irving Berlin* was born Israel Baline, while the famous conductor, *Stokowski*, had been Leopold Boleslowowicz. Vito Farinola might not have made it as a singer, but he has with *Vic Damone*. Can't blame Constance Franconero for adopting *Connie Francis*, nor Frank Paul Lo Vecchio in opting for *Frankie Laine. Mario Lanza* sure beat Alfred Cocozza. We also prefer *Peggy Lee* to Norma Egstrom and *Dean Martin* to Dino Crocetti. And lyrics to the song *Mack the Knife* just wouldn't have worked, if composer Kurt Weill had been forced to use his wife's real name instead of *Lotte Lenya* who was born Caroline Blaumauer.

Who said Beethoven could only compose music? He could also play it...on the violin, the viola, the organ and the clavier. Only not all at the same time!

How many of you think of Ginger Rogers as a singer? When George and Ira Gershwin's *Girl Crazy* hit the Broadway stage with a loud bang in 1930, it was Ginger who introduced two of the hit songs — *Embraceable You* and *But Not For Me.* The leading lady, Ethel Merman sang *I Got Rhythm.*

In the 1933 movie *42nd Street*, Ginger Rogers sang a duet with character actress Una Merkel. That same year, she appeared in *Gold Diggers of 1933* and sang *We're In the Money* in pig latin. Also in

1933, she finally got her big dancing break and went *Flying Down to Rio* with Fred Astaire.

Don't sit there and tell us you didn't know that Zelma Hedrick and Ethel Zimmerman were the singing stars of two major Hollywood musicals of 1953. Zelma, or Kathryn Grayson as she's better known, warbled her way through *Kiss Me Kate*, while Ethel Zimmerman, nee Merman, belted out the music in *Call Me Madam.*

An operatic tenor named Boyce
Shattered fine mirrors with his voice.
At a party with class
He broke all the glass,
Rode home in a windy Rolls Royce.

Self appraisal: Ruth Etting, a popular singer of the twenties and thirties, remembered herself when she landed her first singing role as "just a farm girl, so green the cows could eat me."

She's been a bore ever since she got her act straight!

WHAT PRICE FAME?

How about twenty-five dollars a hair? As late as 1963, Elvis Presley fans could buy a strand of his hair for that price. Presley's barber saved a hundred hairs from the famous head each week and the singer's manager marketed them.

If you had seen a nightclub act featuring the singing of Anthony Tonibetto and the dancing of Davenie Johanna, you would have been watching Tony Bennett and Joey Heatherton before they changed their names.

Every well-publicized person is forced to field many silly questions. Take blind pianist, George Shearing. He was once asked, "Have you been blind all your life?"

"Not yet," was Shearing's sage reply.

A marriage license is one of the few certificates issued for recklessness.

RIDDLE: What did these four personalities from the movie world have in common? Lucy Ann Collier, Francesca Marlene de Charney von Gerber, William Enos and Fredrick Austerlitz.

ANSWER: All four are associated with dancing in motion pictures. The first is the real name of Ann Miller, followed by Mitzi Gaynor, Busby Berkeley and Fred Astaire.

A dancer's names should flow together, as in Freda-staire.

Several things the Chinese Peoples Republic is doing without: *Laverne and Shirley*, porno T-shirts and tuba players. Their lack of the first two items defies logic, but the reason tuba players are scarce is simple. Chiang Ching, Mao Tse-tung's wife, couldn't abide that instrument. Exit tuba players, breathlessly.

Don't argue! The two biggest Hollywood columnists of the 1950's and early 1960's were Louella Parsons and Elda Furry! Okay, so Elda Furry changed her name to ***Hedda Hopper.***

TWOSOMES!

One suspects that actor George Peppard and his ex-wife actress Elizabeth Ashley may not be likely to reconcile when faced with her assessment of their marriage: "I kind of look at it like a car trip across the country — you remember the cities you pass through, but not much about them. George was one of those cities."

One of Hollywood's longest marriages has been that between singer Alvin Morris and dancer Tula Finklea. Their stage names are Tony Martin and Cyd Charisse.

Little did the parents of Doris Kappelhoff and Roy Fitzgerald guess that one day the two would star in such movies as *Pillow Talk* and *Send Me No Flowers.* Aw shucks, you already know they changed their names to Doris Day and Rock Hudson.

Doris Davenport drives a 12-string Toyota which she calls ***The Westerner.***

Back in the early 1960's teenage screen fans went ga-ga over the real life marriage of Sandra Douvain to Robert Waldo Cassotto. That's probably because they had seen them in movies as Sandra Dee and Bobby Darin.

Bela Lugosi never participated in the food-stamp program.

When Sarah Jane Fulks married an ex-sports reporter, even her best friends couldn't guess she would win an Oscar and that he would become a governor. The big award was for her role in *Johnny Belinda* (1948). The world knew the pair as Jane Wyman and Ronald Reagan.

Television is halfway between rare and well done!

CAN'T THEY TALK ENGLISH?

Many American motion pictures are also issued in Britain, but quite often with different titles. For example, the American film *Hallelujah, I'm a Bum* was retitled *Hallelujah, I'm a Tramp* for U.K. movie-goers. Good reason, too. *Bum* is a naughty slang term in Great Britain for the very part of your anatomy upon which you are sitting.

But has anyone ever been able to figure out why Elia Kazan's great 1963 film *America, America* was retitled in England as *The Anatolian Smile.* Sure Kazan came from Anatolian Turkey, but did Hollywood fear that the British had never heard of America? Probably the work of the same genius who retitled *Christmas in Connecticut* to *Indiscretion.*

Of course, it works the other way, too — British films being retitled for the American market. That's how their *Night of the Eagle* became *Burn, Witch, Burn.*

He was not very happy with his singing voice until he found out how miserable it makes others.

DROPPING NAMES!

We imagine there are some annoying aspects to having a name which starts out as if it were headed in a predictable direction and then quite abruptly ends in mid-air. The British actor Alastair Sim has such a name.

Picture Mr. Sim at a cocktail party of Americans who may not know him.

"Hello, there," a guest says. "I'm Art Hutton and you're...?"

"Alastair Sim."

"Afraid I didn't catch that. Mr. Sim what?"

"Alastair Sim."

"Sorry, I still missed the last part."

"Alastair Sim, period."

"Oh, Mr. Simperiod," he beams with his new knowledge, then motioning his wife forward, introduces, "Honey, I'd like you to meet Mr. Alastair Simperiod."

RIDDLE: Did billionaire Howard Hughes ever produce a real good movie?

ANSWER: Three of the motion pictures Hughes produced are considered classics of their type — *Scarface* (gangster), *Hell's Angels* (war in the air) and *The Front Page* (newspaper). In the category of using a movie to promote a new face and new bust (Jane Russell), Hughes' 1944 film *The Outlaw* is another classic of sorts. He also directed that one.

After nodding to the actor, she says, "I've just met a gentleman with a similar last name, Mr. Simperiod...Herbert Lomperiod."

Roman poet, Horace, wrote, "He died a pauper in the midst of wealth," two thousand years ago. It's almost as if he had known Howard Hughes.

DON'T WORRY! ALEXANDER THE GREAT WAS LEFT-HANDED, TOO!

Yes, and a host of other rather distinguished persons, as well. Queen Victoria, Ben Franklin and Charlemagne were port-siders.

The movie world has had its share of left-handers, such as Charlie Chaplin, Robert Redford, Rod Steiger, Marilyn Monroe, Rock Hudson, Harpo Marx and Danny Kaye.

In the musical world, Cole Porter, Judy Garland, Anthony Newley and half the Beatles (Paul McCartney and Ringo Starr) were, or are, lefties.

It's a bit more difficult to recall famous left-handed artists, but there's nothing shabby about a group which includes Leonardo da Vinci, Raphael, Hans Holbein, Paul Klee and Pablo Picasso.

Comedians Don Rickles, Dickie Smothers, George Gobel, Dick Van Dyke and Carol Burnett all share left-handedness.

The sports world abounds in famous left-handers, but here are two you probably didn't know about — Ben Hogan and Arnold Palmer. *Oh, they did switch over for golf.*

How about left-handed politicians? In view of their political leanings, the least likely lefties have been Herbert Hoover, Ronald Reagan and Gerald Ford.

Habeas Corpus is two towns in Texas with one lawyer in each.

TOO YOUNG TO DIE...

It says something about the quality of our lives when we are deeply affected by the death of a famous entertainer. But it is a much more personal matter when a famous personage dies young — 'there but for the grace of God go I, etc.'

Three of Hollywood's biggest box-office names died in their twenties. James Dean was only twenty-four when he was killed on a motorcycle. Jean Harlow died at twenty-six and Valentino at twenty-nine.

Screen stars who died in their thirties include three from silent film days — Marie Prevost, John Gilbert and Jeanne Eagles. Then there were Marilyn Monroe, Carole Lombard, John Garfield, Maria Montez and Jayne Mansfield — Lombard in an airplane crash and Mansfield in an auto smash-up.

Among the big names who did not reach fifty are Steve Cochrane, Jeffrey Hunter, Jeff Chandler, Judy Holliday, Vivien Leigh, Linda Darnell, Tyrone Power, Elvis Presley and George Reeves. Inasmuch as Cochrane, Hunter, Chandler and Power were associated with vigorous action dramas, their deaths reminded fans of their own physical mortality. But it hit even harder with Presley's death, for obvious reasons; and because Reeves had been best known as *Superman*, the impact was great.

The passing of celebrities will always have the effect of having been robbed of some inner part of ourselves. Such was certainly the impact felt with the deaths of Gary Cooper, Clark Gable and Bing Crosby.

A drug overdose has killed hundreds of thousands, and some have been famous. A handful whose deaths were attributed, at least in part, to drugs includes Gia Scala, Inger Stevens, George Sanders, Billie Holliday, Lenny Bruce, Albert Dekker, Judy Garland and silent film star Jeanne Eagles.

Ranking high on the list of concise put-downs would be New York drama critic Walter Kerr's "He has delusions of adequacy."

Remember the early 1960's when giddy young girls were simply dying to see every movie starring Merle Johnson? Not, Van, Merle Johnson. For the movies, he changed it to Troy Donahue.

Johnny Cash carries credit cards!

Harlean sounds as if someone were creating a name from the name of Hollywood's famous platinum blonde, Jean Harlow. Actually, Jean Harlow's real name had been Harlean Carpenter.

RIDDLE: Where would you go to see the special talents of Katharine Hepburn, Henry Fonda, James Cagney, Charleton Heston, Elke Sommer, Alfred Hitchcock, Dinah Shore and Jonathan Winters?

ANSWER: Go to a movie or an art gallery — they all paint!

THE LITTLE LADY DESERVES THE BEST!

In researching material about given names our staff has run across books on the names of saints, books on biblical names, books that give the meaning of Teutonic, Celtic, Persian, Indo-Aryan, Romance Language and Oriental Names and books that list everything under the sun which might be utilized as a name for some innocent child. But no Polynesian names.

So in the interests of fair play, and especially for girls, here is a brief list of possibilities from the Hawaiian language with their meanings in parentheses:

Nani (beautiful)
Melokia (melody)
Nia (calm)
Niele (curiosity)
Lino (dazzling)
Kaimana (diamond)
Miona (swift hiding)
Kea (fair)
Ilikea (fair skin)
Kualana (famous)
Nanea (fascinating)
Nahele (forest)
Kiele (gardenia)
Lani (heavenly)
Nalohia (hidden)
Kaona (hidden meaning)
Meli (honey)
Maluna (lofty)
Nohea (lovely)
Mei (month of May)
Luana (be at leisure)
Aumoe (midnight)
Mahina (moon)
Kaoli (morning glory)
Mauna (mountain)
Moana (sea)
Alani (orange)
Manuhia (peaceful)
Ulana (braid)
Melia (plumeria plant)
Mailani (praise)
Kalali (proud)
Moena (resting)
Iolana (soar)
Keia or Neia (this)
Lanakila (victory)
Mahana (warm)
Li'a (yearning)

Aloha!

CHAPTER THREE

In The Beginning...

We're led to believe that almost everything had a beginning, although any reason for this being important escapes us. If compilations of *firsts* and *biggests* and *longests* help sell beer and ale, fine; but God help us if we attach significance to such things. Ask yourself, "Where is the man who invented the milking machine today?" If any living creature remembers him, it would be some octogenarian cow...and that memory would be tinged with hatred, no doubt.

Yet we're obsessed by the initial occurrence of all matter of trivia. Take the first aviator to negotiate the Alps...successfully, that is. His name was George Chavez and he pulled it off in 1910. And what did it get him? Dead is what it got him, because he crashed at the end of the flight.

Of course, if your ambition is to become a professional smart-ass, there's no surer way of attaining your goal than to memorize every first you can get your limited mind on. Make your first *first* this one: Godfrey de Bouillon led the very first crusade from 1096 to 1100. He was really trying to invent the first condensed soup cube, but he got sidetracked by a pack of Saracens.

Quick, jot this down while it's still hot: the first agricultural college was established in 1797. The folks in Hofwyl, Switzerland howl that theirs was first; but pay some heed to the boosters of Krumau, Czechoslovakia — they're backing up their claim with a mummified agronomist.

In the category of *My God, What If It Had Never Happened* we're offering the discovery of Kentucky's Mammoth Cave. An unnamed woman let it out that she had stumbled across the cavern in the summer of 1799 while scouting around for petrified rooster gizzards. In 1809, a hunter named Hutchings said it was while trailing a bear he had maimed, that he accidentally found Mammoth Cave. And the Indians of the region say, "Hell, we've known about that dumb place for centuries. One whole tribe lived there until the bats drove them...well, batty."

By all means avoid *firsts* that people care nothing about, such as who discovered pasteurization (we already know it was Irving Skim). Stick with good stuff like: Who was the first mother to say to her child, "Don't eat the mercury, dear; it's covered with tuna?" You'll get the attention you deserve if you're the first one on your block to spill the beans about the Milam Building in San Antonio, Texas being the first air-conditioned office building in the whole U.S. of A. You can punch up the story with the date if you wish: January 1, 1928.

Better bone up on bathtub *firsts*, too. It's always a big item. We can start you out with this much. Back in 1842, a Cincinnati man named Adam Thompson, who had discovered a process for converting cotton into currency, treated himself to a trip to England. There he heard of the most amazing thing since the baling hook: the Prime Minister of Great Britain not only owned, but actually used, a contraption called a bathtub. Thompson moved Heaven and Earth, not to mention two plumbers and a bathtub salesman, until he bought one.

He proudly unveiled America's first bathtub at a stag party on December 20, 1842 (a date ranking right up there with the discovery of flea powder). All of his guests tried it out. Unfortunately, the bathwater and the story of the wild doings leaked out. Hah! And today's *hot-tub* addicts think they started these shenanigans. No sooner had the newspapers fulfilled their duty to let the people know, than medical men and politicians jumped all over Mr. Thompson.

Doctors prognosticated a wave of pneumonia that would make the Black Plague look like a case of sniffles. Politicians vowed legislation to restrict further use of the infernal device. A minister predicted the end of the world and threw himself off a barn into a pile of manure where he fractured his sternum.

When the news spread to other cities, there was hell to pay. In Philadelphia, they considered an ordinance *banning bathing in a tub* between November and March (probably accounting for the winter aroma of the city in those years). Boston went further, passing an ordinance absolutely forbidding any use of a bathtub without professional medical consultation. The state of Virginia, with sovereign majesty, promptly laid down a tax of thirty-dollars a year on bathtubs, and threatened enormous increases in water rates for any bathtub addicts.

Now, that's what we call a *first* worth remembering.

In America, a plumber can become President of the U.S., if he's willing to take a cut in pay.

BATH STORY WITH THE RING OF TRUTH!

You think hot tubs are a craze. In ancient Rome, the Emperor Diocletian had a bath built that accommodated over 2,000 bathers at one time. It was such a hit, they eventually built five more.

One problem: they didn't change the water...just added some now and then. For sheer size the rings around those tubs were something else! They must have been harder to remove than any ring around the collar.

Rolling those who are stoned will get you nothing but moss.

BUSINESS FIRSTS YOU'LL NEED TO KNOW!

The first major merger in the *portable-sanitary-facility* industry occurred when Sani-Kan of Crofton, Maryland was taken over by Johnny-On-The-Spot, Inc. of Buffalo, New York. Comments on this development were heard from Comfort Castles in Massachusetts, Potty House in Illinois and Kwik-John in Missouri.

Meanwhile, in Troy, New York, Stephen Van Rensselaer, the Patroon of Rensselaerwick, had founded America's first private technical institute — Rensselaer Polytechnic Institute. We're a little late in getting this news to you. It happened in 1824.

The first International Industrial Exposition was held in the

RIDDLE: Has any worthwhile literature been written in a bathtub?

ANSWER: Perhaps, but it would have been washed away by now. If you meant written *while* in a bathtub, that would be *Cyrano de Bergerac*. The very wrinkled author was Edmond Rostand.

Crystal Palace in London in 1851. Buttonhooks and moustache curlers were two of the big items displayed.

You can lead whores through water, but you can't make them shrink.

THEY NEVER HAD IT SO GOOD!

Two hundred years ago, Cuban tobacco processors hired musicians and singers to perform for the workers in the tobacco sheds.

It wasn't until 1850 that the first cigarette factory opened. That was in St. Petersburg, Russia. Primitive conditions...not a single balaleika player.

Leonid Breshnev is the only person we know of who owns a time-locked cigarette case. It opens but once each sixty nerve-wracking minutes.

AHEAD OF HIS TIME!

The very first patent issued in this country went to a certain Samuel Hopkins in 1790. It was for a process of making pot and pearlash. At first we were astounded by Mr. Hopkins' foresight — a true grass pioneer. Then we discovered that he had in mind *potash* and its purified form — *pearlash*. Poor old Hopkins...he could have hit it big.

When Captain John Smith wasn't busy being saved by Pocohontas, he was manufacturing wood panels for making wainscoating. And for that endeavor he gets the honor of being America's first exporter of manufactured goods.

My father taught me to work; he did not teach me to love it.
A. Lincoln

WHO STARTED THAT THREE-ON-A-MATCH SCARE?

Some say the so-called Swedish *Match King* of the 1920's fostered the superstition to boost match sales. Others, undoubtedly equally ill-informed, say it comes from the Russian practice of lighting three altar candles from a single flame at funeral services — thus, to light three of anything else from a single flame would bring bad luck. Judging from the rapidity with which most matches burn, we think it stems from a desire to avoid burning the hell out of one's fingers.

Patriotic phrase that lives in the minds of men: Lucky Strike Green Has Gone To War!

THE MATERIAL THINGS!

When Charles Cross and E.J. Bevan, two British chemists, came up with an artificial silk in 1882, they called it *rayon*. As a silk substitute, it ruled the roost until duPont produced *nylon* in 1938.

But real silk! Well, now, the real credit must go to the silkworm. And a somewhat futile existence it is — the little devil is fed and pampered so it will weave a nice cocoon. The moment the cocoon is finished, humans go to great lengths to unwind it.

He made a slick purse from a sow's ear.

Blue jeans, unlike most clothing, seem to be more highly prized when faded and frazzled. If you owned some of the first jean cloth, it would be some 350 years old, because it was made in Jaen, Spain, where it all started.

The famous American feminist Amelia Jenks Bloomer is usually given credit for the creation of the bloomer. However, she was the first to admit that she got the idea from a Mrs. Elizabeth Smith. But who'd want to wear a pair of *smiths*?

NONSENSE

Bouncie, bouncie, ballie,
I lost the leg off my dollie;
My mother came out
And gave me a clout
That turned my petticoat inside out.

ROCKING RIGHT ALONG!

The English furniture designer, Thomas Sheraton (1751-1806), gets credit for the first rolltop desk and the first set of twin beds.

William Morris created the first morris chair.

Furniture historians now brand as *rubbish* the old theory that Egbert Foot and Nancy Stool collaborated in making the first footstool.

Mark down 1774 as the year the first rocking chair was made in America.

And the antimacassar — that lace doily they used to put over the arms and backs of upholstered furniture — was the first effective method of counteracting greasy kid stuff.

RIDDLE: What was that strange glow in Fredonia, N.Y. in 1824?

ANSWER: We weren't there, but an older associate says it was the first time natural gas was used for illumination in the U.S.

LET BEN DO IT!

While Ben Franklin was busy setting up the first lightning rod in 1752, or inventing bifocal glasses and a stove, he found time to be the Deputy Postmaster for the American Colonies. He probably would have invented the first spectacles of *any* type, but someone had already done that in the 13th Century.

A lazy man has simply made a choice between envy and industry.

AND THE REST GREW LIKE TOPSY!

The first city in the U.S. which was laid out with the plan to be a state capital was Raleigh, North Carolina. And the only other one was Indianapolis, Indiana.

Credit for being the first chain-store operation goes to the Great Atlantic and Pacific Tea Company (A & P). They began it all in 1858, three years before R.H. Macy opened the first true department store. Woolworth came along with the five and dime store in 1879; Marshall Field got into the department store game in 1881; and J.C. Penney Stores started up in 1902. While we're speaking of commerce and free enterprise; during Prohibition, there were approximately 36,000 speakeasies in New York City.

A dark brown taste, a burning thirst,
A head that's ready to split and burst...
No time for mirth, no time for laughter —
The cold gray dawn of the morning after.
George Ade

GOTHAM IS SO SOPHISTICATED!

We used to think *Gotham* was a sophisticated term for New York City, too. Ain't so. The first Gotham was an English village. In the 13th Century, its citizens were so foolish they were sarcastically referred to as 'the wise men of Gotham.' Washington Irving picked it up and applied it, with the same derision in mind, to the inhabitants of New York City. Hah!

Don't churn your milk over spoiled butter.

WHERE THERE'S A WILL, THERE'S A WAY!

The first public building to be completed on schedule was the

Roman *Colosseum.* The strong-willed Romans had a neat way of seeing that construction of the 87,000-seat amphitheater was finished on time — they used 12,000 Christians and Jews to do the work. First big job to come in under budget, too, since they paid nothing for labor. It shows us: if the purpose has merit, it will be accomplished.

Nome wasn't built out of hay.

Everyone knows the Home Insurance Company erected the first so-called *skyscraper* in Chicago in 1885. The ten-story wonder was such a hit, they added two more floors later on.

How excited were you when you learned that the *first brick* building constructed in Illinois was located at Kaskaskia? Did you flip when you also discovered that the first Illinois Territory legislature met there? You just may be weird.

Speaking of bridges — and nearly everyone does these days — the first suspension bridge across the Niagara Gorge employed a very scientific system for getting the metal cables from one side to the other. They began by paying a small boy $10 to fly his kite across the gorge at the appropriate spot. The kite string was tied to a tree on the far side. Then these clever engineers used the kite string to carry across a stronger line, then the line carried a rope and finally the heavy metal cable was carried across by the rope. The boy's name was Homer Walsh; can't recall who the engineer was.

Don't ask someone else to do a task you wouldn't be willing to foul up on your own.

RIDDLE: Has Paris's Latin Quarter always been known for Bohemian behavior?

ANSWER: The University of Paris is located in that sector. Originally all courses were given in Latin, and students paraded around the area singing Latin songs.

FASTER, MR. PENN, FASTER!

Back in 1682, William Penn was the first colonist to try out the Delaware Indians' *walking purchase plan*. Agreeing that the Delaware River would be the eastern boundary of the parcel he was buying, the Indians said the western limit would be as far as he could walk in three days.

Either Penn was out of shape or generous, because he quit walking west after a day and a half. He had covered forty miles. Just think, if he'd been in training, he might have made it halfway to Ohio.

A lass and her favorite beau
Went out on the river to reau;
But a blizzard came through,
And turned them quite blue,
And filled their reauboat with sneau.

CAN'T TELL THE WOOFERS FROM THE TWEETERS!

Not being of an inventive mind, we were dismayed to hear from a hi-fi salesman that plain old stereo was on its way out. He then proceeded to baffle us with the *in* item — *quadruplex*.

We were a bit less impressed with the advances of modern electronic wizardry a few weeks later, when we read that old Tom Edison had invented a technique for sending four telegraph messages simultaneously through a single wire. He called his invention a *quadruplex*. The year was 1874.

Noise proves nothing; often a hen who has merely laid an egg cackles as if she had laid an asteroid.

Mark Twain

MOON, JUNE, SPOON, CROON!

In response to an outpouring of emotional interest, the original *Tin Pan Alley* — where the composers of popular songs had their offices — was in New York City on West 46th Street, extending from Broadway to Eighth Avenue. Song-pluggers battering away on upright pianos gave the place its name.

Benny Goodman did not give Bill and Helen Seethaler clarinet lessons! That's final!

AND THE RAIN ONLY FALLS AT NIGHT!

When land developers began selling southern California to the nation in the 1860's, that was one of their claims. Others included tales of a single grape-vine that bore 22,000 pounds of grapes in one season, 20-foot high tomato vines, one rose bush with 200,000 blossoms *all at once*, a 250-pound squash, 15-foot high lilies, 6-foot long cucumbers and 12-foot high geraniums. The gullible of the nation were astounded to learn that melons in southern California grew so fast they had to be harvested on horseback; and corn had such a rapid growth rate, it pulled itself out of the ground by its own roots, and then was able to live for days on the glorious climate alone.

One developer said, "We sold 'em the climate and threw the land in free."

But then the real-estate boom of the 1880's made the earlier hoopla of the first landboom seem mild. Two railroads which owned great tracts of barren land in southern California began excursions to California from almost every railhead in the midwest. A price war ensued and finally a person could ride from, say, Missouri to southern California for *one dollar* in 1887 (it had been $125 in 1885).

When the trains arrived, the developers descended, arranging barbecues, scenic trips and, of course, a visit to the subdivision. In a four-year period, 1884-1888, one hundred and seven new towns were laid out in Los Angeles County. When the boom collapsed in mid-1889, only forty-five survived. In the wake of the land binge, there were towns such as *Chicago Park* with 2,290 lots and one inhabitant; *Nadeau*, 4,470 lots and no citizens; *Sunset*, 2,010 lots and a watchman; and *Fairview*, which had a hotel, a bathhouse, two miles of railroad that led to nowhere and nary an inhabitant.

Oddly enough, some of the wild claims were almost true. Lucky Baldwin's Santa Anita Ranch in the 1880's produced a ton of butter a week, 440,000 gallons of wine and brandy a year, 44,000 boxes of oranges and lemons and 175,000 sacks of grain. Baldwin said he could raise anything but his mortgage payments.

By 1900, they were at it again. The Los Angeles Chamber of Commerce sent a special train around the nation. A million people went through the train to see photographs of California scenery, model homes and tons of statistics.

Money has roots like a weevil.

THE MONEY TREE!

In most parts of the world, any item that people considered valuable, yet reasonably available, was used for money. The Aleuts of

Alaska used fish hooks, for example. In the Fiji Islands, whale teeth doubled for money, while tribes in West Africa used elephant tails. American Colonists used nails as an exchange medium since they were quite scarce.

When Canada was a French Colony, they began using playing cards for money. The highest denomination was a whole card; then there were half-cards and quarter-cards. Each card or card portion bore the colonial treasurer's seal and the governor's signature. The playing-card money lasted from 1685 until the British defeated the French in 1759.

And there once was a real *money tree*. The Malayans made replicas of trees from tin. Whenever a Malayan was called upon to pay for something, he broke off the required number of 'leaves' from his money tree.

'Deficit spending' is when your Congressman calls you collect.

HOW LONG DOES MONEY LAST?

We don't mean how long does *your* bankroll last. We're referring to the life of our *paper money*.

The average one-dollar bill will hold up for about six months; a two-dollar bill for eleven months; thirteen months is about as much as you can expect for a five-dollar bill; eighteen months for a ten-spot and thirty months for a twenty-dollar bill.

By the way, in the matter of redeeming bills from which a piece is missing, here's the law: if sixty percent of the bill is intact, it's worth its face value; if you still have between forty and sixty percent, you can get half the value; when there's less than forty percent, throw it away.

I beg your pardon, I never promised you Rose Gardner.

TAKE A LITTLE, GIVE A LITTLE...CONFEDERATE STYLE!

As soon as Louisiana seceded from the Union in 1861, the Confederacy took over the U.S. Mint in New Orleans, latching onto all its contents, including a nice quantity of gold bullion.

Meanwhile, the Union grabbed Robert E. Lee's place in Arlington, Virginia just across the Potomac from the Capitol. They didn't give it back either, converting it eventually into Arlington National Cemetery.

The U.S. Mint coined its first silver dollar in 1794. It was worth 100 cents.

WEALTHY G.I.'s?

In the beginning, the U.S.Army didn't bother with such frills as combat pay. They figured combat was the very reason for having an army. But, you know civilians — always out for a buck. So, in 1847 — in the Middle of the Mexican War — the army staggered the imagination of its troops with a two-dollar-a-month bonus for combat service.

It's amazing how few legal questions arise over a pauper's estate.

FAD IS A SHORT WORD FOR BIG MONEY!

If you were to go through an American attic, you'd find ample proof that we have been first in fads. An average American family dating back to 1915 probably still has a ouija board, a Mah Jongg set, a miniature golf scorecard, a yo-yo, a packet of bubble gum trading-cards, some silly putty, a Hula Hoop, a Davy Crockett coonskin cap, a Hopalong Cassidy record, a Superman comic book and perhaps a Parcheesi board. And each item cost money.

The Chinese were playing Mah Jongg in the 6th Century B.C. but, when it hit America in 1922, a nation went bananas. Although it peaked out in 1924, over a million and a half sets were sold in 1923...some for as much as $500.

When Bill Boyd, who had starred in over sixty low-budget Hopalong Cassidy movies from 1934 to 1947, bought all rights from author Clarence Mulford in 1948, he couldn't have dreamed of the ensuing explosion. In 1951, Boyd was raking in two million dollars from Hoppy radio shows, TV shows, personal appearances, commercial tie-in products, records and almost 15 million Hoppy comic

RIDDLE: What is the greatest inflation any currency has undergone?

ANSWER: The Hungarian *pengo*, originally pegged at seventeen and a half cents in our money, became so inflated in 1946 that notes were printed for 100 quintillion pengos.

books.

The pattern that Hopalong Cassidy followed had already been laid down by *Superman* which had bimonthly comic-book sales topping a million and a half in 1938. By 1940, *Superman* was printed in thirteen languages in seventy-six countries. Unlike most fads, *Superman* has continued as a commercial success.

The Davy Crockett madness, although concentrating almost all its wallop in seven months of 1955, racked up its share of firsts: 14 million books sold; 4 million *Ballad of Davy Crockett* records; $100 million in merchandise, mainly frontier-style clothing from coonskin caps to moccasins; and then add on the revenue for the TV series and the Disney movies.

Little did the Australians know that when the bamboo hoop they twirled about their middles came out in plastic form in America (in mid-1957) that over 20 million hula hoops would be sold in less than a year and a half.

Miniature golf debuted in 1927. In 1930, there were over 40,000 courses in operation and, Americans were plunking out *225 million depression dollars* to play the game.

The yo-yo, in one form or another, had been around since before Christ. It cropped up in America in the 1930's and was a fairly big fad. But in 1961, the demand suddenly became so great that the leading manufacturer sold in excess of 15 million in that one year.

We certainly still see a lot of bubble gum around to this day, but we don't know if it approaches the $30 million annual sales it once had. The skateboard is another fad that refused to die. Of course, ever since the invention of the roller skate, kids have been fastening them to boards. Today, as any parent can testify, a skateboard can cost a bundle, so the number being sold probably doesn't approach the big skateboard year of 1965. One California company was knocking out 100,000 of them a day that year and the industry's gross annual sales topped $100 million.

But for the one or two fads that have managed to last, there have been dozens that vanished into thin air. And when a fad stopped dead without warning, many manufacturers and retailers went on a diet of peculiar and unwanted merchandise. Would you put catsup or mayonnaise on a coonskin cap?

An idea isn't responsible for the people who believe in it.
Don Marquis

REVOLVING PENSION — AN ALMOST FIRST!

As a class, the elderly were probably hit harder by the great depression of the 1930's than any other single group. So, it was natural that millions of Americans over 60 looked to a certain Dr. Francis Townsend as a savior in 1933.

Dr. Townsend's approach — called the *Townsend Plan of Old Age Revolving Pensions* — was to give each American $200 a month as soon as a citizen reached 60, with the stipulation that the full amount be spent each month. A cursory study would indicate that the Townsend Plan would provide for the elderly while simultaneously bolstering the economy. It grew a bit fuzzy when it came to the problem of financing the plan. Townsend's thought was a 2 percent federal sales tax.

By 1937, despite the Federal Social Security Act of 1935, Townsend was claiming twenty-million followers. It is known he had several hundred-thousand members who paid 10 cents a month in dues, and his weekly newspaper, with a circulation of a quarter of a million, was loaded with advertising...mainly for patent medicines.

Eventually the doctor underwent a Congressional investigation which indicated that he and a partner had probably profited handsomely from the plan. As the real impact of social security began to be felt, support for the Townsend Plan dwindled. Townsend, himself, damned social security mightily but, ironically, *collected* it from 1948 until his death in 1960.

Just because poverty is no sin, it's a mistake to believe it must be a virtue.

ANOTHER DAY, ANOTHER DOLLAR THREE-EIGHTY!

One reason goods were cheap on the Eastern seaboard in the 1840's was that factories hired children for far less than adults. Then, in 1842, the do-gooders spoiled it in Massachusetts by restricting factory working-time to a skimpy ten hours a day for children under twelve. Driven beyond all reason by their generosity, the Bay State legislators extended the restriction to cover women factory workers in 1847.

The foul contagion spread as state after state was pushed into treating women and children like people. In a mere ninety-six years, we had valid federal legislation on the matter.

All work and no pay makes Jack madder than hell!

RIDDLE: Who was the first American workman to receive fringe benefits?

ANSWER: That would be Hobart Smirt, an insulation applicator, whose employers (in 1947) cut his wages but allowed him all the rock-wool he could eat.

FIRST TIME IN YOUR AREA: BOTULISM AT HALF PRICE!

The British government, concerned about what food processors might be up to, enacted some *pure food* laws in 1860. America, not be outdone, scurried into action with a *state pure* law in Michigan in 1895. In a mere three years, Wisconsin followed suit. And, praise be, we had a federal statute on the books by 1906.

Why are cows smarter than all the scientists put together?
Only a cow knows how to convert grass into milk.

DOUBLE INDEMNITY IF ATTACKED BY A WHALE!

A chap in Hartford, Connecticut had the first accident policy — $5,000 if he were accidentally killed walking between his home and the post office. Premiums weren't bad, though — 2 cents a month!

We heard a rumor that *Night Life of Las Vegas* will insure you against all losses at blackjack...the only stipulation is that you don't play.

The only dependable fortune-teller I have known is the life-insurance man. He tells you what is going to happen and it does.

Theodore Roosevelt

FIRSTS THAT SHOULDN'T HAVE LASTED, EVEN AT FIRST!

Either Clark Kent or his alter ego.

Bongo drums and those who bong them.

TV commercials in which animals appear to discuss their masters with a vicious condescension bordering on reality.

Little girls who sell cookies outside cocktail bars in the middle of the afternoon.

Great hordes of expensively uniformed college students stumbling about during the half-time of football games in a vain effort to form some intricate design on the gridiron: such as a circle, while rendering some well-known melody in a totally undecipherable fashion.

Noisy breakfast foods.

Boutiques, whatever in the hell they are.

Rubber stamps in the hands of postal employees who enjoy the crunch of imprinting the word FRAGILE on packages that *were* just a moment before.

Maitre d's who gaze about their deserted tables, stroke their chins philosophically and then announce, "We *might* be able to seat you in about fifteen minutes...meanwhile, the cocktail lounge is just on your left."

Mineral water, as if most water today didn't already have enough minerals in it.

Gourmet restaurants located in bowling alleys.

Any item of apparel referred to as *togs*.

Tiny tots who can name every product in your household by its brand name.

Chain saws.

All so-called *lifetime* products...especially those guaranteed for six months.

Life-insurance salesmen who apologize for reminding you that no one lives forever, but keep on reminding you through the full three hours of the *half-hour* appointment they made with you.

Senility.

Can anyone remember when times were not hard — and money was not scarce.

R. W. Emerson

WELL, MY GOOD MAN, SO YOU'RE GOODMAN GOODMAN!

English gentlemen, physicians and ministers of the 17th Century were entitled to use *Mr.* before their names; and their wives were allowed *Mrs.* That left two classes below: servants, who were addressed as *Goodman* so-and-so and *Goodwife* so-and-so. (What do you think of that, Benny?)

Heritage: He that boasts of his descent is like the potato; the best part of him is under ground.

Thos. Overbury

The first federal census in the United States was taken in 1790, eleven years ahead of the first census in Great Britain. Then there was Turkey's first census in 1928: every Turk except for the census takers themselves and the troops guarding them, was confined to his home for the entire day.

RIDDLE: Thomas Jefferson was this nation's first Secretary of State, second Vice-President, and third President. He also helped frame the Constitution and the Declaration of Independence. He was a farmer, architect and inventor. What other president bore the first name Thomas?

ANSWER: ***Thomas*** **Woodrow Wilson! Wilson dropped the first name.**

In 1776, when Maryland took a census of its own, one of the categories was *revered senior.* It turns out the term meant grandmother.

Proverb: The worst of some days is the best of others.

IF YOU CAN'T BEAT 'EM, QUIT!

No sense attempting to establish who was the first person to see a good bandwagon and hop on it. We rather favor the 15th Century Frenchman, Jean, comte de Dunois. Joan of Arc's first stop on her famed military campaign was Orleans. Dunois was in charge of the city's defense. When Joan whipped him good, he joined her. Now, whether it was this action or some accident of birth, Dunois had come to be known as the Bastard of Orleans.

This book has too much plot and not enough story.
Sam Goldwyn

STICKY BUSINESS!

If you've been planning to send a congratulatory letter to the person who invented *tarring and feathering,* don't. He's long gone. It was Richard Lion-Heart in 1190. On shipboard during the Third Crusade, Richard directed that a thief should be punished by having his head shaved, then covered with boiling pitch and finally feathers scattered over the pitch. Just in case the poor devil didn't get the notion he was in trouble, they also put him off the ship at the next land they came to. However, that may have been preferable to going on with the Crusade.

"Mankind censures injustice," in the words of Plato, "fearing that they may be the victims of it and not because they shrink from commiting it."

If you've had the impression that the United States is always ahead of the rest of the world in scientific matters, you should know that an English physician performed the first appendectomy in 1838. Forty-eight years later, the U.S. celebrated (is that the word?) its first appendectomy.

The art of medicine consists of amusing the patient while nature cures the disease.

SCIENCE MARCHES ON AND ON!

Dr. Timmy Miggles, the eleven-year old surgeon who astonished the medical world with its first elbow transplant, told a gathering of Druids yesterday that he is planning to grow azaleas on the roof of his mouth as soon as there's a break in the weather.

Ignorance is bliss. So why aren't more people happy?

ON YOUR FEET, YOU LITTLE BEAST!

In the world of mammals, the newborn wildebeest of Africa is probably the first to learn mobility. Three minutes after birth it's up and around. In *one* day the newborn is able to keep up with the herd...a feat which some humans *we* know can't accomplish in a lifetime.

There wouldn't be so many jackasses in this country if hadn't been for the King of Spain. He sent the first to George Washington.

TAKE A BOW, LADIES!

American-born women with political 'curtain raisers': Mrs. Rebecca Felton, first female U.S. Senator, *appointed* in 1922; first woman *elected* to the Senate was Mrs. Hattie Caraway in 1932; first member of her sex to win a seat in the House of Representatives was Jeanette Rankin in 1916; Mrs. Nellie Ross was the country's first woman governor...in Wyoming, 1925.

And the first woman to become a Member of the British Parliament was Lady Astor, who was born in Virginia as Nancy Langhorne.

Pioneers in another area were France's Baroness de la Roche who got her airplane pilot's license in 1909. America's first woman licensed pilot was Harriet Quinby in 1911. And a mere three years later, Catherine Stinson opened a flying school in San Antonio, Texas.

Don't forget Elizabeth Blackwell! She was America's first woman M.D. in 1849.

So that's what M.D. stands for...Madame Doctor.

E PLURIBUS UNUM TIMES THREE!

We came by that motto, meaning *one out of many*, as the result of a committee appointed by Congress in 1776. The committee members

RIDDLE: What's the connection between Frances Perkins and David Farragut?

ANSWER: Since Frances Perkins was our first woman cabinet officer (Secretary of Labor in 1933) and David Farragut was our first Admiral (1866), the only connection we can imagine is that neither ever visited Madagascar.

were Thomas Jefferson, Ben Franklin and John Adams. We never could get it exactly straight, but we think it was Jefferson who suggested *Pluribus*, Franklin contributed *Unum* and, after much thought, Adams came up with the *E.*

The ***poinsettia*** *is the very first flower to be named after a U.S. Secretary of War — Joel R. Poinsett. (Remember: you read it here first.)*

SEPARATION OF POWERS!

Every Easter-time the kids in Washington D.C. had a ball rolling eggs on the lawns of the Capitol. Along came President Rutherford B. Hayes's wife in 1878 and, before Congress knew what hit them, the egg-rolling affair had been kidnapped and taken to the White House lawn where it remains.

"Assist me up and, in coming down, I will shift for myself," said at the scaffold by Sir Thomas More in 1535.

BELFRY DWELLERS!

Marcus Dwindle was the first man of Welsh-French parentage to transport a cage of live bats from Albuquerque, New Mexico to Racine, Wisconsin in a converted Pierce Arrow touring car. Upon his arrival in Racine, he discovered the Wisconsin bat market had collapsed. It also cost him $73.50 to have the Pierce Arrow reupholstered. This was in 1925.

Nine years later, almost to the day, his niece, Leatrice Squish, became the first woman to ride a glass bicycle through the lobby of a resort hotel in French Lick, Indiana.

Listen to a couple of witnesses to an accident and you'll have your doubts about history.

I COULD HAVE DANCED ALL YEAR!

Whether it was 'bathtub gin' or some other mysterious force, individual Americans began behaving oddly in the 1920's. First, a fellow named Alvin *Shipwreck* Kelly began sitting atop flagpoles for a living in 1924. In a promotional stunt during December, 1929, Kelly

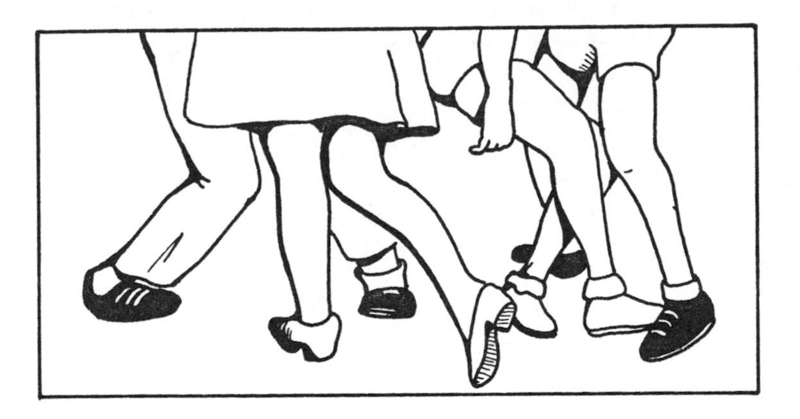

perched on a flagpole on top of New York City's Paramount Theater through sleet, snow and sub-zero temperatures; and, defying superstition, came down after *13 days, 13 hours and 13 minutes.*

In 1928, a promoter named Milton *Doc* Crandall put on a dance marathon in Madison Square Garden that drew 18,000 spectators in a single day. After 20 days, the New York Board of Health closed him down. But he was back in 1929 with another dance marathon plus a perpetual rocking-chair contest...with Shipwreck Kelly squatting on an 8-foot platform fifty feet above the roof.

Marathon dancing spread from New York to the rest of the nation. An Ohio girl danced non-stop for a bit over ninety hours. But the longest marathon dance (the contestants got a 15-minute break each hour) occurred in West Palm Beach, Florida in 1934 — 3,600 hours (that's a 150 days). The winner was Jean Reed, who was to become movie star June Havoc. She won $40 for her 150-day stint.

Sociologists say the zany antics of the 1930's relieved the tensions of the Depression...and that relief took every marathon form one can think of — tree-sitting, raw-egg swallowing, talking, piano playing, goldfish swallowing, hoop-rolling and eating of every conceivable food.

Nowadays, the motivation seems to be to get oneself into a record book — premeditated craziness that, to us, lacks the flair and spontaneity Shipwreck Kelly initiated.

As for what you're calling hard luck — well, we made New England out of it. That and codfish.

Stephen Vincent Benet

RIDDLE: When did Labor Day start?

ANSWER: The Knights of Labor started an annual parade in New York City in 1882. Colorado set up a legal Labor Day holiday in 1887.

THE POWER OF ELECTRICITY!

It was Boston, not New York City, which had the first U.S. subway...in 1897. New York had its own electrical first in Auburn in 1890, when they pulled the switch in Auburn Prison on William Kemmler.

However, Boston electrified the entertainment world, in 1883, when the Gaiety Museum presented the first vaudeville show.

In 1927, Billy Poogle was first to dive from a ninety-foot tower into a prune Danish.

WHERE WERE YOU JANUARY 16, 1547?

We missed it, too — the coronation of Ivan IV, the first Czar of Russia.

We also had an invitation to watch Wilhelm Roentgen discover the X-ray in 1895, but we were still watching Louis Tiffany do some lamps in his new *favrile* enameled glass.

By the way, in 1545, two years before Ivan began acting so terrible over there in Russia, some of the boys in Padua, Italy were putting together the first botanical gardens. And 386 years later — August 18, 1931, to be exact — the U.S. Patent Office issued the first *plant* patent...for a rose, of course.

Things you missed, in the 1870's, included Alphonse Bertillon's invention of fingerprint identification in France (1879), and the deaths of 63-year-old Chang and Eng, the first known Siamese twins, in 1874.

In the library at Alexandria around 200 B.C., they were laying 8 to 5 that Eratosthenes couldn't come within a country mile of estimating the earth's circumference. He fooled them. Missed it by less than two-fifths of a degree!

Sorry you weren't able to attend the grand opening of the Pleistocene Epoc. After the ribbon-cutting, they held a drawing. We won a mastodon.

A weed is a plant whose virtues have not yet been discovered.
R. W. Emerson

FLAGGING THE FLAGS!

The British flag is called the Union Jack because its adoption in 1801 celebrated the union of Great Britain with Ireland. That makes the American flag older, except for the addition of stars as new states were admitted to the union. The oldest flag is that of Denmark which became the national emblem of the Danes in the year 1219. And that noble friend of the United States, Lafayette, was responsible for the French flag in 1789.

Who stole the Swiss flag? The Red Cross! Perhaps *stole* is too strong. In the last century, constant wars produced enormous numbers of sick and wounded throughout Europe. Finally, in 1863, representatives from fourteen nations met in Geneva, Switzerland to form an organization to cope with the carnage of war. Inasmuch as they were meeting in Switzerland, whose flag has a white cross on a red field, they chose the opposite effect — *a red cross on a white field* — as their emblem.

In some parts of Ireland the sleep which knows no waking is followed by a wake which knows no sleeping.
Mary W. Little

Although we adopted the eagle as a national emblem in 1783, it certainly wasn't a first. Russia had it before then. Some of the Roman legions used an eagle on their standards because Jupiter was associated with the majestic bird.

It is a sin to believe evil of others, but it is seldom a mistake.
Mencken

In addition to the Revolutionary War, we've got King George III to thank for granting a royal charter to the United States' first Chamber of Commerce which was in New York City in 1770.

The Chamber of Commerce is an American institution, right? Not by a long shot. The French had one going in Marseilles in 1599, one hundred and seventy-one years ahead of America's first one.

Spooner was a great Donford ox
Who, mounted upon his boap sox,
Lalked at great tength
About Strengland's ength
Claimed they came from taking wong lalks.

CLUB FORMATIONS!

Would you believe that the Daughters of Rebekah, a woman's organization, was founded by a man in 1857 at South Bend, Indiana. His name was Schuyler Colfax and he was later to become Vice-President of the United States under Grant. Mr. Colfax stated that the purpose of the Daughters of Rebekah was *"to reconcile women to the pledge of secrecy made by their husbands by inducing them to take similar obligations."*

What do you think Schuyler's chances of being elected to public office would be today?

The Benevolent and Protective Order of Elks began in New York City as The Jolly Corks and was for actors only.

The Society of the Cincinnati was organized in 1783 but *not in Cincinnati.* It started in Fishkill, New York with former officers of the Continental Army to perpetuate the friendships and dangers they shared in the Revolutionary War. George Washington was their first President-General. How come *Cincinnati?* They took it from the Roman hero Cincinnatus who left his farm in 458 B.C. to lead the Roman legions against their enemies and who returned to his farm after victory. Since many Revolutionary War officers had done the same, the name was apt. As Isaiah said: "They shall beat their swords into plowshares."

George Washington was also in on the establishment of another famous organization — the Order of the Purple Heart — formed in 1782 to honor Revolutionary War heroes for military merit. Herbert Hoover re-established the order in 1932.

Wise men talk because they have something to say; fools, because they have to say something. *Plato*

BIG BENJIE!

Ben Franklin has more firsts to his credit than almost any American you can name. But his *Poor Richard's Almanac* isn't one of them. The Greeks around the time of Alexander the Great had them. Handwritten almanacs appeared in Europe as early as the 13th Century. An astronomer named Purbach put out a printed one in the 15th Century. Franklin wasn't even first in America. A chap named William Pierce collared that honor in 1639.

The world's first circulating library was established in 1731. And, as you might have guessed, Ben set it up in Philadelphia. One of his lesser known *firsts* was the *Philadelphia Zeitung* — first foreign language newspaper — in 1732.

The first successful ascent of the Matterhorn was made in 1865. Leader of the party was a chap named Whymper. Thought you should know.

EXTRA! EXTRA!

We don't claim to be the first to tell you that the oldest newspaper was the Peking News, which opened up shop in 363 and closed down on account of war in 1935. But who else remembers their first headline — *MANDARIN BITES CHOW?*

Dartmouth University got the drop on everyone else by publishing the first college newspaper in 1800. Daniel Webster was one of the editors.

Johann Gutenberg is generally credited with inventing movable type. In 1456, he printed what has been variously known as the 42-line Bible (each page was set in two columns of 42 lines), the Mazarin Bible (one of the copies showed up much later in Cardinal Mazarin's library) and the Gutenberg Bible. However, exactly 700 years before, the Japanese had printed a million copies of a Buddhist prayer using wooden type. The Japanese Empress Kokes had ordered the job, and it probably ranks as the first runaway best seller, too.

It's easier to appreciate the complex electronic network of news transmission facilities of such organizations as AP and UPI when one realizes that the first such organization sent its news stories from Paris to London and Brussels by *carrier pigeon* in 1840.

Scotland gets credit for having the first newsboys. They really combined their work, passing along local gossip as they sold their papers. They were called *caddies.* We added that to heighten your confusion.

In Scotland there's a monster called the Lox Mess.

Let 'Er Rip, Van Winkle! Washington Irving (1783-1859) was one of the first American authors to be recognized in Europe as having literary merit.

The first Sherlock Holmes was invented by A. Conan Doyle in 1887. Elementary!

GILBERT WROTE THE WORDS. DID SULLIVAN WRITE THE LYRICS?

Nonsense! The words *are* the lyrics! Example: Sullivan composed the melody to which we sing *Hail, Hail The Gang's All Here*; Gilbert did not write the words. He wrote other words to that tune for *The Pirates of Penzance* in 1879.

We were going to tell you that *The Chocolate Soldier* was a musical adaptation of George Bernard Shaw's *Arms and the Man,* but

RIDDLE: Which president was the first to be born in the United States of America?

ANSWER: That would be your Martin Van Buren, born in 1782. Those presidents before Van Buren, who were born in this country, technically were born in the British Colonies of America.

we've decided not to, right now.

Between us, we cover all knowledge; he knows all that can be known and I know the rest.

Twain on Kipling

FIRSTS WE'LL NEVER HEAR THE LAST OF...EDUCATIONALLY!

Now that everybody is asking the question, "Who was England's first Poet Laureate?" we'll get into it. On one side we have Old English Nit-Pickers who opt for Chaucer in 1328. Middle-of-the-Roaders support Ben Jonson in 1617. The Latter-Day Numbheads are standing firm with Dryden in 1670. We know for a fact it would have been Thaddeus Cwylp in 1532, but his mother wouldn't let him out of the house.

Tidbits from the educational larder: The University of San Marcos, founded in 1551 at Lima, Peru, says it's the oldest university in the western hemisphere. Harvard offered the first college scholarship in the United States in 1643, but the money came from a certain Lady Mowlson of England. Otago University at Dunedin, New Zealand claimed to be the southern-most university in the world. The Carlisle Indian School opened in an old army post in 1880, but the War Department took it back in 1918.

The University of Miami held the first underwater classes, using glass-bottom boats to study marine biology. Cornell beat the rest of the world to the punch when it offered a four-year course in hotel administration in 1922.

William and Mary College certainly sounds like a coeducational institution; however, it took from 1693 to 1918 before girls were accepted. The world's first formal educational program for dentists began at the Baltimore College of Dental Surgery in 1840. Michigan State, founded in 1857, is the country's oldest agricultural college. England's venerable Cambridge initiated the detestable practice of written exams in 1702. And the first school for delinquent girls got under way in 1854 in Massachusetts.

I find that the three major administrative problems on a campus are sex for the students, athletics for the alumni, and parking for the faculty.

Clark Kerr, President of U.C. Berkeley, 1958

Sequoia National Park and the giant trees that grow there were named after a Cherokee half-breed named George Gist. Of course his Cherokee name was Sequoia. He's also famous for his invention of the first American Indian Alphabet.

The first Corsican to serve as Russian Ambassador to France (in 1814) was Carlo Andrea Pozzo di Borgo. The second...

Millions of students have cursed the day Latin came into existence. But the old Romans did all of us some favors, too. They originated the exclamation point, for one. First, when they wanted a sentence to be read with the power of joy, they put the two letters of *Io*, their word for joy, one atop the other at the end of the sentence...slowly it evolved into ! They invented the question mark in much the same fashion; stacking the first and last letters of *questio*, it became ?.

If you think all college fraternities have Greek names, you just don't know that the very first college fraternity in America was the Flat Hat Club at William and Mary in 1750. Members could be recognized by the peculiar shape of their heads.

A literary critic is a person who has the courage to crucify others for doing that which he can not.

ORTHOGRAPHICALLY SPEAKING!

The art of spelling correctly — orthography — has had more downs and ups. But the English language makes all the others look like pikers. Spelling was erratic enough prior to the Norman Conquest of the 11th Century. After that historical event, French was the language of culture in England; the language of the Anglo-Saxons continued in parallel, but French scribes were writing it down in their own fashion. And, French words were coming into English, too.

It should come as no surprise that orthography hasn't been on speaking terms with English for very long. In 1604, a Robert Cawdrey published the first English dictionary, aptly titled *A Table Alphabeticall of Hard Words.* Prior to that, people spelled English about any way they damned well pleased. Cawdrey's guide had only 3,000 entries or so.

The first work that packed some authoritative punch as to spelling, usage and pronunciation was Samuel Johnson's *A Dictionary*

RIDDLE: Was Confucius the first to introduce the three R's into education?

ANSWER: No! Confucius taught six things to the upper classes — rites, history, music, mathematics, archery and horsemanship. All snap courses.

of the English Language, published in 1755.

Nowadays, we seem to have sunk back into a pre-Johnsonian slime in which correct spelling on the part of the young is endangered if not defunct.

First kid who spells **cat** *correctly gets a Mercedes...or a Cougar...or...*

We'd have to classify Issac Pitman as a guy who wasn't afraid of competition. The first shorthand system dates from 1588. When Pitman devised his in 1837, there were over two hundred others in existence.

Facts: Ammunition of the professional bore.

IT IS WRITTEN!

The *Spencerian Writing System* — that flowing, ornately handsome style taught to most American schoolchildren in the latter part of the 18th Century — was developed by brothers, Platte Rogers Spencer and Lyman Paul Spencer.

In the 1860's, Congress commissioned Platte Spencer to make a copy of the Declaration of Independence in the *Spencerian* style. The fee agreed upon was *$5,000* — princely enough to enable Platte to retire.

It usually takes more than 2 weeks to prepare a good impromptu speech.
M. Twain

The first manual alphabet for the deaf was devised in the 1600's by George Dalarno. But it wasn't until 1755 that the first school for the deaf was established in Paris.

Do not do unto others as you think they should do unto you. Their tastes may not be the same.
George Bernard Shaw

Most people are unappreciative. For instance, whenever a person uses the equal sign (=), he should be thanking a Mr. Richter, late of the Sixteenth Century. He got tired of writing "is equal to" every time his arithmetic called for it. So he started making two short parallel lines — one equal to the other.

Scorpios: kick the hell out of any Geminis you see today!

YE DREADFUL TEA SHOPPE!

If you've been pondering the origin of that dreary bit of commercial cuteness in which shopkeepers use *ye* in the place of *the*, hearken! The Old English alphabet had a letter for the dipthong *th*, which they called a *thorn*. Deplorably, when written, the *thorn* resembled the letter *y*. Dunderheads with weakened vision read *the* as *ye* and the accursed thing caught on.

Proverb: A dog has never called a man and then beaten him.

OUR FIRST IS FIRSTER THAN YOUR FIRST MAIL!

We say the first telegraph office went into operation before the United States printed its first postage stamps. And we're right! Samuel F.B. Morse opened the first telegraph office in the nation's capitol in 1844, three years ahead of the 5-cent Ben Franklin and the 10-cent George Washington stamps.

Of course, there are those who claim the postal service was always slow. After all, if they had nice stamps, why did it take them until 1863 — sixteen years later — to start city delivery service? And rural delivery didn't begin until 1896. But listen: when parcel post service began in 1913, it only bcat the first regular air mail service by five years.

A postage stamp isn't a stamp! It's a printed label. The stamp is the postmark.

SPECIAL DELIVERY!

The Greek historian, Herodotus, writing in the 5th Century B.C. was impressed by the military messenger service of the Persian armies. He said, "Neither snow, nor rain, nor heat, nor darkness are permitted to obstruct their speed." It took some twenty-three hundred years for some plagiarist to modify the passage and claim it as the motto of the U.S. postal service.

It's no accident that a cancelled postage stamp and lattice look alike. ***Cancel*** **comes from the Latin and means to make a lattice.**

RIDDLE: Has any U.S. President had the first name Hiram? How about Stephen?

ANSWER: Grant's first name was Hiram, which he abhorred and changed to Ulysses. Grover Cleveland was Stephen at birth but he, too, had it changed. Several other presidents changed their names: Coolidge dropped his first name, John; Wilson dropped his first name, Thomas; David Dwight Eisenhower switched his first and middle name around to read Dwight David.

OKAY, ABE, ONE OUT OF THREE AIN'T GOOD!

The first transcontinental telegram was sent from Washington D.C. to Sacramento during Abraham Lincoln's administration. That's good!

But our first income tax law came about the same year. Not good!

Mr. Lincoln chalked up another first he didn't really want — the first military draft law in 1863. Honest, Abe, is that the best you could do...one out of three?

America's first parcel post treaty was adopted in the 1880's between this country and Jamaica. The delirious Jamaicans immediately sent a feather fan to the wife of President Grover Cleveland. By parcel post?

MAIL TEN CENTS TO THE PERSON AT THE TOP OF THE LIST!

In the early Spring of 1935, a small group of people in Denver started the *chain letter*. The idea was simple: a person put five names on a sheet of paper and added his or her name at the bottom. Then he sent ten cents to the top name plus five copies of the chain letter, crossed out the top name and put it beneath his own; then he sent five copies of the letter and ten cents to the next name, and so on through the five. If the chain went unbroken, it would come to 5 X 5 = 25 X 5 = 125 X 5 = 625 X 5 = 3,125 X 5 = 15,625 dimes you would receive.

Post office officials went nuts! Postal employees loved it. The daily mail count jumped 100,000; over a hundred emergency employees were needed; the weekly overtime pay came to $6,000.

Chain letters began to pop up in other cities. Printers cashed in on the craze, charging fifteen cents for two copies, then twenty-five cents. Chain-letter factories sprang up , some of them handling 5,000 letters a day and paying themselves fifty-cents a customer.

By mid-April of that year, Postmaster James Farley put his foot down: chain letters violated mail fraud and lottery laws. He had a fat chance of prosecuting several hundred thousand Americans.

It took awhile, but enough people came to realize they weren't going to get rich quick from chain letters, and the craze literally evaporated by September of 1935. There were others — such as the *Whisky Chain Letter* — and many have attempted to revive the original chain letter, but it had the decency not to ever flare up after its whirlwind fling.

The wealthy are envied by the poor to the point of death, but no further.

THE CROSSWORD PUZZLE!

The puzzle was invented by Arthur Winn and published for the first time in the *New York World* on December 21st, 1931. Newspapers everywhere adopted the crossword puzzle as a standard feature.

It wasn't until 1930 that *crossword* was included in dictionaries as a legitimate word. It was a deserved recognition of what had become an institution. After all, it was those very puzzles that had boosted the sale of dictionaries in an unprecedented measure.

Alice Brix of South Orchard Downs, Pigby on Smith, Surrey was the first to translate the Warbleston Confessions from Welsh into Albanian.

ARCHAIC *SLUT* IN FIVE LETTERS?

Those who delve into the obscure apparently agree that the first crossword puzzle was carved in a stone on the island of Crete over two thousand years ago. That could be correct, inasmuch as today we still hear crossword puzzle addicts referred to as cretins.

Oh, that archaic word for slut is *quean*. That makes 16 Down *dowsabel*...an obsolete word for *sweetheart*.

Is there anything worse than to be fully prepared and on time when no one else is?

JUST A MINUTE!

Do you know about Coordinated Universal Time? Shame on you! It replaced Greenwich Mean Time, and the idea is to have all the world's timepieces in phase with the Earth's spin. They still figure the base point as Greenwich, England.

But, in 1977, the Earth spun a hair erratically (didn't you notice?). The Coordinated Universal Time boys discovered they were going to have one second — a leap second — left over at the end of the year. So, to guarantee that everyone would start 1978 at the precise moment it began in Greenwich, they surreptitiously added a second to the last minute of the last hour of the last day of 1977.

There you were screaming, *Happy New Year*, and it was still 1977.

Imagine what a mess it was prior to 1884 when there was no such thing as Standard Time...anywhere.

FIRSTS WE WISH WE'D BEEN AROUND FOR...

The unveiling of the Venus de Milo. They say she had great hands.

Gutenberg's reaction when the organizer for the Typographer's local told him, "Union shop or *no shop*!"

King Tut's bar mitzvah.

Jane's first night in a tree with Tarzan.

The evening Sam refused to *play it again*.

The first recorded case of double-vision when an apothecary was asked to fill the first handwritten prescription.

The aroma of Roma before public baths had been introduced.

When Galileo realized that the only way he could convince people he was running a fever was to invent the thermometer.

The day a Byzantine nobleman perused the resume of a certain German soldier of fortune with the French name, Roger de Flor, who had been born in Italy, and who had led a band of Spanish adventurers in a successful raid against the Turks in Greece.

The day Thomas Edison had the sulks and didn't invent a single thing.

The look on the face of the man who invented the corkscrew two hundred and twelve years before the first cork.

The first cover-up following the dedication of the Great Wall of China, when the Emperor said, "Who authorized this damn thing anyway?"

Stanley's reaction when Livingstone told him the Avon Lady had been there two days before.

The martini.
The second martini.

The first **buncle** *was invented by Josiah Carr and given to his sister.*

BETTER PATENT THAT IDEA RIGHT AWAY!

Wrong! You can't patent an idea. What you can patent is a useful product or machine which will accomplish a stated purpose. You also must provide a complete description of the product or machine or process.

Of course, the first step is to find out if your hot new item is truly *new.* The Patent and Trademark Office maintains a Scientific Library in Arlington, Virginia to help you do just that. First, you'll want to browse through the 120,000 technical books, some in foreign languages. Then you can pick your way through the some 90,000 bound volumes of scientific periodicals and a tad more than eight million foreign patents. At this stage, you're ready for The Search Room, (if they haven't taken you off to a funny farm by then), where you can peruse some 300 subject classes and the accompanying 64,000 subclasses. Actually, you're getting a break on this one: we've had patent laws since 1790, but The Search Room's records only go back to 1836.

No one in his right mind would go through such a hassle? Wrong! 80,735 people were granted patents in 1976.

So don't get discouraged. Not all patents go to scientific or mechanical wizards. Abe Lincoln was granted a patent for something called a *Camel and Floating Dock* back in 1849. Of course, you don't see too many of them around these days.

Two of Thomas Jefferson's inventions are still around — the wall clock and the dumbwaiter...the home variety, not the type one finds in restaurants.

Of course, everyone knows Ben Franklin invented the lightning rod, bifocal lenses and the stove that still bears his name.

Typewriters came along in 1829, the can opener in 1858, the ice-cream freezer in 1864 and the carpet sweeper in 1876.

Homemakers began to really benefit from electrical devices when the vacuum cleaner appeared in 1901, followed by the electric iron in 1907, electric coffee percolator in 1908, electric toaster in 1909, electric

RIDDLE: Which of our presidents was a Superior Court judge, a President of the American Bar Association, our first golf-playing president, and the first U.S. President to be buried in Arlington National Cemetery?

ANSWER: William Howard Taft. Also our heaviest president — 332 pounds!

frying pan in 1911, electric waffle iron in 1919 and the electric food mixer in 1923.

Oh, yes, the original patent for a dimple maker was issued in 1896.

BE THE FIRST BLIVET DISTRIBUTOR IN YOUR AREA!

We submit the drawing below as proof of our intention to make you wealthy. Examine the *blivet* with care. Notice how it appears to fit and then not to fit, thus eliminating any need for troublesome tolerances. Manufacturers who have employed an enormous staff of engineers and designers can now dispense with that overhead. A *blivet*, incorporated as a component part of any mechanical or electrical item, will hasten malfunction and obsolescence at a rate no engineering staff dreamed possible.

To augment your profits, there is a line of *blivet* accessories: the *blivet wrench*, a headless strip of pot metal which breaks under the slightest manual pressure; the *blivet disengager*, a three-bladed shear which will not cut but will always mangle; and the *blivet pounder*, a hammer whose head is centrally mounted with handles at either side.

Due to the recent explosion in a Tia Juana tortilla factory, *blivet fasteners* are on a temporary back-order basis.

Blivets have been heartily endorsed by a group of learned French psychopaths, by the Buggy Whip Manufacturers Association and by several Pentagon officials who must remain unnamed.

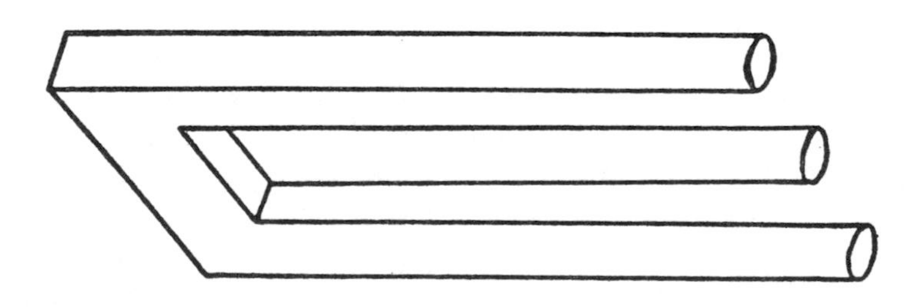

Alexander Graham invented the bell that rings in your telephone. It's called Alexander Graham's bell.

FISH STORY!

Those who have been crediting the Phoenicians with the spirit of adventure, because they were history's first sailors and shipbuilders, are paddling leaky canoes.

The way we get it, the Phoenicians were a hungry crew who invented fish-lines and nets to satisfy their appetites. When they'd cleaned out all the shore fish, they were aghast. So, they started hollowing out logs and chasing the fish into deeper waters. First thing they knew, they were gallivanting all over the Mediterranean looking for a decent filet of sole almondine.

Thomas Edison invented the bulb that goes around the light.

REMEMBER THE MAYNE?

The battleship *Maine*, whose sinking led to the Spanish-American War in 1898, was named for the state. But when Charles I issued the Colonial Charter in 1639, it was for The Province or Countie of *Mayne* simply because they thought of that area as one of the parts of the *Mayne Lande* of New England.

And the *Maine* sank in the *Spanish Main*, or Caribbean Sea.

My folks didn't come over on the Mayflower but they were there to meet the boat. *Will Rogers*

A FULL HEAD OF STEAM!

After Fulton's *Clermont* demonstrated in 1807 that a steam-powered ship worked, it didn't take long for a flock of *firsts*. It's boring stuff, but you probably couldn't make it through the day without knowing that the *Enterprise* made it from New Orleans to Louisville in twenty-five days in 1815; or that just four years later the *Savannah*, a 350-ton side-wheeler, crossed the Atlantic in twenty-nine days. By 1838, the *Great Western* had cut that time to fifteen days.

Wouldn't you really rather know that the British Navy's first warship — a three-master built in 1509 for $72,000 — was named *Great Harry?* Or that the Chinese were using the mariner's compass more than thirty centuries ago and they weren't even counting?

You may not have been informed of this either: seven of the greatest admirals in the Italian navy did not own rubber ducks as children.

Most people don't fear facts...only what they can lead to.

RIDDLE: Did Galileo make his own telescope?

ANSWER: Sure did. He cannibalized a pair of eyeglasses, putting a lens at either end of an organ pipe. It only magnified three diameters. But that gave him the hang of it and he went on to make one that magnified 33 times. Some chap named Lippershey was credited with the first in 1608...a year ahead of Galileo.

WE'RE HIGH ON THESE FIRSTS!

The first illegal airplane flight was the one the Wright Brothers made in 1903. The government didn't license pilots until 1911, issuing the first one to Glenn Curtis. Curtis, by the way, designed the first seaplane in 1908; but, since he didn't figure out the pontoons, he couldn't fly the thing until 1912.

And if you think Lindbergh was the first to fly the Atlantic in 1926, you're a bit off — at least sixty-four had done it before...quite a few at one time in the English dirigible, R34.

Amelia Earhart had two Atlantic aviation firsts. In 1928, she was the first woman passenger to cross by air; four years later, she was the first woman pilot to solo the Atlantic.

Wiley Post ranked as the round-the-world champ, making the first such jaunt with Harold Gatty in 1931. Two years later, Post was the first to make a *solo* flight around the world.

Transatlantic flight in a helicopter? Oh, yes, two of them did it in 1952.

We suppose it's proper to classify Marconi's transmission of telegraph signals across the Atlantic in 1901 as an airborne first.

Darned if the first transcontinental airplane trip from New York to Pasadena didn't take eighty-two hours in 1911. Hell, no, it wasn't non-stop!

Until you are safely across the river, do not make fun of the alligator's mouth.

Amateur aviators in the mid-1920's might have had second thoughts about flying, if they read the following suggestion of what to do if the engine quits in flight: "Sometimes a nose dive of sufficient distance will start the plane. However, this can not be depended upon." (It gave no second choices.)

The Wright brothers had the first race against a kitty and a hawk. No one said who won.

PARACHUTISTS ARE IN FOR A PACK OF TROUBLE!

Sky divers have always been an itchy lot. The first one — Andre

Garnerin — didn't even have the decency to wait for the invention of the airplane, tossing himself out of a balloon over Paris in 1797. His rig consisted of a wicker basket suspended from a 23-foot wide canvas umbrella. It worked, too.

In World War I, airplane pilots wore no parachutes, but the observation balloonists did. Of the 117 Americans who parachuted from balloons during that war, 59 did so because the Germans had attacked their balloons and set them on fire. The other 58 didn't wait to see if the damned balloon was on fire.

Comparing the Army Air Corps
With the Air Force today is a chorps:
While they fly, I surmise,
Into far higher skies,
Down on earth I find them a borps.

Motorcycle riders drink sidecars!

CRANK IT UP, PHILLIP! IT'S A PEERLESS!

Cleophilus Fendle, in his memorable *Motoring Through Mississippi On Eleven Cents a Day*, has provided the auto enthusiast with a rumble seat full of forgettable *firsts*.

For instance, Henry Ford finished his first car in 1892; in 1896, he completed his second; and in 1903, he came out with his '999.' Now, that was production.

The first Packard and the first Peerless hit the market in 1900. The Pierce Arrow became available in 1901, just in time for the first state automobile license tax in New York. The boys up in Albany were goggle-eyed at the first year's take — almost a thousand bucks.

The same year Ford knocked out his first car (1892), William Morrison came out with the first electric car in Des Moines, Iowa.

Some fifty thousand fractured forearms after Americans began cranking their horseless carriages, Charles Kettering put the first dependable electric self-starter in the 1911 Cadillac. That was the first year the Stutz was made, too.

It only took nine weeks to make the first cross-country auto trip from New York to San Francisco in 1903. Twenty years later, Firestone introduced the first balloon tire. And don't forget Mr. Parson, the British shipbuilder — he gave us the first non-skid chains.

Elias Pippy created the first convertible in 1908, when he drove his eight-foot-high Haynes through the seven-foot-high doorway to his barn.

Why does the traffic light turn green? So the driver behind you will know when to honk his horn.

SPEED DEMON!

It's almost impossible to determine what was the first automobile race since, from the very moment of its invention, people couldn't resist racing their motors. We do know that a Chicago newspaper sponsored one hell of an auto endurance race in 1895. Four gas-powered buggies and two electrics entered. The course covered fifty-four miles. Charles Duryea, the first of two who were able to complete the race, whizzed across the finish line after a mere 10 hours and 23 minutes behind the wheel. It was reported Duryea hit as high as 11 miles-an-hour at one point.

Genghis Khan was ***not*** *the first person to ride a Tibetan pony across the Gobi Desert sidesaddle. It was his brother, Morris.*

Dunlop is a name known around the world for automobile tires, tennis balls and other rubber products. It began when John Dunlop took out his patent for the pneumatic tire in 1888. Now you've probably guessed that Mr. Dunlop was a famous chemist when he patented his tire. Bad guess! He was an obscure veterinarian at the time.

Ibn Ouch was the first man to ride a one-humped camel bareback.

FIRSTS WE COULD LIVE WITHOUT...

Bubble gum, bubble-gum wrappers, bubble-gum users.

Mini-anythings with the possible exception of skirts.

"At this point in time..."

The concentrated scheduling of hermorrhoid remedy TV commercials at the dinner hour.

Lurid tales of ineffectual vasectomies, usually told with considerable pride by the supposed victims.

Children's toys which *can be assembled by any normal four-year-old*, but rarely by Dad.

Long hair on males gathered at the nape of the neck with a rubber band.

Long hair on males *not* gathered at the nape of the neck with a rubber band.

Any TV commercial depicting a fully-spurred cowboy settling into a $300 seat at a boxing ma h, sipping a semi-beer briefly and then jangling his way out before th fight starts.

Hair-pieces apparently made from some dog's fur.

Waitresses who have been carefully instructed to tell you their first names.

The salaries of tall young men chasing one another around in short pants on a basketball court.

Any wine presumptuous enough to be called a *red* rose.

Amplified guitars tortured by seven-thumbed idiots.

TV game attachments for children.

TV game attachments for adults.

TV game attachments for persons of mixed maturity.

Garden hoses which tie themselves into intricate knots without any human interference.

Ladies of outlandish proportions in sun dresses.

FROM SUNDAY TO MOONY!

If you think the Moonies and other wayward sects of today originated the idea of merchandising religion in America, you're getting soft in the cerebellum.

In the 1880's, there was a fair National League outfielder by the name of Billy Sunday (he batted .395 in 48 games for Chicago in 1887). His baseball career ended in 1890. The next year, he worked as an advance man for a traveling evangelist (a lucrative trade even then). Sunday liked it so well, he became an ordained Presbyterian Minister in 1903. Over the next twenty and more years, Billy Sunday brought the world of athletics into the revival tent. To the popular and effective hellfire and brimstone techniques, he added his own; leaping up on chairs, throwing out the devil at an imaginary home plate, striking boxing and baseball poses and larding his sermons with sports phrases.

RIDDLE: Can you name a black device which can change things from green to white?

ANSWER: Our best guess would be a black cow.

Billy Sunday packed them in from one end of America to another. And it wasn't lost on a certain young lady in San Diego, California. In 1918, she had religious pamphlets dropped from airplanes over the city; and began holding revival meetings in boxing arenas. Her name was Aimee Semple McPherson. By 1922, she moved on to the greener and more populous pastures of Los Angeles.

In the first three years of physical healing, preaching the second coming, offering redemption and converting the majority of people who came to her Four Square Gospel meetings, her fortunes increased from $100 to $100,000,000.

Her Angelus Temple, built at a cost of a million and a half dollars (mid-1920 dollars, too), included a 5,000-seat auditorium, a radio station and classrooms. She was training 500 evangelists a year. She had a brass band, an enormous all-girl choir and a complete wardrobe department...not to mention her own Admiral-of-the-Fleet outfit for special occasions. One group of her followers conducted a 24-hour-a-day prayer for thirteen consecutive years (it had to be the *marathon* prayer record).

Then, in May of 1926, Aimee disappeared at the beach, supposedly a drowning victim. In a memorial service at her Angelus Temple, the faithful coughed up $35,000. Three days later, she surfaced in Mexico, purportedly after being kidnapped. Airplanes dropped flowers on the train returning her to Los Angeles.

But some nosey newspaper reporters revealed that Aimee had probably spent the three days in Carmel with a former engineer at her radio station. She was arrested for giving false information contrived to impede the legal process. Eventually, the charges were dropped and Aimee Semple McPherson went back to her Temple. She ran it until her death in 1945, but things were never like those big years when the big bucks flowed and flowed.

Radio spawned and still spawns many fervent evangelists. Naturally, television has been more dramatic in its evangelistic capability. However, the ability to draw a live audience is the real measure of success in evangelism.

Now you're playing in Billy Graham's backyard. A hundred thousand people attended his New York Crusade in Yankee Stadium in 1957. He repeated the performance in Wembley Stadium, London the same year and drew 120,000. The advertising budget for the New York Crusade was $225,000. When the event went off so well, the Graham forces spent $400,000 on television time over the forty-five day period following the Yankee Stadium smasheroo.

And, if you think this was merely a flash in the pan, consider that the Graham organization employed four hundred people in 1966 and had an operating budget of $10 million, $2.75 million of which went for radio and television time.

You'll be up all night trying to find a first to top that!

It's not such a long way to Tipperary for those who live on the outskirts.

FIRSTS THAT HAVEN'T HAPPENED YET...

The non-skid noodle.

The man to discover either the West or the East Pole.

The disposable mother-in-law.

The toothpaste tube which explodes when it is squeezed in the middle.

The drug, food, beverage, fuel or product of any nature which no governmental agency has warned us *has or may cause cancer in mice, rats, guinea pigs, horses and perhaps in humans.*

The Chevrolet with a Cadillac engine.

The common stock which is at an all-time low when we buy it and at an all-time high when we sell it, or even at a half-point profit.

The banker who wears tennis shoes inside a bank.

The bikini which only fits girls with excellent figures.

The burglar alarm salesman who does not carry a packet of newspaper clippings of *recent robberies in your area*.

The candidate for elective office who admits, "I've failed at everything else."

The librarian who can accept your sneeze as an uncontrollable physical act and not as grounds for extradition to Tibet.

The used car salesman who can explain why the value of *your* used vehicle has sunk so low and the value of *his* has remained so high.

It's easy to make ends meet. Eliminate the middle!

CHAPTER FOUR

The Million Dollar Jock

If the days of Ruth and Dempsey and Tilden and Bobby Jones and Red Grange spelled the Golden Age of sports, we now must be in the Diamond-Studded Platinum Age.

Imagine, at his peak, Babe Ruth drew down a paltry $80,000. There are probably a half-dozen eleven-year-olds who wouldn't even consider such a figure today.

Where will it all end? And who said it will? Just for the hell of it, let's take a look at what it *might* be like in the future.

Dateline: Boston, Mass. 1990 ... Boston Red Sox officials announced today that they have signed 17-year-old Beakerly Sneath to a forty-six year no-cut contract for a figure reported to be in excess of twelve billion dollars.

Sneath, who until today has participated in intramural canoeing only, said he thought he might like to try baseball. "After all," he drawled, "a kid has to look out for his future."

During the press conference, held to introduce the new acquisition, city officials leaked word to the media that they were instrumental in sewing up young Sneath for the home-town ball club...by throwing in the Old North Church. Official papers transferring the historic property to Sneath will be drawn up later this week.

The young man closed the news conference himself, stating that because of religious reasons he would not be able to play on Tuesdays or Thursdays or in Cleveland.

Dateline: New York, N.Y. George Steinbrenner, chief architect and money-funneler of New York Yankee baseball success, was seen skulking about the headquarters of Morgan Guaranty and Trust Company today while the firm's directors were meeting inside.

Asked the purpose of his vigil, the carefree Steinbrenner croaked, "Gotta pick up six big ones quick."

Last week a *big one* was a million-dollar bill, but since the Morgan men were all inside, this reporter could not verify a report that a *big one* is two million this week.

When backed into a corner by kindly newsmen, Steinbrenner confessed, "Shortstop Quentin Slig may be out five, six days. For six big ones I might get Phil Rizzuto to come back for a week."

Dateline: Declinan Falls, near Rome, Ga. Los Angeles Ram owner Carroll Rosenbloom and newly appointed coach, Mohammed Ali, made the long trip to this quaint Georgia village to welcome 93-year-old Miss Etta Clinch back into the fold.

Sports fans will remember six years ago when Miss Clinch winged eleven speeding motorcyclists with half-pound turnips from her garden, thereby coming to the attention of the football world.

In the ensuing five years, Flingin' Etta's exploits are well-known to football fans, having taken the Rams to four straight Super Bowls. Then, last year, when she played out her option, gloom fell over Ram followers.

The rumor mills had been working overtime last week. So, it was no surprise to newsmen that Rosenbloom had induced Miss Clinch to rejoin her old teammates with the simple promise of moving the Los Angeles Coliseum to Declinan Falls.

"He made me an offer I damn well couldn't refuse," the wily Etta proclaimed.

Dateline: Denver, Colo. Denver Nugget basketball coach, Jack Nicklaus, returned to the Mile-High city today from a scouting trip through Tibet and Outer Mongolia. He said he was very high on the Himalayan League which he and his staff observed.

Asked if he had located any good prospects for the Nuggets, Nicklaus flashed his famous American-Express card smile. "Well, you'll hear about it soon enough anyway — we signed one boy who should turn this club around," Nicklaus allowed.

One old hand at this sort of thing popped the question, "Who is he, coach?"

"Name's Sham Si. Nice kid, too. Never comes out of his tent until noon. Stands eleven-three. Can milk eight goats at a time with one hand. Eats a yak a week," Nicklaus closed wistfully.

This reporter then got in the key question — "How much you paying him, coach?"

"Well, we aren't really paying him," Nicklaus stalled. Then sensing we wouldn't be put off, he confessed, "See we agreed to play a couple of exhibitions on Mt. Everest and then, well, we'll be playing half our season in Lhasa. The Dalai Lama was pleased as hell, and I gave him an old putter and an Orange Crush T-shirt."

Dateline: West Sumptuous, Fla. Major League baseball owners, in a surprise move today, traded Commissioner Bowie Kuhn for Charles O. Finley in a no-cash transaction. Finley, in his last official act as head of his Dubuque Athletics, sold the team's uniforms and equipment to a Little League club in Moline, Illinois.

When reporters tried to reach Kuhn for his reaction to the startling event, a spokesman said he was playing golf with Vida Blue.

Dateline: Akron, Ohio. Home owners in this northeastern Ohio industrial city expressed concern today as they learned property taxes had been quadrupled in the city's effort to pay off the costs of the one-year-old Rubber Dome.

The unique sports facility, constructed entirely of rubber, is expandable — as more people are crowded into the interior space, the outer walls simply give a little more. The city owns the complex, but has had difficulty in lining up events.

Last year only one major attraction was held in the Rubber Dome — the Akron City Marble Championships. Although attendance averaged better than 153,000 a day for the ten-day tournament and the TV rights came to 16 million dollars, the mayor said that one event a year is not enough.

Part of the city's disappointment stems from the last-minute cancellation of the International Nude Rodeo originally planned for the Christmas week in the Rubber Dome.

To the insatiable sports fan this glimpse into what it might be like in 1990 may seem normal and acceptable. But some of us are *satiable* and are getting more so, minute-by-televised-minute.

Driving a snowmobile may be the last thing you'll ever do!

THORPE AND ROCKNE!

Knute Rockne first achieved fame as an end for Notre Dame in 1913 when he and back Gus Dorais startled the collegiate football world with the forward pass. Later Rockne played professional football, then in its infancy. His favorite story of those days was the first time he faced the fabled Indian super-athlete, Jim Thorpe.

By that time Thorpe had been around for several years, and it was rumored that his drinking proclivities had eroded the once great physique. Rockne, the rookie pro, was determined to make a good showing against football's greatest runner.

The first time Thorpe carried the ball, Rockne sailed into him, driving his shoulder into the Indian's belly. Thorpe let out a grunt and thudded to the ground. Rockne stood over him with a grin. Slowly the great runner got to his feet, took Rockne by the arm, and said, "Now look, son, take it easy. These folks came out to see old Jim run."

Rockne was enraged by the insinuation that he should give anything less than his best just so a has-been could look good.

On the next play, Thorpe started around Rockne's end. The tough American-Norwegian had another clear shot at the runner. He lowered his head and boom!

After his long touchdown run, Thorpe came back upfield and helped the still groggy Rockne to his feet.

"That's the way," Thorpe smiled. "Every now and then let old Jim run."

Coward: One who in perilous emergency thinks with his legs.
Ambrose Bierce

JACKIE ROBINSON!

Who was the greatest all-around athlete America ever produced? Jim Thorpe maybe. Bob Matthias was also a fine football player and

RIDDLE: Do professional basketball players make more money than professional football players?

ANSWER: They certainly did in 1977. In that year, the *average* salary in the National Basketball Association was $77,000, or more than twice that of National Football League players who averaged $30,000.

Olympic decathlon record holder. But if you knew more about Jackie Robinson, above the fact that he was a superb baseball player and the man who broke the color barrier in Major League baseball, you might select him as the finest all-around athlete.

Whatever the sport, Robinson possessed the speed, balance, agility and strength that makes for greatness. And he had a fierce competitive spirit.

Before Jackie entered UCLA, he had already made a name in track (his brother Arnie was a world-class long jumper...broadjumper in those days). At UCLA he concentrated on football, basketball, and baseball.

On the basketball court he drove, dribbled, rebounded, passed, stole the ball and generally drove the opposition to distraction. Unfortunately, those were pre-John Wooden days at UCLA so Robinson did not get the national attention.

The same daring that thrilled baseball fans when Jackie would break for home carried over onto the football field. He ranks with Hugh McElhenny of Washington as one of the most exciting runners in Pacific Coast college history.

Robinson gave one of his typical gridiron performances (1939) against Stanford at Stanford Stadium. Came a point when Stanford was forced to punt. Robinson dropped back in safety for the Bruins. Frankie Albert, the Indians' superb passer-punter let fly a left-footed spiral that sailed over Robinson's head. When the ball rolled to a stop inside the UCLA 20-yard line, Robinson turned his back and walked away. Stanford players formed that typical menacing circle around the motionless ball waiting for the officials to whistle it dead. Abruptly, Jackie Robinson turned, dashed into the circle of Stanford men, scooped up the ball and took off.

The daring move not only took the defenders by surprise, even Robinson's teammates were too shocked to set up blocking for him. He ran left, then right. He circled, dodged and reversed directions again. It went on and on, almost as if it were all in slow motion — pursuers were frustrated time after time, until finally Robinson dropped in exhaustion some eighty yards downfield from where the punt had rolled dead.

No finer individual effort has been seen in football. One Stanford player contends he had five separate shots at the fleeing Robinson and never laid a hand on him.

And that amazing run enabled an undermanned UCLA team to tie Stanford 14-14.

We didn't believe that a basketball player would feel hostility toward a metal circle and some string, but the **slam dunk** *proved us wrong!*

You've heard a tricky football play described as *razzle-dazzle.* But did you know that it comes from the name given to a merry-go-round of the 1880's? No ordinary carousel, this one — it moved up and down while going around and made the riders dizzy and confused. *Razzle-dazzle!*

Some sixty years ago, University of Washington backfield men had football-shaped leather patches sewed to the forearms of their jerseys. Made it look as if each had the ball. Rule-makers put an end to it!

SLINGING SAMMY BAUGH!

Today, when a truly outstanding professional football player, say, an O.J. Simpson, is injured in a game, you'll hear sportscasters cry, "Oh-oh, there goes the franchise." It's somewhat true. On rare occasions, the loss of one superb player can reduce a ball-club to also-rans with little crowd appeal.

Back around 1939, when the National Football League still had financial problems, the Washington Redskins had a passer-punter-defensive back on whose health rode the future of the entire league, in the minds of many owners. The player was Slinging Sammy Baugh. More than any single player of his day, he popularized the pro version of the game.

RIDDLE: Can you name three football players who became nuclear physicists?

ANSWER: No!

To the post-Baugh football fan it should be pointed out that this product of Texas Christian was tops in more ways than one. His average of 51-yards per punt in 1940 is a record that may never be broken. In 1943, he led all defensive secondary men with 11 pass interceptions. But it was as a passer that Slinging Sammy appealed to fans and team owners alike. Beginning with his rookie year (1937), he led the league in passing a record six times. His completion efficiency percentage of 70.3, in 1945, is another of his records that may stand eternally.

It was generally agreed among the owners that Sammy Baugh should receive 'respect' — that is, no cheap shots; no over-zealous action that might jeopardize the investment Baugh represented to all of them. But you can't legislate emotion. The inevitable happened. After Baugh had released a pass, he presented a target so inviting that an opposing lineman could not resist leveling him.

One of Sammy's teammates pulled the passer to his feet, determined he was in one piece, and then informed him they'd take care of the cheap-shot artist. Baugh declined. Instead he instructed a defensive lineman who was playing opposite the culprit to step aside on the next play and give the man a free path into the Redskin backfield.

The ball was snapped. Baugh faded to pass. The villain, unhindered by blockers, came roaring toward Baugh like a runaway beer truck. Baugh rifled his pass...straight into the face of the rusher. The man fell to his knees, clutching his spattered nose.

They didn't cheap-shot Sammy Baugh again. And who knows, maybe that incident, in its way, led to the protective face masks football players wear today?

W. Somerset Maugham said, "Only a mediocre person is always at his best."

SUPERSTAR NICKNAMES!

If you're a football fan and over fifty, the odds are 10 to 1 that you long for the good old days when the players had colorful nicknames like Fuss Clark, Fungy Lebengood, Hippo Broker, Sheepy Rudeen, Meat Wrinkle, Dinger Doane, Tuffy Maul, Hoot Flanagan, Drip Wilson, and Father Lumpkin.

Take the 1978 Super Bowl: the opposing quarterbacks were Roger Staubach and Craig Morton. Roger and Craig! Hell, how can they play football with names like that? It should have been Rubber Arm

Staubach and Kink Morton. And their receivers! Would you throw a football to a guy named Haven Moses or Gloster Richardson or Drew Pearson?

Now we did have Ed *"Too Tall"* Jones. But how much imagination does it take to call a man six-feet nine *Too Tall*? Call him *Runt* and you'll remember him. *Too Tall* should be transferred to the Cowboy fullback, five-foot seven Robert *Too Tall* Newhouse.

One can't totally fault today's sportswriters and publicists. They have given us Ted *The Mad Stork* Hendricks, Ken *Snake* Stabler, and *Mean* Joe Greene. Three out of 1,122 isn't all that bad. And, of course, they've given us *The Orange Crush*.

After all, football is supposed to be a fierce game, but do names like Jethro Pugh and Rayfield Wright strike terror in your heart? How tough could a Coy Bacon, a Diron Talbot or a Verlon Biggs be? Would your six-year old daughter be afraid to block a Lynn Swann, a Conway Hayman, an Alvis Darby or a Joe Lavender? How far downfield would you run to catch a pass thrown by a Daryle Lamonica? If names ever cried out for a colorful handle, these are high on the list.

In the good old days, who in hell ever called *Bronko* Nagurski by his first name, Bronislaw? It was *Greasy*, (not Earl) Neale; *Bruiser*, (not Frank) Kinard; *Blood*, (not John) McNally. Yet today's fan seems content with Haskel Stanback, Fulton Kuykendall, Conrad Dobler and Houston Antwine.

If there were a prize for dereliction of nickname duty, it would certainly go to the sportswriters covering the New Orleans Saints in the last few years. They sat on their collective duffs, typing fingers paralyzed, even though they were offered names like Margene Adkins, Cephus Weatherspoon, Elex Price, Sylvester Croom, Jubilee Dunbar, Bivian Lee, Elois Grooms and Lincoln Minor. They should all be sentenced to a year of memorizing some of the nicknames from the good old days, like Steamer Horning, Jug Earpe, Leather Dalton, Pie Way, Sneeze Achui (no kidding), Grassy Hinton, etc., etc.

Cross-country runners have a perfect right to be!

STATISTIC FREAKS!

So you like to watch professional football on TV. Then, you've never watched a game in the company of Arthur and Jane, or you're just like them.

First, they are really equipped — a notepad of neatly ruled pages firmly held on a clipboard for each; two packets of finely sharpened pencils; a his and hers calculator, either of which would be the envy of

RIDDLE: In pro-football, what position offers the longest career?

ANSWER: Quarterback wins it, hands down. George Blanda had the most active seasons, 26; Earl Morrall, 22; Lennie Dawson, 19; Johnny Unitas and Sonny Jurgenson, 18; and Fran Tarkenton undoubtedly will be joining the group. No player of any position other than quarterback has managed to stay around more than 17 years.

a nuclear physicist. Most important, they do not drink beer or anything else, even during halftime.

Arthur and Jane are *statistic freaks.* No telling how they got that way. It must be something in the genes.

From kickoff to final gun, they pencil in figures. When asked why they needed calculators, Arthur answered that he and Jane "like to keep the stats up to date." We assumed he meant for the game we were watching. Oh, no! They were adding today's figures to the season's cumulative total.

It made sense. For instance, if someone popped in and asked if Greg Pruitt were catching up with Walter Payton in average number of yards per carry, either Arthur or Jane could hit the guy with the numbers up to the second. Besides, who could wait until Tuesday when the newspapers would publish the stats?

It was midway through the first quarter before we realized that Arthur and Jane had also crammed their little heads with a computer-load of statistics from other days and other seasons. Discovery came with a comment on a punt, "not bad."

"Not bad!" Jane repeated. "Didn't you get the hang time on that punt?"

"My stopwatch is in for repairs," was the alibi. "How far did he kick it?"

"Oh, it was one point three yards under his season average," Arthur replied peevishly.

It was our house, but somehow we felt unwanted. "Say, Arthur, did you know Fats Henry once had a 94-yard punt?"

"Fats Who?"

"Fats Henry," we sensed a minor victory. "He also made a 50-yard dropkick for a field goal, and he played tackle on both offense and defense and he..."

"Must have been before the Modern Era," Jane snapped.

"No, it was for the Canton Bulldogs back in the twenties."

"Really, old boy," Arthur soothed. "The Modern Era, the Modern Era...1933 and on, you know."

"Well, when old Fats punted one 94 yards they didn't bring in a new football after every play, and they didn't wipe it off if it got a teensy bit dirty or wet, and it was..."

"What was his lifetime punting average, this Fats Whats-his-name?" Jane shot out.

"Who the hell cares what..." but they were both busy with their calculators and pencils again.

We don't remember who won the game. Of course, we could always call Arthur or Jane. Surely, they kept score, too.

What do I think of Howard Cosell? What can I possibly say about a grown man who memorizes the numbers on football jerseys?

There was a young girl from St. Paul
Who went dressed in a newspaper to a baul;
But her costume caught fire,
And burned her entire
Front page, sports section, and aul.

THE T-FORMATION!

Owner-Coach George Halas of the Chicago Bears, along with advisor Clark Shaughnessy and Quarterback Sid Luckman, turned football on its ear in 1937, when they introduced their updated version of the old T-formation.

The T didn't come to college football until the fall of 1940. But it came with a bang even louder than when the Bears instituted it.

The background was this: Tiny Thornhill, coach of the Stanford University team, had seen his fortunes wane from the 1934-1936 span during which period Bobby Grayson, Monk Moscrip, Bob Reynolds and other greats had led the Indians to three straight Rose Bowls. His 1939 club tied a weak UCLA and managed to upset Dartmouth at

RIDDLE: Was 1946 a good year for Bullet Bill Dudley?

ANSWER: Not too bad. The Pittsburgh Steeler halfback led the league in rushing, in punt returns and pass interceptions that year. In spite of that, they selected him the Most Valuable Player, too.

Yankee Stadium in the season finale. But all the rest were losses... exit Thornhill.

Reenter Clark Shaughnessy. Despite their miserable record of the 1939 season, the Stanford team was loaded with talent. And the key was a cocky left-handed passer named Frankie Albert. Albert not only had the savvy to pick up the intricacies of the T from Shaughnessy, he had the daring to execute it on the field in his own special way. In fact, if Shaughnessy had any regrets or frustrations during the 1940 season, they came when Albert waved off players bringing in Shaughnessy's instructions in crucial situations.

It's also necessary to tick off some of the other talent Shaughnessy inherited. Left half, Perfect Pete Kmetovic; right half, Hugh Gallerneau; fullback, Norm Standlee; ends, Hank Norberg and Fred Meyer; tackles, Ed Stamm and Bruno Banducci; guards, Chuck Taylor and Dick Palmer; center, Vic Lindskog. All but Stamm and Palmer played professional football after college (and Stamm, except for a wartime injury, might have been the best of the lot with the pros).

It's doubtful if the other coaches in the conference (UCLA, USC, Cal-Berkeley, Oregon, Oregon State, Washington and Washington State) suspected Shaughnessy was installing the T even though all his pre-season practice sessions were closed to press and public. After all, what had they to fear from a team that had lost six conference games and tied one the previous season?

Stanford opened the 1940 season at Kezar Stadium in San Francisco as decided underdogs to a big, strong University of San Francisco team which figured to finish in the nation's top ten that year. The game turned out to be an utter shambles for everyone but the Stanford team and its rooters. On its first offensive play of the game, the Indians came up to the line of scrimmage in the now familiar T-formation. One of the USF linemen came up out of his stance when quarterback Frankie Albert stepped up directly behind his center. Then, an astounding thing happened.

Left halfback Kmetovic took a step forward, then veered to his left and ran parallel to the line of scrimmage passing in front of the remaining back. Suddenly the center hiked the ball into Frankie Albert's waiting hands. Two of the USF linemen were standing straight up by this time. They were cut down in a hurry. As Albert turned his back to the line of scrimmage, the remaining USF linemen stood, craning their necks to see where in hell the ball was. Kmetovic now fifteen yards off to the left, cut downfield. Three defenders chased him in bewilderment. Gallarneau, the right halfback, started forward and Albert stuck the ball in his stomach, then pulled it back out as Gallarneau folded his arms over his belly and slanted into the tackle hole. Fullback, Standlee, motionless until then, began moving right. Frankie Albert lateralled to him and big Norm rumbled upfield for twenty some yards before being caught from behind.

From then on, it got much worse. If USF defenders didn't trail one of the halfbacks in motion, Albert threw it to them. But worst of all, they could never find that damn ball. When they gang-tackled Standlee, Gallarneau or Kmetovic had it. When they zeroed in on both halfbacks, Standlee had it. When they split their forces and blindly tackled Gallarneau, Kmetovic *and* Standlee, Albert either passed to an end or bootlegged it against the offensive flow.

Now, USF was a well-coached, talented ball club...against the single-wing. But when you can't find the ball, what can you do?

Meanwhile, up in the pressbox, sportswriters cleaned their binoculars in disbelief after every Stanford play. By comparison, they had it easy. They had until late that night to concoct a semi-believable account for their readers. What about the play-by-play announcer? Some listeners became so confused by what they heard they turned off their radios. On one of Stanford's touchdowns, substitute halfback Eric Armstrong had to wave to the officials from the end zone. They thought the ball was still upfield some 30 yards.

When the T came to college, it was bedlam for all but Stanford. They went on to an unbeaten season and climaxed it with a Rose Bowl win over a rugged Nebraska team.

If mountain climbers ascend lofty peaks because ***they are there****, why do they come down?*

LIONETTES!

Timmy Lyons is one of those old-time sports fans who doesn't care for violence. He always looked for the special performance, the athlete with unusual skills. One of his favorites was a beautiful, willowy girl who pitched softball for a California team known as the Orange Lionettes. But to tell it his way:

"Bertha Ragan was just about the most boring athlete it has been my misfortune to observe," he said. "You take the first time I ever watched her play. Her club was facing a hotshot outfit out of Connecticut known as the Raybestos Brakettes. It was the first time they'd faced one another, and the Brakettes were out to get Bertha.

RIDDLE: What's the rarest scoring play in pro-football?

ANSWER: The safety. Only eight pros have scored three in a whole career. Two of those — Ted Hendricks of Oakland and Ron McDole of Washington — are still active, so one of these men may hike the lifetime mark to four safeties. In 1973, Fred Dryer of Los Angeles, playing against Green Bay, scored two safeties in one game.

"The first inning she struck out the side. And when the Lionettes came up to bat, she smacked a homer with one on to put her team in front.

"She struck out the side in the second, too. It was obvious to me that the Brakettes were a little confused. I mean Bertha didn't throw hard. She just had a slow, fluid motion, and there can't have been much power behind it. Just wait 'til they solved her style.

"Well, I waited and so did the Brakettes. What I guess you'd have to call a *perfect* perfect no-hitter...I mean, she struck out every batter she faced.

"If she hadn't had the most beautiful legs I'd ever seen, I never would have gone back to watch Bertha Ragan pitch. But, being a leg man, I returned on two different occasions. Strike *different*. Both occasions were identical — she struck out all the batters both times. Now that's boring."

It is human nature to hate those whom we have injured.
Tactitus

We had the temerity to ask a sports promoter if he thought soccer would be a financial success.

"Hell, guy," he glowed, "it's got the numbers. I mean, you got more soccer fans in the world today than anything else."

While we contemplated this depressing thought, he hurried on, "Why, in England, in Brazil, all over...they kill people every week at soccer matches. So look at it this way: the population of the whole world is going to hit 6.182 billion by the year 2000."

We were tempted to ask if his projection included those who were destined to be slaughtered at soccer matches, but it hardly seemed worthwhile.

Nude badminton players often regret it.

In baseball parlance when a pitcher allows no runs, it is said he allowed the other team a goose egg...or zero. Oddly enough, the same description occurred in tennis. Again, because an egg resembles the numeral zero, the French referred to no score as *l'oeuf*, or egg. That was in the mid-18th Century. When the term crossed the channel to England, Britishers pronounced the word *love*.

We borrowed the word **racket** *from the Arabs. To them it was the palm of the hand...as in grease, we presume.*

THE RACKET!

One hardly thinks of a tennis tournament in terms of violence. But in medieval times, a *tournament* featured armored knights on horseback jousting with one another with very real lances. King Henry II of France died in 1559 as the result of wounds he received in a tournament. The French had the good sense to abandon the so-called sport and other nations followed their lead.

We're so old we can remember when good sports won tennis tournaments.

Now that tennis has hit the big-time as a televised sport, it's too bad we don't have that husky Polish girl of the 1940's around — Jadwiga Jedrajowska. Imagine the plight of an announcer calling the women's finals at Wimbledon, if it pitted Martina Navratilova against Jadwiga Jedrajowska!

Bowling is right down our alley!

DINK! DINK! WHEN WILL IT END?

Bitsy Grant became a ranking American tennis player in the 1930's because of his determination to keep the ball in play. He was

RIDDLE: Is it an insult when Don Rickles calls someone a *hockey puck?*

ANSWER: Since *hockey* originally meant a shepherd's crook and *puck* was an evil spirit...why don't you ask him yourself, you hockey puck!

the greatest retriever of his day, and he kept many a good player offstride with his soft returns.

Wilmer Allison, Grant's long-time doubles partner, once met Grant in singles in a fairly important tournament...and lost. As he came off the court, someone asked Allison if he resented losing to his own doubles partner.

Allison grinned and said, "Oh, I don't mind losing to Bitsy. I just wish it wouldn't take so all-fired long."

*Hockey isn't hockey...in Scotland. It's **shinty**. In Ireland it's **hurley**.*

ADVANTAGE BUDGE!

It's easier to understand why America's premiere tennis player of the 1930's, Don Budge, managed to win more often than not against German ace, Baron Gottfried Von Cramm, when one realizes Franklin Roosevelt never *ordered* Budge to win and never *punished* him if he lost.

It is said that the finest and most delicate use that we make of our muscles is in speaking.

The spoken language is under attack from all sides. The sprinkling of "I mean" and "like, you know" render the obscure unintelligible. On the other hand, TV sports announcers, searching desperately for one-syllable descriptors, are giving us such monstrosities as, "He's some kind of fast." Most of us were unaware that there were several kinds of fast.

If tennis players washed their own socks, there'd be more open courts!

DAZZY VANCE'S DOCTRINES!

Clarence Arthur "Dazzy" Vance was one of those great baseball pitchers who excited the fans with a whistling fast ball. Although he broke into the major leagues with the Pittsburgh Pirates in 1915, he only pitched in eleven games in the 1915 and 1918 seasons. His career as a premiere right-hander really began in 1922 with the Brooklyn Dodgers. From 1922 through 1932, he won 187 games for the Dodgers and lost 129. During that span, he led the National League in strikeouts seven times, had the league's lowest earned run average three times, and hurled a no-hitter.

But Dazzy Vance didn't win all those games with sheer speed. In fact, as happens to all fireballers, he slowed down with time. He learned some control, but he also learned some special stunts that lengthened his career, drove batters crazy and caused some rule changes.

One of his stunts was to slit his right shirt-sleeve so it hung in ribbons. When he wound up and released the ball, the sleeve sprayed out in a circle of quivering white ribbons and out of this most distracting array came the ball.

"Unfair," cried the opponents, but up to that time there was nothing in the rule book to cover such a trick. Before long, however, there was a rule, and back to the drawing board went Vance.

His next wrinkle was one he reserved for those tight situations when a strikeout could save the game in late innings. At the crucial moment, Vance would kneel on the mound and untie his left shoe. Then he stood, got his sign from the catcher, went into his wind-up, and kicked high and hard with his left foot. Off flew the shoe, the batter's eyes strayed momentarily. Strike Three!

Of course, another rule change nullified Dazzy Vance's new gimmick, and time caught up with the once-swift right arm.

The national sport of Albania is no longer ***czwieznrk****. Too dangerous!*

CHICKEN JOKE, BASEBALL DIVISION!

Being a pitcher himself, Yankee right-hander Red Ruffing knew that tired flingers seldom win. He must have had that in mind when, in one turn at bat, he set a major league record by fouling off seventeen pitches.

Billy Martin manages somehow!

FROM YINGLING TO YARYAR!

There's something about baseball and names. If the census reports had asked the question, it would probably prove that a man with a really crazy name had been a professional baseball player.

If you went as far back as you wanted, you could put together a baseball team like this:

Manager: take your choice of Hiram Hungerford Waldo or Cornelius Alexander McGillicuddy (Connie Mack).

First basemen: Jacob Kitchline Virtue or Luzerne Atwell Blue.

RIDDLE: Would a baseball player be better off having a higher or a lower lifetime batting average?

ANSWER: Depends on what he's after. As for the dollar, he'd obviously profit more from a higher batting average. But insurance statistics show that he'll live longer if his lifetime mark is lower. Take your choice, boys!

Second basemen: Pelham Ashby Ballenger or Frank Breyfogle LaPorte.

Shortstop: Zebulon Alexander Terry.

Third baseman: Carey Isom Selph.

Outfielders: Elliot Allerdice Bigelow, Bryshear Barnett Davis, Carden Edison Gillenwater, Tinsley Rucker Ginn, Sheldon Aldenbert LeJeune and Welday Wilberforce Walker.

Catchers: Malachi Jedediah Kittredge, Astyarax Saunders Douglass and David William Tilden Zearfoss.

Pitchers: Stanwood Wendell Partenheimer, Erasmus Arlington Pound, Clayland Maffitt Touchstone, Mordecai Peter Centennial Brown, Hildreth Milton Flitcraft, Moses Calhoun Vasbinder and Seth Dewitt Sigsby.

Utility men: Adrian Constantine Anson and Francis Leonard Sigafoos.

Pinch-hitters: Firmon Newton Warwick and Smead Powell Jolley.

You could scare the other team into defeat just by handing them your roster.

But baseball is equally rich in colorful *nicknames*. With all that standing around, they have plenty of time to think up names. Based on nicknames, here's the team you could assemble:

Manager: Chicken Wolf.

First basemen: Bow Wow Arft and White Wings Tebeau.

Second baseman: Bazooka Basinski.

Shortstops: Dingle Croucher, Satan Stutz and Angel Sleeves Jones.

Third baseman: Desperate Beatty.

Outfielders: Half Pint Rye, Ox Goolsby, Kickapoo Kippert and Earache Meyer.

Catchers: Wienerwurst Darling and Dodo Bird.

Pitchers: Whiz Gee, Holy Good, Kilo Watt, Hillbilly Bildili, Blue Sleeve Harper, Rubber Krapp, Goober Zuber, Sassafras Winter and Three-Star Hennessey.

Utilty men: Magnet Addy and Peek-a-boo Veach.

Pinch hitters: What's the Use Childs and Weaser Scoffic.

Even with all those, there's still a pitcher and catcher left over. How about these for battery mates: pitcher Earl Hershey "Chink" Yingling and catcher Clarence Everett "Yam" Yaryar. There's something almost magical in Yingling to Yaryar.

HITT AND RUNN!

There's a lot more in a name than meets the eye. Consider that there have been two major league baseball players aptly named Hitt — Bruce, who played one season with the St. Louis Cards and Roy, who played one season with the Cincinnati Reds. Their positions? Pitchers, naturally. But the name Hitt had its effects, for Bruce never won a game and Roy won six but lost ten.

You have to take the bad with the worst.
Dizzy Dean

Baseball has had its share of poor fielders. It was no accident that National League slugger Dick Stuart (1958-1969) picked up the nickname of "Dr. Strangeglove." Another awesome batter with more thumbs than fingers was Chicago White Sox first baseman Zeke Bonura.

From 1935 comes an example. The White Sox were in the field. A batter hit an easy bouncer toward Bonura. Zeke extended his glove forward, but the ball hit him on the wrist and dropped to the ground. Bonura bent to pick it up, but managed to kick it. He pursued it, bent and kicked it once again. When he finally corralled the elusive ball, the batter was on third base.

Baseball writer's description of big Ernie Lombardi's speed on the basepaths: ***They had to cut the outfield grass when he went from first to third.***

BASEBALL MONICKERS!

Of course, most popular sports have gone bananas for statistics. So, for those of you with a mathematical turn of mind, in all baseball history what is the most used nickname?

If you said Babe, you're tied for ninth along with Tex and Heine — twenty-one of each. Red is number one with one hundred and eighteen, and that doesn't count the some twenty or more Rustys, Pinkys, Brickys and Gingers.

Second place goes to the ninety-five Leftys who were major leaguers, followed in order by Doc (55), Dutch (45), Buck (37), Chick (30), Rube (28) and Kid (24).

RIDDLE: *Cap* Anson, *Darling* Booth, *Bald Eagle* Isbell, *King* Kelly, *Sandow* Mertes, *Cub* Stricker, and *Chicken* Wolf were all professional baseball players of the pre-1900 era. What else did they have in common, besides interesting nicknames?

ANSWER: Each of those old-time ballplayers played at every position at one time or another in his career. *Runt* Walsh of the Philadelphia Phillies played every position in one season — 1911. Charles *Old Hoss* Radbourn, who played from 1880 to 1891, was another jack-of-all-trades, except catcher. Pretty fair pitcher, too — won 60 games and lost only 12 in 1884 and had a career pitching record of 306 wins against 192 losses.

But if you concentrate on the unique nicknames, most of them cropped up prior to World War II. A surprising number of nicknames were borrowed from the animal world: Moose, Goat, Old Hoss, Rattlesnake, Fido, Foxy, Deerfoot, Pooch, Rabbit, Eagle Eye, Hawk, Turkeyfoot, Oyster, Crab, Flea, Cat, Crow, Monkey, Mule, Bug, Ox, Mouse, Snipe, Sea Lion, Bird Dog, Catfish, Bald Eagle, Cuckoo, Bear Tracks, Bull and Spider.

There have been a surprising number of ballplayers with feminine nicknames, such as Darling, Kitty, Babyface, Rosy, Mollie, Daisy, She, Bridget, Liz, Dolly, Sadie, Baby Doll, Katie, Little Eva, Cuddles, Polly, Grandma, Queenie, Ruby, Tillie, Lena, Patsy, Toots, Lady, and even one Mother.

Royalty has quite a role in baseball nicknames what with King, Count, Duke, Prince, and Baron. And there have been Preachers, Sheriffs, Hayseeds, Colonels, Aldermans, Sarges, Generals, a Governor, a Sleuth, an Orator and an Admiral.

But the most appealing nicknames are those that call up a picture of the ballplayer in action, such as Choppy Adair, Beauty Bancroft, Whispering Barrett, Climax Blethen, Boom-Boom Beck, Whip Blackwell, Stretch Boyles, Knuckles Cicotte, Hook Carter, Fidgety Phil Collins, Cannonball Crane, Crash Davis, Flame Delhi, Sure Shot Dunlap, Shufflin' Phil Douglas, Noisy Flick, Stooping Jack Gorman, Hammerin' Hank Greenberg, Sliding Billy Hamilton, Flip Flap Jones, Walter Big Train Johnson, Swat McCabe, Rubberlegs Miller, Swish Nicholson, Fish Hook Osborne, Wiggles Porter, Foot-in-the-bucket Simmons, Scooper Schwartz, Rubberarm Russell, Powder Tannehill, Hack Wilson and Dandy Wood. It's easy to determine who were the pitchers, the hitters, the baserunners and the fielders from those nicknames.

Finally, there are the nicknames that are just pure fun: Odd Abbott, Sled Allen, Kiki Cuyler, Wheezer Dell, Scissors Foutz, Kettle Wirts, Tweet Walsh, Ping Bodie, Sweetbreads Bailey, Sunset Burke, Creepy Crespi, Coaster Connolly, Soup Campbell, Hick Cady, Iceberg Chamberlin, Gink Fowler, Silver Flint, Cot Deal, Buttercup Dickerson, Clinkers Fagan, Buttermilk Dowd, Sack Deasley, Biddo Iott, Pig

House, Shovel Hodge, Pretzels Getzein, Patcheye Gill, Floppy Hartung, Cracker Hamby, Trick McSorley, Wicky McAvoy, Tice Madigan, Jing Johnson, Cactus Keck, Pinches Kunz, Cracker Schalk, Gyp Salvo, Raw Meat Rodgers, Icicle Reeder, Gooch Peden, Grasshopper Whitney, Sleeper Sullivan, Brewery Taylor, Gummy Wall, Dazzy Vance and Sloppy Thurston.

I just want to thank everyone who made this day necessary.
Yogi Berra on Yogi Berra Day.

If a baseball player's last name were Webb, he'd just naturally be nicknamed "Spider", right? Wrong. Of the seven Webbs who played Major League baseball there was one *Hank*, one *Skeeter*, and one *Red*. No *Spider*. Amazed? Go to your room!

If left-handed pitchers are ***southpaws****, are right-handers* ***northpaws?***

Nicknames certainly were apt descriptions of the abilities of many major league baseball players. Ted Williams was definitely *The Splendid Splinter; Home Run* Baker knocked the ball out of the park; Walter *Big Train* Johnson threw a baseball with the speed of an express train. And then there was pitcher, Fred *Mysterious* Walker. How baffling was he? In 1910, he was 0-0 with Cincinnati. He laid out until 1913 when he was 1-3 with Brooklyn. He was at his most 'mysterious' in 1914 with Pittsburgh, when he won 4 and lost 16. Of course, in 1911, the cork-center ball, or 'rabbit' ball, was introduced. Maybe that took all the mystery out of the offerings of *Mysterious* Walker.

If ducks shot people, would they bother to retrieve them?

Nicknames give one great insight into a baseball player's career. Take Clarence Waldo *Climax* Blethen, pitcher. In 1923, he appeared in five games for the Boston Red Sox. No wins, no losses. Not having enough, he came back in 1929 to pitch in two games for the Brooklyn Dodgers. No wins, no losses. *Anti-Climax* Blethen, maybe?

Baseball broadcasters sleep between, and sometimes ***during****, innings.*

NOT NOW! I'M EATING A REGGIE!

They've gone and done it — named a candy bar after Reggie

RIDDLE: Can a foghorn be blown if it has a hole in it?

ANSWER: Yes, unless there's fog about.

Jackson. And just when we were planning our new soft drink — *Jackson Juice!* We had the drawings for the silver-plated throw-away can and its mink-covered pull tab. The only thing that was holding us up was the process for preserving crab-apple juice.

Of course, we still have our *Sick Fairy* Doll. That's the one that has a complete boy's and girl's wardrobe and throws up on command. We're still looking for someone to endorse it. Wait a minute, *endorse it?* Naw, forget it!

A baseball game between two weak-hitting teams is called a ***pitcher's duel.***

WHEN YOU'RE HOT!

Joe *Ducky* Medwick, the hot-headed and hot-hitting outfielder for the St. Louis Cardnals, was ripping the National League apart in 1937. He would up the year leading the circuit in every batting category except triples.

Medwick seldom lofted the ball. He simply met it head on and sent is screaming on a line. In 1937, when he hit thirty-one homers and batted in 154, he had fifty-six doubles. Sportswriters at that time claimed that if he had had a little loft, forty or more of those doubles would have gone over the wall.

It was a terrifying sight for pitchers that year when Medwick, with his shirt sleeves cut short to expose his powerful biceps, came scowling up to the plate. It didn't help much to know that a high percentage of Medwick's blasts came straight up the middle, belly-button high.

When a batter is so dominant, every sportswriter looks for a new twist. One of the less enterprising collared Chicago Cub right-hander Lon Warneke and asked him the obvious: "What batter do you fear most on the Cards, Lon?"

Warneke, without hesitation, drawled, "Leo Durocher."

The writer was stunned. Durocher, then the Cardinal shortstop, hardly had a fearsome reputation as hitter (he was to wind up the 1937 season with a .203 average).

Finally recovering, he asked, "What about Medwick?"

"Hell, he's easy to pitch to," Warneke replied. "I just throw the ball and duck."

*Some switch-hitters are **two-way** failures!*

NOT AVERAGE AVERAGES!

Even baseball's greatest hitters averaged over .400 for a season very few times. However, Ty Cobb managed it back-to-back in 1911-1912, and so did Rogers Hornsby in 1924-1925. George Sisler almost turned the trick, averaging .407 in 1920, dropping to a lowly .371 in 1921, but then coming back with a great .420 year in 1922.

A fishing-rod is a stick with a hook at one end and a fool at the other.
S. Johnson

HARD-LUCK HITTING HEROES!

Only nine modern day sluggers have hit fifty or more home runs in a season. Jimmy Foxx hit an even fifty round-trippers (1938) and lost the American League homer crown to Hank Greenburg by eight. Foxx, himself, hit fifty-eight (1932) to win the homer derby. Mickey Mantle had a similar fate. In 1956, his fifty-two four-baggers won the AL title but, in 1961 when he hit fifty-four, he was seven behind teammate Roger Maris.

Fate has also been unkind in the annual scramble for the highest batting average. Would you think of Ty Cobb as such a victim? After all, he won the American League batting title twelve times and had the highest lifetime batting average of any player — .367. Yet, on four separate occasions, Ty Cobb hit well above his average and did not win the batting crown. In 1916, his .371 was well behind Tris Speaker's .386. He hit a whopping .389 (1921) and came in second to Harry Heilmann's .394. The next year, he had the third .400-plus season of his career — .401 — and wasn't even close to George Sisler's .420. And in 1925, when he managed a healthy .378, Heilmann hit for a .393 average.

Maybe it's hard to feel sorry for a Ty Cobb with all his laurels, but what about *Shoeless* Joe Jackson of the Cleveland Indians? This superb batter is third on the all-time list with a .356 lifetime mark and yet he never won the batting title. Consider the tough string he had in 1911-12-13. Jackson batted .408 (1911) while Ty Cobb was averaging .420; came up with a .395 (1912), while Cobb was hitting .410; followed with a fine .373 (1913), but again Cobb was on top with .390.

But if there had been a hard-luck trophy, surely Tris Speaker of the Boston Red Sox and Cleveland Indians would have won it hands down. Imagine a batter who hit for an average of .344 lifetime, eighteen seasons over .300, and yet won the American League batting race just once (1916). His .383 (1912 was beaten by both Cobb and Jackson; the same two beat his .366 average of 1913. In 1920, his .388 was far behind Sisler's 407, just as his 1922 average of .378 was far short of Sisler's .420. In 1923 Heilmann spoiled his .380 by batting .403; and Heilmann topped him again (1925) with a .393 to Speaker's mere .389.

The Yankees, as I told you later, are in a slump.
Dizzy Dean

THE BABE!

Trivia buffs already know that the 1914-1915 Boston Red Sox had two hard-hitting pitchers — Babe Ruth and *Smokey* Joe Wood. In 1915, when they confined themselves to pitching, Ruth won 18 and lost six, while Wood won 14 and lost 5. By 1921, both were better known for their batting skills — Ruth hitting .378 for the Yankees and Wood hitting .366 for the Cleveland Indians. Ruth also had 59 home runs and 171 runs-batted-in that year.

Babe Ruth swatted over fifty homers in a season four times — in 1920 and 1921, and agina in 1927 and 1928. But in 1918, a year in which he pitched and won thirteen and lost seven for the Boston Red Sox, he tied for the home run title with Tilly Walker of the Philadelphia A's with just eleven.

Pipesmokers adore an ***idiosyncrasy*** *because it means* ***their own private mixture.***

The Cincinnati Reds were the first baseball team to host a night game way back in 1935. The Chicago Cubs have never played a home game at night for the simple reason that Wrigley Field has no lights.

Oh, yes, the Reds were also the first baseball club to wear short pants. Prior to that time — 1863 — all players wore ankle-length pants.

Maury Wills wasn't so hot! He never stole first base once!

FROM BAD NEWS TO BIG POISON!

Sports nuts are at their zaniest when it comes to records and since organized baseball has the longest continuous history in the United States, it is the most fruitful ground for record-mania. Here are samples of what the afflicted find fascinating:

James *Bad News* Galloway of the 1912 St. Louis Cardinals lived up to his name by batting .187 for the season...his one and only in the majors. Wonder why?

Herrick *Spoke* Emery played the outfield for five games with Philadelphia Phillies, (1924) batted a resounding .667 and was never heard of again.

Aloysius Harry Szymanski, an American League outfielder, (1924 to 1944) won the league batting title once, the RBI title once, batted .392 (1927), had eleven seasons batting over .300 (eight of them in a row) and had a lifetime batting average of .334. You say you never heard of him? Maybe you did under the name he used on the field — Al Simmons, old *Foot-in-the-Bucket.*

Richard Nixon played outfield for three National League teams and had a lifetime batting average of .276. No, not *that* Richard Nixon, but Albert Richard *Humpty-Dumpty* Nixon (1915-1928). Judging from his nickname, he, too, had a great fall.

And everybody knows *Derby Day Bill* Clymer who played three major league games at shortstop and never had a hit. Must have had his mind on the races.

Who would think that most baseball fans would forget a combination outfielder-infielder who had a lifetime batting average of a whooping .336, batted over .300 in twelve of his fourteen major league seasons...eight of those consecutively. Yet few people know of Jackson *Old Hoss* Stephenson (1921-1934) of the Cleveland Indians and Chicago Cubs.

Of course, all fans know about Billy Williams and Ted Williams, but another pretty good man with the stick was Ken Williams (1915-1929) of the St. Louis Browns and Boston Red Sox. Starting with 1919, he batted over .300 in ten of the next eleven seasons, won both a homer and RBI title and had a lifetime average of .319. And Cy Williams (1912-1930) of the Chicago Cubs and Philadelphia Phillies wasn't too bad at the plate, batting over .300 six full seasons and winning the National League home run crown twice (41 in 1923).

What tale of hitters would be complete without the Throneberry brothers — Maynard Faye and *Marvelous* Marv? In his eight years, Maynard averaged .236. Marv managed .237 in seven seasons, but achieved final fame in his last two seasons as first baseman for the New York Mets.

A Major League pitcher must first learn how to fiddle with his clothing!

OH BROTHER!

Major League baseball has had many famous brother combinations: Mort and Walker Cooper, Lloyd and Paul Waner, Wes and Rick Ferrell and Dizzy and Daffy Dean. What do you think were the relationships of American League pitchers Charles William Fischer and William Charles Fischer and National League catcher William Charles Fischer? You're right, they were no relation to one another, nor were they related to two other National League pitchers named Fischer.

Lloyd *Little Poison* Waner and Paul *Big Poison* Waner were the most potent brother combination in major league history. Outfielders for the Pittsburgh Pirates, the Waners terrorized pitchers from the late '20s to 1945. Lloyd batted over .300 in ten seasons and compiled a lifetime mark of .316, while brother Paul topped the .300 mark fourteen times — twelve seasons in a row at one stretch — and had a career batting average of .333.

Skiers eat speed wax!

Stan Musial was one of fourteen batters to hit 475 or more home runs in a career. But Musial is the only one of the fourteen who never led his league in home runs a single season. Willie Mays, on the other hand, won the National League homer crown four times, but he never led the league in runs batted in.

Where do baseball players get all that saliva?

PITCHERS' ACCOUNTS!

Baseball fans know all about the famous pitchers — Cy Young, Christy Mathewson, Lefty Grove, Sandy Koufax, Bob Feller, Tom Seaver, Catfish Hunter and all the others with gaudy records. So it's time to find out about some less than famous major league pitchers with interesting records.

In the 1890's, there was *Coldwater Jim* Hughey who earned his nickname the hard way. In 1898, he won 7 and lost 24 games. But he came right back in 1899 with 5 wins and 29 losses which helped him attain a career record of 29 wins versus 84 losses. 1891 was his best season — he won 1 and lost 1.

One wonders how St. Louis Browns pitcher Fred *Lucky* Glade got his monicker. In 1905, he won 6 and lost 24. From 1902 to 1908, he won 53 and lost 68. Lucky?

Glade was luckier than some, however. Take Steve *Splinter* Gerkin, who pitched one season for the Philadelphia Athletics, winning none and losing 12.

Then there was Fred *Tricky* Nichols who compiled a record of 28 wins and 73 losses from 1875 to 1882. His first year was his trickiest: he won 4 and lost 28. *Tricky* also tried his hand at batting. Alas, his lifetime average was .154.

John *Phenomenal* Smith was another old-timer (1884-1891) whose performance belied his nickname with a record of 61 wins against 82 losses. His most phenomenal year was 1887 when he won 29 games. Unfortunately, he also lost 29. Perhaps the fact that he played under the name of Smith rather than his real name, Gammon, explains something.

But how about Elmer *Spitball* Stricklett (1904-1907)? How could a spitballer fail? Stricklett figured out a way: 34 wins and 53 losses.

And you heard about Eric *Swat* Erickson? Sounds like a hard-hitter, but evidently *Swat* was what happened to him rather than what he did. In his seven seasons, he never had a winning year, winding up with 33 wins and 58 losses.

If ever a nickname haunted a player, consider Aloysius *Wish* Egan. In three seasons in the bigs, he got 8 wins and 27 losses.

However, there were some *winning* pitchers you might not know, like Charles *Kid* Nichols (1890-1906). His first year he won 27 games; then he followed with four straight years in which he won over 30 games; came back with another 27-game winner; and then had another string of 30 wins or more for three years running. The next year he dropped off to a mere 20 wins, but ten straight years of 20 or more wins isn't bad. Neither was his lifetime record of 361 wins versus 204 losses.

It takes a brave fellow to play in Atlanta!

Few baseball fans know of Harry Stovey, perhaps because he played from 1880 to 1893. But he had to have been a hell of a ballplayer, batting over .300 eight straight years, and .320 lifetime. In 1884, he batted .404 and in 1887, .402; but he didn't win the batting title either year. Stovey was also quite a thief. He stole 96 bases in 1886, 143 in 1887, and 156 in 1888.

Allison, the Cincinnati Red catcher of 1869, was the first to wear a glove on his left hand.

The first time admission was ever charged to see a baseball game was on July 20, 1859. The game was played between teams from Brooklyn and New York, taking place on the Fashion Race Course, Long Island. Over 1,500 people paid 50 cents to watch the contest.

Statisticians: your days are numbered!

BASEBALL'S BATTLE OF THE STATS!

Want an end to all this nonsense about who was the greatest offensive star in baseball history? Simple! The statistics will do it for you.

First, there are the basic offensive categories: batting average, runs scored, hits, two-base hits, three-base hits, home runs, runs batted in and bases stolen. But, instead of taking the lifetime leaders in each category, compare players on the basis of the number of times each led his league in the eight categories, allowing one point for each league title.

Here's how it charts:

	Avg.	Runs	Hits	2B	3B	HR	RBI	SB	Total League Titles
Cobb	12	5	7	3	4	1	4	6	42
Musial	7	5	6	8	5	0	2	0	33
Hornsby	7	5	4	4	2	2	4	0	30
Wagner*	8	2	1	7	3	0	3	5	29
Ruth	1	8	0	0	0	12	6	0	27
T. Williams	6	6	0	2	0	4	4	0	20
Aaron	2	3	2	3	0	4	4	0	18
Klein	1	3	2	2	0	4	2	1	16
Gehrig	1	4	1	1	1	3	5	0	16
Mays	1	2	1	0	3	4	0	4	15
Rose	3	4	4	3	0	0	0	0	14
Lajoie*	3	1	4	5	0	0	1	0	14
S. Crawford*	0	1	0	1	5	3	3	0	13
Yastremski	3	3	2	3	0	1	1	0	13
Mantle	1	6	0	0	1	4	1	0	13
Medwick	1	1	2	3	1	1	3	0	12
P. Waner	3	2	2	2	2	0	1	0	12
Speaker	1	0	2	8	0	0	0	0	11
Sisler	2	1	2	0	1	0	0	4	10

*RBI's records were not kept until 1907.

Is the chart a good measure? Where are Jimmy Foxx, Joe DiMaggio, Roberto Clemente? They simply didn't outplay the ballplayers of their own times.

Now extract a few items from the chart. Ty Cobb was the only player to lead his league in every single category at one time or another. Cobb was the only player to lead his league in seven of the eight categories in a single year (1911). Cobb topped the American League in six categories in 1909 — a figure matched only by Honus Wagner, Rogers Hornsby (twice), Joe Medwick and Stan Musial. Players who led their respective leagues in five categories in a season (not including the above) were: Napoleon Lajoie, George Sisler, Chuck Klein, Carl Yastremski and George Stirnweiss.

This should end all the arguments, until some other nut adds slugging percentages, times on base, bases on balls, etc., etc., etc.

Ross Youngs, New York Giant outfielder from 1917 to 1926 batted over .300 in nine of his ten seasons for a lifetime mark of .322. He died at age 30.

HIT PARADE!

The major leaguer who averages better than .300 for a whole season achieves instant fame, right? Then how come so few people remember Heinie Manush who batted over .300 thirteen times and had a lifetime mark of .331? Where are the fans of Fatty Fothergill who topped the magic .300 in ten of his twelve seasons and had a career .326 (a point higher than Joe DiMaggio's lifetime mark)? Does anyone still talk about Baby Doll Jackson, even though he averaged in excess of .300 eight times (seven in a row) and was .311 lifetime?

You don't read much about Harry Heilmann either, although he had twelve .300-plus seasons in a row, including one .403 year. And his lifetime mark was the same as Babe Ruth's — .342. Sam Rice had fourteen .300 years and was .322 lifetime, but he's as well-known as Edd Roush who went over .300 thirteen years (eleven straight), and was .323 lifetime. People do remember John McGraw, but as the tough manager of the New York Giants rather than as a slugging third baseman who had nine straight seasons over .300 and a rousing career .334.

Everyone remembers Ty Cobb with twenty-three straight seasons over .300, and Honus Wagner's seventeen in a row, and Rogers Hornsby's thirteen in a row; but Wee Willie Keeler hit at better than a .300 clip sixteen straight years, including a fantastic .432, and who knows him? And let's hear it for Zack Wheat who had fourteen .300-plus seasons and a career average of .317.

Hunting: When a man wants to murder a tiger, he calls it sport; when a tiger wants to murder him, he calls it ferocity.

G. B. Shaw

RUSHING ABOUT IN ALL DIRECTIONS!

15th Century Englishmen became fascinated with a game the French played with a *palle* (ball) and a *maille* (mallet). The game was played in an alley with an iron ring at either end. Object: drive the ball with the mallet through the opponent's ring.

The British built an alley of their own in London and named it after the game — *Pall Mall.* Of course, they pronounced it *Pell Mell.* From the furious scuffling and shin-cracking action we get *pellmell.*

The yak roams Tibetan plateaus
With a mitten to cover his neaus.
Lest his strength you impugn,
You should know he's immugn,
In all other parts, to the sneaus.

CHIN UP!

Heavyweight boxers have succeeded with a variety of special skills. Jack Dempsey was the epitome of savage power. Gene Tunney and Billy Conn were the artists of speed and finesse. Joe Louis was the cool killer; Rocky Marciano, the charging bull.

There was a heavyweight in the mid-1930's named *Steamboat* Doyle. He didn't achieve any particular fame. In fact, his bulging waistline indicated he never had his eye on the title. But he had a technique all his own.

At the opening bell, *Steamboat* Doyle waddled out to the center of the ring and stuck out his chin. At first his opponent took it for a trick and held back. But such a tempting target was too much to resist. Wham!

Miraculously Doyle was still on his feet. Worse yet, he still had his arms at his sides, and he pushed out that inviting chin once more. Wham! Wham!

And Doyle was still standing. Now he turned his chin a bit to one side and held his glove up to his jawline indicating to his bewildered opponent that he simply hadn't found the right spot yet. Wham, wham, wham in quick succession.

There stood Doyle, grinning. And so it went, until the opponent got so armweary he could not raise a glove above his beltline. Then *Steamboat* stepped in and made quick work of it, sometimes only having to push an exhausted foe to the canvas.

Steamboat, wherever you are: chin up!

EPITAPH:
Here Lies James Earl-
The Pugilist-who on the
11th of April 1788
gave in.

THE BROWN BOMBER!

Back in the mid-1930's, boxing fans began to hear about an up-and-coming heavyweight prospect in the midwest. He was putting together a string of knockout victories, but the cynics said he had only faced palookas. Wait until he got in the ring with a real contender and then there'd be no more talk about Joe Louis, The Brown Bomber.

And the day did come. Louis was matched with the tenth-ranking heavyweight in the country, a cute boxer with lots of experience named Lee Ramage. The fight was set for Los Angeles. Ramage was a California product, so the fans were all behind him.

One boxing writer who had been building Ramage up for a title fight looked upon this as a good steppingstone for his boy. He couldn't hold back a sneer when, after an uneventful first round of Ramage's left jabs and no returns, the young Louis asked his corner man if he couldn't go out and take his man in the second.

The writer's scorn skyrocketed when young Joe was advised to wait, he'd be told when to take his man. After every round, Louis asked again, and each time his corner man told him to be patient.

It was scheduled for ten rounds and, midway through the bout, Ramage had piled up all the points with his sharp jab and his fancy footwork. The sportswriter had settled back in his seat near Louis' corner. At the end of the round, he leaned forward to see if the request and denial routine would be repeated.

RIDDLE: The 1926 and 1927 heavyweight title fights between Gene Tunney and Jack Dempsey produced the first and second 'million dollar' gates in boxing. Which of the two received the most money for these fights?

ANSWER: Dempsey's end of the purse in the first fight topped Tunney's by over half a million dollars but, in the two fights combined, Tunney earned $1,194,445 to Dempsey's $1,136,868. Only fair. Tunney won both fights!

This time, the corner man simply winked at Louis and said quietly, "Now."

The boxing writer was still laughing when a short left hook almost lifted Ramage off the floor. The following right cross caught him squarely between jaw and cheekbone. Accounts differ as to whether Louis threw another left. It was academic. Ramage was out cold before he hit the canvas.

The boxing writer's story in the morning paper was filled with phrases such as 'the ferocity of an animal tantalized beyond endurance,' 'cool, expressionless assassin of the ring,' 'exploded like a bomb' and at least a dozen uses of *The Brown Bomber.* But no description of the actual blows that ended the fight. He simply hadn't seen them. But not seeing was believing when young Joe Louis finally got the go-ahead.

A boxer was sweet Nellie's beau,
Always fit and ready to geau.
But now she's bereft.
Her arms he has left —
Victim of a very leau bleau.

You may be astounded while watching those weight-lifting behemoths in the super heavyweight class. But if you'd been around in 500 B.C., you'd have seen Milo of Croton carry a full-grown ox around the Greek stadium of Of Olympia. Later the same day, he devoured the entire ox at one sitting.

He fought him with a tooth and a toenail.

THE SECRET EVERY GOLF PRO KNOWS!

Deep in his frustrated heart every amateur golfer knows the professionals are withholding the one secret that could make him a superb player.

Several years ago, when we had persistent dreams of trouncing Jack Nicklaus in the U.S. Open, although we had yet to break 86, an itinerant golf pro came to our offices. In a conspiratorial tone, he told us that he was breaking the professional golfer's code, but that he thought it about time good, decent, golf-fearing amateurs learned

THE SECRET.

We have never parted with $100 so joyously. The itinerant pro then charted a new stance for us on butcher paper, and gave us *THE SECRET*. We were to press the club handle with the thumb of the left hand until we sensed we could feel the knuckle of the first finger on the underside of the club. We practiced diligently in the office for three days. Then our secret-giver took us to a driving range where we hit two buckets of balls.

In no time at all we were hitting straight and far with every club. Overcome with gratitude, we pressed another $50 on the pro. He thanked us, and then implored us not to mention *THE SECRET* to anyone. As if we were about to share such an advantage!

The following Thursday, as I joined my regular foursome on the first tee, I had difficulty keeping down a greedy hilarity. But the game went slowly, each player fussing endlessly over every shot. Finally, when one of them appeared to have gone into a cataleptic trance as he addressed the ball, a second of the group growled, "What the hell are you trying to do, Jack?"

Jack looked up helplessly and blurted, "I can't feel the knuckle with my thumb." Then he looked away quickly and reddened.

Slowly it dawned on us. *We had each bought THE SECRET.* Inasmuch as they all claimed to have paid only $75, we simply nodded. Relax, Jack Nicklaus!

Golfers will never take a single drink after a round...ten, maybe!

AROUND THE LINKS IN EIGHTY SHANKS!

To a baseball player, stealing second and then discovering one of your own teammates is already on that base is shattering; but, it probably won't happen again. A tennis player may be chagrined for the moment at fanning an easy overhead, but the odds are he'll not repeat the boner. The *gutter ball* embarrasses a bowler, but he can correct. In all sports, there is but one error which can *not* be anticipated — the golfer's *shank*! Even more disconcerting is that there is no assurance it won't recur on the very next stroke.

The destructive power of the *shank* is so awesome we have never heard a golfer say the word aloud while out on the course. In fact, most golfers, even when safely in the clubhouse, prefer to use the euphemism — a *lateral*. This applies to others' misfortune, as well, since the atrocious *shank* is highly contagious.

Golf has rules for everything else. Why can't they outlaw the *shank*?

RIDDLE: Are *foible* and *forte* related in any way?

ANSWER: Sure! The weakest portion of a fencing foil is the *foible* and the strongest part is the *forte*. Foiled you, didn't we?

Jack Nicklaus is really a set of identical triplets!

GOLF, ANYONE?

Golf comes from a Dutch word for hockey stick. *Caddy* came from the French *cadet*. Mary Queen of Scots was responsible for that one. And, typical avid golfer that she was, she managed to get in several rounds only a couple of days after her husband was murdered. Fore!

Half of the children who play golf are over forty-five.

THANKS A LOT!

More years ago than we care to remember, we had the pleasure of playing in a golf pro-am with the late Porky Ed Oliver. Oliver was known for two outstanding characteristics — he played extremely well despite his portliness and he was a thoroughly good-humored gentleman.

On the 18th hole, Oliver had bunkered his approach. He stood in the trap, sand-wedge poised just above the ball. Just as he began to take the clubhead back, a small boy darted out of the crowd around the green and blurted out, "Can I have your autograph?"

Ed managed to stop his swing with considerable effort. He turned, winked at the kid and said, "In just a moment, son." He readdressed the ball and made his stroke. But he had lost just enough concentration to spoil the shot — it hit the lip of the bunker and trickled back into the sand.

Oliver sighed, then said, "Okay, son, I'll give you that autograph now."

The boy looked from Oliver to the ball still in the trap, then back at Oliver before he said, "No, thanks!"

He was brave in the heart, but weak in the knees.

THE MADDENING GAME OF GOLF!

Golf has been called the *blame game*. Golfers would always shoot par or below if it were not for rocks, tree limbs, wet grass, hard greens, his noisy partners, soft greens, cart tracks, finicky rules, too much wind, low-flying aircraft, not enough wind and poorly designed equipment. We've yet to hear a golfer blame himself.

So, if nature has conspired to defeat him at every turn, why does he play? To relax! Overlooking the fact that his swing has more flaws than a barrel of crockery seconds and that his practice sessions are limited to solidifying his mistakes, he has about as much chance of succeeding at golf as he does of driving railroad spikes with a strand of spaghetti. Therefore, it must be the alternating fits of trembling rage and utter despondency which relax him.

After all, it must be therapeutic for a man to escape from a business or profession at which he is reasonably competent and attempt to conquer a game at which he is unreasonably inept.

Is it just possible the amateur golfer *doesn't* find it relaxing at all? We first felt that such a possibility existed when we heard a once-a-week golfer say, "Thank God I only have to play this damned game on Wednesdays!"

Of all amateur golfers, perhaps only comedian Jimmy Durante really relaxed on the links. The story goes that as Durante returned to the clubhouse and was asked what he shot, he invariably answered, "Had a 74." What he neglected to explain was that whenever his score reached 74, he stopped and came back to the clubhouse. On good days, he sometimes got as far as the 14th hole.

Golf courses have eighteen holes because a little misery is never enough.

ACE!

At last count, professional golfer Art Wall had made thirty-nine holes-in-one, far outclassing anyone we've heard of. Seventeen of those aces have come on one hole at his home course in North Carolina. Asked to comment on this phenomenal feat, Wall replied simply, "It's a nice little hole."

When Charlie Spray was told that, in golf, putting is half the game, he gave up the other half.

PUTT AND RUN!

A fine amateur golfer of the 1950's, Dr. Bud Taylor, had just returned from playing in his first British Amateur. We asked how he liked golf in England?

"It's awfully windy most of the time," he replied, "and so you have to make a few adjustments. For instance, I learned to keep a dime in my hand when I putted. I'd hit the putt and then take off after it. The split-second the ball came to a momentary stop, I'd spot the dime behind it and pick it up. Before I learned that stunt, I had the wind blow a couple of putts right back at me."

RIDDLE: Can a golfer score a *double eagle* on a three-par hole?

ANSWER: Since a *double eagle* is three under par, it's not likely. However, we've met some atrocious golfers who were superb scorekeepers. It is not beyond imagination for this type to give themselves a *zero*. The honest method of getting a *double eagle* on a three-par is to skip the hole altogether.

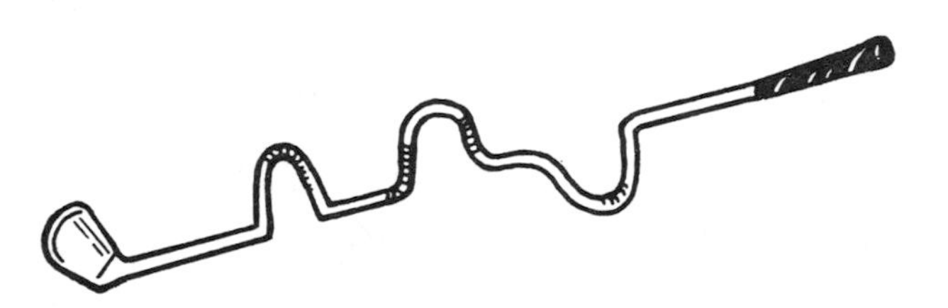

DIRTY BRACKAFRATZ!

Golf has reduced more than one addict to a howling mania of equipment destruction and language that would sear the cover off your Maxfly. The most publicized angry man was Tommy Bolt, nicknamed *Terrible-tempered Tommy.*

At the end of the third round in one professional tourney, Bolt came stomping off the final green. A reporter, disregarding the steam emanating from Bolt's ears, bravely asked, "What did you have today, Tommy?"

Bolt paused, then growled, "Three, dammit. Three!" and marched off.

The reporter was confused. He caught up with another member of the Bolt threesome. "He said he had three...for the last hole...that what he meant?"

"No, for the whole round." he said. "He wrapped his six-iron around a cypress on the third, tossed his four-wood into the lake on the fifth, folded his two-iron in half on the eighth and then he got mad."

The first women's golf tournament took place in Great Britain in 1893. We'd tell you who won, but it's considered bad form.

GENTLY, BABY!

Have you ever golfed with a man who speaks to his clubs and his golf ball? It's bad enough to listen to a man imploring his club to "Go straight on through the ball now" and to beg the ball: "Right over that trap, now...and bite!'' But to have the damned clubs and ball obey is downright infuriating.

We finally saw such a player get his come-uppance on the steep 16th green. His ball had come to rest a scant twenty inches above the hole. Even as we approached the green, he was chattering, ''Okay, putter, just a tap, just a tap.''

Then a strange sequence took place. One of the foursome took the troublesome fellow aside on some pretext. We watched the third man take a wad of chewing gum from his mouth, stick it atop a tee, drive tee and gum into the green just beside the man's ball; then, he moved the ball onto the gum and pressed down firmly.

When the moment arrived, the fellow kept repeating, ''Just a tap,'' eyeing the treacherous downhill putt. Then he stroked gently. The ball wiggled, no more. As he backed off, then turned his back on the offending ball, the gum and tee were removed. We never did tell him...and he missed the putt again!

Bob Hope drives a golf ball to work!

HEY, BAGGY PANTS!

It's difficult to imagine how the golfing pants of the 1920's and early 1930's, called the *plus fours*, could have been considered an improvement, but they were. It seems that, prior to the *plus fours*, knickerbockers had been in vogue on the links. But they restricted free knee action, so the apparel industry obligingly added four inches to the length of the knickerbockers. Knickers plus four inches for blousing — *plus fours!*

Cary Middlecoff played fast, but he had very slow clubs!

DISADVANTAGED!

Years ago we played an occasional round of golf with a phys-ed teacher who had lost his left arm in an accident. He played an exceptional game, considering.

During one of our infrequent games, another fellow was along. This man was having a rough day, topping and slicing incessantly... and slowly coming to a boil. About then our phys-ed friend hit a particularly fine tee shot. We complimented him. Our third member grunted in disgust, ''Hell, I could hit it like that, too, if I didn't have any damned left arm to keep straight.''

RIDDLE: What happens when a golfer *four-putts* a green?

ANSWER: After the first wave of nausea, an apoplectic stroke!

God invented golf to teach man futility.

NEEDLE, NEEDLE, WHO'S GOT THE NEEDLE!

As any dictionary will tell you, a *needle* is a sharp instrument used for puncturing. In golf, the *needler* punctures an opponent's confidence in an inventive variety of ways.

In the pro ranks immediately following World War II, the reigning *needle* champion was Lloyd Mangrum. The other pros knew it, but it gave them no immunity.

Shortly after a young Gene Littler had brought his flawless swing onto the professional circuit, he found himself in a threesome with Mangrum and another veteran. After Littler had hit his fifth fairway-splitting tee shot of the day, Mangrum turned to the other older pro and said loud enough for the young pro to hear, "Beats me how he can keep it straight with his right thumb in that position." Now, Littler knew it was the *needle*, yet, on the next tee, he examined his grip on his driver. Was it wrapped over a bit? Perhaps, so he made a small adjustment. He had hit his last straight drive of the day.

Within earshot of a golfer whose habit was to attack the golf ball, much in Arnold Palmer style, Mangrum wished aloud, "If I could only get away with lunging at it like that." The lunger had an atrocious round.

On many golf greens, especially in the southwest, poana grass can intrude. When it does, putts don't necessarily follow a green's natural contour. It makes *reading* a green ticklish, even hopeless at times. In one tournament at a crucial point, Mangrum bent down and examined a patch of grass and then murmured to no one in particular, "I see the poana's back." A few unnecessary three-putt greens ensued.

When words failed to implant the seed of doubt, Mangrum resorted to the *status needle*. It's traditional for the low scorer to have the honors on the following tee, but it wasn't mandatory. Mangrum was not above hurrying off to the next tee and hitting first when not rightfully entitled. An opponent who said nothing seethed inside. Those who challenged Mangrum on the point were informed, "It isn't *when* you hit it that counts...it's *how*."

As one pro put it, "I don't mind *giving* blood, but Lloyd *takes* it without asking!"

A woman in Puyallup, Washington claims Gerald Ford has never hit her with a golf ball. Hard to believe!

Slow golfers bathe in casual water.

A MISS IS BETTER THAN A MILE!

Who is the nut who wrote the golf rules? Player A drives the ball 265 yards, but it stops one-sixteenth of an inch into the out-of-bounds area and he loses two strokes. Player B misses the ball entirely and only loses one stroke; in addition, he doesn't have to walk 265 yards to verify his bad luck.

Men who tell their wives they play golf for the exercise always ride in golf carts.

Consistently bad luck never seemed to dull the fervor that Joe Frisco, the stammering comedian, had for horse racing.

Late one afternoon, Joe showed up at a bar frequented by horse-playing companions. A buddy greeted him and asked him how he had made out that day.

"Oh, I h-h-had a g-g-good day. I g-g-got a r-r-ride home," Joe offered.

Luck is what the other golfer uses to overcome your skill.

For skill, hat's off to Snapper Garrison, a jockey who held his horse back until the last furlong and then surprised everyone with *a Garrison finish.*

Social note: Genghis Khan and Attila the Hun played polo!

THROW HIM A SEABISCUIT!

Radio sportscaster Bill Stern was famous for his exciting descriptions of sports action, if not for his accuracy. In the heat of a football broadcast, Stern began calling off the yard-markers as a back broke into the clear. Unfortunately, he kept shouting the wrong name. His spotter kept poking him to indicate that it was Jones, not Smith, who had the ball. He finally got Stern's attention. Without hesitation, he screamed out, "Smith crosses the fifteen, laterals off to Jones, and Jones scores." Since it was radio, who knew the difference?

Some time later Stern got an assignment to announce one of the country's premiere horse races. His partner on the air was to be gravel-voiced Clem McCarthy. McCarthy knew horse racing, while Stern did not.

RIDDLE: Where did we get the word *tout*, as in a race-track *tout*?

ANSWER: Psst! Come here! We're going to let you in on a good thing. *Tout* comes from a Scotch word meaning to peep, or spy. Originally, a *tout* was a fellow who snuck in to watch horses run time-trials and who ferreted out any information that might help him in betting. Later, a *tout* offered a betting tip on the tacit understanding you would share your winnings with him. Losses, it was understood, you bear alone.

Before the broadcast, Stern asked the old pro if there was anything special he should know before they went on the air.

McCarthy, a man of tact, said, "Well, Bill, jockeys are a bit too small to lateral off a horse."

Mortimer Kibble gave up water polo when his horse drowned.

THE GAMES LANGUAGE PLAYS!

Amusements — ancient and recent — have contributed some interesting expressions to the language.

When jousting was considered great sport, the horses had to be mammoth strong beasts to support a knight in full armor. Naturally, knights had considerable social status — thus, *on his high horse* indicated a person who thought himself superior.

To show the white feather has a rather superstitious background: if a fighting cock had a single white feather, he was thought to be cowardly.

Radio made its contribution, too. We get *on the nose* from a radio director's signal to performers that their timing for length is perfect.

*Horses sweat and men perspire, but ladies only **glow**.*

THE HUNNERT DOLLAR KID!

Dear Artie,

I could rite my heart out and not scratch the top of the troubles which fell all over me when I hit this Sunny California. Insted let me suffice to give you a thumbnose skech of what has happened to me in the erstwhile since arriving.

My very second day, I'm casing where L.A. broads may do a little whistle-wetting, when in front of a joint called The Dragon's Flagon, a guy bunks my arm...like at the track when some yance is trying to tout you off on some nag or other. Quick like a flashlite, he ducks into the saloon, but not before I lamp him good.

Artie, feathers wouldn't have knocked me down better, on account of who he was — not no one else but a guy I ain't seen in a coot's age — *The Hunnert Dollar Kid.* I figger he didn't give me a tumble cuz he had a mark inside this joint...and that bunk on the arm was to screw me into the score him and me can make.

But, let me regress, Artie, to how me and the Kid operated. The way the Kid set up his Store was to locate a saloon where guys were not reverse to a little wager. This one time it was a baseball crowd. So the Kid, he picks out maybe three out of fifty newspaper clippings he had...all of them on baseball. This he stuffs in his righthand coat pocket and me and him goes into the saloon, but like our eyes had not never set on each other in our lives.

Pretty soon the Kid's putting a bad mouth on the Immoral Babe and Joe DiMag and Mickey Mantle, saying how they was less than hot. Natcherly, some rube finally gets a hot collar and hollers maybe the Kid knows so much he's got himself a better Yankee.

The Kid, at this junction, pulls out his wad, peels off a couple of twenties and says, "For my dough, no Yankee ever breathed which was so grand as Ellis Peagarden."

While them marks is breaking their arms to cover the dough the Kid spread out on the bar, the Kid's taking one of his three clippings and putting it over in his leftside coat pocket.

Once the dough's all up, I steps to the Kid's side and fish out the clipping. Then I announce to one and every how I heard their little argument and how maybe I can settle it for them with a newspaper item I just happen to have on me. Then I reads them how, in 1919, the Weehawken Chamber of Commerce voted that a kid born there, name of Ellis Peagarden, was "the grandest Yankee of them all."

Anyway, that's history that's passed up. Back at this Dragon's Flagon, I go marching rite in, knowing the Kid's up to his old tricks. And sure is enough, he's waving around his wad and yelling, "King's Banana won more races on California tracks than any other cutlet of horse flesh." And just like times of older, the marks is busting several guts to get on this sure thing.

Then's when I comes up and sticks my mitt into the Kid's leftside pocket. But, honest engine, *there ain't no clipping*, but what there *was* was an arm on me.

So what I need, Artie is bail money for this pickpocket rap. One other thing — if you see the hide or hair of The Hunnert Dollar Kid, warn him off this Sunny California, cuz he's got a dead double-ringer for hisself out here.

Your sinceer buddy, Freddie Sellers

RIDDLE: Did a professional athlete ever miss his senior prom because of his sports life?

ANSWER: We know one who did — super-jockey Steve Cauthen! In 1977, Cauthen could have held his own senior prom. He became the first rider in history to boot home over six million dollars in purses in a single year. He was also the first jockey to win the Associated Press's Athlete of the Year award and the AP has been doing it for forty-seven years. Not bad for a 17-year-old.

The top event in whores racing is the Summer Syphilis Stakes!

CHAPTER FIVE

Frankly, Dear Eve, I Don't Give A Damn!

Given this suitcase full of trivia and an I.Q. bordering on the imbecilic, you, too, can astound bartenders, baffle gynecologists and rank high as a specialist in general nitwittery.

So, button up your underwear, dust off your libido and romp with us in the search for your lost marbles.

It takes more than 3,000 elephants to make piano keys for a single year of production. They work in a well-lighted fifteen-acre room, take hay-breaks every two hours and are represented by the Pachyderms Amalgamated Key Workers Union.

You can stop expecting people to grow old gracefully. It's the first time most of them have ever tried it.

Dancing pumps made from gila monster hides are definitely out this year!

The Western Regional Tongue-Biting Contest had to be postponed, due to a nationwide shortage of contrition.

Ornithologists, in a fit of relevance, announce that bird-watchers may use *titlark* and *pipit* interchangeably for that cute little tyke.

There's still sting to the famous remark Tom Mix once made to Hoot Gibson: "There are 216 bones in an average horse, unless you count the teeth...in which case, it is 256."

It takes four tons of grapes to make just one ton of raisins. Then, they go into the artificial wrinkling machine.

We feel a certain sense of loss upon discovering that when they took the *poon* out of *lam*, they destroyed almost all the *tang.*

Project for a rainy afternoon: count the feathers on your pet tom turkey. If he's full-grown, you should come up with a total of 3,850 to 3,900. But don't take our word for it...keep counting!

Field Marshal Grigori Potemkin said Catherine wasn't all that great.

How on earth did George Hepplewhite manage to make any worthwhile furniture back in the 18th Century before the invention of plastic seat covers and plywood?

Actuaries have finally released the long sought statistic that the common housefly has a maximum life expectancy of 62 days...and is a damn poor insurance risk after forty days.

A banker in Limp Rock, Utah made a humorous remark in 1888.

Imagine the frustration of Marvin Pheeter: he invented the bumper sticker in 1862 and then had to wait around for almost forty years before he found a place to put it.

Our Congress-watcher reports that heavy rains in Washington D.C. have frequently resulted in *quorums.*

Someone once commented that John Barrymore was so conceited he hated to exhale in public.

The older aren't necessarily wiser. They've simply slowed down to the point that it may take them all day to make the same mistakes they used to make in a jiffy. Jiffy-drivers know the mistakes we're talking about.

Don't take any bets that Isaac Bickerstaff wasn't a good writer.

That's a phony name Jonathan Swift used when he was off his feed.

Speaking of whales, a skilled *flencher* can strip the blubber off a full-grown whale in sixteen hours and three minutes. Less than that if the whale consents.

Fortunately the trend of people dancing on parquet tables in their golf shoes is on the wane.

We now have incontestable proof that Mammy's little baby did *not* love shortnin' bread! The kid *preferred* it to sowbelly and okra.

In 1894, the kids in downtown Munich wouldn't touch their sauerkraut until Mama read them Marie von Ebner-Eschenbach's best-selling dog story, *Krambambuli.*

Three members of Gamblers Anonymous gave up trying to convert 83-year-old Lydia Strongarm. Sleeping in shifts, they kept a two-week vigil as Lydia played six nickel-slot machines simultaneously. Thomas Trickle, leader of the team, said, "We'd have fallen asleep sooner, but she hit 337 jackpots...and what with all those bells ringing and coins jangling..."

Scottish kings in the 12th Century lived in *Holyrood.* Disgruntled at never being offered a screen test, they moved out.

Housefly data keeps pouring in. Now, we learn the little devils may take as many as 8,760 steps in under a minute...moving less than a foot in the process. And we thought teen-agers made a lot of useless, nervous movements.

Don't be taken in by the question *What is something blue, that is red when it's green?* That would be your basic unripened blueberry!

Travel agents announce you can now visit the head-hunting *Jivaro* of Ecuador in perfect safety. Just offer them peanut shells. They think the shells contain powerful spirits. But, knock off any snide remarks about their collection of shrunken heads...unless you want to change hat-size in a hurry.

Cornballs will want to know the Indians already were cultivating the *dent, sugar, flint* and *pod* strains of corn when the first whites came flocking in.

Next time you feel all shriveled with ennui, make plans to be in the Virgin Islands on June 19th. That's the date they celebrate being granted political and legal status. It's called *Organic Act Day.* Come as you are!

Remember: Mother Lode was panning for gold before you were born!

RIDDLE: *Stove* should be good enough. Why do we also have *ranges?*

ANSWER: Chalk it up to rank commercialism. Wood and coal-burning stoves had four units or plates. Damned things wouldn't wear out, though. So, the big stove boys tried to create obsolescence with a six-plate model. They swaggered around crowing that it had more cooking *range*.

Tonight, before plopping your quivering hulk onto the mattress, give thanks to the Egyptians who had the first beds, to the Greeks who added the headboard and to the Romans who made the first metal bedsteads of bronze. Then, thank us for telling you this thrilling news!

If you've been hearing the call of ***kissytwit****, phone your analyst!*

SQUARING THE HOLLYWOOD SQUARES!

Questions we wish Peter Marshall would ask his Hollywood Squares:

— If 15 percent is an acceptable restaurant tip, is it alright to just leave 15 percent of your food untouched?

— Is it true the coal miners were striking for *softer* coal?

— The Western Wig-Warmers Association says hair-pieces should not be preheated in microwave ovens unless the oven has a special control button for that specific purpose. Is that true?

— Is bronc-busting apt to make one crotchety?

— Alligators appear to smile. How far can they be trusted?

— A horseshoe throwing expert claims no game will be officially sanctioned unless the shoe has been detached from the horse. Is he right?

— The National Society for the Preservation of Profanity has just dropped *egad, aw shucks* and *oh fudge* from their preferred list. Is this fair?

— If flooding the nasal passages with fermented fig juice cures *Popinjay's disease,* how long must one continue the treatment?

— Are President Carter's teeth all payed for now?

— Someone gave us a *dingbat* for St. Swithin's Day. Where can we find *dings* to bat with it?

— When making pizza from re-vulcanized bicycle tires, should the valve stem be removed?

— We find removing unwanted hair with a corkscrew is quite painful. Is there any other way to do this, or are we just squeamish?

— We understand Paul Lynde has never tasted fricasseed caribou ear. Is he prejudiced or something?

Underneath those baggy pants beats a heart of gold! Sam, did you say that, too?

IT BEARS REPEATING!

Where else but in America would tens of thousands of people pay money for a recording whose only words were *John* and *Martha?* Yet, while casting stones, we recall that, during our loquacious youth, we laid out some cash just so we could hear a gigantic chorus wail the single word *Guadalajara* over and over.

As a musician he was a dog. His Bach was worse than his Haydn.

MAESTRO, PLEASE!

Don't allow people to tell you that the psychedelic bit with the strange lights is a musical innovation. Hell, early this century, the Russian composer, Alexander Scriabin, was insisting that a changing play of colored lights be projected on a screen while the orchestra was whaling away at his *Prometheus.*

The composer, old Papa Haydn
Went huntin' more for the raydn.
When he came home without game,
He would then pun to his dame,
"Sorry! They all seem to be haydn."

MUSIC TO YOUR EARS!

George Bernard Shaw had the dubious pleasure of attending the performance of a string ensemble. A friend informed him, "These men have been playing together for twelve years."

Shaw, in mock surprise, said, "Surely we've been here longer than that."

EPITAPH

Here lies one Merideth, organist, blown out of breath,
Who lived a merry life, and died a Merideth.

WITHOUT RHYME OR REASON!

If you were to examine the seven dozen or so decently painted portraits of Christopher Columbus, you still wouldn't have a very accurate idea of what he looked like. Now, *why* you ask?

Well, because Columbus never posed for his portrait. Too busy with his egg trick. In fact, none of the Columbus portraits were painted during his lifetime. So *he* didn't know and *we* can't know if any of them were good likenesses.

RIDDLE: Was George Ade an American humorist?

ANSWER: Sure was! Mr. Ade (1866-1944), among other funnies penned this line: The music teacher came twice a week to bridge the gap between Dorothy and Chopin.

A stripper named Angeline Duvall
Came dressed as a Viola to a ball;
But a man clad as Caesar,
In an effort to squeeze her,
Snapped her Fret, her G-string and all.

Don't expect to find out how long orchestra conductors have been using a baton. All we know is that in the Fifteenth Century the director of the Sistine Choir in Rome beat time with a roll of paper. Budget problem!

Musical leprechauns let themselves in at night with minor keys.

No comment! Some ninny with a threadbare mind and a loose bobbin thought he had the best of two worlds when he invented a musical sewing machine which actually stitched in time.

Jeff and Cybele, leave home! Cacophony is here to stay!

I'VE HEARD THAT SONG BEFORE!

What's unique about the melody of *America* is that it's not unique at all. Same tune can be found in Great Britain's *God Save the King* and in songs from other countries. In fact, music historians say it's a very old melody, proving the good songs really last.

Suggested signs for symphony hall doors: Emergency Exit in case of Brahms!

TRAVEL NOTE!

When jazz pianist, Harry "The Hipster" Gibson arrived in Hollywood, he was asked if it were his first trip out West. Gibson cried, excitedly, "Man, this is my first trip *above ground!*"

Bloops, pardon my radio! "And now, stay stewed for the nudes."

MUSIC QUIZ!

Was it Duke Ellington who hopped off the A train and wrote *Mood Vertigo?* No!

If Tony Bennett won't sing *I Left My Heart on Alcatraz, Tier 3, Cell 592, Down in the Corner Underneath the Wash Basin,* then who will? Hum a few bars and we'll try it.

Hebrew Proverb good any Wednesday: when a man is young he writes songs; grown up, he speaks in proverbs; in old age, he teaches pessimism.

SMELLING SALTS NEEDED!

One of our staff fainted dead away when he first read this tip for homemakers: drop your nuts in boiling water for three to five minutes and they will be easier to crack when they cool off.

Bachelordom: when you raced for the sport and not to win a permanent trophy!

PHILOSOPHICAL!

See if you can guess the occupation of the man who wrote: *By all means, marry; if you get a good wife, you'll become happy; if you get a bad one, you'll become a philosopher.* You're right...he was a philosopher...Socrates, by name.

Many people cry at weddings. If you're not the groom, you'll get over it!

TOMMY CARLYLE WENT AND DID IT!

When British historian, Thomas Carlyle, got married, fellow writer, Samuel Butler was greatly pleased. He said, "It was very good

RIDDLE: How come February has only twenty-eight days?

ANSWER: Politics, pure and simple! Back when all Romans dressed as women, they had already named a month for Julius Caesar when Augustus came along and demanded a month to call his own. So, the Senate gave him the one after Big Julie's. But, July had thirty-one days and the following month only thirty. To placate Big Augie, they snipped a day off February's twenty-nine and tacked it onto August. Meanwhile, back at the Forum...

of God to let Carlyle and Mrs. Carlyle marry one another and so make *two* people miserable instead of four."

The only way Abner Doubleday could get out of the house was to invent baseball.

A MAN OF PARTS!

A chap we know, who thinks the zenith of female accomplishment is canning fruit, was recently killing a cocktail party with weighty aphorisms about the glories of housewifery. The desperate hostess finally intervened: "Frank, if you should ever need an organ transplant — preferably nothing minor — don't consider one of mine. Your body would reject it...on principle."

Oscar Wilde described a gentleman as ***someone who is never unintentionally rude.***

SING IT AGAIN, BLANCHE!

We can understand why men might be a bit in awe of opera singer Blanche Thebom. So, when meeting men, she tries to put them at ease by telling them she's in the lingerie line.

Almost all women have learned the knack of making pips squeak.

FORTY, FORTY, NASTY FORTY!

George Hummer is perplexed! Seven years ago he gave his wife a lavish gift on her thirty-ninth birthday, and she still hasn't reached forty. Relax, George. You should be proud of her for taking a stand. Some vacillate, although seldom in public.

Divorce is a bore. Ranks right up there with marriage!

EPITAPH
Here lies my wife: here let her lie!
Now she's at rest and so am I.

B. Franklin advised affairs with older women, saying, ***They are so grateful!***

BURNING EARS DEPARTMENT, HUSBAND DIVISION!

By skulking about at needlepoint parties and canasta festivals, we picked up some ego-crushing opinions of husbands. We offer them without comment:

"My husband is as strong as an ox...and almost as smart."

"Egbert has a mind like a mirror — it takes in everything...and gets it all backward."

"He screwed up his courage just like he screws up everything else."

"Frank used to trot right in when I whistled for him. Now he just rolls over and plays dead."

"Matthew is a laugh on the outside, but a crime on the inside."

"There's nothing wrong with being mediocre, especially since Harold is so good at it."

When the psychiatrist told Mrs. Rimp that her husband had lost his marbles, she merely sighed and said, "Oh, well, he never used them much anyway."

WARM YOUR BUNS OVER THIS!

We doubt if there are any husbands...still living...who knock pipe ashes in candy bowls or put their shoes on upholstered furniture or have any annoying habits. However, if a husband should inadvertently acquire some charmless pattern and then give it up, wouldn't you begin to wonder what had replaced it?

RIDDLE: If *bigamy* is having one wife too many, what is *monogamy?*

ANSWER: Same thing!

All husbands are alike. They just have different faces so we can tell them apart.

Epitaph for Brigham Young:
Born on this spot 1801
A man of much courage
And superb equipment.

QUIET! GENIUS AT WORK!

Ferdinand Dimplestuffer, in the midst of inventing the cup, struck a snag. On which side should he put the handle? Mustering up his courage, he asked his wife.

"Why, I think the *outside* would be best, dear."

Any mother, who has prayed for the rain to stop so her children could play outside, can understand how mother kangaroos feel.

QUIET! GENIUS AT DINNER!

If you don't think we're a bit of damned lucky to have the electric light and the phonograph and a few other handy items, then you don't know about Thomas Edison's wife and her palate-tickling menus. First of all, she claimed she knew perfectly well what was best for Tom...and that he would be grateful for whatever she put out. At the time, she had him on a diet of spinach, carrots, sardines and milk. Then, in a fit of redundancy, she said he wasn't much of an eater anyway. Wonder why?

After years of suppression, it's out: Priscilla Alden's maiden name was Mullens! Whew!

AWAKE! THE CHAUVINISM'S BLOOMING AGAIN!

Dorothy Parker, when told President Coolidge had died, said, "How could they tell?"

An optimistic housewife is one who follows a trail of ants *out* of the house.

Boomer Sooner has been heard to brag that his wife doesn't care how long he stays out...in the daytime.

We can certainly sympathize with Charley Appleknocker: a considerable quantity of first-rate fruit was knocked to the ground when his wife hanged herself from the apple tree.

Don't blame Cedric Whim for getting angry every time his wife reminds him he isn't half the man his mother was.

If your father were alive, he'd be turning over in his grave.

THE WET LOOK!

Seriously, ladies, if you want your new print dress to look its vivid best, wear it sopping wet! You see, the water drops settle down between the threads of the fabric and refract more light. Now that you have that straight, a cure for pneumonia is...

EPITAPH
What I like about Clive
Is that he is no longer alive.
There is a great deal to be said
For being dead.

H.H. Munro on cooks: The cook was a good cook, as cooks go, and as cooks go, she went.

STINGY?

Well, you could have knocked us over with an overdrawn check when we found out that simple little metal pins used to be very expensive. In fact, only the wife of a loaded gent could afford to buy them. The part of the budget she tapped for this extravagance she called her *pin money*.

Go ahead and tip the canoe...Tyler fell out a half-hour ago!

POLITICS MAKES STRANGE POSTMASTERS — Frank Hubbard!

Are you constantly astonished by the alert manner in which politicians marshall the facts and then take definitive stands on all issues? For example, two U.S. Senators were about to leave the Capitol building in a driving rain. One remarked, "Do you think it will ever stop?" His companion tugged at his chin, smiled and then scowled. "Well," he began, "as far as I know, it always has."

Foot-draggers? Aren't we seriously considering converting to the metric system? Just because Congress legalized its use in 1866 doesn't mean they aren't moving forward.

George the Third
Ought never to have occurred.
One can only wonder
At so grotesque a blunder.

RIDDLE: Was Teodor Josef Konrad Korzeniowski a feminist?

ANSWER: Who the hell is...oh, you mean the Polish-born author of *Lord Jim*, Joseph Conrad. Yeah, you could say he was a feminist, at least when he said, "Being a woman is a terribly difficult task, since it consists principally in dealing with men."

Most presidents, being shrewd politicians, kept a pet or two around the White House...dogs, cats, guinea pigs and horses, for instance.But, Theodore Roosevelt must have felt if pets improved the old image, he'd give them something to judge him by. In addition to the garden variety of pet, T.R. also had a rat, a kangaroo and an alligator on the executive premises. It could have been more crowded, but someone talked him into donating to the zoo his leopard, baboon, zebra and a couple of black bears.

An honest man is one who stays bought.

Government, as is true with most sports, has definite action patterns. For instance, we have a *standing* army, Congress *sits* and a president *occupies* the White House. As for rules governing the sport of governing, George Bernard Shaw had a good one: *A government that robs Peter to pay Paul can always depend upon the support of Paul.*

If you think political life is all chuckles, you've never read the Congressional Record.

Defying tradition, the French diplomat, Talleyrand, came straight to the point...on the vital matter of how he liked his coffee: "It must be pure as an angel, strong as love, black as the devil and hot as hell." All well and good, Mr. T., but what about Prussia?

England's Henry IV excluded lawyers from the Parliament of 1404. The barristers immediately dubbed it the 'Parliament of Dunces.' Stout fellows!

PRISONER OF LOVE!

He stood beside the huge elm watching her approach. Her dark hair swayed lightly in the twilight breeze. She smiled as she neared him.

She moved behind him, placed her long, slender fingers on his shoulder, and, as he held his breath, she whispered three of the most beautiful words in the English language into his waiting ear — "You're under arrest!"

DO'S AND DON'T'S OF LAWYER SELECTION!

As sure as we're standing here in our burlap jockey shorts (all we own after an *out-of-court* settlement) someday you, too, must pick an attorney. Don't do it willy-nilly. In the first place, *Willy* is out of town whenever you need him and *Nilly* has been disbarred.

Reviewing our track record of forty-two losses and one hung jury, we know what we're going to look for next time. So, follow these hard-won rules:

DON'T:

Mistake youthful enthusiasm for a bad case of fee thirst.

Engage a barrister in expensive English woolens, unless you're dedicated to replenishing his wardrobe.

Pick an attorney with more than eleven letters in his or her first name.

Let appearances of being perpetually sloshed fool you; the odds are ten, two and even that he is merely perpetually sloshed.

Think of caution as a virtue. In our last legal outing — we'd been run down by a neighbor's garden tractor while shaving — our new mouthpiece's response was, "Did you have speed-limit signs posted on your bathroom door?"

DO:

Look for thrift. For example, if you propose that a lawyer take your case on a contingency basis and he sobs uncontrollably, you've located a thrifty guy!

Size up his vivacity. If he has the general demeanor of a drunken caribou caught in a revolving door, imagine what a dramatic courtroom performer he'll be.

Check his record. If he's never won a case, think how hard he'll be trying.

Make sure he has a sense of humor. If he doesn't exhibit this openly, look for such telltale signs as a diploma from the Woody Allen School of Law.

EPITAPH

Beneath this smooth stone,
By the bone of his bone,
Sleeps Mr. Jonathan Gill,
By lies when alive
This Attorney did thrive,
And now that he's dead he lies still.

RIDDLE: Who said, *A conservative is a man who sits and thinks...mostly sits?*

ANSWER: Woodrow Wilson said it, underscoring another description which stated that a conservative was a person who thinks nothing should be done for the *first* time.

Winston Churchill said, "A fanatic is one who can't change his mind and won't change the subject."

BRIEFLY!

An appellate court judge, spying the bulky document an attorney had under his arm, said acidly, "If that's a *brief*, sir, you misconstrue the word."

Momentarily taken aback, the lawyer recovered to explain, "I'm sorry it's so long, your Honor, but I didn't have much time to prepare it."

In many primitive societies, a person too old and silly to be productive wanders off into the wilderness to die. Whereas, in America, they become judges.

CALL IN THE EXPERTS!

Nowadays an *expert* must be just the right age: too old to think he knows everything, but too young to admit it.

He must regulate his behavior according to the two cardinal fears of experts: First, if asked to tell everything he knows, that he'll come in under the current record of two minutes flat; second, because he has heard that a little knowledge can be dangerous, he is in constant peril.

"It is the trade of lawyers to question everything, yield nothing and to talk by the hour." Thus spake Thomas Jefferson.

Henri Frederic Amiel once said, *Doing easily what others find difficult is talent; doing what is impossible for talent is genius.*

The albatross
Is at a loss
To figure why
A man can't fly!

SOMEWHERE EAST OF SEATTLE!

Triviaddicts, arm yourself against the upstager! When you run headlong into another trivia buff at a social function, do not attempt to top him — his freakish tidbits may be more obscure than yours. Take a tack similar to the overmatched tennis player who bolstered his meager ability by wearing black tennis socks.

Emmett Glissando swears on a stack of outdated almanacs that the following happened to him.

Emmett was wowing a comfie gathering with such picayune goodies as, "While Ceylonese ebony is appropriately black, the Jamaican variety is quite green," when this buffoon suddenly spouted forth with:

An elegant dandy named Bligh
In the john, had re-knotted his tie.
What embarrassed him most,
When he rose for a toast,
Was his shirt-tail caught in his fly.

Well, you know how limerickers are once they get up a full head of drivel. Our friend listened helplessly through thirteen or so, before he was hit with the perfect counter-move.

Clutching the chap by the lapel, Emmett cried, "You're just the guy I've been looking for. There's this perfectly marvelous limerick...but I can only remember the first two lines."

"Oh, well, how does it go?" the unsuspecting limerick-freak asked.

"*There was a young man from Seattle,*" Emmett said slowly, "*who went East in a carload of cattle*...but then I go blank."

Emmett had him hooked. The fellow kept mumbling the lines over and over, finally retreating to a quiet corner where he could concentrate on the problem. Three times he came out of the corner to offer a possible third line, but Emmett rebuffed him and then told him to keep at it.

It probably ended the man's party career. But limericks...really!

RIDDLE: Should one trust the advice of a person who can't make up his mind?

ANSWER: Yes...and...no!

We often pardon those who bore us, but never those whom we bore.
LaRochefoucauld

THE DILETTANTE!

The world would be all right if it weren't for experts and committees. Way back in the 19th Century, Samuel Butler wrote: "An expert is one who knows more about less and less." And Bertrand Russell followed that one with, "The fundamental cause of trouble in the world today is that the stupid are cocksure while the intelligent are full of doubt." Then, if you put several experts together, things get even worse. J.B. Hughes hit it right on the head with, "If Moses had been a committee, the Israelites would still be Egypt."

But don't get the idea that man is without redeeming qualities. Just the other day we heard about a man who practiced thrift to the end. On his deathbed, he learned that his coffin had been made too short. He turned to his wife with a tight smile and said, "I'll scrooch up a mite, then."

Anyway, perfection can be hazardous. Anatole France knew that when he said, "People who have no weaknesses are terrible; there's no way of taking advantage of them."

So, to thine own self be true and, as the old Spanish proverb goes: If three people say you're an ass, put on a bridle!

If fiction writers were paid in relation to the merit of their efforts and not by the word, most novels would be short stories...and there would be damned few of them!

Experience is the name everyone gives to their mistakes.
Oscar Wilde

BRICK-A-BRACK!

Now that you're making your own bricks, let us give you some coloring tips. If white bricks are your bag, mix your clay with lime. For red bricks, go out and get iron-bearing clay. Mix the above two together to get cream-colored ones. Magnesia in clay is what's needed for brown bricks. Now, if you mix magnesia and iron together...good, God, man: just go out and buy bricks.

The secret of being a bore is to tell everything.
Voltaire

Archeologists claim to have traced the bagpipe back to ancient Greece and maintain it was known to the Romans, too. The modern Italians have their version, simpler but just as damned noisy as the Scotch and Irish varieties.

Any mention of the bagpipe reminds us of a conversation we overhead between a father and son at highland fling. The boy asked his father what the men were doing with the strange instruments.

"Skirling," his dense old Dad answered.

"How soon will they die?" the boy asked.

All of us, when well, give good advice to the sick.
Terluce

The *finger bowl* was brought to America for the first time by Thomas Jefferson.

The *finger* was brought to Wimbledon, England for the first time by either Ilie Nastasie or Jimmy Connors. Witnesses differ in their accounts of the historic occasion.

Military intelligence implies the same improbability as virgin whore.

Consider the plight of the fellow charged with keeping the Vatican's door knobs nice and shiny. There are some 1,100 rooms in the Vatican. So, if each had two doors and each door has two knobs, that would come to about — hey, man, that's a career, not a job.

If Joseph Califano, why can't you?

IT'S IRRELEVANT!

Gray-eyed people, sit up and take notice. Lord Byron, Bismarck and Napoleon had gray eyes, too. The jury is still out on Frederick the Great and George Washington — some said they had gray eyes, others claimed blue and there have always been the fence-straddlers who voted for gray-blue.

The wise guy who claimed eye color determines a man's personality and his life's work evidently didn't realize that Raphael, Beethoven, Voltaire, Gladstone, Goethe, Julius Caesar, Dante, Rich Little and Nixon all had brown eyes.

Medical explanations have a way of knocking romantic notions in the head. Take the dimple: medical men say it's caused by the skin sticking to the tissue beneath.

RIDDLE: Attention pore-counters: how many are there in the human body?

ANSWER: Those nimble-fingered rascals who assemble such vital statistics say we have two billion pores. Hard to believe that Wilt Chamberlain and Mickey Rooney have the same number of pores.

Children learn by emulating their parents, which is often unfortunate.

Why is it we can never lay our hands on a copy of *Tom Swift and his Pulsating Ornithopter* when we want to ? And before you pretend you're shocked, an *ornithopter* is an aircraft with flapping wings.

Most of us would rather be known as eccentric than imperfect.

FITS LIKE A GLOVE!

As with any apparel item, the manufacturers of gloves go on averages. They figure that a man's middle finger is the key. Its length should match the width of a man's hand as well as the length of the hand from the base of the fingers to the wrist. For men with short middle fingers, the glove will be shorter and not so wide. But, with ladies' gloves, they assume the hand will be slimmer and the fingers longer. So, put 'er there, pal, and get out the tape measure.

An undertaker is a man who knows, down deep, he'll see you sooner or later.

Medical types tell us that when a person is at the very peak of mental alertness, he's still only about twenty-five percent conscious of what his body is up to. That's one thing to be thankful about.

The qualities we have do not make us so ridiculous as those we affect to have.

LaRochefoucauld

YOU CAN BANK ON IT!

You can tell a banker by his actions. He's the fellow who lends you an umbrella in fair weather and takes it back at the first hint of rain.

However, borrowers should take heart: if you owe a bank enough money, you own the joint.

On the whole money game, A.W. Pinero said, "A financier is a pawnbroker with imagination."

Yes, you have a perfect right to be insulted if a Britisher says to you, "a farthing for your thoughts." After all a farthing is a mere ***quarter*** *of a penny.*

A banker was discoursing to a young employee on the proprieties of banking. "For one thing, in forty-two years at the bank I have never approved a loan to a man I called *friend*."

"Does that mean," the young man asked, "that if a man borrows money, you wouldn't call him friend...even if it's borrowers that make a bank run?"

"No question about it, borrowers make a bank, just like hogs make a feed dealer, but he doesn't have to sleep in the sty with them."

We're overpaying him, but he's worth it.
(A Goldwynism according to some.)

Here's a poem Black Bart left at the scene of one of his stagecoach robberies:

Now I lay me down to sleep
To Wait the coming morrow,
Perhaps success, perhaps defeat
And everlasting sorrow.
I've labored long and hard for bread
For honor and for riches
But on my corns too long you've tread
You fine-haired sons of bitches.

CARPENTER! STICK TO YOUR LATHS!

So you're going to build a housc! First, listen to how Ambrose Bierce defined an architect: "One who drafts a plan for your house, and plans a draft of your money."

You're going ahead anyway? In the book of Luke it says, "Which of you, intending to build a tower, sitteth not down first, and counteth the cost, whether he have sufficient to finish it?" (Oh, finish!)

What is a cynic? A man who knows the price of everything and the value of nothing.

Oscar Wilde

VULNERABLE!

Bridge expert, Charles Lockridge, was stuck with an inferior partner. At one stage in the game, having botched a hand miserably, the man answered Lockridge's disgusted look with a belligerent, "How would *you* have played it?"

Without hesitation, Lockridge replied, "Under an assumed name."

A budget is to your money what a speedometer is to your car.

You can bet on it. An *eisteddfod* is a meeting of Welsh bards. Now you know why we've asked you all to come here today.

Virtue has never been as respectable as money.
M. Twain

WHERE, MR. GREELEY?

Everyone knows that New York newspaper editor Horace Greeley said, *"Go West, young man."* The question is: to whom did he say it? And the answer is: a New York preacher named Josiah Bushnell Grinnell. Grinnell took Greeley's advice, too; got as far west as Iowa, stopped and founded a town and a college, both named Grinnell.

Now that we're in Iowa, we might as well tell you that the circus family — the seven Ringling brothers — came from McGregor, Iowa. They put on shows in their own backyard and eventually hooked up with P.T Barnum. Alf Ringling's favorite backyard stint was to balance a plowshare on his chin.

A snapshot fanatic is a person will take everything but a hint.

A literary scholar once claimed that Sir James Barrie got the name *Wendy* from a little girl's attempt to say the word *friendly*. If that were true, wouldn't we think of his characters as *Peter Pan* and *Fwendly.* Has a certain ring!

Irishman George Bernard Shaw said, "An Englishman thinks he is moral when he is only uncomfortable."

SMILE WHEN YOU SAY THAT, PARDNER!

If you're skiing in the mountains of Northern California and a Wintun Indian steps up and says to you, "Yallo Bally," *smile*! He's calling you a snow spirit. If he's not a Wintun, well...

In the land of the blind, one-eyed kings are wild.

I GOT THOSE CALIFORNIA TIREDS!

Met a freaky gal down by the Frisco Bay —
With her wet, hard eyes and her teeth all astray,
Hair full of cockleburrs hanging down her back,
Extra set of jeans in a plastic sack.
Tiptoe, Steptoe, Epsom Salt —
Don't blame me for the San Andreas Fault.

Down the big Sierra in a pea-green fog,
Freaky gal a-chasin' a bear and a hog.
Bear hit the millrace, hog hit the sluice,
Gal hit the rump of a pinto cayuse!
Tiptoe, Steptoe, Epsom Salt —
Don't blame me for the San Andreas Fault.

Freaky gal 'n me got a sucker's hunch:
Bought a hardpan acre for the price of lunch.
Couldn't wish any water, couldn't bore a hole;
Couldn't grow wire, might have growed coal.
Tiptoe, Steptoe, Epsom Salt —
Don't blame me for the San Andreas Fault.

Now we got food stamps and the ol' welfare,
A psychedelic van and a kitchen chair.
So it's Freaky 'n me, hand in hand —
One week in Vegas, the next in Disneyland!
Tiptoe, Steptoe, Epsom Salt —
Don't blame me for the San Andreas Fault.

Damn those torpedos! Where's the head?

Would you feel safer as a train passenger if you knew that the translated name of a certain well-known railroad is the Atchison, Topeka, and the Holy Faith?

Some adults are people who got tired of growing up and started growing sideways.

RIDDLE: Is a diet of worms beneficial?

ANSWER: It wasn't for Martin Luther. The *Diet of Worms* was the name of the council called by Emperor Charles V, (top dog in the Holy Roman Empire) to give the Protestant heretic what for.

YOU SOUND LIKE BIG HILL PEOPLE TO US!

It comes as no news that many states have Indian names. But wouldn't it be more interesting if we used the English translations of those names? For instance, Nebraska would become *Spreading Out* and its citizens, *Outspreaders*. We would know Alaska as *Great Land* and Missouri simply as *Canoe*. *Good Morning* would replace Idaho, Illinois would become *Man* and Minnesota would be transformed into *Cloudy Water*. And *Big Hill People*? That's what Massachusetts means. We had to explain this in case any of our readers are *Canoeists*.

Gertrude Susk does not now and never has lived in Ewan, Washington.

SOMETHING TO SHOUT UNDER!

A bartender from Juice, Louisiana informs us that sound travels about three times faster in alcohol than it does in the air at zero degrees centigrade. Of course, there's a noticeable slur, undoubtedly attributable to the speed. And for you teetotallers: sounds in water race along about four times faster than in air.

Fate makes our relatives, choice makes our friends.
Jacques De Little

YOU SAID IT!

After forty years of reading quotations on everything from *addle* to *zip*, this handful stuck with us:

Sinclair Lewis — "People will buy anything that's one to a customer."

Oscar Wilde — "He hasn't an enemy in the world and none of his friends like him."

Benjamin Disraeli — "He was distinguished for ignorance; for he had only one idea and that was wrong."

William James — "A great many people think they are thinking when they are merely rearranging their prejudices."

Small boy, reviewing the cowboy movie he'd just seen: "...and the bad guys got thrown in the horsegoo."

THE HORSEY SET!

The big event each year at Pimlico Race Track in Maryland is the running of the Preakness. Why do they call it that, you ask? We're informed that, in 1870, one of Pimlico's big races was called the Dinner Party Stakes. That year, a horse named *Preakness* won it. In 1873, after calling it the Dixie Stakes for two years, they changed the name to The Preakness. (Another thing: don't order steak at a race track.)

He put a sprinkler in the stable so he could give his horse a free rain.

During the Civil War, one of General Grant's favorite horses was named *Jeff Davis*. He was the one with the long spur marks across his flanks.

To have a great man for a friend seems pleasant to those who never tried it; those who have, fear it.

Horace

When the horseless carriage began to replace the kind with horses, people taxed their tiny minds for a name for the new creation. They came up with *cabine, ipsomotor, carleck, autovic, kineter, autogo, sineque* and *autokinet* among others. *Sineque*! You're welcome.

Pride goeth before a guffaw!

Back in 1926, the U.S. Bureau of Standards saw fit to announce that radio broadcasting has no influence (harmful or otherwise) on people, plants or the weather. Which all goes to prove that weathermen never listened to *Just Plain Bill* or *Myrt and Marge.*

That lovely, slimy variety of seaweed called ***kelp*** *has been known to grow almost a quarter of a mile in length. Nuff said!*

SOMETHING FISHY!

A *yearling* may be a one-year-old cow to some, but it's also a one-year-old fish. Fish work their way up to it...starting out as *fry* and then becoming *fingerling*. All of which leads us to tell you that while shad and salmon leave saltwater to spawn in fresh water, the contrary eel does it the other way around.

RIDDLE: If a little oyster can produce ten million eggs, how many can a great big oyster produce?

ANSWER: Ho hum, maybe fifty-nine million. Who in the hell do you suppose sits around and counts oyster eggs? Must have a lot on his mind.

THE WET SET!

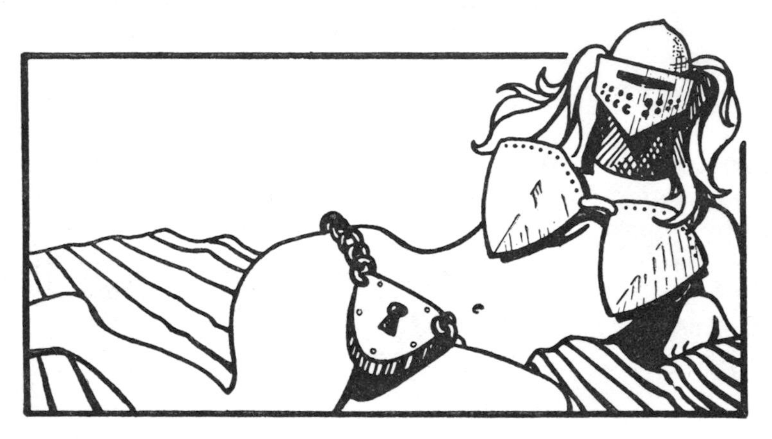

Browsing through the Seattle Times for June 13, 1968 we were startled to see an advertisement announcing a sale of some nine thousand modified bikinis and one and two-piece high-style swimsuits. We'll admit there's nothing so remarkable about seeing a sale advertised in a newspaper, but the name of the advertiser was the *Pacific Iron and Metal Company* with foundries or showrooms or whatever in Seattle and Everett.

Why is it very few swimmers will go in the water when it begins to rain?

Now that you've acquired a boat, we're going to tell you how to compute its tonnage. Take its length and multiply by its breadth and then multiply that by its depth and then multiply that by .75 and then divide the whole thing by 100. Those who forgot to divide by 100 are sinking.

Polite sailors say, "Ahoy, there." Others use nautical terms.

Those who have been bad-mouthing the good old Pacific Ocean should be apprised of this wet item: if Mt. Everest were plopped down in the deepest section of the Pacific Ocean, its tip would still be a half-mile under water.

How does seaweed know exactly where you want to swim?

TIME FOR BED. OOLACHANS OUT!

The *oolachan* is a useful little fish found in the Pacific coastal waters north of Oregon. The Alaskan Indians dry the oolachan and then run a strip of dry bark through it. Because it's so oily, it makes a good candle and is also called the *candlefish*. So light your *oolachan* and settle down with the *Igloo Tribune*.

Anchors, away! You broke my snorkel!

Inasmuch as the Mississippi is referred to in song as *Old Man River*, the Rhone in France should be called *Young Man River* — in some places it whips along at 40 miles an hour.

Before we forget: when you're trying to determine which is the left bank or right bank of a river, simply face downstream.

And don't ask which is the world's longest river. We're too damned busy trying to tell which is our right and which is our left.

Incidentally, we are not to be credited with the story that George Washington threw his buck across the Potomac but held onto his doe.

Up until we conned Hawaii into joining the Union, spots in Oregon and Washington had the nation's heaviest annual rainfall — in the neighborhood of twelve to thirteen feet, and that's a wet neighborhood. But ach du lieber, Hawaiians can name you a dozen spots that average twenty-five feet and more annually, and forty feet a year occurs in some spots. *Dot is vet.*

People who dedicate an entire summer to acquiring a tan must have pointless winters.

You can bet your purse, shoes and wallet that people who keep alligators for pets are extremely patient. It takes your basic, fun-loving alligator fifteen years to reach a length of two feet. Of course, his rate of growth depends somewhat on what you feed him and how much. (Try a steady diet of noisy teenagers and we promise that you'll be pleased with the results.

If none of them ever got away, men would stop fishing!

RIDDLE: Does the best whalebone come from the whale's rib bones?

ANSWER: Technically, none of it comes from the body of the whale. Whalebone, called *baleen*, is a series of bony plates extending downward from the whale's upper jaw and forming a sieve through which he strains his food. (This, ya had to know?)

Watch out! The tide rises over fifty feet in Canada's Bay of Fundy.

If you've been tying flies all winter, you'll be flabbergasted to learn that fish rise to bait more often because of the smell than the sight. We haven't the foggiest as to the specific smell they find most entrancing. Now you can untie your flies and take up bowling.

If you think swimming will help you become graceful, watch how penguins and ducks walk.

DON'T SPOUT OFF!

It's utter nonsense that whales take in a mouthful of water and then spout it out through their nostrils. The way we hear it, while the whale's submerged and holding his breath, the air he's holding becomes saturated with moisture. Just before he surfaces, he exhales...*really exhales*. When that stream of moisture-laden air hits the cooler air of the atmosphere, condensation occurs. And that's what you see. That's a whale of an explanation!

The tortoise is the one that lives on land and the turtle is his aquatic relative. All of which means that *sea turtle* is redundant. We thought so.

A heavy rain is a ***downpour****. No rain is an* ***uppour****.*

Very few scientists are willing to admit that if Christopher Columbus had altered his course a mere one-twentieth of a degree each day of his famous voyage, he would have fallen off the edge of the Earth before discovering the New World.

We don't know why it's said that a ship engaged in coastal trade is said to be ***enrolled*** *while one in foreign trade is* ***registered****. We are sure we don't care.*

BIRD TALK!

Attention goose-feather addicts! If you want ten pounds of goose feathers, you're going to need sixty geese. On the other hand, if you'd like something truly exotic such as a pillow stuffed with peacock tail feathers, you are going to get a measly eighteen feathers per peacock. They are not very comfy anyway...those peacock tail feather pillows. Also, they're six feet long.

Ticklish Humble Pie: Some editor ate crow and left the feathers on.

Obviously the swan, crow, eagle, crocodile, turtle and elephant know something we don't: quite a few of these creatures live to be more than 100 years old. For some time we thought the elephant's longevity stemmed from his diet, but after trying to consume a hundred pounds of hay daily we gave up the notion.

Early birds get worms!

Is there anything sillier than a bird drinking water. But, for some reason, the pigeon, which can be pretty silly in other ways, doesn't have to throw its head back and let the water trickle down its throat. It simply sucks up liquids.

Barring B-B guns and stray cats, your average robin lives to ten or fifteen years. By the way, he only sings about ten weeks out of the year.

How long have you been wanting to know that the robin is an altricial bird? That long? Well, it means their young are born without feathers and are helpless. Now the pheasant and the duck are precocial, meaning the young have down and can go right out to find their own meals. (Think *that* over, sonny boy.)

WILD FRONTIERS AND COONSKIN CAPS!

We read the following news story filed from Whangarei, New Zealand...we kid you not.

> *New Zealand ornithologists say they have positively identified and photographed the Magenta Petrel, a species of bird whose existence has never before been confirmed.*
>
> *It was first seen 110 years ago by an Italian, 500 miles east of Chatham Island, which lies east of New Zealand's South Island.*
>
> *He sketched it and named it the Magenta Petrel. But his sighting has never been verified.*

RIDDLE: Hummingbirds really do hum, but why?

ANSWER: When they hear a tune they like, they can't help themselves. But seriousness aside, folks, it's the rapid beating of their wings that creates the hum.

Now an ornithological expedition headed by David Crockett, of Whangarei, claims to have attracted three of the birds with a bright light during a search on Chatham Island last month.

They could not risk harming them by trying to catch them, but Crockett said the identification was positive. The next job will be to find the bird's nesting burrow. Very commendable, friend.

All-Occasion Conversation Stopper: Do you think the rain will hurt the rhubarb?

There was a young maid from Madras,
Who had a magnificent ass;
Not rounded and pink,
As you probably think...
It was gray, had long ears and ate grass.

Beefeaters are members of England's Royal Guard whose fancy headdress adorns a well-known gin. But a *beef-eater* is also a clever little bird who rides on the back of the rhinoceros, feasting off insects who are also along for the ride.

You'll get an average of seventeen pounds of honey every year from a bee hive, but only if you wear gloves.

THE STING!

Results of the annual Sting Power survey are in: old hornet is still on top when it comes to being venomous; yellow jacket is a fair second, followed by wasp and honey bee. Tarantula and Black Widow spiders were disqualified for being *arachnids*.

Texans take notice: In Africa there are locusts four inches long that often lunch on mice.

If you can figure out why the Circassian walnut tree is known in the United States as the English walnut, we'll owe you a tube of elephant lard for your complexion.

You could walk up a vertical pane of glass with ease if you had feet which form a vacuum. That's how flies do it.

THE ANTHROPODS HAVE LANDED!

If ever a group needed a union, it would be the drone bees. Up at dawn, busy as a bee all day and then hit the comb. No wonder they only live for a few months — nine at the outside — while the Queen sits on her thorax all day making with the eggs and lives three years.

However, if you really think the queen bee lies around the hive being waited on, wing and mandible, remember that she lays two thousand eggs a day.

Native American of the Week: the sassafras tree! Hickory came in second.

GARDEN VARIETY!

If you have a nice stand of maple on your property, have you ever considered infesting them with a certain parasite? It won't hurt the wood, but it will cause swelling growths. Then, when the wood is cut, you'll discover you have *bird's-eye* maple...and a handsome profit.

A-tisket a-tasket, we think we've blown a gasket!

Being sticklers for accuracy, we're quite perturbed about the name of the Australian bottle tree. On the one hand, its trunk is assuredly shaped as a bottle. Aborigines, on the other hand, tap fluid from the tree to make a native beverage. So, is it a bottle tree because of its appearance or because it contains a drink? Golly, we wish we knew for sure!

Today many think being lost in the woods is a special new freedom.

RIDDLE: Why do mocking birds keep repeating the same tune?

ANSWER: You've got the wrong bird. Mocking birds have been known to switch tunes ninety times in ten minutes. A little hard to follow, but impressive.

Spanish explorer Coronado is credited with discovering Arizona's Painted Desert in 1540. It has yet to be established who painted it.

LOVE THAT SCENT!

The next time you're about to plunk down sixty dollars for an ounce of some exotic perfume, consider that it probably contains *ambergris*. The dictionary, in politest terms, says *ambergris* is the morbid secretion of a sperm whale. They're trying to tell you that the whale threw up!

If you're planning to make your own perfume, take heed. To produce one ounce of attar of roses you'll need 4,000 pounds of rose petals.

Don't get upset, but the poinsettia has small yellow flowers. Those bright scarlet items aren't petals but leaves surrounding the small blossom.

Mildred Brislane, if you're reading this right now, write a thank you note to your Aunt Carrie in Dubuque.

CITY SLICKER!

Country folk delighted in putting down strangers.

One city dweller innocently asked a farmer how he kept the cows out of his corn field.

"I just don't plant no outside rows," the farmer informed him.

And another know-it-all from the big city pointed to a large leafy tree, and said, "Bet you don't get more than two baskets of peaches from that tree."

The farmer gazed at the tree, pulling at his chin whiskers while he pondered city-bred wisdom. Finally, he said, "You may be right...seein' as to how that's an ash tree."

I have never made but one prayer to God, a very short one: "O, Lord, make my enemies ridiculous," and God granted it. Voltaire

IT'S FRUITY!

All of you who said the *cantaloupe* was named for Irving Cantaloupe, go to the back of the room. It was named for a town in Italy. No, not *Florence Cantalupo,* just Cantalupo.

The banana has a few things in common with wheat. Both contain a small quantity of iodine and both are perennial herbs. The banana, even though it can grow as high as thirty feet, is still classified as an herb because it never develops a tough, woody tissue.

Joy is a fruit that Americans eat green.
Amando Zegri

A British lady, writing a Swiss priest about vacation housing in his village, asked if a W.C. (her euphemism for *water closet*) were available. Thinking W.C. stood for *Wayside Chapel*, the priest wrote that it was 9 miles from town, seated 219, was open on Thursday and Sunday only and had organ music.

We think this drawing might have satisfied both parties as a W.C.

Alphonse, an arthritic Basque,
Phollowed girls whenever they'd asque.
Once, in a maid's room,
He was phraught with gloom:
"I phear I'm not up to the tasque."
(*We're* **not** *saying he's phruity.*)

The difference between you and a peach is quite apparent. If there's a long dry spell followed by rain, the inside of the peach grows faster than the skin and the peach cracks. *Your* cracking skin is strictly a dry weather phenomenon...or hereditary.

Dorothy Parker, commenting on the Halloween game of ducking for apples — Change one letter and you have the story of my life.

Don't forget that the grapefruit, largest of the citrus fruits, is related to the kumquat, smallest of the group.

In the United States we squeeze lemons to make lemonade. In England they squash lemons to get lemon squash. (Will wonders never cease?)

RIDDLE: What's the difference between lightning bugs and glowworms?

ANSWER: A matter of sex: the male of the species is the lightning bug; the wingless female is your basic glowworm.

GIRL TALK!

If you ever wondered why Lewis Carroll's famous fantasy was titled *Alice in Wonderland* and not Max or Fred, he gave us a clue when he said, "I am fond of children — except boys!" Sounds as if he wouldn't have minded living under a *gynarchy* — a government of women.

How do you like children? Boiled in oil.
W.C. Fields

You would think younger mothers would have the most multiple births since, physically, they're better suited for extended labor. But it isn't so in America, where women between thirty-five and thirty-nine are the champs at twin-bearing, triplet-bearing and up.

On July 8, 1926 a baby was born in Crump, Tennessee with no penis. Fortunately, it turned out to be a girl.

Okay, ladies, how about a nice Bronx cheer for Lord Chesterfield and his endearing line, "Women are to be talked to as below men and above children."

Bad news runs in the family.

It could, understandably, have been Lord Chesterfield who, on his deathbed, asked his wife if he could have a slice of the apple pie she had just baked. "Nope," she said with finality, "Saving it for the funeral."

Grover Cleveland knew how to please women, too. In 1905, he wrote in the Ladies Home Journal, "Sensible and responsible women do not want the vote. The relative positions to be assumed by man and woman in the working out of our civilization were assigned long ago by a higher intelligence than ours." Duck, Grover!

It must have been remarks such as the above which led a 17th Century French noblewoman, the Marquise de Sevigne, to write to her daughter, "The more I see of men the better I like dogs."

Then there's the thought of that old French phrase-maker, Montaigne: "Women are not altogether in the wrong when they refuse the rules of life prescribed to the world, for men only have established them and without their consent." And that may have prompted

Frances Gage to write, "Wife, mother, nurse, seamstress, cook, housekeeper, chambermaid, laundress and scrubwoman doing the work of many for the sake of being supported."

It could have been Sam Goldwyn who said, "Give me two years, and I'll make her an overnight star."

A California television announcer introduced a filmed public service announcement with, *"Now Beverly Shills for the opera."* Well, if you're going to hire a shill, we can't think of a better one.

Any woman who enjoys dancing cheek-to-cheek with her escort must be unaware that the average man has fifteen thousand whiskers. Now that can smart.

When you examine two fish of the same species, the darker one is the female. Evidently this doesn't work with people. Example: Deborah Samson dressed herself in men's clothing and enlisted in the Continental Army as Robert Shirtliffe. She fooled the military authorities for the entire Revolutionary War. Don't ask us how she fooled her tent-mates.

Remember the good old days when no one was trying to get his head straight.

BOYS WILL BE BOYS!

We know a man so old he can remember when charity was a virtue and not a tax deduction. Same man claims you're only as old as your arteries.

Did you ever stop to think how many male mosquitos are killed every year just because of mistaken identity? Only the female of that species has the right equipment for biting and drawing off blood. The males are just buzzing around wondering what's for dinner.

Speaking of meals, London solicitors were once in the habit of dining in a Flat Street pub named *The Devil*. Before leaving the office, each hung a sign on his door saying, *"Gone to the Devil."*

Do you know why some men's underwear were called BVD's? Simple! The manufacturer's name was *Beverly, Voris and Day*, but what guy could yell out to his wife, "Hey, did you put starch in my Beverly, Voris and Day's?"

Another initials question: what do the letters *T.D.* on a clay pipe

RIDDLE: Which came first...the hat or the hatband?

ANSWER: Funny world, isn't it. Ages ago, the Egyptians kept their long hair out of their mashed potatoes, by catching it up with a band which they tied under their chins. The hat came later and they kept the band for decoration.

stand for? Seems there was a Massachusetts industrialist back in the 19th Century who was balmy over clay pipes. He made a generous donation to a clay pipe-maker and they put his initials on them. Oh, his name was Timothy Dexter. He was balmy in other ways, too. He once wrote an entire book with nary a punctuation mark.

Then there's the dentist who had this inscribed on his headstone:

Stranger! Approach this spot with gravity!
John Brown is filling his last cavity.

Arthur Trefawley posed for three hat-rack advertisements. Then he had his teeth fixed. Now he's quite useless, Arthur is.

WELL, FURROW MY BROW!

Some nut wrote to tell us thirteen muscles are involved in smiling and fifty in frowning. The way it adds up, one good frown is worth almost four smiles. If you're too poorly coordinated to frown, growl a little.

Once a punster, always a punster as in this epitaph:
There's a man who was not born,
His father was not before him.
He did not live, he did not die,
His epitaph is not o'er him.
Who was he? Mr. Nott!

The approximate chemical analysis of a man 5 feet 8 inches in height, weighing 148 pounds, would be: Oxygen, 92.4 pounds; hydrogen, 14.6; carbon, 31.6; nitrogen, 4.6; phosphorus, 1.4; calcium, 2.8; sulphur, 0.24; chlorine, 1.12; sodium, 0.12; iron, 1.02; potassium, 0.34; magnesium, 0.04; fluorine, 0.02; total 148.30 pounds. (Beware of the six-footers!)

The man who is a pessimist before 48 knows too much; the man who is an optimist after 48 knows too little. *Mark Twain*

William Pitt *The Younger* was only twenty-four when he became England's Prime Minister in 1783 — a record. His father, William Pitt *The Older* had been forced to resign as Prime Minister fifteen years earlier because of a bad case of the crazies.

ANOTHER RECORD!

If you've been wondering which year was known as the *year of the big snow,* Californians will tell you it was in 1879 and 1880 when 783 inches of snow fell in the Sierra Nevada. (If you're talking to a publisher, it was the year Clifford Irving sold his Howard Hughes book.)

Hell is the place where the satisfied compare disappointments.
Philip Moeller

Every time we read that someone reported a hailstone that weighed one pound and seven ounces or measured fourteen inches in circumference, we're astounded at how well prepared some people are. When it starts hailing around our place, we never can find the damned scales or tape measure.

In the latest sugar-content rankings, dates are out in front of raisins by six percent and raisins lead figs by thirteen percent. Zap!

LET'S HEAR IT FOR THE TOWER OF PISA!

Having reached the magic figure of seventeen feet out of whack by 1976, the Tower of Pisa up and refused to lean any more in 1977. Of course, it took the old girl 804 years to decide to stand still.

Flash! The Earth's surface is curving about eight inches per mile...rain or shine.

THE SIZE OF IT!

Abraham Lincoln, George Washington, Lyndon Johnson, Thomas Jefferson and Andrew Jackson are a few of our presidents who were over six feet tall. That is not meant to imply short is bad, because John Quincy Adams and James Madison were short. And our short naval heroes include Admiral Farragut and John Paul Jones. That's about the size of it.

ALEXANDER THE GREAT'S EPITAPH:
Here a mound suffices for one whom
the world was not large enough.

Every man desires to live long, but no man would be old.
Jonathan Swift

RIDDLE: Why are polo fields 900 feet long by 450 feet wide?

ANSWER: We didn't know they were. Not at all horsy, don't you know.

The world's tallest midget was said to be Everett Spisker of Lean Falls, Ohio. He stood five-feet six inches when fully grown. His younger brother, Dwight, who was an inch shorter than Everett, was later proclaimed the world's shortest giant. The two brothers lost their life savings in an abortive attempt to raise caribou in Florida, and little has been heard of them since.

Chastity's a good deal like promiscuity — same old thing day after day!

If the Romans during the reign of Augustus Caesar are to be believed, a big attraction was a pair of giant human bodies. One was a man and the other a woman...and both were said to be 10-feet, 2-inches.

Metrically, my dear, a dekameter multiplied by a hectometer equals a kilometer.

We didn't know that the island of New Guinea was 303,000 square miles in area, ranking it second largest of the world's islands. But we were absolutely diminished to hear that Greenland's area is 826,000 square miles...give or take a frozen square mile or two.

The Trans-Siberian Railroad from Leningrad to Vladivostok stretches 5,481 miles. If you stay home, it won't seem nearly that long.

CONCRETE FACTS!

Triviality forces us to inform you that the first concrete road was laid down in Bellefontaine, Ohio. It took from 1893 to 1894 to pour 4,400 square yards of concrete. Let's see, if it was only ten feet wide, the new road would have been a whopping 440 yards long...or a quarter of a mile...or less than half a kilometer. My God, another one of those time-and-material jobs!

For sheer brevity, there's Dorothy Parker's own epitaph:
Excuse my dust.
And there's only one shorter:
Thorpe's
Corpse.
Exit laughing!

The astronomical unit is exactly 92,900,000 miles long. Or, to put it another way, it's ninety-three million times as far as it is from the starting point of an auto trip to the first time someone needs a rest room.

No guest can stay three continuous days without becoming an annoyance. *Plautus*

Ask a native New Yorker what stood on the site of the Empire State Building before that colossus was erected, and you'll get a blank stare. As any Kansan can tell you, it was the original Waldorf-Astoria Hotel.

He carved his way through a wall of genealogy, dragging his canoe behind him.

Is the Death Valley of California much larger than the Shenandoah Valley of Virginia and West Virginia? It's smaller by about half — 50 miles long versus about 100 for the Shenandoah Valley. Both valleys average about 25 miles in width. Terrific!

Moonies: Moonlight is equivalent to the output of a 100-candlepower light at sixty-six feet.

The world's largest lake is the Great Sahara Lake in North Africa. There is a reactionary group of geographers which refuses to accept the Great Sahara Lake as a lake on the flimsy basis that it contains no water. Are we to deny a great natural wonder its rightful place in the atlas simply because it has been the unfortunate victim of drought?

He rented some air for his curses.

We were about ready to go for the information that the Buddhist monastery in Hanie, Tibet (elevation 16,000 feet) is the highest inhabited spot on Earth. Then we learned that Washington's *Tacoma* is an Indian word meaning highest. What do you know? Tacoma is at sea level.

A full moon occurs twice in the same month ten times in 28 years, on an average.

RIDDLE: Can the government come and claim all the meteorites that fall on private property?

ANSWER: Hell no! The courts say they're yours, especially the *big* one that flattened the house, the barn and seven outbuildings.

THE SKY'S THE LIMIT!

Of course, stars are not really pointed. Since the Earth's atmosphere is not uniform, light passing through it from outer space appears to scintillate, or spark. We thought you should know, Sparky!

It must have been a travel agent who discovered that the Earth is three million miles closer to the Sun on July 1st than it is on January 1st.

GOING AROUND IN CIRCLES!

At an altitude of 100 miles, you can make a circular orbit of the Earth in roughly eighty-seven minutes. It will take you approximately twenty minutes longer if your orbit is 1,000 feet above the Earth. Before making dates, check your altitude...and your parachute.

Why didn't anyone tell us before? 338,452 Austro-Hungarians emigrated to the United States in 1907. Nine percent of them were left-handed.

MOON OVER MURMANSK!

People who worry about such things tell us that, in arctic and antarctic regions, the full moon rides along above the horizon for about two weeks in the winter; then, it dips below the horizon for some two weeks, when it's new. In the summer, it's just the other way around. We're lost!

The road to ignorance is paved with good editions.
G.B. Shaw

If someone asks you if there were eleven eclipses of the Moon in 1927, tell them no. In the first place, there are never more than three lunar eclipses in a single year...none in some years; in the second place, why is he bothering you with what happened in 1927?

Play this on your ocharina: the raccoon was once known as the wash-bear.

THE ANIMAL ACT!

The character who claimed that the loudest animal sounds in the world are produced by the lion, wolf, elephant and bull elk has never been to a Shriner's convention.

The next time you're feeling all mixed up, consider the plight of the reindeer: he grazes the same way cattle do; he flocks together as sheep do; and the rest of the time he acts like a horse, except when he's making a pig of himself.

Yes, Morgan, pigs will eat snakes. No one knows if they enjoy it.

Please don't think any the less of pigs and cows for oozing sweat from their noses. It's the only place the poor devils have sweat glands.

Animal Lover: It was the last Strauss who stroked the camel's back.

WOULD YOU BELIEVE...

Many years ago in the Himalayan highlands, the locals would get together and have a lively discussion over the relative merits of the *yak* and the *zebu*. Of course, both provided reasonable transportation and passable milk, but it was the matter of beauty which caused argument. *Yak* fanciers were especially taken with the fringe of long hair on the *yak's* underbelly and lower legs. Contrarily, *zebu* partisans pointed with pride to their favorite's smooth hump, drooping ears and magnificent dewlap.

The more they argued, the more adamant each side became. Finally, they appointed a committee to decidc the issue. Unlike most legislative bodies, this one acted promptly. They bred a bull *yak* to a *zebu* cow. Then, proving they weren't all that different from other committees, they named their new creation the *zobo.*

Actually, this is sheer fable, but how else is one to account for the *zobo?* He really is a hybrid of *yak* and *zebu*, but we're sure the choice was never his.

Never lie to a sleeping dog.

Did you see a fox fly by just now? Not likely. Could have been one of those fruit-eating bats with a face like a fox. The unwashed have taken to calling them *flying foxes*.

It takes a quick needle to sew up the eye of a camel.

That South African antelope called the *gemsbok* gets enough moisture from the succulent plants it feeds on so that it never drinks water. It's known as the Dean Martin of antelopes.

RIDDLE: If a bull is mated to a cow, will she have pups?

ANSWER: Seals wouldn't have it any other way.

For your cocktail party ice-breakers, take your pick from these:

You probably don't realize that monkeys and cats have tears ducts. Eh? No they don't cry in anguish, Madam, only to lubricate their eyes.

The meteorite that did such a bang-up job on a farmyard near Paragould, Arkansas back in 1930 weighed 820 pounds.

Our resident skunk expert says the little critters are not at all afraid to eat bees and wasps.

FOOD, AGAIN?

Did you ever sit up half the night trying to figure out how certain peanuts have been salted *in* the shell? Quite simple. First the whole peanuts, shells and all, are boiled in a salt solution, then dried and roasted. Knocks out your *elf* theory, doesn't it.

The rule is, jam tomorrow and jam yesterday — but never jam today.
Lewis Carroll

A PERSON COULD GET STUFFED!

We're on a diet, so it's rather painful to mention that Thanksgiving is celebrated three times every year in North America. Since 1734, the Dutch Schwenfelder Society in Pennsylvania has given thanks for their deliverance from European religious persecution on September 24th. Then comes Canada's Thanksgiving Day on the second Monday in October. The third Thanksgiving Day, due to legislative obfuscation, falls on an undefinable day in November. The following day all surviving turkeys give thanks.

It is a difficult matter to argue with the belly, since it has no ears.
Cato

STOP EDITORIALIZING AND GIVE THE NEWS!

A listener to radio station KCBS in San Francisco was mildly interested to hear that California Governor Jerry Brown, while on a whirlwind tour of Great Britain, was invited by Prince Charles to dine at Buckingham Palace. The newswoman went on to explain that, in November of 1977, the Governor had treated Prince Charles to a lunch of cold cuts in Sacramento. Our listener was then startled by the newswoman's closing line, intended to clear up the mysterious royal invitation: "Prince Charles reciprocated the hostility."

Americans used to eat gobs of *crane*-berries...every Thanksgiving. You see, cranberries grow from a long, curved stalk which resembles a crane's neck. Of course, they also resemble a stork's neck, in which case...

Pancakes, pancakes, Baker Man,
Call Aunt Jemima quick as you can!

If you think the custom of waiters in fancy establishments wearing white gloves is a sanitary measure, you're all wet. The dummy who designed the Palace of Versailles put the kitchens so damned far from the royal chambers that all the food arrived ice cold. So they began serving on pre-heated silver trays. Thc servants had to wear gloves to prevent burns.

Since Worcestershire sauce is made primarily from soy beans, wouldn't it have been less confusing if we had called it soy sauce from the outset?

For Gizzard Lovers Only! This ought to open up a whole new world of gourmet dining for you: besides poultry — insects, shellfish, reptiles and fish have gizzards. (Vivid, man, that's too vivid.)

Diddle-diddle dumpling! Mice in the john.

Remember the *vinegarroons* your mother used to bake? We hope not! To those in the know, a *vinegarroon* is a venomous whip scorpion that gives off a vinegary smell when upset.

On occasions when there's a bit of ***flotsam*** *left over from your* ***jetsam,*** *use it as a topping for ice cream.*

CARRY ME BACK TO OLD BULIMIA!

Starvation will certainly lead to excessive hunger. Another form is called *bulimia*...that's when you never feel satisfied, no matter how much you eat. Next time you go out for Chinese food, watch out for the *bulimia.*

The good ship 'Lollipop' took a licking and hasn't been seen since.

RIDDLE: Is the phrase *I don't give a fig* the slogan of the Fig Growers Cooperative?

ANSWER: Surely you jest! The only thing we know on the subject is that a fig tree is capable of producing two fruit crops a year. The second bearing comes from separate shoots of the same tree. Now we don't give a fig either.

FOLK SONG:
I bought my wife two cows and a steer,
Nickeltin' nickeltin new but new.
They all went dry in the fall of the year,
It is to be walloped a bangoree.
Halliday, walliday, bangor, noodlety,
Hoffle come trosselmy, bangoree.
She milks the milk in the slop-pail,
She strains the milk through her shift-tail.
She makes the butter both green and gray,
The cheese takes leg and walks away.
She takes her butter to Huckleberry Town,
The print of her foot in every pound.

CHAPTER SIX

Gesundheit, And Pass The Tranquilizers!

The bank calls to say you're overdrawn, the cat just had a litter of five, Amy and John have been exposed to chicken pox, the station wagon's battery just went dead and your mother-in-law arrives Friday. Oh, the tension. Take a tranquilizer!

You've exhibited that, for all his civilization, man is still a superstitious creature. Our minds still react to forces we don't understand with irrational fear. And in this helpless state, we still call upon magic.

Tranquilizers a magic potion? You bet! They don't enable you to understand the source of your tension-creating fears. They simply dispel those fears temporarily through a chemical reaction. Rubbing cold lamb fat behind your left ear and saying, *Beetle, beetle, don't you crawl* would have the same effect if you believed in it. As hypnotists will tell you, it's next to impossible to hypnotize a person who does not believe he can be put under.

Many vestiges of bygone superstition exist today in customs. It's considered a polite custom to say, *God bless you* when someone sneezes. Why?

As far back as ancient Grecian times, men believed a sneeze blew out some of the breath of life. So they implored the Gods to intervene. The German Gesundheit (your health) conveys the same thought. This fear of losing the breath of life resulted in another custom we still practice: covering the mouth when yawning to prevent the precious breath from leaving. Within the last hundred years, some superstitious people held a dying person's nose and mouth to prevent his spirit from being exhaled. This practice often had the opposite result they were seeking.

So we say to you, "Gesundheit, and pass the tranquilizers!"

We fear things in proportion to our ignorance of them.
Livy

PICK YOUR FAVORITE *MANCY!*

Wind, water, smoke, fire — you name it, and somebody built a fortune-telling scheme around it. Those who practiced *aeromancy* observed wind and weather for good omens, and were smart enough to predict everything *but* the weather. The charlatans who gazed into crystal balls for a fee are engaging in *gastromancy*, although it sounds as if they should be examining your stomach. *Necromancy* is the art of examining skulls for omens. In *hydromancy*, the big item is liquid. Then there are the ultra-specialists: in *pyromancy*, the flames and embers of a fire are seen as indicators of all sorts of good and bad things; but they pay no attention to the smoke...that's an art all by itself, called *capnomancy*.

There's no *mancy* ending in *augury*, but it's a fortune-telling gimmick all the same — predicting from the examination of the bones of snakes and birds.

Hope and fear are inseparable.
La Rochefoucauld

H.L. Mencken once wrote of an imaginary band of primitive people seeking refuge from a flood atop the highest hill in their vicinity. As the raging waters rose nearer and nearer their hilltop, they grew more fearful. Finally, one of the band became hysterical. He began slapping at the water with his hands, yelling at it. At that critical moment, the flood began to subside. The others clustered around the hysterical man, looking at him with a certain awe.

Mencken went on to propose such an event as the beginning of the class of priests or medicine men.

Wealthy Egyptians used to dress their children in ragged clothing to prevent someone becoming envious and giving the kid the evil eye.

OFF WITH YOUR DUDS!

As late as the 1930's, bands of a certain religious sect would crop up in the news. Their formal name was New Ground Christians, but since they often rolled about on the earth in a religious frenzy, they came to be called Holy Rollers. And they weren't your average religious sect, often seeking to increase the power of belief by holding services in the nude.

As you might imagine, this got them in a peck of trouble. One such band marched through a small Iowa town, in the altogether, hoping to recruit new members. Instead, the local lawmen rushed them off to the hoosegow where they almost froze their scriptures off.

He went from hags to bitches.

MIRROR, MIRROR ON THE WALL...PLEASE DON'T FALL!

In this day when so many products seem to wear out or break or become obsolete overnight, the manufacturers of mirrors are claiming *foul.* Seems people take damned good care of their mirrors. Superstition is killing the replacement market.

If you happen to break a mirror and just can't face seven lousy years, go out and look for a five-dollar bill. Finding one kills the curse. And if it doesn't, at least you'll have the price of a new mirror...a small one.

The superstition which holds that breaking a mirror brings bad luck stems from the days when mirrors were used to forecast the future. It was believed that mirrors did not break accidentally, but that the gods caused them to break so mere mortals would not be able to see into the future. Speaking of bad luck, the opal was thought to be a real bummer for centuries. It began in the Fourteenth Century during the Black Plague. The tales were told of opals worn by plague victims

RIDDLE: What does it mean if you sneeze before getting up on a Sunday morning?

ANSWER: That's a surefire sign that a wedding is on the offing. Kerchoo!

becoming excessively brilliant and then losing all their luster when the victim died. Presto, the opal was bad luck. (But who doesn't want to own one, anyway?)

Some say it's good luck to find a pin, especially a safety pin; on the other hand, some recite, "Pick up a pin, pick up sorrow."

AMERICANS SUPERSTITIOUS?

"Uh-uh, I dropped my scissors. Pick them up for me. It's bad luck if I do it."

"Don't cut his fingernails. He isn't a year old yet. Want him to grow up a thief?"

"You can't marry *him* — his last name starts with the same letter as yours. Remember what they say: 'Change the name but not the letter, marry for worse instead of better' and that's the truth."

"Clean the chimney, Jack. Tomorrow is New Year's Day...we want to be able to let all the good luck in."

Yep, all those are American superstitions. Oh, sometimes, when we ran out of good ones, we imported a new batch from the 'old country.'

It's good luck if a swallow builds its nest under your eaves. Watch out if he leaves — that means your place is going to burn down.

Keep your eye out for crows, too. If a lone crow starts cawing around your place, the only way you can avoid a calamity is to take your hat off. When you see a crow in flight, make a wish. If he flies to the left, that's bad; and if he flies to the right, be on guard. If he soars out of sight without flapping his wings, your wish will come true; but, if he flaps, the only way you can salvage the wish is to look away quickly.

Now, if you'd like to get rid of warts, you have a wide range of choices. You can tie a knot in a string and hide it; or you can bury a rooster's comb; or you can rub the warts with a peeled apple and then feed the apple to a pig; or steal a bite of beefsteak and bury it where three roads meet; or you can even take one pebble for every wart, tie the pebbles in a bag and then throw it away...which may be difficult if you're living in a city apartment.

And, if you see someone walking around with a buzzard's head tied around his neck, think nothing of it. He's only trying to cure his headache.

Superstition is the damnedest thing! Spilling salt may not fill you with terror, but the chances are many of you still toss a pinch over your shoulder...just in case. Let's try to unravel this little mystery.

We're in a simple household several centuries ago. During the morning meal, someone spills salt. Later that day, the youngest daughter breaks her arm. What had they done to anger the secret forces which then caused the broken arm? Spilling the salt was the only extraordinary event they can recall.

Several days later, salt is spilled again. Fearfully, the mother picks up a pinch and tosses it over her shoulder. The next day their cow, which had been dry for a month, suddenly begins to give milk again. Ah-ha! Soon all their neighbors who knew that spilling salt was bad luck learned that tossing a pinch over the shoulder appeased the evil forces.

We can't help but believe that many superstitions have passed into custom by some similar set of fortuitous circumstances. Why else would New Englanders of a not too distant time rub onions on the chest of a person with a lung infection? Or bathe sore eyes in tea? Or grease the soles of their feet to prevent head colds? Or wear salt pork around their necks to ward off a sore throat. Or carry a peeled potato in their pockets to ease their rheumatism?

Some of their superstitious acts had some medicinal value, such as rubbing bee stings with mud and placing mashed potatoes on a burn. A syrup of fir balsam may have eased a cough. Hell, maybe even putting pepper in your stockings fought off chills, but we can't see the value of sticking a kerosene-soaked feather down ones' throat when it's sore.

*Americans once thought the foul-smelling herb, **asafetida**, placed in a bag and suspended from a neck chain would cure a cold. It **did** keep others at a distance!*

UNEXPECTED VISITORS?

Do you have the fear of someone dropping in unexpectedly? My dear, a little old-fashioned superstition can give you ample warning.

For example, if scissors fall and stick point downward in your freshly polished oak floor, a stranger will soon appear. If your hand itches, company is on its way; if it's the right hand, it will be a friend.

A visitor will come calling on the day you see a robin in the early morning. Of course, two knives and forks accidentally set beside a plate spell company (the mere fact that you're setting the table should have indicated something). There are even ways of telling the sex of an impending caller: a dropped fork tells you it's a woman; or it will be a man if you drop a knife. Children of indeterminate sex will arrive if you drop a spoon. Hey, watch it, gal, you dropped four knives!

If you want a guest for tea, just let the lid of the teapot stand open.

Be forewarned about visitors on New Year's Day. If the first one is a dark man, you're in for good luck. But, if the year's first caller is a woman — blonde, brunette, redhead or totally bald — that's a sure sign of disaster. Also, don't let them take anything from the house that day unless they brought something to take its place.

Spilling salt is still a bad omen to some. In Japan, it's spilling rice.

DIRECTION POINTERS!

If you spot a knife lying on the ground, don't pick it up if the point is toward you. We wonder if it would be alright if we walked around it and picked it up from the other side, or would that be cheating?

A money superstition points out that if you fold your money away from you, that's where it will go. However, folding your money toward you is a sign there will be more coming your way. Our problem has always been that we could never hang on to it long enough to fold it.

Picking up a glove is bad luck. Not picking it up is expensive.

OUR SUPERSTITIOUS THESPIANS!

Carole Lombard's good-luck charm was a smooth pebble Clark Gable had given her. Bette Davis is said to favor a gold beetle. Irishman Pat O'Brien is true to the old sod by carrying a four-leaf clover; and another Irisher, George Brent, relied on an old Irish shilling.

Al Jolson was one of many actors who always wore old clothes on an opening night.

Hey, Alfred, don't put your hat under the bed; it's bad luck!

WHAT HAPPENED TO OUR LUCKY KNEE?

Gamblers on their way into the casino at Monte Carlo once had a habit of rubbing the knee-joint of a bronze equestrian statue in front of the building for luck. Along came a new manager. Wanting to put everything in apple-pie order, he had workmen paint over the bronze horse's knee-joint where superstitious gamblers had worn away the patina.

Well, neatness was one thing, but painting over their good luck caused the casino patrons to boycott the place. The manager had to have the paint scraped away before he could induce them back into the casino.

There's something about a closet that makes a skeleton terribly restless. *Wilson Mizner*

IF THE SHOE SQUEAKS, WEAR IT!

Actors and actresses in stage productions have so many superstitions it's rather remarkable that they ever get the thing on at all.

For instance, it's a no-no for an actress to knit on stage. In a musical, the only way to remedy the bad omen of spilling powder is to have a chorus girl dance on it. Whistling in dressing rooms is strictly taboo. On the other hand, squeaky shoes and wigs bring good luck; and falling on stage means a long engagement (the outwardly contradictory expression *break a leg* stems from the same belief).

Set designers are warned to avoid yellow curtains and artificial flowers are considered much safer than real ones. And never open an umbrella on stage. Of course, there's no need to — it seldom rains inside theaters.

On May 10th in 1849, a riot broke out during a performance of *Macbeth*. Ever since, it has been taboo to quote a line from *Macbeth* on May 10th. Fortunately for theatergoers, they waive the ban for professional productions of *Macbeth*.

Actors and actresses consider it a bad omen to change costumes if a play is a hit, in some cases wearing them until they literally fall apart.

RIDDLE: What does it mean if your shoelace is untied?

ANSWER: One of two things — either someone is talking about you or your shoe is about to fall off.

An actor we know swears that when you are about to enter a theater to try out for a part and if you turn the stage door handle the wrong way, it is wise to forget the tryout. Go home and come back the following day.

When thespians are on the road with a touring company, they have another curious fancy: it's bad luck to leave soap behind in one's hotel room. Hotel owners say the legend apparently applies to towels, as well, in some cases even to the bed linen.

A drama critic once said, "If there were no such thing as superstition, theatrical people would have invented it."

Call the casino manager! Sylva Skwarek rolled a fourteen!

STOP RUBBING THAT MOONSTONE AND DEAL!

We've seen bridge players get up and walk out, if a black ace is accidentally dropped on the floor. Others are convinced that a cross-eyed player will make them lose. And, don't be surprised if you get a dirty look from a card-player, when you put your foot on the rung of his chair or peek over his shoulder.

If you've been astounded by the insensitivity of gamblers, you can believe they would follow the old Monte Carlo superstition. When an unlucky player commits suicide, they would rush into the Baccarat game and bet against the bank!

The traditional green covers on gaming tables were not decorator touches. Gamblers believe it's bad luck to play on a bare table.

Multiply your license number by your Social Security number; add six; multiply the sum by your zip code. You'll have the odds against your winning the Irish Sweepstakes, plus or minus your mother-in-law's weight.

HOT TIP!

Waiters have their share of irrationalities. As you might have guessed, most of their fears have to do with their tips.

Getting a big tip early in one's shift is a sure sign the rest of the day will be lean. Breaking a dish can cost tips, too; and dropping a whole stack can get a waiter fired.

Some waiters pull back the chair to seat a customer and open the napkin not so much out of courtesy but superstition.

On the other hand, customers consider it a very bad omen to get a waiter who deserves no tip at all.

The four of clubs is such a bad-luck card it is called 'the devil's bedstead.'

These days, most people look to the government to ease their money shortage, find cures for disease and lengthen our stay on Earth. In medieval times, they turned to the chemists or, more properly, to the alchemists. The legendary *Philosopher's Stone* was the grail they sought — rub it on lead and get gold, cure disease and get life eternal.

Wear a topaz if you want new friends. Brushing your teeth might help, too.

An alchemist philling a phial,
Phound the phlavor exceedingly vial.
"Phive phrogs and some phruit,
Plus a phricasseed newt...
Oops, I have left out the bial."

IT'S A PHOBIA!

The late Howard Hughes was a *pathophobiac.* In simpler terms, he had an unreasoning fear of germs and disease. There's a special name for almost any fear one might imagine. Supposedly most women suffer from *myophobia* — a fear of mice. Everyone must have *taphephobia*, which is the fear of being buried alive. Those with an irrational fear of fire are *pyrophobiacs*. Most of us have a superstitious respect for the number 13, but if it scares the hell out of you, then you're a *triskaidekaphobiac,* no less.

It is said that Mussolini had *claustrophobia* — the fear of confined spaces — and so he had enormous offices. We've never heard of a trapeze artist who had *acrophobia* — fear of heights — but many people suffer from it. Perhaps all good housekeepers have a bit of *mysophobia* — a fear of dirt.

A child who can't fall asleep without a light in his room is a victim of *nyctophobia*, or fear of the dark. *Agoraphobia* is almost unknown in farmers, because that's a fear of wide-open spaces. But everyone has *thanatophobia* to one degree or another, because that's the fear of death.

But the phobia to end all phobias is *phobophobia* — the fear of fear itself.

To be frighteningly repulsive in Scotland is to be ***ugsome****! You bet!*

RIDDLE: Is the number 7 really lucky?

ANSWER: Depends upon whether you are an optimist or a pessimist. The optimist cites the Bible — God completed the world on the seventh day and there were seven days of plenty. The pessimist also cites the good book — there were seven days of famine.

When one is feeling insecure, it is natural to wish for the approval of rational people. However, nothing bolsters the moral so quickly as the disapproval of a single neurotic.

You're in for a stretch of bad luck, if you hear an owl screeching or a rooster crowing at night. You must also avoid stepping on cracks in the sidewalk, killing spiders, dropping combs, stepping over snakes or breaking mirrors. To start your day propitiously, get out of bed on the *right* side (not the left), don't laugh before breakfast and don't burn the toast. The last two may be difficult to manage. After all, the reason many husbands don't laugh before breakfast is because their wives *do* burn the toast.

Tip For Hitchhikers: pick up a pin with the head facing you and you'll get a lift in a jiffy. If you don't want to ride in a jiffy, forget it!

CLOCK-WATCHERS!

In olden times, many religions involved sun worship. And they told time with sundials. It then became a custom to perform certain acts *clockwise* — that is, in the east-west path of the Sun. Some cooks insist that beating cake batter or cream in a *clockwise* motion insures success. And superstitious card players try to change their luck by walking around their chairs...*clockwise* only!

Styes are easy to cure. Rub your eye three times with a plain, gold wedding band. If your eyelid turns green, you'll know your gold ring isn't really gold.

THOSE EVIL SPIRITS!

The ancient Egyptians had ladders so it isn't surprising to learn that they were afraid to walk under one. Seems they didn't want to take the chance that a god might be coming down or going up the ladder at that unfortunate moment.

The Scotch once believed that, to prevent evil spirits from coming into one's house, quantities of garlic should be hung about. In fact, it discouraged *anyone* from coming in.

It could mean disaster if you and a friend pass around opposite sides of an object when you're walking together. We wonder what people did in the days before the magic words *bread and butter* dispelled a lot of bad luck.

Naming ships is fraught with superstition. What boat owner in his right mind would call his vessel the *Lusitania* or the *Maine* or the *Morro Castle?* Nor would he include *fog, reef* or *ice*. It's advisable to select a name with happy connotations and, as a further protection against evil spirits, try to pick a name with seven letters. Then cross your fingers and cast off!

You can still see the ancient oriental sign of creation — yin and yang — in the flag of South Korea.

THE NUMEROLOGISTS!

The Bible is fertile ground for numerologists. For instance, they point out the significance of *40*: Jesus fasted 40 days and was seen again 40 days after the resurrection; Jonah gave Nineveh a 40-day period in which to repent; the flood raged on for days, then Noah waited 40 more before opening the Ark's windows; Elijah was nourished by the ravens for 40 days; and Moses spent 40 days on the mount.

However, in some ways, the Bible confounds the numerologist. In the Epistles of Peter, the First, it states, "...a few, that is eight souls, were saved by water." Is a *few* always eight?

Then there's that biblical method of counting years, as with Methuselah living to the age of 969. The famous British historian, H.G. Wells, felt that the Bible was referring to lunar months, not years. Makes sense. On that basis, Methuselah lived to be 74 years and 7 months.

Numerologists: take five!

NUMEROLOGY WITH A HONG KONG TWIST!

Chinese fortune-tellers had a handy reference guide known as the *book of classics.* In it were all manner of numerological and astrological interpretations. But, when a lovesick man came to find out if a certain girl had favorable signs matching his, the fortune-teller didn't simply open the book and give the kid a reading. After all, if a person was willing to spend money for this sort of thing, he deserved a bit of excitement.

The fortune-teller put a bundle of numbered sticks into a cup and shook the cup until one stick popped out. Then he read the number,

RIDDLE: Did Americans really believe in witches?

ANSWER: Sadly enough they did around Salem, Massachusetts in 1691-1692. Those infamous *witchcraft* trials cost twenty-one lives — nineteen so-called witches were hanged and two died in prison. And it was all legal, since that state had passed a law in 1641 making the practice of witchcraft a capital crime.

By the way, the British employed a curious technique in seeking to destroy the widespread belief in witches. They passed a law in 1736 that denied legal status to all witches.

gazed wistfully into the distance and finally looked up the matching number in his *book of classics*. Good show!

GO FOR YOUR NUMBER!

Egyptian priests of the 15th Century B.C., running low on ways to scare the hell out of the populace, hit on the numbers game. In no time, they were telling fortunes, warning of constant disaster and stirring up trouble in general. They convinced people that all numbers under ten were extremely significant and the odd numbers were the most potent.

Even a nice guy like the Greek mathematician, Pythagoras, couldn't resist toying with numbers.

The upshot of the whole farce was that, for centuries, those who swallowed the bait wouldn't even tell a stranger their names, for fear he'd figure out some numerical method of sicking evil spirits on them.

Knowing you're too bright to be conned, the way you figure the numerical significance of names is to add up the numbers corresponding to the letters:

A	B	C	D	E	F	G	H	I	J	K	L	M	N	O	P	Q	R	S	T	U	V	W	X	Y	Z
1	2	3	4	5	6	7	8	9	1	2	3	4	5	6	7	8	9	1	2	3	4	5	6	7	8

Practice on Julius Caesar: the letters of his name total forty; knock off the zero and you have four. Had it been forty-two, add four and two for a six.

Now, here's what the various numbers portend. *One* is the symbol of man and of creation (pagans used one as the phallic symbol). People born on the first day of the month are said to have a devil-may-care attitude; but if your address is *one*, you're supposed to be a spendthrift (shouldn't be hard). *Two* is woman's symbol and doubles for love. Couples living at Number *Two* are scheduled to fight.

Three is one of the biggies! Before Christ, it was unlucky — the old one about death coming in threes was so strong, ancient magic words and phrases were always repeated three times. After Christ, *three* did a turnabout, probably from association with the Holy Trinity; and good things, such as gifts and letters from friends, were supposed to occur in threes.

Pythagoras was a staunch supporter of *four* as a good number because he had a theory that all matter was composed of the four elements...air, earth, fire and water. It's not a hot number in Japan, however — too close to the Chinese word for death.

If one thing is consistent about numerology it is its inconsistency. Take *five:* the ancients thought it was an omen of the end. It softened up a bit in early Greek and Roman civilizations; and then the Christians came along and gave *five* a good name because of the five wounds of Christ and the five books of Moses.

Someone born on the sixth of the month had fortune-telling powers, it was claimed. But *six* was unlucky for a dishonest person. We can't find out what number might be lucky for the dishonest. You'll have to take your chances.

As far back as the Chaldeans, *seven* has been considered lucky. Astrologists are sold on *seven*, because they cooked up the way man's life is controlled in seven phases by the planets: up to four years, Moon; Mercury rules from four to ten; Venus, ten to fifteen; fifteen to twenty is the Sun's area; manhood of indeterminate length is ruled by Mars; plain old age is Jupiter's province; and decrepitude, when you shouldn't care much, is Saturn's bailiwick. But before you get too stuck on *seven*, remember that Hitler went ape over it, attacking Greece, Yugoslavia, Poland, Austria, Holland and Russia on the *seventh.*

After *seven*, it's a welcome relief to discover that *eight* means very little, except for those who read *survival* into it, because of the eight on Noah's Ark.

Guess why *nine* is lucky? It's three threes. Good number for spell-breaking, too, according to the old Anglo-Saxons.

Ten, twelve and *thirteen* have biblical overtones — ten commandments, twelve apostles and then thirteen at the Last Supper. *Eleven*, some say, is unlucky, but they can't say why. Obviously, they're not dice-shooters.

Nowadays, twenty is getting a bad name, because someone pointed out that from 1840 on, each U.S. President elected at twenty-year intervals has died in office — the last being Kennedy, elected in 1960.

When the whipped owl cries, evening is night.

RIDDLE: Is the Witch's Sabbath held at regular times?

ANSWER: Pull up your broom and we'll tell you. The year's first Witch's Sabbath, called *Candlemas*, is held February 2nd (also Ground Hog Day); *Roodmas*, the second scheduled meeting, is held April 30; then comes *Lammas* on August 1st and *Hallowe'en* on October 31st. Don't be late...the brew will get cold!

OFF WITH YOUR DUDS AGAIN!

In case you recently moved into a section of the United States where cyclones are known to occur, you might do what some backwoods folks used to do for protection.

At the first sign, one of the adults whipped off his or her clothes, grabbed a knife and ran stark naked in the direction of the oncoming cyclone holding the knife out front. You see, this split the wind so it just went around your house rather than *through* it. This practice may account for the large number of cyclone false alarms in some areas.

If you see someone standing in the fork of a road in Ozark hill-country and singing, "Sty, sty, leave my eye," run like hell. The next line is, "And catch the first one passing by."

MOON WEATHER!

If you want to know what the weather is going to be like, you can watch TV or the Moon. The latter may be more entertaining and even more accurate. It will be a wet month if a crescent Moon is upright because the water can spill out; but, if the crescent is horizontal, no rain...since it can't spill out.

Keep an eye on the ring around the Moon, too. The number of stars within the ring will tell you how many days before a storm will occur. Five stars inside the ring means cold weather.

While you're out there gazing at the Moon, be on the lookout for shooting stars. When you see one, make a wish...especially for money.

(What else?) Comets, however, bring bad luck. After all, where's Halley today?

We read somewhere that moonshine makes a razor dull. Trouble is, it didn't specify whether it was the light from the Moon or white lightning.

KINIK-KINIK, HERE COMES WINTER!

Some of the Indians of western America developed a foolproof method of forecasting the mildness or severity of winter. They observed bears.

It seems there was a certain yeasty berry bears adored. It was called the *kinik-kinik*. It was a phenomenon of nature that when the winter ahead was to be mild, the kinik-kinik produced a modest amount of yeast; in advance of a long, hard winter, it produced a large quantity of yeast.

Along came the bears, followed by Indian bear-watchers. When the bears, gorging themselves on kinik-kinik berries became only sedately drunk, the Indians could be sure of a nice winter. But, when the bears got rip-roaring drunk, climbed slender aspen and roared at the sky until the tree broke and then fell on their drunken backsides, a rough winter was in the offing.

It makes one wonder if those bears hibernated after all, or simply spent the winter hung over.

Some people tossed their dogs outside, when a storm came up, because they feared their tails acted as lightning rods.

THE BIRDS ARE COMING!

If superstition counts for anything, bird-watchers ought to be accurate weather forecasters. In general, sea hawks mean fair weather, unless they fly low which indicates rain followed by a rainbow. A friendly robin isn't good — spells a long, hard winter. Let the robin find his own friends.

When turkeys begin stretching their necks and staring up into the sky, put your raincoat on. Do the same if the pigeons start flying in circles over a lake or river. And there's this poetic prediction: Crow on the fence, rain will go hence; crow on the ground, rain will come down.

No matter what the weather, it will change, if the turtle doves begin making a racket.

RIDDLE: We know bears, bats, hamsters and dormice hibernate.Do any other animals hibernate?

ANSWER: Hell, we're still back on *bats*, but we get it from a badger we know that he takes a winter snooze, too.

Then there's the cuckoo. Mostly his crazy antics will lead you astray, but come the first of May, get out your compass, then listen. If his first call comes from the *west*, that's good luck and good weather; from the *south* indicates good weather for crops; from the *north* foretells a sad harvest and all other manner of tragedy. If you hear the cuckoo's first call from the *east*, forget all about the weather — he's telling you of a great romance in the season ahead.

Keeping a pet canary is all right. But, if a strange canary flies into your house, it supposedly foretells a death in the family. In fact, it applies to any strange bird inside a home. The superstition is said to account for the fact many people would not have wallpaper depicting birds.

Speaking of birds, if a sparrow builds its nest above your window, you're scheduled to take a trip. Smart little bird.

Also, keep in mind that when the peacock bawls, you'll soon have rain and squalls.

If it hadn't been for astrology, he might have gone through life blaming ***himself*** *for his stupidity.*

THE GROUND HOG CLUB!

Outside the little Pennsylvania community of Punxsutawney there's a hill named Gobbler's Knob, known as the *weather capital of the world*. Back in 1898, seven fun-loving fellows climbed Gobbler's Knob to drink a little beer and eat ground hog — a local delicacy. They had so much fun, they repeated the outing every year and came to be known as the *Ground Hog Club.*

Eventually, they settled on February 2nd for the big doings. On that day, they kept their eyes peeled for ground hogs. If the little devils didn't see their shadows, it meant an early Spring. If they *did* see their shadows, they went scampering back into their burrows for another six weeks of hibernation — thus, more Winter and a delayed Spring.

Here's to the ground hog, tried and true,
For he's a weatherman through and through!

IT MAY BE FLORA TO YOU, BUT IT WAS BAD LUCK TO THEM!

Oh, yes, the superstitious couldn't leave the plant world alone either. Some people ate chicory in the belief it would make them invisible. Looking at a fern could cause thunder and lightning. People who feared snakes took to wearing onions around their necks. Poppies could make women fertile, or drive away a discarded lover... depending upon your mood, we suppose. Cowslips were supposed to cure amnesia. And, in some unimaginable fashion, a cyclamen dispelled the sadness for a girl who had been jilted.

Never get rid of that croaking frog; if he stays around long enough, it's good-luck insurance. (We got that straight out of grandma's mouth.)

PASS THAT GIN, SON, THE MARIGOLDS ARE IN BLOOM!

Pick flowers before they're in full bloom and you can expect to get a stye in your eye.

Don't go prettying up the hen house with primroses...it stops the setting hens and their eggs won't hatch.

You could go temporarily blind if you stare at poppies.

You'll get blind in another way, if you gaze hypnotized at marigolds, especially in March — brings on the drinking habit, don't you know.

He that tiptoes through the tulips is not quite right.

OF COURSE, THE HORSE!

1978 is the Year of the Horse, according to oriental astrology. We mention it only because we admire the oriental preservation of one's time. Occidental astrology, as it operates today, can save you spending half your time over complex horoscopes covering the day, week, month, etc. In fact, we think one prediction for the whole year is so good, we'll go it one better. How about an astrological era of four years duration?

It also adds the element of suspense because, under our plan, the next era wouldn't be known to anyone until after the presidential election. Right now, we're in the *Era of the Peanut.* In 1980, we might have Phase Two of the Peanut Era, but we might not. 1968, in case you've forgotten, began the *Era of the Scalawag.* The era really lived up to its name in Phase Two, from 1972 on.

On the remote chance you may not buy our concept, the least we can do is print the oriental years and appropriate birth years, so you'll know where you are:

Year of the Horse: 1978, 1966, 1954, 1942, 1930...keep subtracting twelve.

1979 will be the Year of the Sheep (again go backward by twelve);

RIDDLE: Was tea ever given to pigs?

ANSWER: You bet. Farmers used to think a little alfalfa tea was good for their hogs. Now, get your snout out of the crumpets and pay attention!

1980 is set for the Year of the Monkey; 1981, Year of the Cock; 1982, Year of the Dog; 1983, Year of the Boar; 1984, Year of the Rat; 1985, Year of the Ox; 1986, Year of the Tiger; 1987, Year of the Rabbit; 1988, Year of the Dragon; and 1989, Year of the Snake.

And what may be the significance of each of these *Years*? Damned near anything you want to read into it, which isn't all that new.

Experts say you can blame racehorses for the notion that a two-dollar bill is bad luck. You know...two-dollar window, slow horse and good-bye two bucks.

Horses might not agree, but most people look upon the horseshoe as a good-luck symbol. Originally it was not so much a good-luck sign as a way to ward off evil forces. According to one tale, St. Dunstan recognized a visitor as Satan. The Saint promptly nailed him to the wall and went to work on his hoof. Satan begged him to stop. St. Dunstan did on the promise the devil would never show up again wherever a horseshoe was hung.

Met any nice sheep lately? Too bad! They say it's good luck to meet a flock of sheep, so keep your eyes open.

MINERS' MOUSE!

Did you know that mice are smarter than men? At least many miners thought so. They kept pet mice to warn them of cave-ins or gas. If the mice scampered out of the mine, the miners were right on their heels.

And in the days when donkeys pulled the ore cars, miners put great stock in their intelligence. Perhaps because the donkeys moved about in the dark so well. At any rate, if a donkey refused to pull an ore train of ten cars, the miners settled for nine cars. They figured the beast knew something.

Birds are afraid of snakes, right? Not always. The Great Crested Flycatcher has the vile habit of lining its nest with snake skins. Nice decorator touch, though.

If a cricket makes your home his home, you're in for good luck. And don't ever kill a cricket, especially on Sunday. Remember: crickets can forecast the weather, tell you when friends are coming and predict when someone will die.

***Stridulation** began with crickets. It's how they make that chirping.*

COCK-A-DOODLE-DOO! ARREST THAT MAN!

In the middle ages, they had their own version of the police line-up. First, they put a rooster under a bucket. Then each of the suspects marched up in turn and touched the bucket. If the cock crowed at one person's touch, the jig was up...and his goose cooked.

Down by the river is a little bag of bees,
Hanging from the limbs of the cottonwood trees.
Shake the little bag and you'll find out,
How little-bitty bees can make you shout.
Sting-away, sting-away,
Sip, sack, see;
Sting-away, sting-away,
Lawdy me!

WAKE UP, QUEENIE! UNCLE JAKE DIED!

For all we know there still may be some people who follow an odd custom...telling the bees of any death of a family member. Some felt it had to be repeated three times; some draped the beehive in black. If a family neglected to tell the bees, the hive, strangely, was abandoned.

The sting of a wasp is said to cure complacency!

HERE'S TO CATTLE AND EGG PRICES!

An Austrian peasant couple's future depended upon their success at raising cattle and poultry. An old superstition called for the couple to eat a special cake after the wedding. Baked into the cake were eggshells and cowhairs. Anyone who could swallow that concoction should find farming a cinch!

Eternal hope: A hen trying to hatch a pet rock.

CRACKERS ABOUT ANIMALS!

We used to think the elbow was the *crazy bone* but, after hearing about some of man's superstitions, we're convinced the skull is the real crazy bone.

Consider the mental equilibrium of a person who would wear an adder skin inside his hat to prevent headaches. Or criminals who thought that keeping a dead toad in their pocket insured them against arrest. And wouldn't you have loved being a child of parents who believed that horsehairs chopped up, mixed with butter and spread on bread would protect your health.

Some people forced their children to ride donkeys to cure whooping cough. And carrying a rabbit's foot wasn't good enough for some — it had to be the right forefoot of the rabbit...even then, it only worked if you kept it in your left pocket.

Attention cowboys: Put a horsehair lariat around your blanket, when you're sleeping out on the range, and the rattlesnakes won't crawl into your bedroll.

Indians who once inhabited what are now the upper midwestern states stretched their superstitions to gigantic proportions. These tribesmen built mounds, usually in the shape of animals, to frighten away evil spirits. In Kentucky, mounds in the forms of panthers with 360-foot long tails have been found. A serpent-shaped mound in Ohio runs over a quarter of a mile in length and the jaws are seventy feet wide. They did it up brown in Wisconsin, too, with an eagle-shaped mound. The eagle's wingspread is about three and a third football fields tip-to-tip.

Mountain folk in some parts of the United States still sing:

If you want to get to heaven, let me tell you how to do it:
Grease your feet with a little mutton suet;
Stand right out by the Devil's hand,
And slide right over in the Promised Land.

NOW THE GOIK IS IN YOUR COURT!

A carryover from pagan days still existed in 19th Century Poland.

At spring festivals, they made a dummy representing winter and then got rid of it to guarantee a good planting season. In some areas it was called a *Goik*. The Silesians called it a *maranza* and their favorite stunt was to take it to a neighboring village and dump it there. Of course, their neighbors, being equally superstitious, stole back and returned the *maranza*. It was damned hard to get rid of one permanently.

In medieval Europe, it was thought witches could assume the form of a black cat. However, the ancient Egyptians thought very highly of black felines.

The scarecrow one often saw in cornfields is a superstitious figure. A straw-stuffed figure of a man mounted on a cross was to frighten off crows and evil spirits in general. Can't vouch for the evil spirits, but a lot of crows saw through the subterfuge and ate themselves silly.

We doubt if swans believe it, but humans used to think a swan couldn't hatch eggs in a storm.

To drive away the evil spirits before the Spring planting, Japanese farmers held a bean-throwing festival on the last day of winter. Some still do.

An idealist is one who, on noticing that a rose smells better than a cabbage, concludes that it will also make better soup.

H.L. Menken

Some of the Pennsylvania Dutch still put *hex* signs on their barns. The German word *hexe* means witch, so a *hex* sign wards off evil. And the old expression to *put a hex* on someone indicates a less than friendly act.

In the old days, the railroad tried to catch cows.

STRIP! IT'S PLANTING TIME!

True to their Scotch-Irish heritage, most hill-country people of the southeastern United States are strictly religious. However, here and there traces of certain magical pagan ceremonies could be found even into this century. For instance, an outsider was surprised one evening

RIDDLE: Even though they are part of the United Kingdom, do Scotland and Wales have so-called National flowers?

ANSWER: Yep. Scotland's is the thistle; the leek is Wales' flower.

about dusk to see a group of naked young men and women planting turnips. When he remarked about it to an elderly woman of the area, she passed it off as young people's foolishness, then added, "But they do have the best turnips in these parts."

The same traveler, in another place, found a family who swore there was only one way to be assured of a good cucumber crop: the seeds had to be planted on May first before sunrise by a nude man at the peak of his virility. (Hell, we didn't want cucumbers this year, anyway.)

Barry Moil hasn't missed a ***briss*** *in twenty-seven years! Atta-baby!*

HAIL TO YOU, FISH!

Even though the Navaho and Zuni Indians of the arid southwest were often hard put for food, they would not eat fish. In their dry lands, water was so precious it became sacred. Now, since they believed that fish ate and breathed water, it, too, was sacred. It hadn't always been that way, inasmuch as Zuni meant *fish cannibal.*

Avoid cook-outs when the main course is announced to be ***badger.***

SUTURES, CLAMP, CORMORANT SKIN!

Your family doctor may scoff and cry, "Superstition!" but how does he know that you won't be helping your neuralgia by walking around your bedroom three times in the morning wearing only your left shoe and stocking? And, if he prescribes medicine for you, it'll work a lot better if you take it in the nude.

Tummy upset? Tie a cormorant skin around it until the pain subsides. And, if that doesn't work, put water-lily roots in your wine. No kidding!

The hell with Preparation H. Grandma says sumac seeds will do the job.

You say you have a stye in your eye? Go outside and wait until you hear a swallow sing. Grab the little critter, take him to the nearest stream and wash his eyes. Then let him go. Your stye will go flying away with him.

Then there are some things we recommend only to those with an established resistance to foul odors. One is a little gem to relieve frostbite — apply a poultice of cow manure and milk! Wolf dung mixed with white wine (a *good* year, naturally) is great for colic. Finally, when your sciatica is acting up, slap onto your hip a plaster you've prepared with onions, rum and neat's-foot oil. Maybe the smell will make you forget your ailments.

Up in Maine, they used to say you wouldn't get rheumatism, if you filled your hip pocket with buckshot. If you forgot to do this and the rheumatism hit you, set fire to a turtle shell and then rub the ashes over the afflicted area.

Unless your dentist is superstitious, he probably hasn't heard that rubbing your children's gums with the teeth of a wolf will guarantee their dental health. Hazelnuts clear up sores in the mouth. And for toothaches, take your choice between a snappy mixture of gunpowder and brimstone or a gum prepared by boiling sumac leaves in beer.

There's a home remedy for minor ailments, too. Stop a nosebleed with cobwebs. Rags soaked in boiled hemlock when applied to your head prevent dandruff and falling hair. Sleeping on a bearskin rug knocks out a backache. When the hiccoughs hit you, take a few dill or caraway seeds. For the bald, wash your pate with warm sage tea and watch the hair come in.

Not all legendary beliefs can be brought into play this simply. Sometimes, you must do a bit of work. Let's say your muscles ache and joints are swollen. The thing to do is boil one full-grown bear, rendering the fat to grease. Then apply the bear grease. Be sure you don't use the brains. They're poisonous, we're told.

Skunk grease, obtained in the same way, will cure lameness. To cure fits, pulverize part of a horse's leg — preferably the gambrels — mix the resulting paste with goat's milk and drink. If you didn't have fits before, you might just get them from this.

Now, if you've been hearing that a powder obtained from mashing up codfish bones cures kidney stones, be advised that it works only if you use the center bones.

In case none of these remedies work and you feel you're headed for the great beyond, call up a tattooer. Have him tattoo a pair of vertical lines on your chin. We got this from the Sioux Indians. You see, when your ghost is traveling up the Ghost Road, those two lines prevent an evil spirit from driving your ghost into the ditch.

Oh, and before you go, arrange for a tombstone for your family's sake. It's the only way to prevent you from coming back and stirring up trouble.

Janet and Jess Kraus gave ***epidemiologists*** *to all their friends last Christmas!*

RIDDLE: Which smells more like a rose...a piece of rosewood or a tea rose?

ANSWER: Cut into a chunk of rosewood and you'll get a rose-like whiff. Tea roses smell like tea.

Some superstitions lead to rather obnoxious habits. Spitting for one. Expectorating into the hole before planting a tree or bush is a good-luck charm. Fishermen spit on the bait to make the fish bite. And if you're hunting for a lost object, spit hard in your left palm, slap it with your right index finger and the direction of the splash will guide your search.

Shaking hands with a **Nandi** *tribesman of Uganda used to be a wet proposition. For good luck, he spat in his hand first.* (*Your good luck or his?*)

OUTWARD APPEARANCES!

In Colonial days and for some time thereafter it was thought that teeth set wide apart guaranteed health and wealth; or, if just the two front were gapped, that individual would be a rover.

These beliefs were probably outgrowths of the so-called *science* of physiognomy. Specialists in that neat little deceit examined the shape and size of your head, face, nose, ears, eyebrows, eyes and mouth and then told you what sort of person you were. Evidently a sizable number of people believed in physiognomy, since the English Parliament saw fit to ban it by law in 1743.

At one time you would have been destined to grow up a murderer if you were born with any teeth.

IN ONE EAR AND WHO KNOWS WHERE?

Pay close attention: someone's talking about you *if your ears burn*. A burning left ear means the talk is uncomplimentary and it spells praise when it's your right ear. Then, if there's a *ringing* in your left ear, that's bad news coming; good news for ringing right ears.

Now, there is a way to fight back when your left ear burns. Pinch it good and hard. That causes the unseen gossip to bite her tongue!

Adage: Boned wisdom for weak teeth.
Ambrose Bierce

PIERCE MY EARS! I SEE LAND AHEAD!

Parents used to think they could improve a child's eyesight by piercing its ears. Not quite as confusing as it sounds — in many ancient cultures, amulets worn in the ears were supposed to ward off evil spirits and strengthen one's senses.

At one time, sailors were strong believers that a ring in one pierced ear gave them acute vision. On some occasions it gave them sore ears, too.

Snapping the fingers for luck dates back to ancient times when any sudden noise was useful in frightening off the forces of evil.

LEFT IS NOT RIGHT!

Superstition about left-handedness pervades many cultures. It isn't bad enough that the words for left-handed have been *sinister* in Latin, *gauche* in French and *gawk* in old English, but now we discover the Hawaiians take their word for left — *hema* — and double it to *hemahema* to mean awkward or unskilled.

There was a time in Japan when left-handed children were beaten on that pretext alone. And, if a Japanese woman had hidden her left-handedness before marriage, it was grounds for annulment.

Chiropodists bathe their toes in ***mistle.***

BEAUTY MARKS!

Our informants in the court of Louis XIV report that imitation moles (or *beauty marks*) enhance a lady's pure white skin by contrast.

As to real moles, there's a superstition for almost any location on the body you can think of. If it's on the breast, you're in for a life of poverty. A mole on the arm, live on a farm. A mole on the chin or near the ear is a joyful matter because it spells great riches. Good luck comes to those with a mole on the throat, but if it's on the forehead near the hairline, call your insurance man.

It seems to be a different story with warts. No luck at all is attached to having warts, and that probably explains why there are so many wart cures. We like the one that instructs the warty one to rub the undesirable object with the end of a corn cob; then bore a hole in a tree, stuff the cob in the hole and plug it up. If the wart doesn't disappear, you've got double trouble — you may have killed your tree, too.

In Norse mythology, the first man was created from an ***ash tree*** *and the first woman from an* ***aspen.*** *No word yet whether it was a* ***quaking aspen*** *or not.*

RIDDLE: Are the eyebrows significant?

ANSWER: Assuredly! If they're close together, you'll always live near your present home. Far apart and you'll roam. If your eyebrows are extremely bushy, you may be related to John L. Lewis.

HOLDING HANDS!

We'd be a bit worried about someone who wishes to examine your hand. He may be practising *chirognomy*. That's an old art of judging character by the appearance of the hands. For instance, if you have thick, short fingers, your friendly little chirognomist is saying to himself, "A klutz!" If your fingers taper from a broad base on the other hand (you're strange; your hands don't match) he's sizing you up as witty, even artistic.

If your hands are bony and a bit bent and your knuckles protrude, he figures you're good at solving philosophical problems. Those with frail hands, long tapering fingers and almond-shaped fingernails he can predict will be impractical and idealistic, but with certain intuitive powers.

Then, if he begins to examine the fatty tissue at the base of your fingers (he calls them *mounds*), watch out: that's the mount of Jupiter at the base of your forefinger and can indicate intelligence and caution, while the mount of Mercury at the base of your little finger can signify a practical nature.

Be on the lookout for the chap that starts telling your future from your hand. He's not practicing *chirognomy* at all, but *chiromancy* or *palmistry*.

Finally, there is the super-specialist. He's the one who can learn everything about you merely by examining your fingernails. His art is called *onychomancy*. He can be foiled by sloppy manicuring and fingernail biting.

Beware of people who point with their aftfingers!

You've heard that people with itchy palms are greedy. Probably based on the following warnings: an itching left hand indicates money slipping away, while an itching right hand means it's coming your way.

Stop cutting your nails! Don't you know it's Friday?

NOT BY THE HAIRS OF YOUR CHINNY-CHIN-CHIN!

There was a time when a dimpled chin was more than a cute feature. It was believed it guaranteed that the owners of dimpled chins would never commit murder. However, don't stand too near a man trying to shave down inside that maddening little depression.

When someone talks about me behind my back, it makes my ears turn.

The terrible things they used to say about dragonflies. In Iowa, the dragonflies went after any barefooted person and sewed his toes together. Evidently New England dragonflies were an even meaner breed, swooping down and sewing together nostrils, ears, eyelids and lips. So button your lip, junior, before a dragonfly does it for you!

Don't have a dress fitted with black pins. Bad, bad luck!

GETTING HELP FROM BABIES!

It was once thought that *footlings* — infants born feet-first — would then have lifelong healing powers, especially for rheumatic aches and pains. Babies born by Caesarian section were purported to have the power to see invisible spirits and even to locate buried treasure. In America's southeast, they once believed that the first person to carry an infant outdoors imparted his personality traits to the child. And, in the midwest, a double-crown was a sure sign the child would eventually live on two continents...not simultaneously, we presume.

In parts of England, the very superstitious couldn't wait for baptism, so they drove away evil spirits by dousing the baby's head in rum. A honey shampoo accomplished the same purpose in Wales.

The Spanish once believed water into which a wedding ring had been dropped was a sure cure for sore eyes.

PREDICTING THE FUTURE CAN GET PRETTY HAIRY!

Samson was one of the early believers in associating hair with strength. But in a later time, there were those who felt fearsome spirits could enter the body through the hair, so they couldn't wait to snip it off.

Hair addicts were certain that hair on the back of the hand was a sure sign of getting rich soon.

Mothers used to feed their little girls bread crumbs being certain that such a diet would induce curly hair.

And stop worrying about your hair breaking off. It's almost half as strong as steel.

RIDDLE: Who said, "From birth to age 18 a girl needs good parents...from 18 to 35 she needs good looks...from 35 to 55 she needs a good personality...from 55 on she needs good cash"?

ANSWER: Sophie Tucker said it. And she meant it, too.

There was a time when women with a *widow's peak* surreptitiously shaved it off because its very existence foretold she'd lose her first husband and remarry right afterwards. We presume the first husband didn't object.

Samuel Johnson described a second marriage as "the triumph of hope over experience."

ANOTHER HAIRY ONE!

In Germany and the Ozark area of America, a dandy way to get a headache was to cut off some of your hair and leave it around where a bird might build a nest from it. But, in Morocco, a woman could cure her headache by cutting her hair and draping it over a tree limb.

Some of America's backwoods folk had a hair cure for asthma. First, a hole was bored in a tree trunk. Then the afflicted party was backed up to the tree, and a wad of his or her hair was stuffed into the hole and then snipped off. When the bark grew over the hair-filled hole, the asthma was supposed to disappear. A person could wait quite a spell for this to work, it seems.

She wears spit curls in the morning and bangs at night.

PLAYING IT SAFE!

White men, exploring Borneo in the 1800's, discovered that the *Sarawaks* feared their lives might slip out from their fingertips, so they tied a palm leaf around one wrist. Of course, there was always the danger of the palm leaf coming untied, so they tattooed a palm leaf on the wrist and relaxed.

If a hairpin comes loose in your coiffure, your lover is thinking about you.

DIRE DOINGS IN THE BATH!

At one time in England and some sections of America it was thought bathing would wash away a person's good luck. (Maybe *filthy rich* comes from this.)

Those brave souls who risked all and bathed once or twice a year still listened to such warnings as: he who bathes in May will soon be laid in clay; he who bathes in June will *sing* a merry tune; and he who bathes in July will *dance* a merry tune. Inasmuch as the poesy ends there, we assume no one bathed after July or before June.

There was a time when Welsh coal miners wouldn't wash their backs. They were convinced that, if they did, the roof of the coal pit would fall in on them.

HAIRPIECES!

Sometimes it takes a lot of money to carry a superstition to its most idiotic extremes. Such is the case with wigs.

In ancient times, a full head of hair was a necessity because it frightened off enemies and evil spirits. Bald men, no braver than their hairy cousins, resorted to wigs if they could afford them.

In the 18th Century, the wig blossomed into a fashion craze, especially for women and most especially for those in the court of the French kings. A first-class wigmaker of those days turned out thirty-eight different styles using names such as *pigeon's wing, flying star, wild boar's back, artichoke* and *bell tower.*

As wigs grew in height and intricacy, they became monstrous dust-catchers. And, since the ladies of the day were not the cleanliest and because they often used butter to give their wigs a sheen, wigs were infested with lice and even mice. A day in court was an assault on the nose.

Today, it's the man's turn again, but being bald can be confusing as hell. Do you want a hair transplant? How about an implant? One scarcely hears of switches, rugs or toupees anymore. It's hair replacement, hair weaving, skin graft with hair and who knows what other hair alternatives. If a man doesn't want to buy his way out of baldness, he can *lease* a topper. There are even hair-piece service centers (just fill it up, I had the oil changed last week).

Throughout this hair-raising tale you've undoubtedly noticed that

RIDDLE: Have some primitive tribes admired baldness in their women?

ANSWER: One of the Amazon Indian tribes even made a ceremony of it. While the drums beat and an older male relative lectured a young girl on how to become marriageable, several female relatives pulled out all her hair, a tuft at a time.

it costs money to be hairy. The emergence of the expression *bigwig* to describe the important personage is no accident.

For pretty hair, my darling daughter,
Wash it once in March snow-water.
For the other eleven months,
you'll just have to look tacky.

There are some curious superstitions about water. One old claim is that drinking well-water exclusively will make you grow tall. (Now they tell me.) Then there's, "Wash your hair in summer rain and see your lover once again." For heaven's sake, be careful not to get wet when doing your laundry...it could ordain you'll marry a drunkard.

I fear the man who drinks water. He remembers this morning what the rest of us said last night.

Some call them *water witchers*. Some call them *dowsers.* Some call them uncanny the way they can take a forked stick and locate underground water.

They say mulberry and apple twigs make good dowsing rods, as long as they're taken from a bearing tree.

Once the water has been located, the trick is to determine how deep it is. Here is where dowsers differ. Some carefully count the number of times the dowsing rod dips and then they multiply it by three feet. Others put a glass of water over the spot, dangle a gold ring on a thread in the water and count the numbers of times the ring strikes the sides of the glass.

Unsuccessful water witchers have been heard to say, "It's thirsty work."

If you spent some of your idle hours doing something useful, like weighing water, you'd already know that an inch of water weighs 100 tons per acre.

MOTHER OF MUCH MAGIC!

Mother Russia was a place of many peoples and an equal number of superstitions. The *Turkomans,* for example, were convinced that healthy babies could be assured only if the mothers gave birth while standing. A frail *Turkoman* woman could have a couple of friends support her, but no lying down!

In another part of Russia, they let a bride know what she was in for during the wedding ceremony. The *I do's* were scarcely over, when they put a wreath of wormwood on the bride's head to remind her how bitter married life was going to be. And to remind her of a duty to be totally obedient, she had to knock her head against her new husband's shoe.

Many Russians wouldn't hear of conducting a wedding until all doors, windows and the chimney had been closed against witches.

Some Russian men delighted in a typical superstition of bridegrooms: to wash a bride-to-be's sins away, it was a good idea to have her sleep once with a stranger.

Then there were the *Ostiacs*...a very suspicious lot! If a man began to question his wife's fidelity, in his mind, he could solve the problem simply. He cut some hair from any bear which happened to be standing nearby and handed it to his wife. If she took it without hesitation, his fears had been groundless. Let her refuse the handful of bear hair — and out she went.

So, what prevented a guilty wife from faking it a bit? You don't know your superstition. If a faithless wife even so much as touched one bear hair, that same bear would have come looking for her and would have torn her into very small pieces...even if he were dead, himself.

So, beware of Russians bearing bear hair!

Brides of northern England wept on their wedding days just for luck.

KEEP AN EYE ON THAT DAHOMEY GIRL'S TOES!

There was a time when a Dahomey man had to be observant, if he wanted a happy life and children. A woman with pubic hair growing up to her navel would be lucky to produce more than one child. If she were flat-footed, she'd flatten her husband financially. No hair growing down to the nape of the neck also spelled bankruptcy. Walking with her toes outward was a sure sign she would bring him unhappiness; and the same thing would happen to him, if she let her arms dangle loosely when walking.

What if he spotted all these signs but overlooked the fact that her big toe overlapped the next toe? He was a goner!

If either husband or wife snuck a blade of grass into the marriage bed, the other would die soon.

RIDDLE: When fathers-to-be have sympathetic labor, what is it called?

ANSWER: *Couvade*. Came in handy at one time in parts of England: when an unwed girl went into labor, her father scoured the village for any man sick in bed at the time. He was considered the rightful father. The Basques and the Corsicans believed *couvade* so thoroughly that newborn babes were brought to the father's bed; he was pampered and cared for, while the mother was sent out to work pronto!

We think it would have been far safer to have been a bachelor in Dahomey!

*Is a forgetful lover one who can't remember if it's **his** terectomy or **hers**?*

DO WE SMELL A GROOM!

In the 1800's, you had no trouble sensing that a Swedish bridegroom was in the vicinity. To protect himself from trolls and other evil spirits which might put a curse on his upcoming wedding, he sewed garlic and chives into his clothing.

People with three nostrils smell better.

MARRY YOUR OWN PRACTICAL NURSE!

It's a wise idea to marry a girl with the same last name as yours. It gives her the power to cure measles, scarlet fever and a few other things. Also, you don't have to change your stationery.

German brides and grooms must have had itchy feet in the days when they sprinkled dill seed and salt in their shoes to ward off witchcraft.

STRICTLY FOR THE LADIES!

Do you want to know who your future husband will be? You have a choice of three methods for finding out. First, you can count nine stars for nine nights, and he'll appear. Or, drink a glass of white wine mixed with rose water and then stare at the Moon through a silk scarf and there he'll be. If those two don't work, write the name of your three most likely prospects on three separate slips of paper and put them under your pillow. Before you fall asleep, throw one of the slips away. When you awaken, throw another slip away. That third one has the magic name of Mr. Right. Of course, there was a girl who cheated on this one — put the same name on all three slips!

Walking down certain aisles is considered unlucky by bachelors!

LOVE AND XXXX!

That XXXX for kisses started in medieval times. (Just as today, illiterates put their X-mark on documents.) Then, to give the signature the power of an oath, they were required to kiss the X. Eventually the X came to stand for kiss.

In Burma, sniffing one another's faces takes the place of kissing.

NANGGANANGGA AND THE MISSIONARIES!

Judging from the fact that there are some unmarried Fiji Island men, their god, *Nangganangga* has lost out to Christianity. Before the missionaries brought their civilizing ways, a Fiji Islander knew that *Nangganangga* stood at the gates of the Fijian paradise and turned back all bachelors. Naturally, there weren't any!

If you don't believe that bachelors know more about women than married men do, ask yourself why they are still bachelors.

FATEFUL DAY!

Weddings were looked upon as fateful days in more ways than one. Not all aspects of marriage are fraught with superstition, however: the bride's position at the left of the groom was to keep his sword arm free (a bit unhandy for left-handed grooms). It was strictly business when it came to rings, too. The engagement ring signified that the bride had been bought and paid for. But, from the days when a great many brides were kidnapped, the wedding ring was thought to be a magic circle which prevented anyone from stealing the bride from her owner or groom.

Timing was vital, too. May was a bad-luck month for marriage from the Roman habit of honoring dead spirits in that month. And the English Parliament and the church got together and had a law passed in 1642 which absolutely forbade any marriages between November 27 and January 13, from February 6 to April 18 and between May 16 and June 6.

It was back to business, though, when it came to the wedding certificate. That document was intended to define what food and clothing and other niceties the husband would provide and what the wife's duties were to be. Later on, they added a few provisions to cover a wife's rights, if her husband divorced her or died ahead of her.

Don't overlook the wedding cake, because it was significant, too. In ancient times, it symbolized fertility, and it was a lucky bride who had the wedding cake thrown at her. To Fiji Islanders, eating cake in public could constitute a marriage all by itself.

RIDDLE: Is carrying a bride over the threshold a superstition?

ANSWER: It is, and an old one. In ancient Rome, Vesta was the virgin goddess. So, at the very point of leaving maidenhood, if a bride were to touch the threshold, it would anger Vesta and result in bad luck in the marriage.

NOW, THAT WAS A CROCK AND A HALF!

Whether it was natural exuberance or an easy way to get rid of broken pots, the Prussians felt duty-bound to throw great quantities of cracked crockery against the front door of a newly married couple. The bigger the heap of rubble at one's doorstep, the greater the esteem of their friends.

Do 'bachelor buttons' propagate illicitly?

NO WEDDING BELLS UNLESS...

Before the ceremony in ancient Ireland, the wedding party went to the nearest Druidess who did a little fortune-telling stunt by throwing pebbles in the air and catching them on the back of her hand. If she said things didn't look favorable, the wedding was postponed...or canceled if the couple were overly superstitious.

In many parts of Europe during the Middle Ages, brides were elated if a cat sneezed in their presence the day before a wedding.

A couple couldn't feel safe until they were inside a church. For instance, it was a dreadful omen to meet a priest, rabbit, dog, lizard, cat or snake on your way to the church. Contrarily, it was a bit alright to run into a wolf, spider or toad en route to your wedding.

And the fisherman living in Norfolk and Suffolk weren't about to tempt fate. All their weddings took place at high tide. (Above the waterline, we presume.)

Weddings at sea are concluded with the cry, "Man overboard!"

GOOD HEAVENS! TURN THE SPINNING WHEEL AROUND!

Before a bride in the Black Forest allowed her dowry to be taken off to her husband's house, she took a few required precautions. Five crosses had to be sewn into the wedding bedcover to keep witches away. When her spinning wheel was loaded onto the cart, its side had to face the horses...that is, if she valued painless childbirth. The superstitious rituals didn't end there. Before the dowry-cart was unloaded, the new husband took consecrated chalk and put a magic mark on every item; and, in case some of the local witches had Christian inclinations, he sprinkled all the contents with holy water. (Nothing like a damp bedsheet on the first night.)

Useful wedding gifts are apparently considered bad luck!

MAY THE BEES FLEE FROM YOUR BLOUSE!

We know where the messages inside Chinese fortune cookies come from. The Cantonese used to suspend paper strips from the canopy of the nuptial bed with such goodies as, "May you have a hundred sons and a thousand grandsons." At this point, some brides passed out.

Biting was considered affectionate in China at one time.

UNHAPPY THE BRIDE THE SUN SHINES ON TODAY!

Swedish brides used to have more superstitions than wedding gifts. Rain or a good snowfall was a good sign. To insure easy childbirth, she had to wear very plain shoes, but first her father inserted a silver coin into the left shoe to guarantee her prosperity. She also had to be careful not to tear any of her clothing — that was a sure sign her husband would become a wife-beater.

Finally, to make sure she wore the pants in that household, she bought a pin from one of her bridesmaids. (After all this, she was probably late for the wedding.)

As a safeguard to assure her dominance over her husband-to-be, in case the pin purchase didn't work, she made sure she saw him before he saw her, as the ceremony began. There was yet one more magical act to perform — to make sure her right foot was ahead of his at the altar. (What chance did the poor groom have?)

Slavic peoples once sprinkled corn and hops on a newly married couple for luck.

OUCH! THAT WAS AN ELEVEN TRIPLE-E!

In Scotland, old shoes were thrown at newly wedded couples. But they didn't confine this good-luck act to marriage ceremonies exclusively — they threw their old brogans at anyone beginning a new venture to assure his success.

At one time the lowland Scotch never served green vegetables at a wedding feast or wore green clothing to a marriage. That was the color of elves and sprites who had a reputation for all sorts of mischief.

On the Arabian peninsula, however, a bridegroom was tickled to wear a green turban for several days after the wedding. First, it was

RIDDLE: Did primitives also have superstitions about *marking* unborn children?

ANSWER: Indeed they did. The *Dyaks* of Borneo kept pregnant women away from fire for fear of *spotting* the baby; neither parent could eat fruit or the baby would have colic; and holes bored in wood resulted in a blind infant; and bathing in deep water could cause a baby to suffocate before birth.

Mohammed's sacred color. Second, it indicated to his chums that he had married a virgin. Big item with the good old boys of Arabia.

In Sumatra it was bad luck to add a second wife without paying the first wife 40 guilders.

MORE COLORFUL SUPERSTITIONS!

Green was looked upon as a very unlucky color for a bride or bridesmaids to wear in almost all countries of Europe. In Norway, it was a lucky color for wedding outfits.

The Eskimos were a color-conscious bunch, too. Maidens wore red ribbons to designate their condition to all comers. You could spot a married woman by her blue ribbons. And the unlucky lass who was neither a maiden nor a widow announced her status to the whole Eskimo world with green ribbons.

*The **Rejangs** of Sumatra flattened their children's noses for luck and beauty.*

BLUE BOYS!

Blue was a very significant color to the ancients — it could ward off evil. So boy babies were dressed in blue. Since a girl had far less value to the parents, they clad her in any old color. Pink, as a favorite color for girl babies didn't come along until much later. More discrimination, eh?

In this life there's only one safe time to travel feet-first — at birth.

GIVE US THE DISEASE; WE CAN'T STAND THE CURE!

Imagine covering a red string with hog manure and tieing it around your neck merely to prevent mumps from *going down*. Wouldn't you rather have the measles than a cup of tea made from sheep-droppings boiled in water, strained and then disguised a bit with honey? Epilepsy has to be better than eating a colt's tongue. Yet all these superstitious cures were actually practiced in America.

White and yellow were often associated with death among Asian people.

COLOR HER SILLY!

As sure as we stand here with a white rabbit's foot in one hand and a green four-leaf clover in the other, just about everything on earth colors the superstitious mind.

At one time it was thought that a person's selection of colors in clothing was a dead giveaway. The envious wore *green,* of course. *Yellow* signified silliness or jealousy. You were considered worldly-wise clad in *brown* but, in *orange,* you were thought to be naive, stupid or both. There were *reds* and then there were *reds.* One had to be very discerning to read character correctly in this category. For instance, *crimson* indicated animal passion, while *scarlet* was a sign of anger or other strong emotion. Just *plain red* offered a bit of latitude in judgment — from a sign of love to outright lust. But *bright red* was a simple matter — those were the confident and the courageous.

Just so the bride would not make a fatal error in selecting the color of her gown she was taught this poem:

Married in white, you have chosen alright;
Married in red, you'd be better dead;
Married in yellow, ashamed of the fellow;
Married in blue, your lover is true;
Married in green, ashamed to be seen;
Married in black, you'll ride a hack;
Married in pearl, you'll live in a whirl;
Married in pink, your spirits will sink;
Married in brown, you'll live out of town.

Come to think of it, we don't recall seeing many brides in red, green, black or brown.

A warning to bridesmaids: We know you believe that being a bridesmaid is supposed to mean you will become a bride within a year, but don't stumble as you go up the aisle. That means you'll be an old maid...or clumsy!

APRIL'S CHILDREN: DON'T WEAR EMERALDS!

Amulets were favorite good-luck charms among the ancients, and they often wore their birthstone in the center. Thus, birthstones gained the reputation of promising certain qualities to the wearer. January's *garnet* implies truth and fidelity. Sincerity is indicated by February's *amethyst*, and the Greeks also felt it helped to keep one

RIDDLE: Does a wedding on April Fool's Day have any special significance?

ANSWER: Yep. Means the woman will be boss, which doesn't really set April 1st apart from the other 364 days.

sober. The *bloodstone* supposedly imparted courage to those born in March, while April's *diamond* stood for innocence. Potency in love was in store for May *emerald-wearers.* Those with June birthdays have a great choice: the *pearl* if they're looking for purity; the *agate* if they prefer health and long life...especially protection from poison. There are two July birthstones, too — *ruby* or *carnelian* — but either was said to bring contentment and bravery. The *sardonyx* promised married happiness to August children. And the *sapphire* of September was a lulu — it was Jupiter's magic stone, so it protected the wearer from misery. Hope stemmed from October's *opal* and fidelity from November's *topaz.* Perhaps they had Christmas shopping in mind when they attributed prosperity to December's birthstone, the *turquoise.*

It was considered bad luck to wear birthstones from months other than the month of your birth.

How were young men forced into marriage before the invention of the shotgun?

CHEER UP, WEDNESDAY'S CHILD!

For all you young whippersnappers who haven't heard the poem which forecasts your future by the day of the week on which you were born, here 'tis:

Monday's child is fair of face,
Tuesday's child is full of grace,
Wednesday's child is sorry and sad,
Thursday's child is merry and glad,
Friday's child is loving and giving,
And Saturday's child must work for a living,
But the child that is born on the Sabbath Day
Is bonny and merry and glad and gay.

(If you weren't born on any of the above, we don't know what will become of you.)

Iranians believe Judgment Day will come on a Wednesday, so it's a bad-luck day.

OH, DOCTOR!

An old belief was that it was unlucky to see a doctor on a Friday. We can't see the great good fortune in seeing a doctor on any day.

Another superstition had it that to pay a doctor's bill in full would surely bring on a calamity. Now, there's a superstition we can hold with.

...'tis the eye of childhood that fears a painted devil.
Shakespeare

CHILDERMASS DAY!

December 28 was said to be the day King Herod had the children murdered, and so it became the worst possible date for one's birthday. It was considered an unfortunate day for many other happenings, too. King Edward IV of England felt so strongly about it in 1461, he changed his coronation day to another date. Louis XI ascended the French throne the same year and, he so feared Childermass Day, he never conducted any business on that date.

In a peculiar ritual designed to make children remember Herod's atrocity, many 16th Century Europeans beat their children at the end of Childermass Day.

Even into the 20th Century, no new construction was allowed and no traveling on December 28 in England.

You would have ruined the whole rice harvest in Sumatra if a young virgin didn't start things off!

BLACK UP, KID, THE PILGRIMS ARE HERE!

Lhasa is the holy city to Tibetans. Just in case the pilgrims who came there let their minds stray to matters other than religious meditation, the local women once had to blacken their faces and look tacky in general.

The natives of French Guinea changed their names every time they got sick to fool the evil spirits. It was about as effective as two aspirins.

BURN A *PLAYBOY*, HE'S SINKING FAST!

The Indians of Panama might never have accepted white men if it hadn't been for magazines.

It was their belief that every object possessed a soul. When one of the tribe fell ill, the medicine man rounded up an armload of illustrated magazines and began burning the pages that had pictures. Setting fire to the sheets freed the spirits of each object pictured. These spirits

RIDDLE: What's the best day to move downstairs in an apartment building?

ANSWER: Never move *down* in the same building. For other moves, Wednesdays and Mondays are good. Friday's unlucky as hell. And a Saturday move indicates a short stay. If your moving men are clumsy, there is no good day.

then hung about in front of the sick person's abode. In no time the 'picture objects' became such a source of fascination for the evil spirits, these nasty things forgot all about working their devilment on the victim. Rumor had it that early *National Geographics* were especially good for malaria.

Fear cannot be without hope nor hope without fear.
Spinoza

EVEN UNTO THE GRAVE!

Superstition certainly didn't end with death. One of the big fears was that the soul couldn't escape and would stay behind to bedevil the survivors. To prevent this, the family might open all doors, windows and locks, untie the curtains, turn all mirrors to the wall, remove any pillows made from game-bird feathers, and make sure the deathbed was in parallel with the floorboards. Salt sprinkled on the corpse and a bucket of brine under his bed helped, too.

Coins on the corpse's eyes prevented the bad luck of looking into them, as well as paying the toll fee for entry into the hereafter. Removal from the house was feet first or the soul would be lost. And, since it was bad luck to be the first interred in a new burial ground, the family would secure the corpse of a vagrant or criminal and bury it there first.

Definition of a eulogy: Praise paid for by dying.

STAND STILL, HE'S ABOUT TO RUIN YOUR LIFE!

Hindus took astrology so seriously it forced them into fatalistic views. A child's horoscope, cast by a soothsayer, outlined everything that would happen in the youngster's life — joy, sorrow, disease, accident, marriage date, number of children he or she would have, how many would survive to adulthood and even whether this next generation would shame or honor them.

Since the Hindu referred to this lifetime horoscope constantly, and believed in it, he felt helpless to affect his own destiny in the slightest way. (Nice way to control people, eh?) He did have one alternative — buy his way out of a part of his fate.

Old age is a tyrant who forbids, on penalty of death, all the pleasures of youth. *LaRochefoucauld*

"IT'S IN THE STARS," SAID THE MAN IN THE MOON!

Okay, astrology buffs, you wanted the signs of some famous people, so here they are: *Capricorn,* Paul Revere; *Aquarius*, Abe Lincoln and F.D.R.; *Pisces,* George Washington; *Aries,* Charles Chaplin; *Taurus,* Adolph Hitler and Shirley Temple (some combination); *Gemini,* Al Jolson; *Cancer*, Jack Dempsey; *Leo*, Herbert Hoover; *Virgo,* Greta Garbo; *Libra*, Christopher Columbus; *Scorpio*, Daniel Boone and Paderewski (a lot in common, those two); *Sagittarius,* Winston Churchill.

While we're at it, root crops should be planted in between the Moon's first quarter and the full Moon, leafy plants when the Moon is on the wane, peas in the light of a full Moon and potatoes only in the dark of the Moon, preferably on Good Friday. Also for farmers, the Moon weather forecast:

Pale Moon, doth rain,
Red Moon doth blow,
White Moon doth
Neither rain nor snow.

And if you don't think it's dangerous to sleep out under the moonlight, where do you think we got the words *lunacy, loony* and *moonstruck?*

The seventh son of a seventh son has more aunts and uncles than he needs!

BURY ME NOT ON THE GAY PRAIRIE!

The established regimen for Sioux Indian boys, upon entering manhood, was to be trained in hunting and making war. Sioux mothers, not unlike mothers everywhere, had a natural inclination to protect their sons from the violence and death that often came to Sioux warriors at an early age. Some mothers put their feelings into action, dressing their young sons as women and training them to make clothing, war bonnets, shields and in other women's chores.

When these young men, called *winkte*, were old enough, they erected their tepees in a part of the encampment usually reserved for elderly widows.

Sioux warriors looked down upon the *winkte* for being 'womanly'. But there was respect, too. Clothing and war paraphenalia made by *winkte* usually brought a higher price, because they were better made. Also, there was a superstition that *winkte* possessed a magical power

RIDDLE: Where should you be on September 1, if you wish to attend the Festival of the Hungry Ghost?

ANSWER: Singapore is the spot. Might as well stick around for the Moon Cake Festival. It's another Singapore celebration held September 30.

— dreaming up a secret name for a young boy which would protect him from all danger. Sioux fathers often paid dearly for such a name...a treasured horse, for example. The secret names were thought to have such power they never were spoken aloud. The only ones who ever knew a boy's secret name, aside from himself, were his father and the *winkte.*

The last time we saw Harris, he was young and gay!

UNDER THE VOODOO SPELL!

In the Dahomey area of Africa, the word *voodoo* meant *spirit* or *god.* In Haiti, *voodoo* literally became a religion; but a religion intermixing pagan deities and beliefs with standard Catholic practices. Even though a Haitian must be a Catholic before he can conduct voodoo rites, he doesn't think of it as mixing two religions.

Voodoo *loas* (gods or often, mysteries) are frequently depicted as Catholic saints. The Snake God, *Damballah,* looks like St. Patrick because they know of his ridding Ireland of snakes. *Ouga-ferraille,* God of Iron and War, is a dead ringer for St. James the Greater, complete to the armor.

Other voodoo gods have some very human traits. For instance, *Ageve-Taroyo,* God of the Sea (usually shown as a green-eyed mulatto) can be placated by putting out a glass of champagne for him. *Zaka,* God of Agriculture, is a greedy, suspicious fellow who doesn't trust city slickers. The voodoo Goddess of Feminine Beauty, *Ezili-Freda,* is beautiful, but she's spoiled so rotten she'll spend every cent for her own pleasure. And the God of the Dead, *Baron-Samedi,* is shown in a typical undertaker's outfit — top hat, black suit, black cane but *white* gloves. Three of his symbols are the pick, the shovel and the hoe.

The *crise mystique* — possession by a god — is rather straightforward. The possessed is called a *choal* or God's horse. Once in a trance — real or pretended — he carries on in the fashion of the god possessing him. For instance, if *Damballah,* the Snake God, has hold of him, he'll crawl around on the ground, darting out his tongue.

As to acts of sorcery, the *zombie* is the best known. A *zombie* is supposed to be the possession of a live person by the body and spirit of a dead one. The voodoo sorcerers whip up some other nifties — *galipots, bizagos* and *zobops. Zobops* are any greedy individuals who buy a so-called *burning charm* from a sorcerer. It is said to render them amoral, especially when it comes to robbery. It makes a very convenient excuse for some; there are even *auto-zobops* who travel about in cars to rob. Female vampires are reputed to exist on the blood of infants. So gullible Haitian mothers bathe their babies in a foul-smelling concoction that supposedly "spoils the blood" for thirsty vampires.

***Saffar** was a bad-luck day in Iran. It was the thirteenth of the month.*

CHAPTER SEVEN

Say It Isn't So; And Even If It Is, Don't Say It!

Facts are the rubble of civilization. People, seeing a pile of facts lying about, can't wait to go scrabbling through them, deluding themselves that enough of anything beats a lot of nothing. And once they've taken hold of a fact, nothing will persuade them to let it go. Some take several of these discarded facts and try to make something out of them...such as an argument or a theory. We say, don't ask a fact why he exists; accept him for what he is, and give him a warm corner of your mind. Don't bother to feed him — facts are totally self-sustaining!

Just like the other day, we took out a small portion of our fact collection and thrilled to the joy of rediscovery. We had all but forgotten the immortal words of Leo Tolstoi: *The things I love most are screzha, vanichka, tanya, grinenka, ilya, sasha, andryusha, masha and lyova.* It took us a while to recall that those were the names of his children.

The fact that the River Seine was 541 feet wide as it entered Paris may not quicken your pulse. But, when you realize it is only 446 feet wide when it leaves the city, don't you hunger to know what went on between entrance and exit that caused it to lose 95 feet in width?

Baldness is one of those plain facts people cannot resist tinkering with. The Hungarians imply a great deal in their proverb: *a good man grows gray; others grow bald.* Even the ancient Chinese couldn't pass up taking a swipe at the hairless: *of ten bald men, nine are deceitful and the tenth is stupid.*

Some facts plunge people into a deep depression. We know a chap who wept uncontrollably for two weeks after learning that a cubic foot of gold weighs 1,204 pounds. He had always dreamed of stumbling upon a discarded cubic foot of gold and walking away with it unnoticed.

Archaeologists are always digging up facts. In 1940, they uncovered the skull of an eight-foot-long pig in South Dakota and we've never been able to forget it!

The most maddening facts are the ones coming out of surveys. Have you ever read of a survey in which your answers would have matched the majority opinion? *Who in hell do they ask?* And this isn't new: almost fifty years ago, some ninny with an opinion poll in one hand and a drawn conclusion in the other asked a group (2?) of American sailors what their favorite magazine was. He had the audacity to claim the majority preferred *The National Geographic*. The *Geographic*'s a great magazine, but you show us a crew with that as top choice and we'll show you a ship with one magazine on board.

Then there is a category of facts which we call *anti-facts*, because they run contrary to what you had always thought. For example, we were perfectly content to assume the letter *A* was the first letter in all alphabets. But, no, the *anti-facts* are that it's fourth in the Runic alphabet and thirteenth in the Ethiopian lineup. A hard drinker, we thought, was one who drank a quart of liquor a day; now, we discover it's one who *spills* that much. We also stand corrected — the *vitreous humor* is not half as funny as the *aqueous humor.* Nor do all *houseboys* have *housemothers*, as we'd once concluded. It turns out to be nothing

RIDDLE: Which took longer to build, the Brooklyn Bridge or London Bridge?

ANSWER: Yes! You see, the question wasn't specific. *Old* London Bridge, begun in 1170, took thirty-nine years to build. The Brooklyn Bridge was knocked out in a mere thirteen years. But, the *New* London Bridge (still standing) was started in 1824 and polished off in just seven years. Satisfied?

more than a rumor that *troglodytes* pay no inheritance taxes.

In general, *new* facts should not be given brain room. They may push out an old one you treasure. There are exceptions. For instance, we feel you should memorize the following: many people find themselves *full of wist* these days because there is *no stalgia.*

If you insist upon reading any further, we can only remind you of the words of Lord Byron:

Of all the horrid, hideous notes of woe,
Sadder than owl-songs or the midnight blast,
Is that portentous phrase, "I told you so."

Judge Crater is selling Datsuns in Puberty, Wisconsin!

OUT WITH THE TRUTH! OFF WITH HIS HEAD!

We have a friend...no, an acquaintance...in fact, we can't stand the guy! He has the deplorable habit of telling the whole truth about everyone he knows. Many of us have begged him to lie a little, yet he remains sadistically moral.

A political pundit of the twenties once commented that he had never believed the old adage that 'anyone born in America could become president' until Calvin Coolidge entered the White House.

FIRST AND LAST!

The first place to be named *America* was central Brazil. The last was the United States of America.

The first of our states in alcoholism is Alaska. The last is Iowa.

The first of the three wise monkeys is the one who sees no evil — *Mizaru.* The last speaks no evil and he's *Mazaru.* The guy in the middle, with his hands over his ears, is *Mikazaru.*

The first year there were over 222 thousand women in U.S. armed forces was 1944. It was also the last.

The first donut had no hole, but the center was so gummy the baker couldn't sell them. So he removed the center. The last donut we had was gummy all around the hole.

The first of the three wise men coming from Persia to find Jesus was Kaspar, then Melchior and trailing, Balthasar.

The first part of a rainstorm is rain. What else? The last part, if the drops refract the sunlight just right, is a rainbow.

When a Spanish explorer discovered an arid valley in southern Nevada, the first word that hit him was *llanos*... sterile plains. The last words that would have come to his mind are the words we know it by now — *Las Vegas*...fertile plains (no doubt for casino operators).

Renoff is a Nevada city without limits!

BORDER TO BORDER!

How did the town of *Florala* get its name? Simple. It's on the Florida-Alabama border. The Kansas-Colorado border has its *Kanorado;* Delaware-Maryland, its *Delmar*. *Kenova* borrowed from the meeting point of three states — Kentucky, Ohio, and West Virginia. Of course, Texas holds the record with three communities using its name — *Texico* on the Texas-New Mexico line, *Texhoma* on the border with Oklahoma, and *Texarkana* on the Arkansas line.

But imagine the possibilities still open. Washington and Idaho could share in *Wash-Ida.* Iowa and Nebraska could spawn a community with a name smacking of a college cheer — *Iowaska!* The new city of *Penny* could rise on the Pennsylvania-New York border. Every time you pay your taxes, you would want to be in the Ohio-Kentucky border town of *Ohucky.* And, for a select few, there could be the Virginia-Maryland paradise of *Virginland.*

Hey, Peru! Ecuador is skidding your way at the rate of 9 centimeters a century!

BUSTED DREAM!

Dear to a *triviaddict's* heart are *biggest* and *highest* anything. Remember when Los Angeles bragged of being the biggest city in the world with 458 square miles? And then Jacksonville, Florida snatched the crown away by going to 827 square miles. Well, Juneau, Alaska pulled the rug out from under Jacksonville, picking up Douglas Island to push their square mileage to 3,108.

Then there's the matter of the highest national capital. For years we thought La Paz, Bolivia at 12,000-plus feet above sea level was the champ. Now, we're told La Paz is not really the legal capital of Bolivia. It's Sucre, which is much lower. So, hats off to Lahasa, Tibet, elevation 11,800 feet. Damn!

Dr. P.A. Zahl found 6-inch long beetles in Brazil in 1957.

RIDDLE: Is the *Prado* the largest building in Spain?

ANSWER: The *Prado*, Spain's national art museum in Madrid, is nowhere near as large as the former royal palace outside Madrid — the *Escorial*. In addition to an art gallery and fine library, the Escorial contains a monastery, the royal tombs, a church, a college and the royal palace. Begun in 1563, it took twenty-one years to complete.

A couple in Wyoming were entertaining a gentleman from Texas. After a week of being told how everything in Texas was bigger and better, they took the Texan to Yellowstone National Park to see the great geyser, Old Faithful.

"Now," the Wyoming host said proudly, "tell me you have something like that in Texas."

"No siree!" the Texan answered. "But we've got a plumber who could fix it."

Saudi Arabia denies it plans to build a statue of Joan Orlando in the middle of Lake Michigan!

In what is now Michigan, there lived an Indian chief named Etiwanda. There is an American town named after this chief. And of course, it's in Southern California.

Italy forgot to signal when it turned left!

There's a street in San Mateo County, California with the imposing name *Alameda de las Pulgas.* It's a bit less imposing when translated...Poplar-lined Avenue of the Fleas.

Sign in small cafe: WE DESERVE THE RIGHT TO SERVE REFUSE TO ANYONE! And they did. We tried.

Montana, Idaho and Wyoming all have a chunk of Yellowstone National Park.

ON THE BRINK OF ONE MORE BRINK!

It is believed that the last survivors of the long-lost city of Muscatel were manning the UFO which was sighted last Wednesday during a husking bee outside the community of Lerth, Arkansas. Although scientists admit to some conjecturing on their part, they feel that the small gray cork dropped from the UFO supports their Muscatel-survivor theory. On its top was printed the single word *PIME*. The cork also had a sickly sweet odor. Dr. Heidi Spil, who led the cork recovery team, was so elated at the find she was unprofessionally ill at the site.

A person who hasn't been around is called a square!

THE HIGH AND LOW OF IT!

The highest piece of *terra firma* in Florida is 345 feet above sea level, which is 3,005 feet under the lowest point in Colorado. Thanks to the Rocky Mountains, Colorado's *average* elevation is 6,800 feet, putting the 'mile-high city', Denver, below average. Wyoming's average is just 100 feet less.

On the low side, Delaware beats out Florida with an average elevation of 60 feet over sea level. In fact, Delaware is so low, a Kansas senator once described Delaware as, "A state that has three counties when the tide is out; two, when it's in."

Mt. Mitchell in North Carolina is the highest mountain (6,688 feet) east of the Rocky Mountains, but less than half as high as many peaks in the Rockies. But the highest point on the Atlantic Coast from Massachusetts to Florida is little Todt Hill on Staten Island in New York Harbor. It's a breathtaking 430 feet high.

Remember the good old *Pylae Ciliciae*, or Cilician Gates...that pass through Turkey's Taurus mountains? Without so much as a by-your-leave they've changed the name to *Gulek Bogazi*. Really!

Mt. Nerth, somewhere east of Rangoon, is said to be the world's lowest mountain, rising a mere two inches above sea level.

Famous mountaineer, Glives Billery, when asked why he had climbed Mt. Nerth, replied, "Frankly, old chap, I didn't see it."

Dr. S. Dillon Ripley caught a spiny babbler in Nepal in 1948! Good!

RIDDLE: Many states have taken their names from Indian words. Using a bit of logic, which state meant "few springs" in Indian?

ANSWER: An Indian word for "Few Springs" is Arizonac. Appropriate?

ON A CLEAR DAY IN COSTA RICA!

The latest sucker-bet, geographical division, is that a person can see both the Atlantic and Pacific oceans from one spot. Weather permitting, you can do just that on top of Mt. Irazu (12,600 feet) in Costa Rica.

Before throwing caution to the winds, throw a little precaution!

HIGH ON WHAT MOUNTAIN?

We all know that the heads of Washington, Jefferson, Lincoln and Theodore Roosevelt have been carved into stone in the Black Hills of South Dakota. What's confusing is that this is known as the Mount Rushmore National Memorial, but the mountain, itself, is Harney's Peak. Is anyone else mixed up?

The Canadian town of ***Mammamattawa*** *is so small its citizens must explain that it is located at the confluence of the* ***Kenogami*** *and* ***Kabinakagami*** *rivers.*

CUT THAT ROCK! TOTE THAT STONE!

When the Mormons got ready to build their mammoth Temple in Salt Lake City, they knew right where to go for building material. Up in the Wasatch Range, about twenty miles from the site, there was a whole canyon full of giant granite boulders strewn about by glaciers. With hand drills and chisels, they bored and cut great slabs of granite. Then they'd load up carts, hitch up four pairs of oxen to each cart and set off. Three or four days later they'd be unloading and turning back to the canyon for more. Fortunately for the oxen, after a few years of this fun job, the railroad came through and the granite went by rail after that.

Flowerpot Island *is northeast of* ***Cabot Head*** *and* ***Cape Chin, Ontario, Canada.***

ISLAND WITH NO WATER!

About ten miles inland from the Italian port city of Rimini you'll find the world's oldest existing republic, *San Marino*. It is entirely surrounded by Italy. Maybe it has gone undisturbed since the middle ages because it was overlooked...it's only 23 square miles in area.

Two Mississippi River flood victims, safely on a rooftop, watched beds, chairs and other items float by. All at once they noticed a hat float by and then float back towards them.

"What do you make of that?" one man said.

"It's just my hired hand," the other replied. "He said he'd plow today come Hell or high water."

Talk about wasting water: the Mississippi River discharges more water (into the Gulf of Mexico) than all the rivers of Europe combined.

BRIDGING THE GAP!

Did you know that New York City's *George Washington Bridge*, (spanning the Hudson River) on the hottest day of summer is almost three feet longer than it is on the coldest day of winter? Fortunately, the people who built it knew it would expand and contract that much. Whew!

Lake Buenos Aires is over 1,200 miles from Buenos Aires and is half in Chile.

ISLAND OF ROUGH WATER!

Sable Island, south of Newfoundland and east of Nova Scotia, lies in some of the most feared waters that ships ever attempt to navigate. The area is called *The Graveyard of the Atlantic,* and poor Sable Island is stuck with the unpleasant name of *Isle of Lost Ships...* almost three hundred of them.

In Alberta, Canada, it's only a few miles from Whiskey Gap to the Milk River.

WATERING PLACES!

One of America's scenic wonders is Lake Tahoe, the blue jewel sitting astride the California-Nevada border 6,225 high in the Sierra Nevada.

John Fremont showed it on his map of the region simply as Mountain Lake. Later it was known, unpoetically, as Lake Bigler (after a California governor).

Although most experts agree that *Tahoe* is of Indian origin, they can't agree if it meant "a great deal of water" "deep and blue" or merely "big water."

The Pacific Ocean was first called the South Sea by the Spanish.

RIDDLE: Is the Danube a capital river?

ANSWER: You could say that! It flows through Austria's capital, Vienna; the capital of Hungary, Budapest; and through Belgrade, Yugoslavia's capital. That's about as *capital* as a river can get.

The Atlantic Ocean they called the North Sea. This would seem to indicate that, in the Fifteenth Century, the Sun rose in the north and set in the south; it would also put Alaska in the frozen west of West America, and the Incas of Peru in East America. Well, why not.

Peru's ***Lake Titicaca*** *is South America's largest; Bolivia's* ***Lake Poopo*** *isn't far back.*

If you sailed eastward between Calpe and Abyla, where would you be going? Into the Mediterranean Sea from the Atlantic Ocean. Those were the names for what the Ancients called The Pillars of Hercules. Calpe, now known as Gibraltar, sat on the European side of the Straights of Gibraltar; Abyla, on the African shore.

As long as you're sailing, would it be closer to go from Paris, France to Melbourne, Australia by way of the Panama Canal or the Suez Canal? You'd save close to 800 miles going by way of Suez.

Last time we looked, Metropolis, Nevada had a population of 22.

TAKING THE MYSTERY OUT OF MIRAGES!

Sooner or later every child wants an explanation for a mirage. You tell the little scamp that the air right next to the hot desert sand, being hotter than the air above, reflects light much as water does. Same effect occurs on roads in summer.

The biggest ***ere*** *in our neighborhood is the western* ***hemisph!***

THE COOLING DESERT SUN!

In the Southwest they've known for years that the best way to cool water is to put it out in the Sun. The container they use is a porous earthenware jug, called an *olla*. The cooling results from fast evaporation. Ole to the *olla*.

Donald Olson dug a hole in his answering service and filled it with chlorinated water!

In case you think arctic exploration is a snap, remember that several arctic expeditions set up winter quarters at a place in Greenland called *Thank God Harbor.*

There's a little village in Siberia you'd love. Its name is Verkhoyansk. The region is called the Pole of Cold. Probably because the villagers have noticed that the thermometer sometimes drops to 90 degrees below zero.

Our favorite Pole is Tad!

HO HUM IN OUTER SPACE!

Facts to fall asleep over include: the Sun gives off 600,000 times more light than the Moon, accounting for the rarity of moonburn; the reason the Sun and Moon look to be the same size is that the Sun is about 400 times larger than the Moon and about 400 times further away; and you can stop thinking of it as *our* Sun — we only get about one two-billionth of its radiated energy.

Every shroud has a shiver lying in it.

ASTRONOMICAL MYTH!

The story goes that after the planet *Pluto* was discovered, selecting a name was sticky. They got it down to three — *Minerva, Cronus* and *Pluto*! Listen to the reason given for opting for *Pluto*: all the other planets were named for Roman gods, and they didn't want to break the pattern. Since when wasn't *Minerva* the Roman Goddess of Wisdom? If they meant to exclude females, what are they going to do about *Venus*? We can grasp why *Cronus* was eliminated — not only was he a god from Greek mythology, but he was also the counterpart of the Roman *Saturn*...and in case your telescope is fogged over, we already had a *Saturn*.

All in all, we're probably lucky *Pluto* wasn't named *Jack Scruggs*.

You're leaning the wrong way — the Earth rotates on its axis from west to east.

There's some good news and some bad news about the Caterpillar Club. The bad news is that eligibility required parachuting from a disabled airplane. The good news is that only survivors were admitted to membership.

*Because a **mango** looks like a bird's heart, it's said to be **anacardiaceous**. Hmph!*

RIDDLE: Where in hell is the North Star in October?

ANSWER: Don't know. Locate the Little Dipper. The North Star is the last one in its handle.

Joe Frisco on California climate: S-s-sometimes it's h-h-hot; s-sometimes it's c-c-cold. Y-you never know what to h-h-hock.

COMPARISON SHOPPING!

You'll probably be desolated, but that $15 pedicure you got in New York would have cost you only $3.50 in Sao Paulo, Brazil. In the major cities of the world, toilet tissue costs the most in Munich and the least in Madrid. Tokyo and Rome will nick you $29 for a dozen roses that you can get for $4 in Sao Paulo, but that metropolis charges 25 cents for a newspaper you can't even read and $2.50 for a gallon of gas.

Munich's $33.33 tab for blue jeans is two and half times higher than the Los Angeles price, but the German city is the cheapest for a bottle of Dom Perignon champagne. You could get a two-bedroom apartment in a good area for as little as $600 a month in Rome, whereas in Tokyo they'll ask from $1,400 to $2,500. Oddly, Tokyo asks the least for a double room in a good hotel — $66 — compared to $139 in Paris.

New York and Madrid taxi drivers charge the least; Munich and San Francisco's, the most. Tokyo's the best place to buy soft contact lenses; Los Angeles, the worst. But don't have a telephone installed in Tokyo — it runs $320. In Sao Paulo you have to buy the telephone...for somewhere between $750 and $3,500.

*Unless it moved, **Kakabeka Falls** is still on the **Kaministikwia River** in Ontario, Canada.*

COW UP, MBU, OR RETURN THE MERCHANDISE!

Don't make any wagers that *installment buying* is an American institution. It isn't Russian either. A couple of centuries before we even heard of installment buying, the Zulu tribesmen of Africa were going into debt as regularly as sundial-work. How else could a young Zulu man get a wife?

It worked like this: when he'd picked out his future bride, he casually stopped by her old man's hut with a down payment of four cows. That got him part way home. On the wedding day, the maiden's dad put the bite on the kid for another three cows. Now he had a month or so to try out the merchandise. If she passed muster, he had to make the final two-cow payment.

However, if our young Zulu didn't pony up on time, his loving father-in-law repossessed the bride and kept the first two installments of cows. There he was: brideless, cowless and with a lousy credit rating!

Would it surprise you to learn that **tax** *comes from a Latin word which means to touch sharply? And it hurts for a long time after, too.*

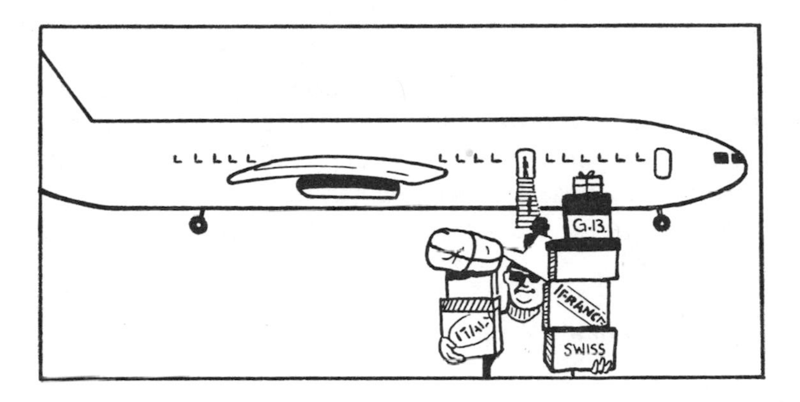

LIVING IT UP IN EUROPE!

In early 1978, the prices of food, booze and clothing in Europe could scare an American but, if he shopped around, he wouldn't fare too badly.

If you value your bucks half as much as the Europeans value your bucks, here's a money-saving itinerary: after breakfast, it's off to Great Britain for a man's suit; then over to Finland for a dress; next, whip down to Italy for cocktails and then double-back to Switzerland or Belgium for cigarettes; and then, it's off to Portugal for dinner.

The bottle of fine Scotch one paid $17.20 for in Sweden cost only $4.80 in Italy. A man's two-piece suit ran $260 in Belgium, but only $80 in England and $90 in Spain. Holland hit the ladies hardest — $85 for a dress; while Finland let the girls off for $26...but that same Scotch, again, ran $17.90 in a Finnish bottle shop.

And food? You shouldn't ask! You could consider yourself lucky if you spent only $90 in a Belgian or Swedish restaurant on a dinner for two. Meanwhile, in Portugal a dinner for two might not top $30.

Follow our plan and you'll save as much as $313 a day, less boat, train, taxi, bus and airplane fares. And you won't have wasted any time in museums, galleries, castles and cathedrals or beautiful countrysides.

RIDDLE: Is it *Doomsday Book* or *Domesday Book?*

ANSWER: Officially, the *Domesday Book*. It was a record of the economic status of England taken by William the Conqueror in 1086. However, since the purpose of this business census was to see how heavily he could tax the country, a great many people must have thought of it as the *Doomsday Book*.

Robert and Tita Weir just returned from a trip through Intestate.

STAND BACK FOR A WINDFALL!

Be prepared! It would be wise to acquire a wooden box whose interior dimensions are five feet wide by five feet deep by ten feet long. That's what you'll need if someone should give you one million silver dollars. If you received such a windfall in one-dollar bills, you'd only need a box three and a half feet wide by two feet deep by 5 feet long.

Never lift a gift horse by the mouth.

JOLLY ODD!

An American executive had recently returned from a four-year stint in his company's London office. Even after four years the British mystified him.

"I mean, there is a suicidal strain in the English. How else can one explain the compulsion to drink beer when it's warm and eat mutton when it's cold?"

The two best times of your life are meal and past!

HOT CHESS FLASH!

American chess champion, Paul Morphy, killed some time in Paris, in 1858, playing against eight French hotshots while he was blindfolded. End report! Hey, wait! Was anyone telling him what was going on with those eight boards? Was Morphy peeking? Did he win any of the games? This is what you get for reading trivia!

You'll never know how few people can count beyond ten until you play blackjack!

SHUT UP AND DEAL!

Card players have a standard explanation for a losing session: their lucky opponents got all the good cards. Some fifty years ago, a consistent loser invented a variation of bridge which he called *Nada*. The object of Nada was to *lose* tricks. A player calculating he could lose eleven of the thirteen tricks bid *nil*; twelve of the thirteen was a *grand nil*; and a bid to lose them all was called a *nada*.

Picture the inveterate Nada player arriving home after an all-night session. His devoted wife asks him how he did.

"Lousy. I couldn't hold anything but good cards all night."

Card players used to call the ace of diamonds the ***Curse of Scotland.***

UNCLE'S NEIGHBOR!

We had a saintly uncle who could not take it upon himself to speak ill of others. However, it was his misfortune to have a neighbor of astronomic thoughtlessness. Uncle Gerald bore it in gentlemanly silence.

At last the boorish neighbor came to borrowing Uncle Gerald's evening newspaper right off the front lawn, soon after it was delivered. Our aunt suggested he go next door and speak to the man.

"I can not abide the sight of the man," he replied, holding himself in. "His countenance has all the northerly aspects of a southbound horse."

If ***Hammer****, South Dakota declared war on* ***Tongs****, Kentucky, they could go at it!*

MATCHING WITS WITH SYDNEY SMITH!

An English clergyman and writer who died way back in 1845 (Sydney Smith) possessed a wit as modern as tomorrow. On one occasion he said that a friend lived so far out in the country "it was twelve miles to a lemon."

When he met the American orator-politician, Daniel Webster, Smith described him as "a steam engine in trousers."

And of talkative fellow author Thomas Macaulay, Smith commented, "He has occasional flashes of silence that make his conversation perfectly delightful."

We know a doctor who won't make house calls even in his own home.

THE TRAVELERS!

A New Yorker was visiting friends in England. After a good deal of sightseeing, his English hosts asked him what he had enjoyed most. When he told them he had been impressed with Magdalen College, he

RIDDLE: Has drought curtailed the vim and vigor of Colorado's ***Horsetail Creek?***

ANSWER: The little town of *Vim* is still at the head of *Horsetail Creek*. We couldn't locate any vigor, but we did find *Energy*, Illinois. Does that help?

was told it was pronounced Maudlin; and when he raved about Glouchester, he was informed it was Gloster.

The following year, his English friends came to New York. After they had traveled about the state, he asked them what had impressed them most.

"Why, I think it would be your Niagara Falls, old boy," the Englishman said.

"I'm afraid I never heard of it," the American replied.

The Englishman was overwhelmed and proceeded to describe the great falls.

"Oh," the American said, "you mean Niffles."

*Florida's **Withlacoochee River** empties into the Gulf of Mexico south of **Waccasassa Bay**.*

The ten-year-old son of a doctor had played hookey from school. The next day, he took one of his father's prescriptions to school and solemnly handed it to the principal. The principal puzzled over it a moment and then said, "Well, I'm glad you feel well enough for school today."

Evidently barbers have always been great chatterers. In the 2nd Century, Plutarch reported that when a certain gentleman was asked by a barber how he wanted his hair to be cut, the man replied, "In silence."

BACHELOR CONFIRMED!

A woman researcher on our staff cried out suddenly one day, "I've just discovered why George Bernard Shaw was a bachelor! Listen to his description of weddings." She read us the following:

"When two people are under the influence of the most violent, most insane, most delusive and most transient of passions, they are required to swear that they will remain in that excited, abnormal and exhausting condition continuously until death do them part."

Anyone who goes to a psychiatrist ought to have his head examined.
Sam Goldwyn

LAST WORDS!

Two men were peering into a casket, viewing the last remains of a mutual friend, when one of them said, "Gee whiz, Marty looks great, doesn't he?"

The other paused, then remarked, "Hell he ought to...he's just back from Palm Springs."

Speaking of things funereal, we were passing by a mortuary not so long ago when a friend came out of the building with a huge grin on his face. We had to ask the reason for his high good humor.

He proceeded to tell us that he had just purchased a casket. Then he described it in loving detail. It sounded magnificent, so we asked him what he paid for such opulence.

"Twelve thousand five hundred," he announced with considerable pride.

Unthinkingly we blurted, "My God, man, for another three hundred you could be buried in a Cadillac."

He bit the bullet at both ends.

EXILE!

Everyone respected my great Uncle Farnsworth. He was one of the last of a breed — the kind, well-bred gentleman. He turned from any condition or action which might possibly injure another. He also held opinions which were not perfectly attuned to the realities of life about him.

It seems two young hoodlums were caught in the act of setting fire to Uncle Farnsworth's coach house. When the arresting officers asked him to sign the complaint, he inquired as to the punishment the culprits might receive. Informed that it could be from five to ten years in prison, Uncle Farnsworth balked.

"Couldn't they simply be banished?" he asked.

*Pool-shooters! Have you considered moving to **Hustler**, Wisconsin?*

HANKY-PANKY ON HOKKAIDO!

Our far-Eastern sleuth has turned up the disconcerting information that forty percent of Japanese housewives now keep secret bank accounts...keep them secret from their husbands, that is.

*A **persnatcher** is one who lifts old bags!*

IT'S A LAW...

Hitch your car to a horse if you're parking for more than 2 hours in Milwaukee, Wisconsin.

Animals wandering the streets of Berea, Kentucky must display a red taillight (try that on your pet porcupine).

Violent or furious ox-driving on city streets is a no-no in Jefferson City, Missouri.

No moose is allowed on the sidewalks of Fairbanks, Alaska. (Can we assume polar bears are okay?)

And don't go hitching your crocodile to a fire hydrant in Detroit, Michigan.

Don't get drunk in Dupont, Pa. They'll give you a legal dose of castor oil.

And you can't roller-skate in the public restrooms of Portland, Oregon...drunk or sober.

You can't set fire to a mule in Maine and, in Brooklyn, N.Y., you're not allowed to put donkeys in bathtubs.

Camels get a break in Arizona. It's illegal to hunt or shoot them.

Rabbits aren't given *total* protection, but you can't hunt them on the main street of Port Allen, Louisiana and, in Los Angeles, Cal., it's illegal to shoot rabbits from a moving trolley car.

Cowboys could get in trouble in Knoxville, Tennessee, if they're caught fishing with a lasso.

And boxers (human) are not allowed to get in the ring with bulls in Washington, D.C.

A blindfolded person is not permitted to drive a car, in Birmingham, Alabama.

Beer drinkers in St. Louis, Mo. can't sit on the curb and guzzle brew from a bucket. (*Standing* on the curb, you might get away with.)

If your pet elephant is caught drinking beer in Natchez, Miss., he'll be thrown or maybe *led* into jail.

Don't ride your horse into a saloon in Prescott, Arizona. However, it's okay in Burns, Oregon, as long as you pay admission.

If you hear the firemen of Marblehead, Mass. singing "yo-ho-ho and a bottle of rum," it's because the law says they are entitled to a 3-gallon jug of the stuff every time they answer an alarm.

In Hawaii, you can't whistle in a bar, but in Kentucky you are required to blow a whistle while operating a still. (Whistling while it works?)

Has anyone noticed that Wyoming women have long arms? Maybe it's because they must be five feet from the bar at all times.

Only eight rabbits can live on the same block in Tuscumbia, Alabama. Enforcement probably involves a daily census.

And the way we restrict chickens! They're not allowed in hotel rooms in Cumberland, Md. But think of the strain on the hens of Norfolk, Virginia, where the only time they can lay eggs is between 8 am. and 4 pm. (Now that's a holding action!)

Don't count your chickens with a hatchet.

NOTE FROM THE BIG TOP!

Agatha Quilm, famed rhinoceros trainer who has attended two quilting bees and a sassafras tea festival in her illustrious career, resigned yesterday from the Fleeg Sisters Circus, screaming at reporters, "I've spent my last day with those horny devils."

Lawyers inflate trial balloons!

IN THE NAME OF SOVIET SCIENCE!

Recently the Russian press reported that a scientist in Georgia (was it Plainsograd?) has discovered how cats can find their way home from a strange and distant place.

He created a maze, even sprinkling gasoline on the floor to nullify any telltale odors. He blindfolded a kitty and carried it through the maze to some food at the end. Then he returned the kitty to the starting point and turned it loose, still blindfolded. Mr. Cat pussyfooted straight to the food.

The illustrious scientist, figuring that the labyrinth canal in the cat's ear was the homing device, surgically removed it. When the experiment was repeated, the cat roamed aimlessly, mewed and tried to claw the blindfold from its eyes.

Think what we know now that we didn't know before. And we have a right to know. And the cat? We're sure he must agree: ain't science grand!

RIDDLE: Are *zebras* black with white stripes or white with black stripes?

ANSWER: This is no easy answer to come by. They had to cross a zebra with a donkey to make sure. We don't know if they called the offspring of this union *zedonks* or *bradonks*, but they all had black stripes on a tan background. Up until then, the average zebra didn't care much, but he loved the experiment.

PEOPLE CATS!

If one provides a cat with an immaculate litter box, at least thirty-two varieties of canned and dry food, innumerable toys and a cosy place to sleep (such as the small of your back), the rewards can be enormous. In a month or so, you will be allowed to stroke your cat...in a prescribed manner and at a time the cat selects. In two months, the baleful stares will be reserved for the times you decide to act kittenish.

Finally, if your devotion has been suitably slavish, your cat will butt its hard little skull into your leg, arch its back and brush its shoulder against you. Affection, at last? Hell, no! The self-centered little beauty is simply transferring some scent from glands around its mouth and ears onto your leg. The purpose is to mark you as personal property. If some interloper should happen along, the scent on you tells him, "This sucker is mine. Scat, cat!"

Hunters beware: male and female caribou and reindeer have horns.

CAT'S EYE!

Sure, cats can see better at night than you can. That's because they can enlarge the pupils of their eyes more than you can, letting in more light.

On a very dark night, a cat's eye is almost totally opened to any light which might occur. Notice that reddish brilliance when a car's headlights flash into a cat's eyes. All the light is passing through the wide-open pupil and reflecting off the retinal lining at the rear of his vision apparatus. And you thought feline night prowlers had red eyes.

Every cow must have a slippery lining.

THEY TAUGHT TURTLES, DIDN'T THEY?

Remember how the Mock Turtle described his education in *Alice in Wonderland?* "I only took the regular course. Realing and Writhing, of course to begin with, and then the different branches of Arithmetic — Ambition, Distraction, Uglification and Derision."

Mary had a little lamb; and it was so good she ate it all, and there was nothing to put in the doggy bag.

LOOK AT DUMBO!

No wonder the African elephant seldom speaks to the Indian elephant. In the first place, he has bigger ears; his tusks are longer and average about twice the weight; his offspring usually weigh about fifty pounds more at birth; and he was never stupid enough to let men train him to do their work.

A little dare from the hog that bit you.

If someone gave you an elephant folio, what would you feed it? The recommendation is not to feed it at all. An elephant folio is a book-sheet folded to make two leaves. A normal folio is 3 1/8" X 4 3/4", while the elephant folio is 23" X 28", even after feeding.

He got bit by the heel of a monster.

PRIVATE EYE SPIES ON COW!

The gods in Greek mythology were a caution! Once, when Zeus had his eye on a pert maiden named Io, his wife, Hera snapped her fingers and turned the girl into a heifer. Then, to make sure the heifer didn't act cute, Hera sent this handy thousand-eyed monster named Argus to keep some of his eyes on her. After awhile, everyone got tired of the game. The heifer became Io again. Argus died from multiple styes. Not a wasteful one, Hera put the eyes in her peacock's tail. And that's a mythical fact!

*Towns to make a menu with: **Fried**, North Dakota and **Rice**, Kansas.*

RIDDLE: Do sheep eat more than cows?

ANSWER: Comparing their appetites to their respective body weights, those gluttonous sheep out-eat cows seven to one!

Cows have to chew a lot of crud before they can give milk.

LOOK WHO'S PEEKING IN OUR THIRD FLOOR WINDOW!

Cows, horses and deer have seven vertebrae in the neck. But the giraffe — well he has seven, too. Only difference is: each of his neck vertebrae is a lot longer than those of his four-legged friends.

If you're fleeing from **Fly, Ohio,** *try* **Scurry,** *Texas!*

GO TRY IT ON THEM!

The poor guinea pig is a victim of his own virtues. He's small and he has a pleasant disposition, so he makes an ideal animal to experiment upon in laboratories. Worse luck for him, he is also susceptible to a lot of things which plague human beings. But if he's so much like human beings, where did he get that pleasant disposition?

Pigs are the cleanest of all farm animals if they are allowed to be so.

OPEN YOUR MOUTH AND COOL OFF, SPOT!

It's not bad manners when a dog who has been running about opens his mouth, lets his tongue loll out and drools all over everything. We don't know who told them, but dogs realize it's the evaporation of saliva on their tongues which cools them off. Besides, a dog's engine runs hotter than a human's — about three degrees hotter...even more for pups.

Don't bite dogs. They have forty-two permanent teeth...ten more than you, if you still have all yours.

IT'S A BIRD! IT'S A PLANE! IT'S AN *ALBORAK!*

Some fancy kid, the *Alborak* — wings, a human face and a peacock's tail. The only thing we ever heard of him doing was carrying Mohammed to heaven.

Now that we've got you in a birdy mood, remember this vital news: it's the upstroke of birds' wings that moves them forward; the downstroke is what keeps them airborne.

And don't fret if your hummingbird's temperature is around 113 degrees Fahrenheit. That's about normal for fast-flyers. Even chickens and other earthbound birds have normal temperatures of 100 degrees.

*The **Ruby-Throated Republican** is the only bird with two **right** wings.*

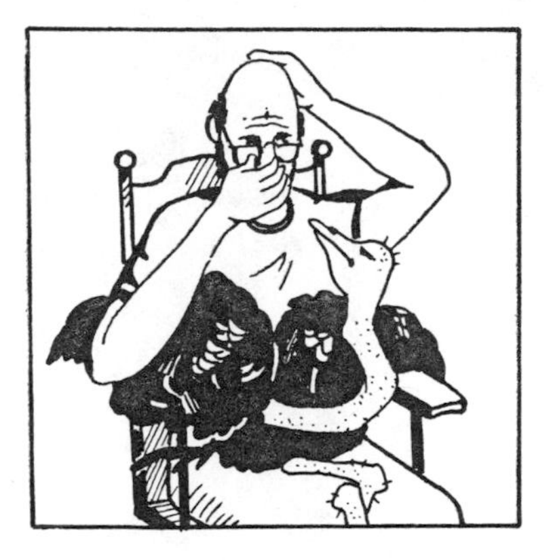

ANIMAL LIFTERS, ATTENTION!

If you're in condition, you ought to be able to snatch an ostrich off its feet. He only weighs about 300 pounds; of course, being eight feet tall, he's a bit awkward. So, you may want to try a lion — a full-grown one tips the scales at about 500 pounds. Watch the claws and fangs!

You say, maybe a hog is more your speed? Depends on which hog. Some of them grow to 1,250 pounds — that's two and a half lions, brother. And then there's his breath to contend with.

Don't let an ostrich sit on your lap no matter how strong your impulse to do so. The ostrich is not always tidy. His dietary habits may give his breath a less than pleasant bouquet.

The hummingbird is a tropical creature, but some of the more than five hundred different species evidently forget that, because hummingbirds have been found in Alaska and at the tip of South America. But, when it gets too cold, they buzz off.

A rare old bird is the Pelican,
His beak holds more than his belican.
He can take in his beak
Enough food for a week;
I'm damned if I know how the helican!

You can tell what a hawk is apt to have for dinner just by looking at him. If he has squarish wings and a broad fan-like tail, he'll go to a

RIDDLE: Why do mosquitos only buzz when they are around a person's ear?

ANSWER: Most humans are ego-stricken, thinking the only events occurring in the world are those of which they are personally aware. The mosquito buzzes all the time it is in flight. We only hear it when it gets close to our hearing apparatus.

place specializing in rodents and insects. But, if he has rounded wings and a long tail, lock up your chickens.

The goose's affection for mankind is demonstrated by pate de foie gras.

BUSY AS A FLY?

Scientists have proved what we knew all along — bees are busy little critters. Imagine this: the honeybee must gather over 29 thousand drops of honey to make a pound of the sticky stuff, and he puts in over 43 thousand miles of flight to do it. But get this: he flaps his wings a mere 240 times a second, while the house fly does 330. The butterfly is the lazy one of the flying insects, averaging eight wing-strokes per second.

If a bee were watching a cowboy movie, could he tell the good guys from the bad guys? You can find out by wearing a black hat near a beehive. Black seems to make a bee madder than a hornet.

It's not too far from 'Yellow Jacket,' Colorado to 'Beehive,' Montana...as the wasp flies.

Thanks to the microscope, man can learn of the most infinitesimal objects. A scientist recently discovered something even smaller than an ant's mouth. Whatever the ant eats. Ugh!

Wake up! We just entered 'Sleepy Eye,' Minnesota!

A husband was teasing his gullible wife by telling her of the amazing zimose spider which begins consuming itself and does not stop until nothing is left. His wife nodded her head to indicate she had followed what he had told her, and then she added, "I've never really seen one, but at least now I know why."

If, as they claim, fleas can jump 200 times their own length, why don't they jump off you and onto someone else?

The anopheles mosquito didn't get the blame for spreading malaria until 1897. Prior to that time, it was thought the disease was caused by bad air, and it was given its name for the two Italian words meaning bad air. And that was in pre-smog days, too.

Don't let the size of fleas fool you. If a flea were the size of a man, he could jump about half a mile with hardly any effort. Think what a bite he'd have, too!

NONSENSE:
There once was a snake
Who lived in Silver Lake.
From the end of his nose
To the tip of his tail
He was twice the length
Of a ten-foot rail
Timma-ri, timma-ro,
Timma-rumma stick a-bumma stick,
Potty-wotty wink,
Come nip-cat, root-hog;
Sing-song kitty,
Won't you ki me ho!

LOST IN THE WOODS!

George Washington may have had art on his mind when he cut down the *cherry* tree, since it's a favorite wood of sculptors. Others they favor are *English walnut, pear* and *oak* of domestic woods; *ebony, rosewood* and *tulipwood* are choice imported hardwoods.

What is done with *persimmon* wood? Today, it shows up in the heads of golf clubs. When auto bodies contained wood, *persimmon* was one of them.

The Honduran *nagaed* has one highly specialized use: it's great for making a marimba.

Is there a wood hard enough to be used for machinery bearings? *Lignum vitae* is not only hard enough but, since its layers of fibers run at oblique angles, it won't split. Makes good mallets and bowling balls, too.

Archers insist the wood of the *yew* makes the best bows. We're too tired to argue with them.

Today, chess pieces are made from everything imaginable, but *boxwood* is still the favored wood. *Boxwood* shows up in another wood product — the manicurist's *orange stick*...which, as you can judge from its name, is also made from *orangewood* and from *lemon.*

Now, hasn't this been enough to drive you up your tree?

*Dieters, never eat more than one **bit** of **tid** at a meal!*

RIDDLE: How many oat kernels are there in a full standard grain sack?

ANSWER: 150,000, give or take a few. What's the matter...can't you count?

It's 280 airline miles between the Louisiana towns of 'Trees' and 'Bush!'

The last time you counted the leaves on your mature apple tree, you should have come up with a total of about 50,000.

Don't keep on feeding plant food to your Alpine willow with high hopes. They very seldom grow taller than six inches.

Deal-tables are always made of fir or pine. Otherwise, it's no deal.

The redwoods of California grow taller than the eucalyptus of Australia, but not by much — say, 360 feet for a record redwood against 346 for eucalyptus.

It takes all the sap from three sugar maples through an average year to produce a gallon of maple syrup.

Sycamores decorticate — that is, they shed their bark.

Towns with something in common: 'Pluckemin,' N.J. and 'Eyebrow,' Saskatchewan.

COFFEE, TEA OR...

Those who have wasted their time chasing down the history of the coffee tree still aren't sure whether it first grew in Arabia or Ethiopia. And here we thought it was a native of Brazil.

Meanwhile, on the tea-front, a single variety of tea plant can produce four distinct teas — Pekoe from the very young leaves, Oolong from one grade of the leaf, Congo from another grade and Souchong from the smallest leaves.

Persians grew alfalfa as far back as 480 B.C. Should be ready to harvest by now.

VEGETABLE PIE!

Our neighborhood botanist says it's proper to call a seed or seedcase a fruit. If he's right, then tomato and pumpkin are fruits. And since rhubarb pie is made from the leafy stalk of that plant, it's a *vegetable* pie. He also says that nuts are fruits as they are a tree's seeds. This doesn't apply to the peanut, which is really a legume...same as a bean or pea. We only call them nuts because they taste like true nuts.

When dining out in 'Burnt Corn,' Alabama, avoid the fritters!

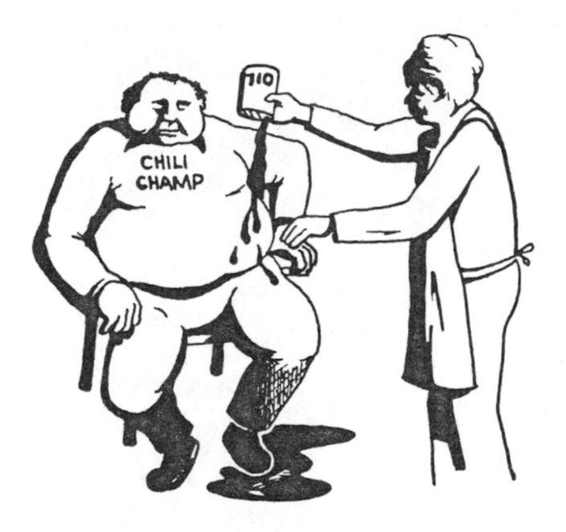

SOCIAL NOTES FROM DOWNTOWN OHIO!

Fat Jimmy Archer got stuck in a chair in Beezy's Chili Parlor and it took two quarts of 30-weight oil and a tempered steel pry bar to get him loose...and he never did get to eat his chili.

Place to visit when you have a cold: 'Stinking Lake,' New Mexico!

Whenever eating a salad made of a pound of avocados and a pound of pineapples, you'll be taking in 532 calories — 20 from the pineapple and the rest from the avocado. You might try smaller helpings.

If you can make a mammoth go to the fountain, let him eat cake.

Mrs. Irving Smickens received this note from Amy Mell: "Dear Mrs. Danny's Mother — I hate your son Danny and, if I hadn't already mailed it, I wouldn't have sent him three cherry tarts for his coming-out party or whatever it is he is having just because he's thirteen."

Long lunch on the Plains: 'Sioux' mothers nursed their children for three years!

THE HEAVIER IT IS, THE LIGHTER IT IS!

Oh, yeah! The dairy fat in cream is lighter than the liquid. So, cream *heavy* with fat is lighter than cream with less fat. Also, explains

RIDDLE: A farmer sells his milk in a 20-gallon can. Over the years, the can has received rough handling and has become badly dented. Would a dented milk can hold a full 20 gallons?

ANSWER: Depends. If the dents were from the inside out, the can would hold more than full measure. But if the can were dented inward, no way to get 20 gallons into it.

why cream rises to the top of milk, in case you'd never noticed this, you homogenized users.

NONSENSE
The sausage is a cunning bird
With feathers long and wavy.
It swims around the frying pan
And makes its nest in gravy.

RESOUNDING PLEASURE!

A belch at an elegant dinner isn't the sort of thing one plans, but it can happen. Should it happen to you, remember how British actor, Monty Woolley handled it in the movie *The Man Who Came To Dinner.* After the unseemly sound, a prim lady next to Woolley looked at him in horror. Arching his brows, Woolley said, "What did you expect, madame, chimes?"

A hen is only an egg's way of making another egg.
Samuel Butler

Recipes specifying *white* pepper may have been concocted by someone who did not know that *white* pepper is simply well-ripened black pepper.

Fish don't swim upstream because they enjoy the extra work. It's just easier to locate their next meal that way.

START A STURGEON FARM!

The Russian sturgeon — the *beluga* or *husco* — could be your financial salvation. Pampered a bit and fed right, the beluga can become twenty or more feet in length and weigh in at better than a ton. Don't be sidetracked by the fact that this may take a few decades; keep your mind on the money to be made. You see, the female sturgeon, with the exception of the *virgin* sturgeon, produces between two and three million eggs. And that, my greedy buddies, is caviar. Now, with caviar selling at $15 an ounce for a low grade, and with lovely Mama sturgeon producing 500 pounds of caviar, you can gross $120,000...to $500,000, if you have a top caviar. Who said the Russians aren't capitalists?

Deceitful is the alligator's grin —
Smiling ear-to-ear as he takes you in!

THREE BODY FACTS YOU CAN LIVE WITHOUT!

One: your hair grows faster when it's warm — thus, faster in the summer than in winter; faster by day than by night. (If you're bald, ignore this item.)

Two: when you get the urge to stretch, it's simply Mother Nature telling you to improve your blood circulation. Cats never turn down a chance to stretch.

Three: if you're average, you have about 3,500 square inches of skin. If all of it is dry and flaking, you're in for a big skin-cream bill.

The only winks we ever got in our youth were tiddly!

THAT SMARTS!

Those grunting karate-choppers know what they're about: the Adams apple is one of the most sensitive areas in the human body. A solid smack and you can't talk, breathe or swallow. The one thing you can do is suffer.

Whacking your head against solid objects isn't much fun either. Did you ever wonder how come a knot raises after such a blow? A hard bump kills some of the elastic tissues covering the skull; so, nature gets rid of the dead tissues by flooding the area with blood (it's the white cells that carry off dead tissue). The more blood needed for the job, the bigger the knot.

Watch your noggin when diving into ***Bumping Lake, Washington!***

PAUL REVERE!

Should you happen to pick up a copy of the Boston Gazette of August 29, 1768, turn to the advertisements. There you'll find one that runs: "Whereas many Persons are so unfortunate as to lose their Fore Teeth by Accident and otherways, to their great Detriment, not only in Looks but in speaking bothe in Public and Private; This is to inform all such that they may have them replaced with false Ones that look as well as the Natural and answer the end in speaking to all Intents by Paul Revere, Goldsmith, near the Head of Dr. Clark's wharf, Boston."

Many people don't smile because their teeth are cheap!

RIDDLE: As far as you can discern, are any of your friends bilabial?

ANSWER: We hope *all* your friends are bilabial. It means having two lips.

ALL IT TAKES IS A SMILE!

The vain ladies of the Anglo-Egyptian Sudan used to file attractive notches into their upper incisors. Then, for drama, they yanked the two lower incisors out.

*A **Baluba** woman of the Congo wasn't beautiful until she had her four incisors knocked out.*

The Annamite women of Vietnam might have been considered beautiful if they hadn't put black lacquer on their teeth; and if they hadn't chewed betel nut and had all that red froth running down their chins. Other than that!

*A man from **Dragon,** Utah lost his upper plate in **False Creek.***

THANKS FOR SHAVING YOUR EYEBROWS!

Since a woman's eyebrows were once considered among her greatest charms, a Japanese husband was pleased when she shaved them off after marriage. This was her way of telling him she wanted to be unattractive to other men. Around the same time, a Japanese bride could add a similar note of fidelity by blackening her teeth. (We would think there should be some limits to removing temptation.)

Just about the sexiest thing a Trobriand Islander did was to bite off his girl's eyelashes. We shouldn't wonder!

SHE LOVES HIM, SHE LOVES HIM NOT!

Once upon a time, the young men of Borneo had a sure-fire way of telling how well they were doing with a young lady. If he were lying on the grass, with his head on her lap, and she began to pluck out his eyebrows with a tweezer, his delight was overwhelming. But he could scarcely contain himself, if she should go on from there and pluck out his eyelashes, as well.

Long, but worthwhile trip: from 'Bled,' Yugoslavia to 'Bliss,' Michigan.

TAKE A SHALLOW BREATH!

If you want to scare yourself half to death, take a look at the amounts of various pollutants in the air where you live. Then figure that, if you are sitting still or lying down, you'll still be inhaling about 126 gallons of air an hour. If you're working, the average quantity shoots up to 1,042 gallons an hour. Maybe the safest course to follow is to *exhale* only.

Hunters! Try 'Decoy,' Kentucky. No luck? Go to 'Duck,' North Carolina!

GET THE BUTTERMILK! SHE'S FRECKLING!

Since winters have always been hard in Finland, summer was courting-time...which meant time to look enticing. In bygone days, a Finnish maiden searched out an anthill, bent over it and took in the mild vapors of formic acid to give her eyes a sparkle.

Then she addressed the problem of freckling. She couldn't stay out of the Sun *all* the time and bonnets were only partial protection. She did avoid touching any speckled bird's eggs, which helped. But the old standby anti-freckling formula was to smear her face with buttermilk! Skoal!

Brides in the Admiralty Islands once wore a coronet of dogs teeth.

OWLS ARE NICE FOR THE FOREHEAD!

Ask any sailor who has submitted to tattooing. Painful. But Burmese tattoo artists of another age were superb and even kindly craftsmen. Of course, at first one could get quite a fright — their tattooing tool was two feet long and had an image of Buddha at one end and four sharp needles at the other. A different colored stain was held in each needle. Then came the good part. The tattoo artist gave his customers enough opium to render them impervious to pain. A couple of hours later, you had as many as twenty detailed and colorful images on your skin. It's not known which the Burmese favored — the tattoos or the anesthetic!

Want a nice dark blue tattoo? Kayan women on Borneo used soot and sugarcane juice to get that hue.

PRAGMATISM ON THE SOLOMON ISLANDS!

Around 1870, a white man, visiting the Solomon Islands, asked a chief why all the men were tattooed. The chief informed him, "For the same reason you wear clothes — to attract the women!"

Watch the road if you're driving from 'Skiddy,' Kansas to 'Slick,' Oklahoma!

IS THAT YOU, OR A TATTOO?

One of the hill tribes of Burma explained their practice of tattooing the faces of their women a shiny black. The tradition stems from one of their legends. It seems a Burmese king once fancied a young girl of this hill tribe and commanded that she be brought to his palace. Her parents couldn't refuse, but they hoped that making her unattractive by tattooing her face black, the King would return her in disgust.

The King, a kinky type, figured two could play that game. He decreed that from then on all the women of that hill tribe had to have black tattooed faces...and he kept the girl.

Tattoo artist: a man who needles you and has the nerve to charge you for it!

HAVE WE GOT A TATTOO FOR YOU!

Moroccan *Berbers* had a tattoo for just about every exigency. One on either temple kept them from oversleeping and cost less than an alarm clock. A tattoo on the knee prevented swollen knee joints. But the one tattoo every male *Berber* prized was one on the hand or arm that made him so attractive to women they were supposed to grant him their favors...gratis.

Good place to go when you're feeling blue: ***Funk,*** *Nebraska!*

AND ONE FOR LATER ON!

Most of the men and women of the *Naga* tribe in Assam were tattooed at one time. Even those who didn't think too highly of skin decoration took a precaution and had one tattoo. This was to enable a husband and wife to identify each other in the next world, when their forms might be changed to members of the animal world. We wonder if it still wasn't a problem: tattooers must have occasionally repeated a design.

Borneo's 'Dyaks' preferred tattoos to clothing. Never needed altering, either!

YOUR FOUR-YEAR-OLD HAS A NICE MOUSTACHE!

We have no idea why the primitive natives of northern Japan — the *Ainu* — tattooed little girls all about the lips, giving the appearance of a moustache. But we see the practical side of their tattooing a wedding ring on a bride's finger.

Eskimos used to greet visitors by licking their faces and hands.

UPLIFTING STORY!

The native men of Nyasaland, unlike many of their African cousins, preferred firm, uplifted female breasts to pendulous ones. Not about to go against male preferences, girls of Nyasaland tied cords just under the nipple of each breast and secured the cords to their heads. Back to the drawing board, Playtex!

Pendulous breasts were once such a rage with the *Hottentots*, a woman carrying an infant on her back had merely to toss her breast over her shoulder to feed it.

When an Inca chief died, his followers killed his favorite wife, his servants and his bodyguard so they could serve him in the next life. (Hardly payed to be loyal.)

MOURNING IS A DRAG!

A widower of the Congo's *Bangala* tribe covered his body with clay, put on women's clothing and then wandered off into the bush for three months of mourning!

There was a time in **Swaziland** *in Africa when there were no widows...for long. The dead husband's brother simply moved the lady into his place.*

THE SHRINKING BRIDE!

Had you been around for the festivities following an old Prussian wedding, you would have seen a relative wash the bride's feet. That was the time to get out, because they then sprinkled the foot-bath water over the guests, the bridal bed, the livestock and all around the house. (Must have had water shortages there.)

Bulgarian brides of the last century took one bath in a lifetime...on their wedding eve.

WOW! WHO DID YOUR NEW COBRA?

There are countless sects within Hinduism. We'd say the *Nairs* were one of the odder sects, their hang-up being serpent worship. *Nair* men arranged the forepart of their hair in the shape of a cobra's hood and shaved the rest off. The women arranged far more elaborate

RIDDLE: Have primitive peoples worn human bones for adornment?

ANSWER: In the 1800's, women on the island of New Britain wore necklaces of human ribs. Sometimes they'd insert them into the lobes of their noses, so they stuck out to either side as a boar's tusks. Pretty as hell!

snake-shaped coiffures. One had to love snakes to fall for a *Nair* girl.

Hindu women suspended a tear-drop gem between the eyebrows to ward off the evil eye.

TEA WAS THE WAY IN PARAGUAY!

Years ago a young Paraguayan either had good-taste buds or he had no idea how he stood with the girl he was wooing. Of course, if she served him *cold* tea, it was time to look elsewhere. When the tea she brewed was flavored with burnt sugar, she had a certain fondness for him. It would pay to stick around.

Cinnamon in the tea was a better sign yet, being the girl's way of saying, "You're the only one I'm thinking of." The next phase of the Paraguayan tea act was tricky. If the boy tasted orange peel in his tea, it meant, "Take me; I'm yours." That was open to interpretation. Sometimes, rather than make a sensitive decision, he preferred tea with honey. That was clear-cut — "I want to marry you."

We almost forgot the *Dear John Tea* — bitter tea...too late, friend.

One food you don't see too many Congressmen eating any more is rice!

OH, TO HAVE BEEN A HOTTENTOT!

A *Hottentot* wedding of the 1800's was a sight to see, but a lot worse to be a part of. The groom sat in one circle with the men; the bride, in a second circle with the women. Then along came the priest. To the surprise of no *Hottentot* but to the horror of a stranger, he pissed on the groom. So the bride would not feel left out, he proceeded to her circle and repeated the act. He did this three times altogether. At least he chanted a prayer for their happiness while all this was going on. (Last one to kiss the bride is a smart egg.)

Cambodian women used to give themselves a 'butch' haircut as soon as they married.

The forest tribes in the Belgian Congo formerly covered their bodies with a red stain and palm oil, in lieu of bathing. Once a month they scraped off the mixture and started over again.

Samoans used to bathe babies in orange juice...fresh, not frozen.

AND NEVER WITH AN OLIVE!

In Nigeria they had a delightful way of being sure a bride entered the groom's house in a state of total purity. Her relatives washed her feet in *gin!*

There's many a slip caused by love in the kip!

ON THE TRAIL OF A RICH SART WOMAN!

Thursday was the day the *Sart* women of Russia used to reserve for washing their thick, dark hair. Quite a task, since they never cut their hair. They had an odd shampoo, too — boiled sour milk.

Had you been visiting the *Sart* last century, there was an easy way to tell the wealthy *Sart* women from the less affluent. The well-to-do ladies washed out the boiled sour milk in hot water.

Ugandan women used to bury their fingernail clippings in a secret forest place.

YOU SAID A NOSEFUL!

Ninety years ago it would have been difficult to resist the *Banaka* woman of French Equatorial Africa...for her lovely costume jewelry, if for no other reason. To make herself irresistible, she bored a nice clean hole through her nose cartilage and inserted a choice cut of fat meat. Oh, to be in Africa when the meat is in the nose!

Icelandic engagement rings were large enough to allow the groom to stick his hand through it and take his bride's hand at the wedding.

GRABBING THE BRASS RING IN BURMA!

You've seen pictures of *Padang* women from Burma with tiers of brass rings around their elongated necks and on their legs and arms. They start when a girl is very young, welding five half-inch thick rings around her neck. At regular intervals, they add more rings. A full-grown *Padang* woman, counting her arm and leg rings, too, was toting some eighty pounds of brass around with her. But...no brass, no love! (Wonder if *Padang* men are required to carry their brides over the threshold?)

Which way do you turn to get out of 'Left Hand,' West Virginia?

RIDDLE: Were public baths in Japan always expensive?

ANSWER: In the last century, they were all free. Every town's streets were lined with troughs where the men and women gathered at the end of the day for a hot bath and a quick round of gossipry.

LOVE YOUR BALL AND CHAIN!

We think the *Herere* women of southwest Africa in days gone by went about things the hard way. First, iron was a rare and costly metal in those parts. So it was a sign of wealth to be able to afford bracelets and anklets of iron. The anklets often weighed as much as forty pounds apiece. Well, you try walking about with forty-pound anklets. The resulting slow gait was very seductive to *Herere* men. Girls, too poor to afford iron anklets, simply imitated the enticing slow walk of their more fortunate sisters. Ankles away!

Love match: bride from ***Cuckoo, Virginia;*** *groom from* ***Crazy Woman Springs, Wyoming!***

SARI, SAROS, SORRY!

A *sari* is that wraparound garment of Hindu women. A *saros* is the eighteen-year and ten-day gap between lunar eclipses. *Sorry* is what we are about the whole thing.

Two thin sweaters will keep you warmer than one thick one because the air between the two is a lousy conductor of heat. Having that air holds the warmth in.

Fascinating statistic without which life would be barren: authentic hula skirts called for the leaves of about 60 *ti plants*, took four hours to weave, and wore out in three to five days of use, depending upon the ratio of shimmy.

Gracias is the appropriate costume for hula dancing!

BEAU BRUMMEL GOES NATIVE!

At one time the native men of the Admiralty Islands wouldn't think of showing up for a festive occasion unless properly attired. His hair had to be combed up stiffly in a wild pompadour. Then a necklace of dog's teeth was a must. Inasmuch as he had artificially distended his ear lobes, he showed them off neatly with notched rings of coconut shell. Next he slipped a sliver of pearl shell through his nose. His G-string was held in place by a colorful woven belt. But the armlets around his biceps were the big item. He covered cloth with a rubbery substance and then, into the gummy mass, stuck little sections of bones...*his dead father's rib bones.* Now, he was ready to show himself to an admiring society!

Since when is a crazy men's tailor a pantaloony?

TO THE POINT!

There being no bushes to beat about on the east coast of Greenland, it used to be acceptable for a man to dash into a girl's tent, grab her by the hair and haul her off to his place. Of course, she had to protect her reputation by letting out great cries of woe to which she hoped he was deaf. *And that was the marriage!*

We must have heard about "The Shaming of the Screw" eleven times but never heard how they did it.

CUSTOM OR NOT, THAT'S OFFENSIVE!

We understand the *Naga* tribesmen of Assam have cleaned up their act since the 1600's. In those days, the *Nagas* had intercourse whenever and wherever they felt like it — on the street, in a crowded bazaar...you name it. With such unfettered sexual habits, it's odd to discover that *Naga* women always covered their breasts.

Scottish lairds at one time demanded the right to sleep with the wife of any vassal on the wedding night. Later on they got tired and accepted money instead.

SHACKING UP IN SARAWAK!

According to tradition some eighty years ago, when a *Sarawak* girl of Borneo became twelve years old, she embarked on a veritable sexual orgy! Any time she spotted one of the local boys she liked, she sent off a girl friend to invite him over to the log house. He hardly had time to wave hello to her parents before she had him bedded down in a corner.

All this frantic promiscuity was sanctioned until she became pregnant — which was the whole object all along. Our overly friendly twelve-year-old then had only one decision to make. The custom dictated that she marry the boy with whom she'd made love most often. Hey, with a string of thirty or so to recall, it wasn't always easy to remember. Besides, who'd been counting?

The oon we hope never makes a comeback is the spit.

RIDDLE: Did *Fiji Islanders* regret giving a daughter in marriage?

ANSWER: It doesn't sound like it! After the wedding, the father-in-law said to the groom, "If you grow tired of her...sell her, kill her, eat her — you are the absolute master." (Sentimental old geezers, eh?)

The father of an Aeta bride in the Philippines poured water over the kneeling pair, then knocked their heads together. The marriage was off to a groggy start.

TAKING A BATH ON THE ROCKS!

The trouble with history is that it remains the same. Did you realize that if the Greeks had sent a messenger with news of the battle at Thermopylae rather than at Marathon, today's big long-distance race would be called the *Boston Thermopylae*? If Napoleon had won at Waterloo and then lost at Antwerp, we'd have expressions such as *he met his Antwerp* and *not through the little corporal* instead of *not through the Iron Duke.* We'd probably see *Beef Bonaparte* on menus instead of *Beef Wellington.*

If General Custer had stayed out of Montana, we'd probably have had a famous battle known as *Sitting Bull's Last Squat.*

If the chef had known that operatic soprano Nellie Melba's real name was Helen Mitchell, we would be able to order *Peach Mitchell* for dessert...and *Mitchell Toast* for breakfast.

Imagine a bartender's reaction if the first distillery had been one county east of Bourbon County, Kentucky in Bath County — you'd be ordering *a bath on the rocks*!

Consider that toilet water might have been named for a German city a few miles north of Cologne...you'd be splashing on *eau de Dusseldorf.*

If a certain Italian explorer had turned north, the capital of Ohio would be *Vespucci.*

It's strictly a geographic accident when it comes to America's favorite food — had it been named for the area rather than the largest city, McDonald's would be serving you *schleswig-holsteiners* instead of hamburgers.

Oh, had the Mayflower only put in a few miles south in Sandwich, we would now have a black-and-white striped chicken known as the *Sandwich Chicken*...and from that a *Sandwich Chicken sandwich.*

And, if Douglas MacArthur hadn't been so bullheaded, we could close this thing with his famous words, *I don't think I care to come back.*

CHAPTER EIGHT

For Your Elucidation

A personal interview with Hannibal had been the planned opening for this chapter. Unfortunately, he was off attending an Alpine elephant-washing festival. So, we must elucidate without him, expanding your knowledge of life's truly important matters.

Speaking of music, a metronome will swing faster at the North or South Pole than it will at the equator. The earth's surface being flatter at those two extremities, the gravity pull is greater. If you know of any musicians planning polar concerts, be sure to warn them of this phenomenon.

At racetracks, it is wise to heed the advice of Jimmy the Gyp and other learned types: never bet less than a hundred dollars on a race! Let us elucidate. Were you to bet two dollars, rather than 100 dollars, on a ten-to-one shot and the horse won, *look at the money you would have lost.*

Study the last words of famous people and you will discover enormous truths. Ponder the infinite wisdom of Jean D'Arc's final utterance — *Fire*! Or Louis XVI, who said, *But I shaved this morning.* Then there's the enigma of Alexander Graham Bell's *I've been disconnected.* And who can forget the final phrase of Attila the Hun, who whispered to his wife, *I've raped, sacked, pillaged...where did I go wrong*?

We suggest you discount the recent news stories purporting that both crabs and leeches live as long as twenty years. There are several in our neighborhood that are fifty if they're a day!

Before retiring, Fundress Chicklets always reviews some inspirational thoughts, which we hereby pass along: The interior surface of the lungs covers 100 times more area than your skin; you could get *tularemia* from wild rabbits, if you're fast; white, unpigmented splotches on the skin are a sign of *vitiligo*; your liver weighs about three and a half pounds; people who sunburn but do not tan suffer from *heliophobia*; your *sartorius* is your longest muscle, running from the top of your hip to the inside of your knee as if something were chasing it.

*Ponce de Leon drank so much water searching for the **Fountain of Youth**, he floated from Florida to Puerto Rico, where he became governor and wealthy...in that order.*

AN OX FOR YOUR THOUGHTS!

Roman farmers used oxen as their medium of exchange, and from the Latin word for oxen, *pecus*, came our word for money-hungry — *pecuniary* — and finally *penny.*

The Incas had silver and gold running out of their ears, but they never used it as an exchange medium. In fact, they had no word for *money* in their language. The Incas played a role in putting the world on the gold standard, however. The gold Pizarro looted and sent back to Spain was what did it.

The primitive natives of the South Pacific Islands had interesting money forms. The Solomon Islanders used porpoise teeth. Snails' shells were the favorite of the Queen Charlotte Islanders. On the Santa Cruz Islands, feathers did very nicely. A New Guinea native with a flock of boars' tusks was wealthy. And Karok tribesmen traded for goods with the scalps of redheaded woodpeckers.

The first colonists to arrive in this country found the Indians had a buying system developed around *wampum peag* — string of beads. Thrifty colonists quickly shortened it to *wampum*. Most *wampum* was made from white winkle shells or clam shells, although some had a blue color. Alas, the white men figured out a way to manufacture the beads, and that was the end of *wampum* as a decent bartering tool.

Tobacco became one of the prevalent exchange forms in the Colonies. Virginia's colonial government even made it a law that taxes and debts be paid in tobacco.

The onion put in some service as money, too. New England trading ships exchanged them for sugar and spices in the West Indies and South America.

Finally, the Colonies made their own money. Massachusetts Colony issued the first coins in 1652 — a shilling, a sixpence and a threepence.

Once money replaced goods in bartering, things were never quite as interesting...except for oddities, such as the three-dollar bill we issued in 1850.

Work is the curse of the drinking classes. Oscar Wilde said it and believed it.

BURNING FACTS!

The Virginia colonists could hardly wait to get into tobacco growing. By 1615, Jamestown not only had tobacco fields, but the stuff was planted in gardens and even in the streets. Oddly enough, the cigarette didn't come along until around the 1840's, and then it was in France and Italy. Mostly it was a fad until 1870.

The Chinese were growing ***hemp*** *in 2800 B.C., but no one knows why.*

JUST A SIMPLE MARTINI!

It may be simple for an expert to make a truly good *martini*, but there's nothing simple about making the ingredients, themselves.

Take *dry vermouth* — just a flavored white wine, eh? Not on your jigger! A fine dry vermouth contains about forty herbs, spices and flower petals from Bengal and *camomile* (of the daisy family with pungent leaves).

A great dry gin is another recipe. In the distillation process, the alcohol vapor rises through racks of botanicals such as *coriander, lemon peel, angelica root, almonds, orris, licorice* and *juniper berries*.

So, stop gulping that martini!

He always dunked hot dogs in his beer, so they called him Frank-in-stein.

RIDDLE: Did a man named Concord create the Concord grape?

ANSWER: No, just a man who *lived* in Concord, Massachussets.

A teetotaler got notably high
On a single jigger of righ.
Then he said, without guile,
"I find the stuff vuile;
And now it is my turn to bigh."

BARING SOME BEER FACTS!

The Egyptians knew a good thing when they drank it. Beer was so closely associated with their goddess of nature, *Isis*, the first breweries were also temples.

The Babylonians thought so highly of their home brew, they even allowed the girls in the harems to have an occasional schooner of suds.

Beer, the favorite beverage for wedding parties in the Middle Ages, came to be called *bride's ale*...and, from there, it was a simple hop and skip to *bridal*.

You probably never would have heard of Plymouth Rock if it hadn't been for beer...or a lack of it. The Mayflower put into shore because the beer was running low.

It's no accident that the instrument for testing beer's alcoholic content is called an *ebulliometer*.

There was a young girl named Anheuser
Who said that no man could surprise her.
But Old Overholt
Gave her virtue a jolt,
And now she is sadder Budweiser.

That morning-after drink referred to as *the hair of the dog that bit you* started as a quasi-medical treatment and superstition of the 16th Century. Supposedly, if you were bitten by a rabid dog, tying some hairs from the mad dog in with the bandage over the bite would make you safe. It didn't work any better than the morning-after drink — it just made some feel better for the moment.

Don't be overly impressed by **lager** *beer. A* **lager** *is a beer-aging storehouse.*

This bit of doggerel on five reasons for drinking was attributed to a Seventeenth Century English churchman named Aldrich:

Good wine, a friend, because I'm dry
Or lest I should be bye and bye
Or any other reason why.

The tab a person ran up for drinks was once called a *scot*. When the drinks were on the house, one got off *scot-free*.

Absinthe makes the heart go yonder.

FERMENT MY PALM SAP, IT'S A TODDY!

Toddy comes from a Hindu word for palm tree, because the first such beverages were made from the fermented sap of the palm tree.

Punch comes from India, too. They called it *panch*, their word for five, since it had five ingredients — arrak (potent rum-distillate), sugar, tea, lemon and water.

If you want to add zest to any drink, put in lemon peel...*zeste* is French for lemon or orange peel.

Liquor didn't necessarily pack a wallop — in Latin, it's any fluid at all. *Bourbon* did, as soon as the first still in Bourbon County, Kentucky started turning the new whisky out.

Doctors once prescribed the oil from a certain plant for curing worms, so it came to be called *wormwood*. Wormwood oil, anise for flavor and alcohol make up *absinthe*. Absinthe addiction got so bad in France, the stuff was banned in 1915.

A final toast to the 18th Century English sportswriter, Pierce Egan, who gave us the *Tom and Jerry*. That holiday spirit took its name from the two characters in Egan's *Life In London, or Days and Nights of Jerry Hawthorne and His Elegant Friend Corinthian Tom.* When the drink appeared, Tom suddenly got top billing.

Wign is a sign of the times,
With a vintner along business ligns:
He sits, picturesque,
At his computerized desque,
While his robots are picking the vigns.

THE TOAST!

People used to put a piece of bread "parched with heat" into beer or wine, thinking it would improve the flavor. When it was discovered that adding the "toast" didn't improve the drink it was left out. Instead, we now *make a toast*.

I knew he drank because he always wore a rye grin.

RIDDLE: If you were in Philadelphia on January 29, 1973 and witnessed contests in dog-kicking, child-hating and olive-dunking in martinis, what would have been the name of the celebration?

ANSWER: That's when Philadelphians threw the W.C. Fields Birthday Party. Perhaps they still hold it — we haven't recovered from the '73 affair.

MOONSHINE!

Two hobos stole a bottle of moonshine liquor and fled on a departing freight train. One of them took the first drink just as the train entered a tunnel.

"How's it taste?" said the other.

"Not bad, but I just went blind," the first hobo groaned.

Claret is the liquor for boys; port for men; but he who aspires to be a hero must drink brandy. *Samuel Johnson*

WHAT...SOBRIETY?

A thirsty traveler walked into a country store with a gallon jug half filled with water. He asked the storekeeper to pour two quarts of whisky into his jug.

When the jug was full, the traveler said, "I'll pay up first of next month."

"I don't give no credit to strangers," howled the storekeeper, snatching the jug and pouring out what he figured were *his* two quarts.

And the traveler went his way, stopping now and then to sip his whisky and water...happily.

The trouble with you, Lennox, is that when you're not drunk, you're sober. *W.B. Yeats*

After the disastrous San Francisco earthquake of 1906, one of the structures still standing was a large sign declaring the joys of Hostetter's Whisky. The paradox motivated someone of that day to write this rhyme:

If God hit San Francisco town
Because we were too frisky,
Why did he knock the churches down
And leave Hostetter's Whisky?

EPITAPH:
Here lies John Turwitt, a learned Divine.
He died in a fit through drinking Port Wine.

SMASHED AGAIN!

People with hangovers would prefer to believe they had been poisoned rather than over-served. Not too long ago in England, that could have been true. In fact, the word *intoxicate* started out meaning *poison put in it*, although it applied to hunting arrows. Later, when poisoning people became a quaint art, doctoring liquor was one of the standard methods. It took mankind a very long time to perceive that the liquor itself might be poisonous.

Hangover: proof that you still are the man you once were.

KISS ME, TIPSY!

In the 3rd Century B.C. a particularly stingy and straight-laced chap named Cato devised a way of finding out if the women of his family had been hitting the wine jug. He kissed them, inhaling deeply all the while. Nice, Cato!

What did the Governor of North Carolina say to the Governor of South Carolina?
"It's a long time between drinks."

THE OLD BARREL, BUTT AND HOGSHEAD RIDDLE!

When ordering ten gallons of wine or more in a single container, remember each is a *cask*, but there are at least seven different *casks*. Here we go:

Keg — holds ten gallons or less.
Barrel — 31½ gallon capacity.
Tierce — 42 gallon container.
Hogshead — two barrels or 63 gallons.
Pipe — two hogsheads or 126 gallons.

RIDDLE: Did any occupant of the White House have the nickname *Lemonade Lucy?*

ANSWER: The wife of President Rutherford B. Hayes would not allow wine, beer or other strong spirits to be served in the White House while she was first lady. She substituted lemonade at receptions and dinners. Thus: "Lemonade Lucy."

Butt — same size as a pipe.

Tun — the economy-size: four hogshead or two pipes or 252 gallons.

For those who prefer their wine in glass containers, a *jeroboam* is about four-fifths of a gallon; a *magnum* is a half gallon.

Now you can put this whole item in your *pipe* and drink it!

EPITAPH:
'Twas as she tript from cask to cask
in at a bung-hole she quickly fell
suffocation was her task
she had no time to say Farewell.

MCCOY STRIKES BACK!

And there's the tale about a well-known fighter of a bygone era, Kid McCoy. It seems he was in a saloon where a drunk was making disparaging remarks about the Kid's ring abilities. Despite warnings from the bartender, the drunk went on and finally crowed he could whip *any* McCoy. The Kid had enough. He quietly decked the drunk, then picked him up and said. "Any McCoy but the *real* McCoy."

If at fires you don't succeed, try gin.

OLD DAN TUCKER!

Old Dan Tucker, he got drunk,
He fell in the fire, and he kicked up a chunk;
The red-hot coals got in his shoe,
And whew-wee! how the ashes flew!

(*Chorus*)

Get out of the way for old Dan Tucker,
He's too late to get his supper.
Get out of the way for old Dan Tucker,
He's too late to get his supper.

Old Dan Tucker was a fine old man,
He washed his face in the frying pan,
He combed his head with a wagon wheel,
And he died with the toothache in his heel.
Daniel Tucker, he's a Quaker,

He drinks buttermilk by the acre,
Supper's over, dishes washed,
Nothing left but a little bit of squash.
Old Dan Tucker was a fine old man,
He used to ride the Derby ram,
He sent him a-whizzin' down the hill,
And if he hasn't sot up, he's a-lyin' there still.

Everyone knows about the organization AA. There was an organization — and perhaps it still exists — which went them two better: AAAA, which stood for the American Association for the Advancement of Atheism.

EPITAPH:
She drank ale, porter, punch and wine,
And lived to age of ninety-nine.

PATCH UP YOUR LOGIC!

Back in the 17th Century, the makers of pitchers had a simple way of testing them. They filled each with water. Since the ones that *wouldn't hold water* couldn't be sold, today we think of a faulty bit of logic as not *holding water.*

The donkey is ideal for freight.
He'll carry equal his weight.
His habits are fine:
He never drinks wine;
He's not known for staying out leight.

MORE WATER!

Arab gem-traders, not beneath promoting their wares, used the term *water* to describe the luster of their pearls and diamonds. By the 18th Century, diamond merchants were grading stones with *of the first water*, of the second water, etc. We still speak of any high quality item as being *of the first water.*

In an Arabic land one could drink a dozen *juleps* without ill effect, since it was their word for rosewater. Don't try it in Kentucky!

Remember: The bartender is the only one on the sober side of the bar.

THE HEART!

Learning by heart means to memorize, right? Wouldn't it be more efficient to learn by mind? Not necessarily. In another age, the heart became known as the dwelling place of human emotions. Therefore, if a person wished to hold in memory those things which had great emotional impact, it was learned by heart.

The only things he didn't regret were those he couldn't remember.

NICE APPLE YOU'VE GOT IN YOUR EYE!

The above may sound uncomfortable but, to the Ancients, the pupil of the eye looked like an apple. They also thought it was a solid body rather than an aperture, and so they often attributed blindness to destruction of the pupil. To this day we speak of things of great personal value as the *apple of our eye.*

There's many a sip on the lip of the cup.

SOMETHING UP YOUR SLEEVE!

Far be it from fashion to follow a sane line. Take sleeves: at one time, it was the fashion to have them so long they reached the floor. In the voluminous folds almost anything could be hidden. That's where we got *to have something up your sleeve.* And, when folks wanted to disguise a laugh or grin, they raised one huge sleeve to hide their expression...they were *laughing up their sleeves.*

As intriguing as a low-cut gown on a starving model.

THAT'S A VERY USELESS CHAPEAU YOU HAVE THERE!

Examine a painting of soldiers of the Revolutionary War period and you're bound to spot one or more of those odd triangular hats with the brim turned up all around. Turned up like that, the brim was useless. From that came an expression to describe rendering a soldier useless — to *knock him into a cocked hat*...as in what others often do to your pet theory.

In the heyday of Panama hats, most of them were made in Ecuador.

The Greeks had another way of saying, "The tooth-straightener had no pulse." They would have said, "The orthodontist was asphyxiated." We don't know when they might have said such a thing, but just in case.

Noah Webster began preparing his American Dictionary of English Language in 1807 and it wasn't published until 1828.

THE GRAMMARIAN!

Your training might one day save your life. Take the case of the young grammarian who was accosted by a psychotic while visiting the zoo.

Grabbing her by the hair and dragging her toward a cage of wild beasts, he screamed, "Would you rather a lion ate you or a gorilla?"

Without a second's hesitation the grammarian replied, "Yes, I'd much prefer that the lion ate the gorilla."

Mother to squawling child: "Shut your mouth and eat!"

BY CANDLELIGHT!

Long before city streets were illuminated, a wealthy man did not go out at night on foot without a servant carrying a candle ahead of him. A servant who got lost was considered worthless...*he can't hold a candle to.*

*We don't know when the **butler** graduated to his present role. We do know he was originally the servant who brought in the wine bottles.*

Language has a way of evolving from the exact to the vague or general. Take the word *quarantine.* Today we think of it as any term of isolation to prevent the spread of a contagious disease. However, in ancient Rome, it was a very definite 40-day period — the legal limit a widow could remain in the house of her dead husband.

*Nietzsche: "Woman was God's **second** mistake."*

IT SEEMS TO US!

The word *focus* arrived at its present meaning in an odd fashion. To the early Romans, the hearth was the center of family life, and *focus* was their word for it. In 1604, the German astronomer and mathematician, Johannes Kepler, observing that light passing through a lens ignited paper, named the burning point of the lens' curve the *focus.*

Drink to me only with thine ears. I'm nearsighted!

Many languages use suffixes to indicate 'little.' The French diminutive *ette* shows up in our word 'blanket.' The Italian *ino* is seen

RIDDLE: Do we use any expressions out of the days when knights were bold?

ANSWER: If you refer to a *free-lance* writer, you are using a medieval expression. Some knights traveled about offering their services to the highest bidder. Owing allegiance to no specific lord, their lances were free for hire.

in 'casino' and 'bambino.' Old English, too, had a diminutive ending — *le. Knuckle* is literally little bone; *kernel*, little corn; and *icicle,* little ice. More imaginative is *puddle*, since *pudd* was the Old English word for ditch.

It's useless to inform creatures who are half-monster, half-cow. It just goes in one ogre and out the udder.

TOWER OF BABEL!

Did you realize that our word *babble* has a biblical backround? As the story goes, God was determined that the Tower of Babel would not be completed. So he saw to it that the workers suddenly began to speak in different languages. Not being able to communicate with one another, they had to stop the construction. Imagine the sound of several thousand different languages being spoken at once. *A babble!*

Then there was the kid who quit sunday school the minute he heard about freedom of religion.

"O.K."

Most explanations of the O.K. are interesting, yet most unlikely. One attributes the expression to an old French term. The other suggests that, in reality, the O.K. is altogether an error. Originally, the letters were not O.K. at all but O.R., which stood for *Order Record,* a once customary endorsement of documents. O.R.!

We heartily admire the judgment of those who judge us to be admirable.

ATLAS!

Some words acquired their meanings in odd ways. Take *atlas* — a book of maps. In Greek mythology, Atlas was a bad giant who was punished by the Gods in a unique fashion. He was forced to stand on the rim of the Earth and hold up the sky for all eternity. Many years later, he was depicted supporting a globe on his head. Finally a cartographer of the 1700's drew a picture of Atlas on the cover of his book of maps — presto, a book of maps became known as an atlas. Just think, if the map-maker had used the Greek God of the Sea on his cover, teachers today would be telling geography students to "look it up in a poseidon."

Pterodactyls were pterrible pto ptouch:
Ptall, ptoptally ptoady, scaly and such;
Nopt ptimorous, nopt ptiny, a bipt of a snake
When he flew, he left in his wake
A ptrail of ptwelve pteardrops — ptoo much!!

LET ME HEAR YOUR SKIN ONCE MORE!

We presume one of the reasons East and West haven't been able to meet is the difference in awareness. Did you know that the classical Chinese classification for nature's sounds are stone, baked earth, silk, metal, gourd, bamboo, wood and skin? Imagine: no traffic clamor, jet aircraft, rock music, howling dogs or squalling babies!

The Mysterious East: The ink which the Chinese invented is called ***India ink.***

YOU'VE HEARD THAT SONG BEFORE!

Damion Indlewilf is slightly psychotic when it comes to the language of popular song titles. Either they should be altered or they should be expanded according to him. He passed these along to us:

My Sweet Unbreakable You
Mary Is A Grand Old Dame
I Hadn't Anyone Til You and It Was Better That Way
Come to Me, My Melon-headed Booby
I've Got Rhythm... and Blues... and Beri-Beri
Alcoa Oe! Song of the Aluminum Islands
Red Dolph, the Rude-Nosed Rheindeer
When I Had Two Lips and You Had a Big Red Nose
I Could Have Danced Alright If You Had Let Me Lead

The ocelot smiles a lot, contemplating what he's not!

CRITICS CORNER, SAMUEL JOHNSON DIVISION!

When asked about another author's work, Johnson said, "I would rather praise it than read it."

Then, probably with a bit of self-assessment, he wrote, "Criticism is a study by which men grow important and formidable at very small expense."

RIDDLE: What does the WTCU have to say about cotton gin?

ANSWER: Not a helluva lot! The *gin* part is simply short for *engine*.

We've also heard that being a critic is one of the few endeavors in which stupidity is not considered a drawback.

WHIRLWIND TOUR!

When Jules Verne published his science-fiction tale *The Tour of the World in Eighty Days,* most people assessed it as just that...fiction.

Sixteen years later, in 1889, an enterprising reporter for the New York World named Nellie Bly set out to prove the globe could be circumnavigated in eighty days. Inasmuch as there were no cars or airplanes, Miss Bly went by boat, train and horse-drawn vehicles. And she made it in seventy-two days, six hours, and eleven minutes. Of course, if the airplane had been in existence, she would have been bumped in Bangkok, missed the connecting flight in Rome and spent another few weeks just on delayed departures.

Never put off a day until tomorrow.

GIMME A ROCK! I'VE GOT AN IDEA!

Once man learned to write, he began recording words on just about anything that stood still — stone, clay, papyrus reeds, sheepskin, wood and finally paper. For books written on exotic materials, one of the oldest known copies of the bible called the *Alexandrian codex* is unique. It was written on antelope skin.

A novelist was asked if he had drawn from his own experiences in his books. "Well, I would have," he said, "but I've been too busy writing to have any."

He is one of those orators of whom it was well said, "Before they get up, they do not know what they are going to say; but when they are speaking, they do not know what they are saying; and when they sit down, they don't know what they have said." Winston Churchill

The last time you sat down to count all the words in Tolstoi's "War and Peace," what total did you get? If you were around the half a million mark, you were close.

Consider this: practically no one these days asks why a book is called a volume. That's because practically no one cares that those clever Egyptians wrote on papyrus in long strips and, when they were finished, they rolled the strip up and tied it neatly. The Latin word for *roll* gave us volume.

Jonathan Swift claimed, "There are men who pretend to understand a book by scouting through the index: as if a traveler should go about to describe a palace when he had seen nothing but the privy."

TRANSLATING THE BIBLE!

The publication of bibles in English had a great deal to do with the popularizing of the language in England. The first English translation was hand-written by John Wycliffe around 1380. But here's an interesting contradiction. In one current American textbook on the use of English, the authors say it was against the law for the English to read Wycliffe's bible; while, in another textbook (also widely used in the 1970's in America) it is claimed Wycliffe did his monumental translation so ordinary people could read it. Are they telling us that, Wycliffe so hungered for a best-seller, he didn't care if his readers went to jail?

The effect of Wycliffe's bible is not felt much today, since it was written in Middle English, that confusing form found in Chaucer's *The Canterbury Tales.* It was the King James Version of the bible, published in 1611, which did so much to spread the use of modern English.

The most sinful places mentioned in the bible are Syphilis and Gonorrhea!

HOBBY WITH A POINT!

Charles Baker, an employee of the U.S. Bureau of Printing and

RIDDLE: Did Oscar Wilde say, "Marriage is the only adventure open to the timid?"

ANSWER: No, that was Voltaire. Wilde said, "Men marry because they are tired; women because they are curious. Both are disappointed."

Engraving, just couldn't leave engraving alone. In his spare time (over a three-year period), he engraved all sixty-nine words plus the punctuation marks of the Lord's Prayer on the head of a pin.

A lazy man knows what he's missing!

NEWSMEN ON PARADE!

Reading the newspaper these days is a schizophrenic pastime at best. One is torn between a belief that the world has gone berserk and an opinion that reporting is a craft often practiced by wayward loonies. Here's a sample from one American metropolitan daily, *on a single day.*

In a story about six unsolved stranglings in Georgia, the last three paragraphs read like this:

> *The last attacks traced to the strangler occurred over the weekend. Police say an intruder was scared off by one woman — although he may have stayed in the house and slipped past police when they arrived.*
>
> *Officers believe he may have slipped away and killed a woman just two blocks away Saturday morning.*
>
> *Boone and Muscogee County Coroner J. Donald Kilgore said they believe the killer sneaked past police, who were called to Ruth Schwob's home early Saturday and, instead, strangled neighbor Mildred Dismukes Brown.*

After one *slipped past,* one *slipped away* and one *sneaked past,* one gets the notion that someone eluded the police. Then, if we read the last paragraph correctly, are we to assume the frustrated police strangled a neighbor?

Then came a headline on the international scene which leads one to believe that some trials are pre-judged:

LEBANON PLANS TO TRY GUILTY IN WAR FLARE-UP

Same newspaper, we caught a small item about a woman from Ghana.

> *Ghana's oldest citizen, 154-year-old Aba Odekye, died at her home village in the country's eastern region last week.*
>
> *Shortly before she died, Mrs. Odekye, whose eldest son is 94, said the secret of long life was to eat vegetables and palm-oil soup, take plenty of long walks — and avoid sex.*

Now we don't know how to account for Mrs. Odekye's 94-year-old son.

We read with alarm that in California some flood control officials had engaged in a cloud-seeding during a flood condition. We felt better when one of the seeders said they had disregarded a forecast of heavy rains because they didn't always believe in the weather reports.

In a story filed from Rio de Janiero, we learned that two members of the recently disbanded punk rock group, *the Sex Pistols*, had added an actor and a 'great train robber Ronald Biggs.' This Biggs, it seems, after conviction for his part in the $7.3 million robbery of England's Royal mail, had escaped and fled to Brazil.

The actor joining the group, dressed in a Nazi uniform, announced to the press conference that they were making a movie that would celebrate "the ending of the Sex Pistols and the creation and beginning of a new group." Now that's a movie we're dying to see!

To fight off our growing nausea and confusion, we turned to the entertainment section. There we happened upon news of a dance company. It read: "Programs today and Friday will contain *Country Dances, The Fugue* and *Sue's Leg*. The program tomorrow will include *Simon Medley, Cacklin' Hen, Mud* and *Eight Jelly Rolls*."

Before we were able to set fire to the paper, a full-page ad hit us. A certain airline was announcing money-saving fares "to 83 *new* cities." And here we thought the building boom had ended.

When you think of the condition of the world today you sometimes wish that Noah had missed the boat.

Bishop Fulton Sheen

DEAD RIGHT!

The term *mortician* came about because undertakers wanted to add a touch of class to their trade. That might lead you to believe that *mausoleum* had a similar history. Uh-uh! Around 350 B.C. Artemesia, widow of the King of Caria, built a very special tomb for her dead husband. His name was Mausolus. Get it?

If you have but one ox, you need but one whiffletree!

POCAHONTAS!

Famous American Indian words you won't recognize: Daughter of the Stars is what Indians meant when they said *Shenandoah*. "She is playful": that's what Powhatan said to the pilgrims in describing his daughter. The word he used was *Pocahontas.* Her real name was

RIDDLE: Is there a similarity between early Greek writing and a plowed field?

ANSWER: Early Greek writing was *exactly* like a plowed field. If the first line read from left to right, the second line read from right to left, and so on. In fact, the Greek name for this form of writing was called *boustrophedon*, meaning turning of the ox, as when a furrow was completed the ox was turned to plow back in the opposite direction. Besides making reading complex, all slanted letters were tilted in the direction of the line.

Matoaka. When Indians said *How*, they weren't asking for instructions. It was simply a greeting. They had no word for good-bye — they simply went, avoiding drawn out leave-taking.

Yell County, Arkansas has been wired for sound!

SPLIT-SECOND TIMING!

How can historians go on unchallenged with statements such as, *The Industrial Revolution occurred between the 18th and 19th Centuries?*

Synchronize your watches, men. The Renaissance is coming up in...30 seconds.

He authored two best-sellers to support his habit of writing badly.

GULLIVER IN THE HALLS OF JUSTICE!

In *Gulliver's Travels*, Jonathan Swift wrote, "It is a maxim among lawyers that whatever hath been done before may legally be done again: and therefore they take a special care to record all the decisions formerly made against common justice and the general reason of mankind. These, under the name of *precedents*, they produce as authorities to justify the most iniquitous opinions; and the judges never fail of directing accordingly."

One man, alone and not too bright, when arguing to prevent personal inconvenience, may overpower a dozen brilliant minds arguing solely from conviction.

WE'LL DRINK TO THAT!

"Some people are so fond of ill-luck that they run half-way to meet it," wrote Douglas Jerrold. And Plutarch quoted Socrates, "If all our misfortunes were laid in one common heap, whence everyone must take an equal portion, most persons would be contented to take their own and depart."

Winston Churchill defined a lie as "a terminal inexactitude."

DOWN THE CRIME-ROWS PATH!

An electric chair operating on AC current was twice as efficient as one using DC.

The New England states are the only ones never to have had a reported lynching.

Piracy and mail robbery were capital crimes in the United States at one time.

The slang term *stool pigeon* comes from the practice of using one pigeon as a decoy to entice other pigeons into a cage.

Before the repeal of Prohibition, about fifty percent of the inmates of federal prisons were liquor-law violators.

The *Tommy-gun* or Thompson sub-machine gun, is closely associated with the gangster depredations in Chicago. Perhaps, then, it's appropriate that the first operative machine gun was invented by a Chicago doctor named *Gatling* in 1862.

No sense wasting time thinking about death... there's plenty of time for that after it's happened.

Clifford Irving, of Howard Hughes hoax notoriety, joined a rather illustrious group of authors when he marched off to jail. St. Paul was one of the earlier authors who spent time behind bars. Then there was John Bunyan, Oscar Wilde, Henry David Thoreau, Sir Walter Raleigh, John Galsworthy and O. Henry.

Oscar Wilde said, "Experience is the name everyone gives to his mistakes."

ONE THING LEADS TO ANOTHER!

"If once a man indulges himself in murder, very soon he comes to think little of robbing; and from robbing he next comes to drinking and Sabbath-breaking, and from that to uncivility and procrastination." So said Thomas De Quincey in the 19th Century.

He had a horror of different collars.

HEY, MIRANDA! WHERE'S THE RIOT?

The Miranda decision resulted in today's rule that law enforcement officers must *read a suspect his rights*. Way back in 1716, the English Parliament enacted a law which promised imprisonment to

RIDDLE: Did American judges ever force convicted criminals to sit on a pelican?

ANSWER: Yes, even Al Capone sat on a pelican — the English word of the Spanish *Alactraz*. Originally, *Alcatraz* meant albatross, but is that any better than sitting on a pelican?

any twelve or more people who "unlawfully, riotously and tumultuously assembled together, to the disturbance of the public peace."

This gem was called The Riot Act. Whenever the minions of the law came upon such a group, they were first required to read them the proclamation outlawing riots. In short, they *read the riot act to them.* If the twelve or more persons went on 'riotously and tumultuously' after hearing the riot act, they were arrested and received sentences from a few years at hard labor to life.

We wonder if they allowed a group of only eleven to raise hell?

A jury is a group of 12 people of average ignorance.
Herbert Spencer

WE WISH WE'D SAID THAT!

Lord Byron concluded, "Society is now one polished horde, formed of two mighty tribes, the Bores and the Bored."

"Nothing in life is so exhilarating as to be shot at without result," according to Winston Churchill.

It was back in the 1st Century B.C. that Horace wrote, "This is a fault common to all singers, that among their friends they are never inclined to sing when they are asked; unasked, they never desist."

The Reverend Henry Ward Beecher
Called a hen a most elegant creature.
Then the hen, pleased with that,
Laid an egg in his hat,
And thus did the hen reward Beecher.

HALF TRUTHS!

Sure, skiing is free! Riding the lift is what costs. Mountain climbers rave on about *ascending* and *arriving*, but they say little of the joys of *descending*. Mad, zany nights before have their inevitable sad, grainy mornings after. Honeymoons and vacations end. Now that we've got you nice and gloomy, play a hand of solitaire!

When you're passing judgment on another, remember that he may be judging you on an equally flimsy collection of facts.

IT'S NOT WHAT IT SEEMS!

Californians who were out of work used to go the Department of Employment office for unemployment checks. Now they go to the *Department of Human Resources.*

Janitors cleaned buildings long, long ago. Now the work is done by *Sanitation Engineers*. Another branch of this same high-sounding group cleans the streets.

A weather report has become an *environmental assessment,* and the weatherman has become a *meteorologist*. Who runs prison systems? *Departments of Correction*! Throwing a shoe at a howling cat in the middle of the night is probably known today as *nocturnal non-programmed noise abatement.*

If everyone sounds like a specialist, some of them really are. How can one get a tooth filled when a listing of dentists warns "Practice Limited To..." orthodontics, periodontics, oral and maxillofacial surgery, prosthondontics, endodontics, pediadontics and perhaps a few more dontics?

Remember the old Eye-Ear-Nose-and-Throat doctor? Today he is an *otorhinolarynogologist.* Hell, you could be dead by the time you learn to pronounce it. Seen a good oncologist lately? He's a tumor man. If your thoracic and vascular man is out of town, who do you call? Do you fear your otologist and your rhinologist might get together and discuss you?

Want A Burglar Alarm For Your Home? Simple. Call a *residential security-system analyst.* The reason you don't see any garbage trucks anymore is because they are *mobile waste-disposal units.* Kennels have become *pet hotels*. Salesmen are *sales engineers.* Did you know nuts

RIDDLE: Was it Ben Franklin who said, "There are three faithful friends — an old wife, an old dog and ready money?"

ANSWER: Sure was. And on infidelity, Franklin had these words: "Where there's marriage without love, there will be love without marriage."

and bolts are *industrial fasteners?* And the guy who runs the drive-in hamburger joint is a *quick-food service specialist*. Even the good old mortician is now a *funeral director* who offers such scientific wonders as world-wide shipping service analysis and social security benefit consultation. Finally, gardeners who weren't satisfied to have become landscapers have now moved into *environmental planning.*

In the 1st Century B.C., Horace wrote, "I labor to be brief and manage to obscure." Things haven't changed much, Horace.

THE CONFUSING HUCKSTERS!

For years ad-writers for perfume companies wracked their scented brains for provocative product names. Apparently they assumed that women are in a constant state of trembling anticipation, filled with secret yearnings of the most lascivious variety. And they were coming to the rescue, offering an aroma which would render all males senseless with passion. In the meantime, the ads would arouse in eager men their basest instincts so that they, too, would race to the nearest perfume counter for an ounce of some odoriferous aphrodisiac to overwhelm a hitherto resistant damsel.

Just in case the audience for their ads were total clods, they pictorialized. Our favorite has been the scene in which a lust-crazed violinist is bending his accompanyist backward over the piano. What woman did not have a secret desire to be attacked by a mad fiddler? What red-blooded American male could not picture himself as the overwhelmed violinist? Presto, your filthiest dreams come true.

Alas, of late, the perfume ads lack fire. Some have even strayed from the sex-demented to the demure. One has seen fit to presume that, in the hearts of men and women, the overweaning desire is to be buddies. Why else name a perfume *Charlie?* Or are we overlooking the feminist thrust? Will there be an *eau de Max?* Or some *now* realism such as a *Georgie Smell?* Or will we soon have Locker-Room Bouquet?

Joshua had fits and a bottle of Geritol.

THE TELEPHONE PEDDLAR!

Is there anything more enjoyable than to be interrupted at dinner by a telephone pitch-man offering you the very last chance in your area to buy a $3,500 mausoleum crypt...prior to need? Unless you learn how to turn off these creeps, you're in for a lifetime of cold steak and potatoes.

Most telephone pitches are memorized or read from a prepared text. Throw the pitch-person (yes, sexual barriers are down in the pitch field) off stride and many of them get lost, stammer and often go back to their pat opening. So, here are a few stride-breakers to get you off the hook and off the phone.

"Excuse me a moment, I think the doctor's coming out of her room now." Works with everyone but the mausoleum crypt and the funeral plots people; with them it backfires.

Throw them a curve with, "Could I interest you in a set of mohair undergarments that haven't been worn in eleven years?"

A giggle, building into a loud laugh, almost always stops them momentarily. After all, you're supposed to be as serious about being sold as they are about selling you.

Any non sequitur that pops into your head works nicely. Our favorite is "Alfred Mason's back in town, you know." Never had a pitch-person yet who didn't have to interrupt himself to find out who Alfred Mason is. When they do ask, use your humblest tones and say, "Oh, I am sorry. I must have the wrong number." Hang up immediately.

The oblique interruption, in another form, can be, "Well, it took you long enough to call back! The downstairs toilet is stopped up again!" Bang the receiver down hard after this gambit. They seldom ring you back.

Giddiness is effective, too. If you get one of those so-called contest calls with a question like, "Who's buried in Grant's Tomb?" be coy and answer, "Oh, I know this is a trick question...so I'll say Harriet Beecher Stowe...no Marvin Stickley!" They'll give you another chance, not realizing you can go on like that forever.

A final stunt that has one disadvantage. As soon as you've determined it's a pitch, say, "I'm sorry, no one is home." and hang up. The disadvantage is that you don't get to see the look on the pitch-person's face.

What with the increasing frequency of telephone solicitations, we think we will begin answering the phone with, "No!"

DRESSED FOR WORK!

We didn't realize so many young people read Henry David Thoreau until we unearthed his statement, "Beware of all enterprises that require new clothes."

We hired a receptionist a while back who, in addition to being inventive with bubble gum, possessed a wardrobe fraught with surprises. One day we judged her to be one of the Rover Boys in drag; the next day she would have looked at home over a steaming cauldron of toads.

As she settled into her task of frightening off anyone foolish enough to enter our offices, she grew more casual. First she gave up hair-combing. Faded blue jeans with frayed bottoms replaced skirts. She went from shoes to sandals to barefeet in a matter of four days. We began to think she'd been trained by the Gypsy Rose Lee School for Secretaries.

Then, just as we were all growing accustomed to the squalor she lent the place, she ran off with a hovel salesman from Kentucky. Her replacement is a disconcertingly neat young lady, obviously not the Thoreau scholar our former helpmate was.

The person to whom you are speaking is not here!

BLOODY FAMILY STORY!

A brother and sister have a closer blood relationship than either of them has to the father or mother. Figure it out: each child has half the mother's blood and half the father's; but, they have all common blood. That means that half-sisters and half-brothers are as closely related as children to each parent. Who started this anyway?

Family Tree: We don't see anything wrong with a person who takes pride in his forefathers (or even his foremothers), but it's damned maddening when he tries to take *credit* for them, too.

He described a Genealogist as one who traces back your family as far as your money will go.

IT'S PHYSICAL!

The early Greeks did a lot of poking around the human body to see what makes us tick. The first part of the blood network they discovered were veins. Then, in the Second Century, a Greek physician found the arterial system. But he thought these vessels were to carry air throughout the body, so he named them after the Greek word for windpipe — *arteria.*

Athletes, particularly long-distance runners, claim to get a *second wind.* The effect is real. At the outset of physical activity, the heart is seeking to adjust to the action of the lungs. When the heart adjusts to the rate of air intake and outgo of the lungs, it is less difficult to maintain the activity level of the body. Oh yeah!

It's the tenth cranial nerve that tells your brain you're thirsty. It's your wife who overrules your tenth cranial nerve at parties.

Reunion: "One may return to the place of his birth; he cannot go back to his youth," wrote John Burroughs. Dammit! He's right.

TENCH-HUT!

The next time you're drafted, remember that forceful commands are voiced with a full breath in the lungs. Timid obedience usually begins on the inhale and is weak at the start, gets even weaker and rises to an unwelcome falsetto.

Preserving one's identity has become instinctive. Even your nose is blessed with this sixth sense. After all, the nose stops growing for that very reason, realizing if it reached twelve inches it would become a foot.

***Whimbrels** of the curlew clan cry out **wheep** whene'er they can!*

DEVOTION TO DUTY, EARLY FEMALE DIVISION!

Those fearsome female fighters, the *Amazons*, got their name from two Greek words meaning without a breast. It is reputed that these martial maidens were so dedicated to being good soldiers that they cut off their right breasts in order to draw their bows more accurately.

For some unaccountable reason Fairy Godfathers are on the increase!

SNEEZING YOUR WAY UP THE SOCIAL LADDER!

It wasn't until around the 15th Century that man got over his fear that sneezing let the breath of life out. In short, he faced the fact that a good sneeze cleared the mind and actually felt good.

Then high society took the sneeze to its collective bosom in the 17th Century. An almost continuous fit of sneezing was heard throughout Europe's castles. The biggest impression a lord could make at a social gathering was to sneeze his head off the whole evening, blasting over wine glasses and blowing fans right out of ladies' hands.

Some of the tallwigs of that day couldn't always come up with the big sneeze at the crucial moment, so they began resorting to a sneaky device — the snuffbox. Oh, the experimenting with various

RIDDLE: How many armless women stand six-feet, three-inches tall?

ANSWER: The only one we know personally is the *Venus de Milo*.

combinations of sneeze-inducing herbs and tobacco was a scientific marvel.

One of the more expensive concoctions to be stuffed up the nose was *The Howler*. The excruciatingly loud racket it produced was known to have sent wolfhounds whimpering into the night. *Lightning* was a good mixture, too. It acted so swiftly a gentleman often blew his snuff all over his companions. *Two Cannons* was the powerhouse snuff, producing an enormous two-sneeze barrage that could knock a lady's wig askew at twenty paces. But Francois Kerchoo, snuff-maker to many of Europe's royal houses, came up with the whopper, called *Kerchoo's Surprise*.

You see, a definite social pattern had evolved. When one gentleman opened his snuffbox, those about him waited to do the same until he had performed. But *Kerchoo's Surprise* was a delayed-action snuff. Mistaking the sneezeless interval as a snuff malfunction, they opened their snuffboxes. Whammo! The ear-crushing explosion emptied every snuffbox in the room, tore the buttons off a footman's waistcoat, knocked in a greenhouse roof a block away and extinguished every candle in the palace.

So, if you hear an object described as *not to be sneezed at*, you know it's something all-fired important. Oh, they had to ban *Kerchoo's Surprise* as a threat to life and property and snuff-taking has never recovered its social status.

A hiccup is a sneeze with a poor sense of direction!

SO YOU WANT TO BE PRESIDENT!

Anyone looking for a blueprint on how to become president of the United States will discover that the paths to the highest office are as diverse as the men who followed them.

Seventeen of our thirty-eight presidents began their political careers in *appointive* positions. Eighteen aspirants jumped into the political swim as *elected* officials.

Four of the successful candidates ran for only one political office — the presidency. They were Zachary Taylor, U.S. Grant, Dwight D. Eisenhower and Herbert Hoover. William Henry Harrison's only elective office prior to becoming president was as a territorial delegate to Congress in 1799.

Since twenty-four of our presidents have been lawyers, it's not surprising that ten of these were attorneys for cities or counties early in their political lives, and two — Taft and Truman — were judges.

What about the vice-presidency as a stepping stone to the top job? Thirteen vice-presidents went up the ladder, but eight of those succeeded to the office because of the death of the president. And Gerald Ford took executive office as a result of the resignation of Nixon.

Eight presidents held cabinet offices; six were Secretaries of State; two were Secretaries of War (Monroe was the only one to have held two different cabinet posts...State and War); one (Hoover) was Secretary of Commerce.

Fourteen of our chiefs were state governors, Jefferson being the first and Carter the most recent. Two — Cleveland and Coolidge — were mayors.

What we've been leading up to is the fact that being a member of Congress has been the most successful route to the White House. Sixteen men who were to become our leaders were senators, starting with Monroe and going through Nixon. But eighteen members of the House of Representatives have become presidents. Actually eleven presidents served in both the House and Senate — Andrew Jackson being the first and Nixon the last, to date.

Who said, "I would rather be right than president?"
Henry Clay (1777-1852)

Most people know that one president — William Howard Taft — also served on the Supreme Court. It had almost happened once before. James Madison appointed John Quincy Adams to the highest court in 1811 and Adams was confirmed. However, he chose not to accept the appointment. Fourteen years later, he was elected to the presidency.

Oddly enough, the president who held the widest variety of major political offices is little-known John Tyler. In addition to the presidency, Tyler was Vice-President, Representative, Senator, Governor (Virginia,twice), and State Legislator (Virginia).

And what happens to the top men in our government after they have left office? Only three followed up with major federal positions. John Quincy Adams served in the House of Representatives; Andrew Johnson was a Senator; and William Howard Taft was Chief Justice of the Supreme Court. So, only two risked defeat at the ballot box after being president.

RIDDLE: Zachary Taylor was one of two U.S. Presidents to serve in the Black Hawk War of 1832. The other was a postmaster, a surveyor and a school teacher prior to his election as president. What would his name be?

ANSWER: Abraham Lincoln is the one. Lincoln was also our tallest president — a full foot taller than our shortest, five-feet, four-inch James Madison.

Eight of our leaders have died in office to date. Not as well-known is the fact that seven vice-presidents have died in office.

Name ten of the fifty-six men who signed the Declaration of Independence!

IT'S ALL RELATIVES!

The closest thing we've ever had to a dynasty in this country was when John Quincy Adams, son of former President John Adams, became president. Next closest was Benjamin Harrison, Grandson of William Henry Harrison. James Madison and Zachary Taylor were second cousins; Theodore and Franklin Roosevelt were fifth cousins.

Nothing so needs reforming as other people's habits.
Mark Twain

It's rumored that George Washington once slept under a square-tester. He probably did so more than once, since a square-tester was one type of canopy for a four-poster. Two other common types are the tent-top and the field-top.

If you want an intelligent answer, ask an intelligent question.

PRESIDENTS IN WAR!

Twenty-five of our presidents served in the armed forces during wartime. Would you have guessed that more presidents served in the Civil War than in any other? Seven fought in that one, while six served during World War II.

Certainly an oddity is the fact that while four presidents fought in the War of 1812, three in both the Revolutionary War and the Mexican War, only two were in World War I — Truman and Eisenhower. Two who served in the little-known Black Hawk War were Zachary Taylor and Lincoln. And Teddy Roosevelt was the only president in the Spanish-American War.

Zachary Taylor was the only president to serve in three wars...War of 1812, Black Hawk War and the Mexican War. Andrew Jackson, Ulysses S. Grant and Eisenhower each served in two wars.

And the first to rise to the rank of Lieutenant General were Washington and Grant.

The inherent virtue of Socialism is the equal sharing of miseries.
W. Churchill

It shouldn't come as any surprise that President James Buchanan had no children, inasmuch as he was the nation's only top leader to remain a bachelor. Five other presidents were childless — Washington (but at least he was father of an entire country), Madison, Jackson, Polk and Harding.

We lost both pages of ***Famous Sayings of President James Polk!***

THE JEFFERSON-BURR DECISION!

The controversial Aaron Burr very nearly became top man in the election of 1800. He and Jefferson tied in the electoral college, so it went to the House of Representatives for a decision. It wasn't until the thirty-fifth ballot that Jefferson won out and Burr became vice-president. That election, by the way, brought about the twelfth amendment which stipulated that voters cast separate ballots for president and vice-president.

One other election went to the House. In 1824, Andrew Jackson picked up 99 electoral votes to John Quincy Adams' 84, but it wasn't a majority. The House, voting on the basis of one vote per state, gave it to Adams by a 13 to 7 margin. The election of 1824 was unique in another way — all four of the presidential candidates were listed as Republicans.

Of all the Scoop Jacksons to choose from, who picked that one?

IS THERE A FATHER IN THE HOUSE?

Since the Speaker of the House of Representatives is not only a very powerful legislative official, but is also in the line of presidential succession, you would think there would be a rule about who is to give a new speaker the oath. Nope, just a tradition that it be administered by the oldest member, in point of service, if he can be awakened in time for the ceremony. This gentleman is called *The Father of the House.* Tradition being what it is, we assume that if the oldest member happened to be a woman, she would still be referred to as the *Father of the House.*

The hardiness of weeds and the frailty of flowers may give some parents cause to doubt the way they are bringing up their children.

RIDDLE: Have any of our presidents been decorated for gallantry?

ANSWER: John F. Kennedy was awarded the Purple Heart, the Navy Medal and the Marine Medal for gallantry. Lyndon B. Johnson was decorated by General Douglas MacArthur with the Silver Star. James Garfield, while not *decorated*, was promoted for gallantry during the Civil War.

Andrew Johnson set a record he didn't want to establish — he had fifteen vetoes overridden, most of any president. Franklin D. Roosevelt holds a veto record, too — the most pocket vetoes...263.

If Washington, D.C. is the 'seat' of government, where's the head?

HISTORICAL NOTES ON A FRAYED CUFF!

President Franklin Pierce's Vice-President, William King, was the only Veep to have the oath of office administered in a foreign country. King became ill in Cuba and the American Consul gave him the oath there. King died after only 25 days in office...the shortest vice-presidential term.

The reason there were no cabinet changes in Zachary Taylor's administration: Taylor died in July of his first year in office.

Although twenty-four American presidents were lawyers, only ten attended law school...and only four of those remained long enough to get a degree in law. Those were Hayes, Taft, Nixon and Ford. Not that graduation from law school guarantees legal skill — Clarence Darrow had no legal sheepskin but a fair ability!

H.R. Haldemann had a two-fuse theory of government — re and con!

June 25, 1950: President Truman had just announced the outbreak of the Korean War. Americans were shocked and confused.

In a Los Angeles cocktail bar, the discussion was going full blast when stuttering comedian Joe Frisco entered. He ordered a drink, then sat back listening to the heated pros and cons. Finally, one of the others turned and asked Joe what he thought.

"It n-n-never would have happened," he struggled, "if H-H-Harry T-T-Truman had been alive."

Pessimism, when you get used to it, is just as agreeable as optimism.
Edmond Clerihew Bentley

THE UNITED STATES OF CHRISTOPHER!

That's what the country should have been named, except that a mapmaker in Germany who had not heard of Columbus' 1492 trip, named the continent after the Italian explorer Amerigo Vespucci. And some of the fifty states have names of very fuzzy origin. Hawaii, for example. No one is sure what the word means. California is said to have come from an old Spanish tale of a mythical island, but scholars don't agree. Kentucky is variously said to mean *meadow land* and *dark and bloody land.* Experts on Indian languages of America can't agree on Missouri either — it may have meant *canoe* or perhaps *big muddy.*

In the U.S., there is more space where nobody is than where anybody is.
Gertrude Stein

Is William Penn, American colonist for whom Pennsylvania is named, buried in the state capital at Harrisburg or in Philadelphia? Not even close. His body and that of his two wives and seven of their eleven children lie in a churchyard near Beaconsfield, England.

Congress consists of two chambers. One is ***bed.***

BRIDGEWORK!

We don't know it it's a record or not, but Allegheny County, Pennsylvania (Pittsburgh's county) has over 500 bridges. Of course, they have three rivers getting in the way of traffic — the Ohio, the Allegheny and the Monongahela — but that's still more than three times as many bridges as there are on the entire Mississippi River.

Does anyone know what happened to Idaho's 'Little Lost River?'

VILLAGE OF SMALL HUTS!

Canada, one of the world's largest countries in land area, is an Iroquois Indian word meaning *village of small huts*. It's all because some French explorers asked some Iroquois what they called the place where they lived. The Indians quite logically gave them the name of their encampment.

Don't tell a Canadian that the Great Lakes belong to the United States. Of the 94,711 square miles of water surface, about thirty-six percent lies in Canada. Four of the Great Lakes are between 572 and 602 feet above sea level, but Lake Ontario is only 246 feet in altitude.

Which one of the Great Lakes lies entirely within the United States? Lake Michigan.

RIDDLE: James Polk was one of our lesser-known presidents. Can you name one of his unique distinctions?

ANSWER: We know of just one: he was the only Speaker of the House of Representatives who ever became president.

The shortest distance from the Atlantic to the Pacific across the United States is between points near Charleston, South Carolina, and San Diego, California, and is 2,152 miles. Boo!

Bloop! After introducing an American territorial official as "the Virgin of Governor's Island," the offending radio announcer was consoled by the fact it was a man.

WHAT'S IN A NAME, EH GM?

We can understand why General Motors would name one of its cars after the French colonial governor of Louisiana, because he also founded the city of Detroit...fellow named *Cadillac.* But when they named another car after an Ottowa Indian chief — Pontiac — did they realize he led the siege of Detroit in the 1760's?

*One **een** leads to another, as in **car and smither.***

THE GOLDEN GATE!

That beautiful inlet, from the sea to San Francisco Bay, was the brainchild of explorer John C. Fremont, and first appeared on his map of the area in 1848. Although the Indians native to the region had an equally poetic name for the spot — "where the sun plunges into the sea" — their word was *Yulypa*. Even Tony Bennett would have trouble with *Yulypa.*

*Do angry clocks get **ticked off?***

Gigi, the cat,
Lived underneath a hat
In the second-story flat
Of Mrs. Albert Platte...
And that's that!

So you think a Scot is a native of Scotland. He is, but the more exact use of *Scot* defines a Gaelic native of northern Ireland who emigrated to Scotland in the Sixth Century. *Scot* came to us from the Latin word for Irishman.

***Genuflecting** is easy. It's **genustraightening** afterward that's hard!*

TAKE ME DOWN TO THE TENDERLOIN!

Most large American cities have an area referred to as *the tenderloin.* Invariably, it's a district rife with prostitution, gambling and like crimes.

In New York City one district, comprised of second-rate hotels, brothels and rough saloons, paid graft to the police as a regular course of business. So, when one particular police captain was transferred into that precinct in the late 1890's, he is said to have remarked, "After chuck for so long, I'm now going to enjoy *tenderloin.*" Presto — a new meaning to an old word.

Rabelais said, "There are more old drunkards than old physicians."

IN FOND MEMORY!

The citizens of Topeka, Kansas weren't about to forget their illustrious saloon-smasher, Carrie Nation. They erected a memorial fountain on the very site of her first arrest.

Ostentation: People buy more TV sets than pianos because there's nothing they can put on the roof to show the neighbors they own a piano.

The *Chase* in Chase Manhattan Bank isn't the name of one of the bank's founders. When it opened in 1877 as the Chase National Bank, the *Chase* was in honor of Abraham Lincoln's Secretary of the Treasury, Salmon B. Chase. Gotcha!

He conserved his energy by never making up his own mind.

RIDDLE: Which western state is named after a valley in Pennsylvania?

ANSWER: Wyoming is an Indian word given first to a valley in Pennsylvania. It means wide plains.

TENT INDUSTRY TENSED FOR COMEBACK!

You don't picture yourself living in a tent? Then maybe you don't know that more than half of today's new houses cost over $50,000, compared to a mere five percent in 1970. With current mortgage rates, you'd better be making $15,000 a year to afford a $30,000 house...assuming you could find that priced house still standing.

How come, you weep? Well, to start with, in the twenty years following 1950 food costs went up 54 percent; fuel costs, 51 percent. But, from 1970 to 1976, food leaped 57 percent in price and fuel costs tripled.

Now, this particular tent will house four people very nicely!

Almost 520 million of India's 650 million people live on less than $7 a month!

WHO SAID ENTERTAINING IS EXPENSIVE?

Are you aware of the availability of chartered 747's? You can fly a group of your friends around the world, with twenty or so stopovers, for a mere $300,000. Look at the economy of it: you'll impress some 372 people; the price includes booze, food and movies. For those of more modest means, how about just a hop to Europe and back for your guests? Fifty-grand should cover it. That's not at all bad when you consider it's about half the price of a Rolls Royce *Camargue*...and only about three times the price of a case of beluga caviar. So what the hell are you waiting for? Bargains like these don't last, you know!

Talk about being born too late: If you had been around in 1904, you could have taken an ocean liner from New York to Europe for $10. Third class, of course.

QUICK, WATSON, THE BAGPIPES!

When Scotland had its own kings, they enjoyed popping down to London now and then to see the bright candles. The English kings, ever hospitable, put these Scots up in a special palace. It came to be called *Scotland Yard.* Many years later — in 1829 — the London metropolitan police built their headquarters on the site.

As long as we're on police, we want to give Chaucer the credit for the word *clue*. The old boy, retelling the ancient legend of Theseus in the Cretan labyrinth, used the old English word for ball of yarn — *clew...clue.*

*The only factions that ever seem to agree are **satis** and **putre**.*

THE YEAR OF THE BLUE SNOW!

Why was it always colder then than now? Well, maybe it just was! We certainly would not have enjoyed a winter vacation in Europe in 1709. That year, it was so cold, the frost went nine feet deep into the ground. The Adriatic Sea froze over. So did some of the coastal areas of the Mediterranean Sea. So, the next time your furnace plays a cold and dirty trick on you, think of 1709 and warm up.

It was Mae West who said, "I used to be Snow White, but I drifted."

BIG BLAST IN SIBERIA!

The next time you wish upon a falling star, put in a small wish that it doesn't fall all the way to Earth. Almost every part of the globe bears a few meteorite scars, such as the one near Winslow, Arizona that is 600 feet deep and a mile wide. But, the meteorite that plopped down in the Yenisei area of central Siberia was so big, its explosion was seen 500 miles away and the heat was felt for 300 miles.

*Watch out for those one-masted Irish fishing boats! They're called **hookers!***

CLOUDY LIQUIDS!

The reason white clouds don't drop rain is the very reason they are white. A mass of very small water droplets reflect light and so appear white, and they are too small to form falling rain. Larger drops of water begin to absorb light, so the cloud grows dark and the drops are heavy enough to fall. Think on it!

The gaseous element helium was so-named because it was first discovered in the atmosphere of the Sun in 1868 and the Greek word

RIDDLE: Which represents the great amount, an ennead or a chiliad?

ANSWER: In the first place, stop talking like an egghead! An *ennead* is a group of nine and a *chiliad* comes in at a thousand, on the nose.

for sun was helio. It wasn't until twenty-seven years later before it was discovered in the Earth's atmosphere.

We ran across a scientist's description of surface tension in liquids: "A phenomenon in which the liquid seeks to minimize its exposed area." As opposed to the phenomenon of the bikini we suppose.

When a cowboy was 'dragging his navel in the sand,' he was leaving fast! With pain!

UP AND DOWN IN THE CAVE!

For the very last time anywhere, the lime deposit that grows *up* from the floor of a cave is a *stalagmite*; the one that grows *down* from the cave roof is his cousin, the *stalactite*. Mix them up once more, and it's out of the cave!

They better not fool around with the atomic bomb — it's dynamite.
Sam Goldwyn

RED, RED, RED SAILS IN THE SUNSET OF 1883!

Remember what a whale of a red the sunsets were in the fall of winter of 1883? Did you ever bother to ask anyone why they were so special? We thought not! That was the year the volcano Krakatoa blew its top, spewing giant batches of volcanic ash into half the world's atmosphere.

If you're a volcano freak, you probably already know that Hawaii's Mauna Kea on Hilo is the highest island mountain in the world (13,825). It's also probably old hat to you that, when Mt. Katmai in Alaska erupted in 1912, the resulting haze was seen as far east as Pennsylvania. Volcanoes seem to like islands. The large island of Java has a hundred and twenty-five, while little Iceland has a hundred and seven.

Resisting an easy task is the surest way of making it difficult.

DOG OR RED LETTER?

Some say summer came to be known as the *dog days* because that's when Sirius, the dog star, rises with the Sun. Others claim it's because summer was when dogs went mad with rabies.

Of *red-letter days* we're certain — as far back as the 15th

Century, calendars had the holy days marked in red...a cause for celebration.

Punctuality is the thief of time.
Oscar Wilde

LIBERTY!

The Liberty Bell was first rung July 4, 1776! Wrong. It was on July 8, 1776, but it was rung to celebrate the adoption of the Declaration of Independence. And it cracked the first time it was rung! Wrong again. It performed perfectly every year until 1835. That year it cracked as it was rung to toll the death knell for Chief Justice John Marshall. It was rung again — in 1944 to signal the Allied invasion of Europe at Normandy on June 6, 1944.

Remember: when it's 9:08 in 'Time,' Illinois, it's too late in 'Midnight,' Mississippi.

'TIS THE SEASON TO BE CONFUSIN'!

The word *calendar* we borrowed from the Latin; but the names of the days of the week are Anglo-Saxon in origin; month names go back to Latin again; but the seasons stem from the Anglo-Saxon, except we also allow the Latin word for fall — *autumn.* And because all these terms are used so commonly, few of us actually know what they mean. So, here's your lesson for today:

The days of the week relate to various Teutonic pagan beliefs and rites. Monday is *moon* day, while Sunday is *sun* day...what else. Tuesday gets its name from the Teutonic war god, *Tiw,* and Wednesday was *Wodin's* day. Thursday means *Thor's* day, and Wodin's wife, *Frigg,* is honored with Friday. Saturday was appropriated from the Romans — day of *Saturn.*

Our months are purely Latin in origin. January is so named for the two-headed god of doors, *Janus*; the two heads are suitable for looking back on the year just completed and looking ahead to the new year. February is a direct adoption from the Roman feast of cleansing — *Februa.* March is simply *Mar's* month. April, being a time when plants begin to open their leaves in fresh growth comes from *appire* — to open. *Maia,* a Roman goddess, gave us May. Then come three months named for famous Romans — June from the *Junius* family, or from *Juno* (some disagreement here), July from *Julius* Caesar and August from *Augustus* Caesar. Inasmuch as the remaining months are named

RIDDLE: Have you ever spent an entire day with a bissextile?

ANSWER: Everyone has! In each Leap Year, February 29th is called the *bissextile*.

from the numbers seven through ten, by all rights, the month following August should be November, or the ninth month. However, the Romans operated on a ten-month year, so our ninth month is the seventh, our tenth month is the eighth...Right on!

We telephone Call, Texas and there is never anyone home!

There'll be a leap year at the beginning of the next century in the year 2000, but none in the year 2100. For some odd reason, the first year of a new century must be divisible by 400 to qualify. So there's to be an eight-year gap between leap years at the end of the twenty-first century. (We don't know anyone who's planning to wait...maybe you do, though.)

California lies in the west, while Missouri lies in all directions.

Maybe you've forgotten: Buzzard's Day — March 15 — is when the buzzards return to Hinkley, Ohio. Before you go sneering at the buzzard, remember that his return to Hinkley beats the swallows going back to Capistrano, California by four or five days.

Time flies when you owe money.

Sure, you know that the pleasant break in the weather just before winter is called Indian summer. But you probably didn't know that the cold spell before Indian summer is called the *squaw winter.*

Ditch the boughs! It's poison ivy! Now, once more...with feeling!

Easter is a Christian holiday, but the name comes from the old Teutonic fertility goddess *Eoster*. Appropriately, her symbols were rabbits and eggs. Whoever thought of the Easter Bunny and Easter eggs as fertility symbols?

Referring to the Christmas season as *yuletide* isn't just quaint. It's pagan. *Yule* was a pagan rite rejoicing at the new sun. Just happened to fall at the time we now know as Christmas.

The 'crab' in crab apple comes from an old English word meaning sour.

Don't get angry, but locomotive engineers didn't blow their train's whistle because of that haunting, nostalgic sound. They were signaling: four whooee's was for decrease speed; five, speed up; and eight meant the brakes were sticking.

Bore: A person who is willing to take your time outlining his thorough ignorance on a variety of subjects.

SPROTEKALEMONATH ALREADY?

If you've wondered why we use Anglo-Saxon derivatives for the days of the week but not for the months of the year, you're about to find out.

First, they tagged each name with *monath*, their word for month. We'll forego that joy and dig right in. March was *Hlyd*, or boisterous...for the winds. Their April was *Eoster*, a pagan feast day. They so loved the long days of May they called it *Thrimilce*...the time they could milk the cows three times a day. June was simply *Sere*...dry. For confusion's sake, their July was *Maea*...meadow-month when they were flowering. August was *Weod*...weed month. September being harvest time, they called it *Haerfest*. *Win*, or wine, was October. Pagans that they were, cattle were sacrificed to the gods in November, so that month got named for sacrifice...*Blot.* December was very sensibly *MidWinter*; although, when they became converted to Christianity, they changed it to *Haligh*...holy month. Their January was *Wulf*, from the fact that the winters were so hard the wolves waltzed right into the villages for food. And finally we come to February or *Sprotekale* — the month when the cabbages began to sprout.

Remember: thirty days has *Haerfest, Eoster, Sere* and *Blot;* all the rest have thirty-one, except *Sprotekale.*

The 100th anniversary is not celebrated! Just totter a little!

SURPRISE! YESTERDAY WAS YOUR ANNIVERSARY!

Forgetting wedding anniversaries is nothing new. Men have been practicing for centuries and now they seem to have it mastered. Yet, even those who remember, probably don't know the traditional gifts for each anniversary. And no wonder — like so many gift-giving occasions, the wedding anniversary has been commercialized to death.

At one time, the appropriate gift for a First Anniversary was

RIDDLE: Have names of Zodiac signs ever been used in popular slang expressions?

ANSWER: ***By jiminy*** **is one: Gemini, the twins!**

something made of paper. Today, it's a clock. China didn't come along until the Twentieth Anniversary in times past; but now they've stepped it up to the second. One gets the notion that merchants today have calculated your best earning years and, they aren't about to wait until you're over the hill, before parting you from a large chunk of your wealth. The Tenth Anniversary is a good example: tin or aluminum gifts used to be ideal for the event; today, only a cheapskate would sail for anything less than diamond jewelry. Couples were content to wait for the Fifteenth Anniversary for crystal. Now it has been moved up to the Third.

The sentiment counted, then. Fruit and flowers were the tokens for a couple's fourth year of married life. Now they're pitching electrical appliances. Diamonds weren't called for until the Sixtieth Anniversary. Nowadays, they aren't a bit shy about insisting that you give diamonds on the Tenth and Thirtieth as well as the Sixtieth and Seventy-fifth anniversaries. After all, you might not make it to the Sixtieth and they can't sell you diamonds after you've departed.

In the past, when two people reached their Twenty-fifth Wedding Anniversary, they had a few cherished items and lots of fond memories, Today, when you reach that milestone, you can open up your own department store!

Arguments are to be avoided: they are always vulgar and often convincing.

Oscar Wilde

When the incapable appoint a group of the impractical to study the inconsequential, we call it a committee. When the results are incoherent, you can bet it will be called a *blue-ribbon* committee.

CHAPTER NINE

Out Of The Past And Into The Soup!

If you tend to belittle that which is old and past its time, tell us if you have ever seen a worn-out wrinkle!

Look upon the past kindly. After all, history is when *others* were screwing things up. How would you know how badly things are *today,* if we weren't here to tell you how it *was?* And remember: If there were no past, there would be no trivia except for what we think of ourselves. Unpleasant thought, eh?

So let us take you by the pudgy hand into a time when a *furlong* was how long an ox could plow a furrow before he had to stop and take a breather, or when an *acre* was the amount of ground a team of oxen could plow in one day. Let us tell you that you are full of prunes when you say Sunday is the Sabbath, because to the Greeks it fell on Monday; Tuesday, for the Persians; Wednesday for the Assyrians; Egyptians observed it on Thursday; the Mohammedans on Friday; and the Jews and Seventh Day Adventists, among others, hold to Saturday Sabbath.

If you've been questioning your own intelligence because you never get Daylight Savings Time straight, be of good cheer. The English woke up in 1752 to the fact that their whole time frame was eleven days out of whack because no one had taken Leap Year into account. So they adopted the present *Gregorian Calendar*. But to rectify the mistake they'd been making for years, September 2nd, 1752 was followed by September 14th. As if that weren't bad enough, the Russians didn't make the change until 1918.

The next time your children complain of long school-hours, tell them how lucky they are not to be living in Shakespeare's time: winter school-hours were daybreak to dusk then; and in the summer it was 6:00 AM to 6:00 PM. We'd advise you not to tell them that Benjamin Franklin attended school for just two years, age 8 to 10.

We know it will do your ego good to find out that historians botched the Battle Of Bunker Hill on June 17, 1775. It wasn't fought on Bunker Hill at all but on nearby Breed's Hill. Luckily, when it came to erecting a monument, they put it on the correct hill. However, it's still a bit confusing to know that the Bunker Hill Monument stands on Breed's Hill.

On historical matters, you're not the only one who doesn't know the names of any of the ships from which the tea was thrown during the Boston Tea Party. Jot them down: *The Eleanor, Beaver* and *Dartmouth*!

And don't give your local planning commission credit for inventing stupidity. A New York City body in 1925 calmly announced that the city would have a population of 18 million by the year 2000 (which doesn't give them much time to get moving). Six hundred years earlier, the Aztecs sent out a committee of experts to locate a site for their city. Imagine this: Mexico City is where it is today because this planning committee saw an eagle perched on a cactus eating a snake.

Some thirty centuries before Christ, quite a few Hindu critics were knocking the game of *chaturanga*...saying it wouldn't last. Typical! The game's the same, the name's known to us as *chess. Checkers* — or, as the British say, *draughts* — is a johnny come-lately by comparison, dating to the 17th Century B.C. in Egypt. Queen Hatasa was rumored to be a checkers freak of the time.

There's nothing new about the American habit of thinking little of home-grown products and ideas either. Take Charles Burton. He built a baby carriage in 1848. Couldn't interest a soul in it. So, he took his idea to England. Quicker than you can say Bob's-your-uncle it caught on. When Queen Victoria ordered one, the Queen of Spain and the King of Egypt jumped right on the pram-wagon. Suddenly America was dying to have this lovely new foreign product. Ho hum!

Yet we still go on changing the good things of the past. The city fathers of New York, as an example, had enough foresight in 1899 to bar horseless carriages from Central Park. A law making that much sense couldn't last...and it didn't.

So, here's to the only sector of history with a real future — the past!

Remember the Nade sisters — Sere and Lemo?

HARD TIMES BREED SOFT TOUCHES!

During the Great Depression of the 1930's, money was hard to come by for most people and easy to come by for a few fast spielers. One such group made a sound assessment early in those lean years — first, most small merchants in small towns could afford very little advertising; second, radio stations — unlike newspapers, which controlled each issue's size by the ad space — had to broadcast a fixed number of hours daily, even if they choked on their own free air-time.

So, the spielers put together a scam known as the *clock deal.* Picture a tin frame two feet high by three feet wide with a glass front and an electric clock mounted on top. Glossy reprints of a news photo went behind the glass. Across the top of the frame was stenciled, "Time to hear the news on..." and the local radio station's call-letters followed. Every merchant who signed up for the *clock deal* received the clock and frame, a fresh news photo every two weeks and his very own radio spot-announcements for a full year.

Before a *clock-deal* operator called in his crew of fast-talking, quick-closing salesmen, he arranged for radio time. While a 30-second spot announcement commonly sold for $2.00 in those days and a one-minute spot for $3.00, the operator had no difficulty in buying full-hour blocks at $12.00 apiece. All he did was sign a one-year contract and pay the whole thing in advance. And filling up the hours that had cost him $12.00 each with $50.00 in spots was no trick at all. Knowledgeable *clock-deal* operators *netted* $1,000 a week in the depression...easily.

The odd thing about the *clock deal* was that everyone loved it! In those pre-television days, the public looked forward to each two-week news photo change; merchants got added foot traffic plus radio advertising. But what about the radio stations when they found out how much the *clock-deal* operator made? All we can say is that most stations begged to have the *clock deal* repeated the next year.

If life were an automobile, experience would be the rear-view mirror.

With high hopes, a watchmaker wrote his own epitaph:

Here lies in a horizontal position
The outside case of a clock and watchmaker
Who departed this life wound up in hope
Of being taken in hand by his maker and
Of being thoroughly cleaned, repaired and
Set a-going in the world to come.

THE ROCK 'EM, SOCK 'EM WORLD OF ADVERTISING!

Calexico, the California city across the international boundary from Mexico's Mexicali, had its very own radio station in 1935. The 100-watt transmitter, the lone turntable and the microphone were housed in a dirt-floored adobe garage. The owner was somewhat informal, remaining barefooted through the hot summer, even though his titles included Chief Engineer, Head Announcer, Program Director, Advertising Manager and President. Most of the programming was in Spanish, since his primary advertising accounts were located in Mexicali.

This radio-mogul broadcast on a very strict schedule. When a record ended, he gave the station's call letters and turned off the transmitter. Then he'd amble across the border and sell or barter a commercial announcement. Back he came, in an hour or two, packing a live chicken and a half-dozen tortillas in a paper bag on which he'd penciled the advertising copy. He turned on the transmitter again and, while waiting for it to warm up, he rehearsed what he'd written on the paper sack.

Then the listeners of Calexico and Mexicali were treated to another record, some on-mike tortilla-munching interspersed with references to someone's *groceria*, another sign-off and, once again, another hour or two of silence.

Chickens can't be too dumb. You never see one buying a used car.

BEAT YOUR RUGS, BABY! THE JUICE IS OFF!

Obviously, the time is coming when the Fossil-Fuel Age will be a fossil, itself. When they turn the juice off, how will we survive? Well, the egg-beater and the meat-grinder worked okay with a little elbow grease. The washboard was rough on knuckles, but it functioned. Of course, when the juice stops, so will the smog...so hanging clothes out to dry will bring back that special just-laundered aroma. We wouldn't be surprised if that flat metal contraption for beating rugs may not beat the hell out of vacuum cleaners. But what are we going to do about refrigerating and freezing foodstuff?

Well, we read recently about a crusty old New Englander who was offering to teach the young how to cut and store ice. He still has all the special tools for this forgotten trade. He claims that ice was once this country's leading export. So...we looked it up.

He's right! The ice industry began in gala style, too. When the first ice shipment from New York arrived in Charleston, South Carolina, the ship was met by a band. About six years later, in 1805, New Englanders were shipping ice to the West Indies. Ten years later, ice-ships from our Atlantic ports were cooling off the citizens in Cuba, Egypt and India.

The old-fashioned icebox didn't have an ice-maker, but it didn't need one. And you ask anyone who was a kid in the days when the iceman came around to deliver, if the most refreshing thing in the whole wide world wasn't a chunk the iceman chipped off and offered you, free?

Maybe the fruit and vegetable man is on his way back, too. Whoopee!

For every five thousand antique collectors there should be at least one young collector.

RIDDLE: We heard of a hen correcting its chick, saying, "You are not a people; you are a chicken. Furthermore chickens do not come from people; they come from eggs." So, the chick asked, "Are eggs born?" What did the hen say?

ANSWER: On the principle that it's always best to be honest with one's young, the mother hen replied, "No, eggs are laid." Naturally, the chick asked if people were laid. The hen paused, then said, "Some people are...others are chicken."

THREE SQUARES AND A ROUND BELLY!

If you think breakfast, lunch and dinner have always been what they are today you've been eating too much styrofoam. The early Anglo-Saxons only ate breakfast and dinner. Then breakfast dropped off to little more than a snack in the 1500's. It made a helluva comeback in the 1700's, becoming such a gorging affair that it lasted from 10:00 AM until 1:00 PM. Things couldn't go on like that, so it shrank back in quantity of groceries consumed and also dropped back to around 8 o'clock.

Dinner went its own merry way. In the 1500's, it was served at 11:00 AM. Then it started edging forward, until it reached 5:00 PM. It stayed there awhile and then by the mid-1800's, it was served as late as 8:00 PM.

So, what was lunch doing while all this was taking place? Not much! It was never more than a handful of something to munch on between halves of the working day until the end of the Victorian era. When the working day was split up into morning and afternoon segments with an hour between the two, there suddenly was enough time to make a pig of one's self.

It's reasonably safe to assume that meals will continue to change. In fact, if America's current dietary preferences rage on unabated, we foresee the day when there will be these three meals: *coffee-juice,* a liquid meal taken while standing, walking or jogging; *taco-time,* a meal eaten with the hands out of a wet waxpaper envelope with discomforting side effects; *frozen glimp,* a meal prepared by quick-thawing an amorphous mass in a radar device, and featuring unidentified frying objects in a sea of reconstituted buffalo gravy.

Bon appetit!

A watch in the pot never boils.

Is there a hostess alive who has not ground her teeth in anger after a dinner party when she finds her best napkins smeared with lipstick and burned with cigarettes?

There is a solution. It isn't even new. The ancient Greeks used asbestos napkins. After the meal, they were simply passed through the fire. Instant laundering, too.

If you see a cook put a pan of vinegar in the oven, you'll know that she believes the old household hint that this will knock out obnoxious cooking odors. You'll also know why the lamb chops are a bit vinegary tonight.

THANKS FOR THE DRUMSTICK!

When Governor Bradford of Massachusetts Colony issued the proclamation that began our holiday, Thanksgiving Day, he still had a problem. What to eat? So he sent four colonists into the woods to rustle up the fixings. They came back with a mixed bag of wild game, but more turkeys than anything else. So, you see, it was all a matter of luck — we might be referring to Thanksgiving as *Deer Day* or *Squirrel Day* or *Rabbit Day* if the turkey hadn't been so handy and cooperative.

Dutch dogs were apt to ***snacken*** *— snap at you! The next time you have a* ***snack*** *remember that...and stop snapping at your food.*

HERE COMES SINTERKLAAS!

In the mid-east around the 4th Century, there was a generous bishop who gave presents to the needy. After he became a saint, his feast day was set for December 6th and known as St. Nicholas's Day. With the passage of time the gift-giving associated with his day was mingled with Christmas. The Dutch colonists brought the tradition to New York where Americans revised *Sinterklaas* to *Santa Claus.*

Massachusetts made Christmas a legal holiday in 1859. Stubborn Yankees!

ODD PATHS!

Those who colonized this country didn't always come from where you'd expect. For instance, the Pilgrims, while predominantly English, Irish and Scotch, set sail for America from Holland. And the first organized settlement of Jews was established by a group that came from Brazil to New York in 1654.

In Saskatchewan, it's over 200 miles from ***Old Wives*** *to* ***Honeymoon.*** *Everywhere else it's a lot farther!*

SO YOU'RE AN ELK!

Where do you think we got that handy little slit in the lapel where Elks and other groups can put their identifying pins? It started with the Hebrew habit of tearing their clothing when mourning the death of a

RIDDLE: Is it common practice to use an icebox to heat food?

ANSWER: Not common, but not unknown either. Iceboxes were used by Admiral Byrd's Antarctic Expedition. It was so damned cold, food outside an icebox froze stiff.

loved one. When it was a mother or father who had died, the Hebrews never repaired the rips as an indication of their eternal loss. The lapel slit is all that remains of the tradition.

You're old when most of the people your age are dead.

PURPLE'S OUT OF SIGHT!

If today's price of wool clothing gives you a three-way migraine, you should have seen the way they used to stick it to the customers.

First, the Phoenicians had a compulsion for emptying the Mediterranean Sea of all swimming creatures. But, in the process, these scamps happened across a shellfish that gave off a purple fluid. In between fishing trips, the Phoenicians turned out a pretty mean bolt of wool. They experimented with the purple stuff and it was an absolute gas! Since these gents hung around the port city of Tyre, the new purple wool came to be known as *Tyrian purple.*

Now, there was big expense in finding these little shellfish, which the Phoenicians proudly passed along to the customer...never telling him they were going fishing anyway.

The Greeks were suckers for the *Tyrian purple*. A well-to-do Greek figured anything that expensive had to make him look dignified.

By the First Century B.C., the Phoenicians had hooked the Romans, too, And they made them pay through the nose, too — a thousand denarii a pound, which roughly translates to $217.50. In no time, the emperor decreed that only royalty could wear the special wool, and it became known as *royal purple*. A private citizen caught wearing *royal purple* got himself charged with treason and suffered all the good things that implied.

Meanwhile, the Phoenicians were laughing so hard they could scarcely work their looms.

So, if you stand still for a big ticket on purple woolen wear, you're being Phoenicianed!

One of the ***ments*** *we always intended to try is* ***aug.***

WHITE HOUSIANA!

In order to raise the money for the building of the White House, the government sold off some land donated for the purpose by Maryland and Virginia. Washington laid the original cornerstone in 1792 and it was ready for occupancy by President John Adams in 1800.

By the way, in the original designs for the city, it was referred to as *The Palace*...no need to explain why this didn't catch on.

Thomas Jefferson, an architect, had submitted plans for the White House anonymously, but they were rejected. So, following his inauguration in 1801, he designed the terraces and colonnades.

We can't find any record of what color the building was in its earliest days. However, after the British burned the place in the War of 1812, the walls left standing were painted white to cover the scorch marks...and it's been white ever since. Even so, it didn't become *The White House* officially until the administration of Theodore Roosevelt. T.R. also added wings to expand the executive offices.

As with most buildings which have had numerous occupants, people were always adding on — the South Portico came in 1823; the East Room in 1826; the North Portico in 1829; the East Wing in 1942; a penthouse and a bomb shelter in 1952; and to correct some sagging, in 1949, they started rebuilding a large section on steel-supporting frames.

"It is only shallow people," wrote Oscar Wilde, "who do not judge by appearances."

SLOW DAYS ON THE CAPITOL MALL!

In 1836, the government accepted Robert Mills' design for the Washington Monument. Twelve years later, Congress issued a grant for the site, but it took them another twenty-eight years to appropriate the money for its construction. It was finally completed in 1884, but it wasn't until 1888 that the public was allowed inside. Hmm, fifty-two years from design acceptance to opening day — that's foot-dragging on a grand scale!

*A **polling place** originally was where **polls** (heads) were counted. A Gallup head?*

DOWN THE LEGISLATIVE TRAIL...EVENTUALLY!

It's advisable not to hold your breath while waiting for a bill to become a federal law. Take a bill starting in the House. First, it goes to the drafting room. Here, allow time for compulsive tinkering. Then it is introduced in the House. Bang, it's referred to committee or committees, in some instances.

What does a committee do? Well, let's say this is a nice simple, one-issue bill calling for the mandatory waterproofing of blue-and-

RIDDLE: In the 19th Century did lots of citizens vote in U.S. Senate elections?

ANSWER: Not one voter ever showed up! That's because U.S. Senators were elected by state legislatures until a 1913 statute called for their popular election.

white striped railroading caps when, and if, worn by engineers, firemen or brakemen on interstate rail-lines spanning two or more states with an *r* in their names. Naturally, the committee wants to learn all possible effects of the proposed legislation prior to debating it. Witnesses must be called. That means two experts on waterproofing, at least one of whom must have had a minimum of eleven years of experience in the waterproofing of the specific cotton drilling from which said railroading caps are constructed. Before the cap manufacturers may be brought in, three color specialists must be heard...just in case blue-and-white is not the most acceptable combination.

Assuming everything has gone swimmingly up to this point, it's time for the committee to sample public reaction. What effect will the caps have on property values adjacent to such railroad lines? Will the morals of school children be adversely affected by waterproofing of said *head* adornments? What are the religious overtones (blue is a distinctly nauseous color to some Buddhist sects)?

The testimony of labor leaders is mandatory, too. Should any American workingman be forced to wear such an object without compensating additional fringe benefits? Railroad executives come next to give their views on the additional cost per ton which must be added to freight charges to alleviate the excessive expense of the new caps.

If the bill survives the witnesses and the ensuing committee debate, it's ready to go to the floor of the House for debate. Now sectionalism comes into play. The Representatives of states with no *r*'s in their names will cry, "Exclusion." One Representative, whose maiden aunt was assaulted by a berserk brakeman wearing a similar cap in the summer of 1911, points to the moral degradation the proposed legislation will cause. Another Representative, whose district has no railroads whatsoever, threatens to block the bill unless its sponsors support his upcoming measure to restrict the importation of Croatian flypaper. Three Congressmen from a large textile-producing state secretly meet to see that the cap contract goes to their state.

On the ridiculous assumption that the debate ends and a vote is taken without the bill being referred back to committee for expedient log-rolling alterations, *it might be passed*. Then it's printed as an *Act of the House* (and it's a hard act to follow).

Now it's time for the bill to be introduced in the Senate, presuming they haven't adjourned by this time. Naturally, the Senate refers it to committee. Here come the witnesses again...only a new set for each aspect. You can't expect Senators to take the word of persons called by lowly Representatives.

On the off chance that the Senate doesn't set up a joint Senate-House confrerees' committee, it might go to the Senate floor for further mangling by debate. It could even be passed by the Senate and sent to the President.

At this juncture, the President starts consulting, directly and through his staff, with key members of both houses of Congress. What will it do to the downstate vote in his home state? What does his wife think of blue? Will the rubber industry cut off their political donations because the damned thing is made of cotton? Has anyone talked to Billy Graham about it?

At last the President sends word to the bill's author that he will sign it. The overjoyed Representative presents the President with a sample cap, which the President dons for the official signing. While the flashbulbs are still going off, someone dampens the spirit of the festive occasion by mentioning that railroad trainmen have had waterproofed blue-and-white striped caps for over thirty years. Yes, but now it's a law!

We endeavor to take pride in faults that we do not wish to correct.
La Rochefoucauld

PUT THE MINT NEAR THE MINES!

At first glance, one wonders why our government ever set up mints in such out-of-the-way places as Dahlonega, Georgia and Carson City, Nevada. Simple! Dahlonega was a major gold-mining center in the 1830's through 1850's, so the raw material was right at hand. The mint closed down when the gold petered out in 1861. The Comstock Lode silver mines were near Carson City, so it had a mint for many years, too...closing again when the mines had been worked out. Denver, which still has an active mint, was chosen originally because of the gold and silver booms of the 1870's and 1880's.

On the ish question, it's evenly split between the angu and the fet factions!

RIDDLE: How many different U.S. Presidents have been in office when there was no national debt?

ANSWER: Just one — Andrew Jackson in 1834.

EUREKA!

The fabled California *Gold Rush* produced a lots of things, from heartbreak to millionaires. One of the prolific producers — the Monument Mine — gave up the biggest nugget. It bent the scales at 1,596 troy ounces. Yet a nugget weighing 199 troy ounces more came out of Australia's Welcome Mine in 1858. Welcome, indeed! In case you're slow on converting troy ounces to pounds, that Australian record-breaker was a neat 141 and a quarter pounds.

*The world's largest **nougat** was baked by Arnie Belf in 1911!*

WELCOME TO FRESNO!

If Fresno, or any other city, has a distinguished visitor, one of the ceremonies is apt to include the Mayor giving the guest the *keys to the city*. This ritual honor goes back to the ancient days when all major cities were walled fortresses. The only entrance was through the gates of the city. So, when they gave a visitor the *keys to their city*, they were saying he was a friend they trusted. If they had a hint of doubt, the keys didn't fit the gates!

*The **parsnip** sings its welcome song at midnight or not at all!*

WISH YOU WERE HERE!

One of the greatest tourist attractions in the world for three centuries has been the *Mumtaz-i-Mahall*. We're certain you've seen dozens of postcards picturing this stunning marble mausoleum built by Shah Jehan to honor his favorite wife. In fact, its name is Persian for *the distinguished one of the palace*. It took eighteen years to build. Oh, yes, you may be more familiar with its current name — the *Taj Mahal*.

Liberace wears spangled ear muffs!

COME ON, LEONARDO!

No one questions the greatness of Leonardo da Vinci's *Last Supper*, but he should have been more careful. Imagine, the great work took two years for the master to complete, and a few years later it began to deteriorate badly. Leonardo simply had a badly prepared plaster ground to work with. The painting has been restored again and again. So, next time, watch it!

*Art thieves returned Bobby Osprey's painting, **Lips Akimbo**, without comment!*

"STEP INTO MY CONVERSATION PIT," SAID THE SPIDER TO THE FLY!

You never had it so good...what with your *conversation pit*, your *family room*, your *powder room*, your *den-office-bedroom for overnight guests* and your *workshop*. Bah! Where in the hell is your smoke room? Where's a lady to put her riding gear? Are you going to heat the whole damned house in a blizzard? What, no cellar? No loft room, either? Where's the wood box? You tell us there isn't a pantry of any kind in your house! Look, kiddo, take away a few of your appliances and you might as well be living in the Middle Ages. Your house is about as specialized as one two-penny nail in a kegful.

A century and more ago, the American farmhouse was built for *living*! Between the back-porch door and the kitchen you'd find the *pillion room* — that's the place for the women folk to stow their riding gear.

One of the kitchens — yes, *one* — was usually just outside the house but connected by a covered walkway. That was your *summer kitchen*. After all, what with bread baking and canning as well as the regular mealtime cooking, who wanted to be in the indoor kitchen in summer heat?

The big indoor kitchen had a host of fascinating rooms nearby. The *milk room* had an obvious purpose. Next to it was the *churn room*, where butter was made and stored (some called it the *buttery*). Then you had a *pantry* (*butler's pantry* if you were living high on the hog), complete with a *dumbwaiter* in case your *invalid room* was on the second floor. (What so-called modern house couldn't use an invalid room?) Also adjoining the kitchen was the *smoke room* for smoking meats. And, of course, the *wash room* was nearby, and it was just for washing. That other room, which we euphemistically call a *washroom* today, was either outside and called a privy, or it had been moved inside where a closet had been and so was called the *water closet*.

See how complete and self-sufficient the kitchen area was. That's why, during bad weather, the whole family could exist in and around the kitchen...or, the *keeping room* as some called it.

No self-respecting farmer went without at least one cellar. The main cellar, under the house, was where you kept food from freezing in winter and from spoiling in summer. In winter, you cut your own ice, hauled it to the house and down into the cellar, where you covered it with sawdust and burlap bags. It lasted all through the following summer when you needed it. In preparation for the spring planting of root crops, such as potatoes, you had an outside cellar called a *root cellar.*

Then, of course, there was the *chapel room* where you meditated and prayed. The *sewing room* really came after an even more practical and productive room called the *loom room.*

Nowadays, with natural childbirth becoming popular again, perhaps we'll even get back to the essential *borning room* of yesteryear.

There was more. The *parlor* (from French *parler*...to talk) was for social occasions only. Some called it a *sitting room.*

If you were to go back to the beginning of the last century, you would find the forerunner of today's *powder room*; except it was called a *powdering room*, because a body had to have a place for powdering wigs and storing them on stands.

And closets? At first, there were none — pegs on the wall were fine for the clothes you needed immediately; big clothes chests solved the storage problem. It wasn't until the late 1700's that ladies began hanging curtains in front of the clothes pegs, and eventually this led to the closet.

Naturally, they had dining rooms, and thankfully, no damned dinettes. And to top off a decent American farmhouse — an *attic.* Great for winter storage of grain and tools you wouldn't need until spring, as well as a catchall for whatever. Then, in summer, the *attic* (*season room* some called it) could serve as an added bedroom.

Farmhouses without bathtubs used big wooden tubs set on the kitchen floor where they'd be handy to the water you heated on the stove.

It's hard to argue with a way of life that called for a special room for each important aspect of living. Now, go back to your *family room* and sulk.

***Ram's horn** and **butterfly** were the names of two early metal door hinges.*

ONE WONDER OF THE WORLD!

At one time an adventurous tourist could have viewed the *Seven Wonders of the World*: the Hanging Gardens of Babylon, the Temple of Artemis at Ephesus, the Tomb of Mausolus at Hallicarnassus, the Colossus of Rhodes, the statue of Zeus at Olympia, the Lighthouse of Alexandria and the Pyramids of Egypt. Babylon's Hanging Gardens vanished a long time ago. In succeeding years, what earthquakes didn't manage to destroy, vandals did. Today, only the Pyramids remain of the original *Seven Wonders of the World.*

Talk about malpractice! Look at the nose job someone did on the Sphinx!

SHIP AHOY!

Some older New England houses used to have a small room set on the flat-topped roof. That was for retired sea captains and their wives. It was called a *Captain's Room* and, naturally, it faced out to sea.

Anybody who can pack up his troubles in one kit bag is damned lucky!

PASS THE COURTING STICK!

New England families that didn't hold with the bundling board, even though it was known to be a first-class fuel-saver, might allow the *courting stick*. This was a hollow wooden tube six to eight feet long. A couple could sit on opposite sides of the fireplace, with a chaperon practically in their laps, and whisper romantic nonsense back and forth to each other through the *courting stick*. We'd probably still have the *courting stick* if it hadn't been for Alexander G. Bell.

Credit W. Somerset Maugham with this one: "American women expect to find in their husbands a perfection that English women only hope to find in their butlers."

PUT THIS IN YOUR PIPE AND SMOKE IT!

Once a young Dutchman could find out if the girl of his choice would accept him by showing up at her parents house three times and asking for a match to light his pipe. The parents pretended he was some sort of nut the first two times, and he wandered off with his unlit pipe. On his third trip, if they had decided to give their blessing to the marriage, they asked him in and gave him a light and a daughter!

RIDDLE: What did Shakespeare say prevents a bad marriage?

ANSWER: "Many a good hanging," was Will's preventive idea.

When England was a Catholic nation, no marriage could be consummated until the bed had been blessed.

HOUSEMAID'S KNEE AND ALL FOR WHAT?

The *Koryak* of the Russian arctic region had a damned strange way for a young man to make his marital intentions known. He simply showed up at the girl's house and, without a word, started doing housework. The girl's father, knowing a good thing, didn't say anything either. We don't know if anyone ever did break the silence, but it's a matter of record that *Koryaks* did get married.

Finally, the undetectable room deodorizer — Stench!

DARK DOINGS IN THE BLACK FOREST!

Natives of Germany's Black Forest region used to have a two-part courting routine divided into the *Come Nights* and the *Trial Nights*...in that order.

The afflicted swain had to enter the girl's bedroom by the window, which got a few of them shot at. There was the object of his desire, on the bed...fully clothed. Turned out, she only wanted to talk. He could have stayed home and talked to his mother and saved an eleven-mile hike. The moment the maiden fell asleep, he had to leave...by the window again.

A few of these *Come Nights* exhausted their conversation, her anticipation and his patience. That's when the *Trial Nights* began. What with a great deal of heavy breathing and girlish cries of, "You're a caution, Klaus," it was pretty wild.

After several of these *Trial Nights*, and about the time the boy has decided to run off and join a monastery, the girl lets him know that all he has to do is threaten to ravish her and she'll give in. Imagine, it took her four or five nights to pass along this information.

If the *Trial Nights* prove too much of a trial and the two call it quits, the girl is free to begin the ordeal with someone else and no damage to her reputation. However, if she goes through a whole series of *Come Night-Trial Night* sessions without any talking, all the gossips in the Black Forest start chattering. What if she puts every young man in the Forest on trial? What will happen to clock-makers?

Most trial marriages can be settled out of wedlock.

STOP HORSING AROUND! WE'RE THIRSTY!

Picture a summer day in ancient Ireland. The country villagers, not having caused too much trouble recently, begin discussing a young girl; finally deciding she ought to be married (she wasn't even around to voice an opinion), they go about picking a husband for her. Maybe it took a whole afternoon, but they got it all settled.

So, the next Sunday some of the young buckos grab the appointed girl and carry her around on their backs, called *horsing* her. Tiring of this bucolic pastime, it's off for a few rounds of drinks...on her, for some perverse reason.

Just as she's beginning to enjoy the party, they pick up and trot off to the hurling field (field hockey). And guess who is one of the participants? The boy they'd picked to be her groom. Now, if he happens to be the winner — although how in the hell one person can win at hurling, we don't understand — they get married then and there. If someone else won, *he* got the girl and the chosen boy was off the hook.

However, the Irish never did like to call off a good game of hurling, so it often required two or three consecutive Sundays of hurling before things were decided. By this time, the girl could have run off to Wales with an octogenarian potato farmer for all they knew. At any rate, this manner of picking the groom was called *goaling the girl*.

And it was a lucky Irish lass who was *horsed* and *goaled* in a single Sunday!

Welsh draymen no longer shout "Cwthllwp" at weddings!

WHAT A YAM COOKER, BUT...

It was relatively easy for a young Solomon Islander to gauge a girl's reaction to him. He simply cooked up a tasty dish of yams and coconuts and left it at her door. When he returned in the morning, the dish told the story: untouched, bye-bye; if money was left in the dish, it told him she liked his cooking, but that was all; but an empty dish and no money meant he had been accepted.

Sick witches go to witch doctors!

WHEN MEETING A MAN, BE ABJECT!

Lousy advice! But it was a custom in Japan, for one. In those times, when a Japanese woman saw a man approaching on the

RIDDLE: What did an umbrella have to do with courting in Brittany?

ANSWER: First, it rains a lot in that northern province of France, so an umbrella is standard equipment for outside courting. But, at one time, a boy desiring to court a girl asked to carry her umbrella. If she had someone else in mind, she left him standing there in the rain.

roadway, she turned aside and covered her mouth with her hand. This prevented him from being polluted by her breath. She also removed her cloth headgear, bowed low to stress her humility and remained in that position until he had passed by.

Landlubbers scrape and bow! Seamen scrape their bows!

HOW WAS THE WINE, ANDROS?

Greece is no different than other countries. Occasionally, lovers stray. In the last century, a Greek maiden rectified such a situation with a touch of magic. First, she had her neighborhood witch go out at midnight and gather some firewood. Then she roasted a bat to ashes over the bewitching flames. The next step was to bury the bat's ashes at a crossroads. Forty nights later, she returned, dug up the ashes and as soon as the time was right she slipped them into the straying lover's wine.

We don't know about you, but we'll be damned if we want to have anything to do with a girl who serves *bat's-ash cocktails.*

The Sun's under...no over the yardarm...oh, hell, drink up!

OH, TO HAVE A QEESTER, NOW THAT SUMMER'S HERE!

Would we kid you? In the 17th Century on Texel, an island in northern Holland, all the houses were built with a convenient opening under the window. This was to allow amorous boys of the neighborhood to sneak into a daughter's bedroom and spend the night in blissful dalliance. It was a recognized custom, called *qeesten.* You guessed it! The boyfriend was called her *qeester.*

*If you thought the **Bunsen burner** was an ancient biscuit warmer, go to bed!*

LIPS THAT WON'T HOLD CHERRY WINE!

The *Pawunwa* Indians of Brazil didn't merely give lip service to beautification. When a young *Pawunwa* girl became of courting age, their lips were pierced and a wooden plug was placed in each. The boys knew she was ready to be wooed.

After her marriage, the plug was removed from the lower lip and a wider incision was made. Then a shiny chunk of quartz was placed in her lower lip so everyone would know she was married. Oh, your aching lips is right!

*In downtown Mesopotamia, around 3001 B.C., wine was called **Blood of the Gods.***

ANYONE WE KNOW?

The *Igorots* of the Philippines used to be head-hunters and all-around nasties. But they were comparative sissies alongside another Philippine tribe, the *Ilongots*. At one time, an *Ilongot* boy would have his marriage proposal turned down flat, unless he first gave the girl a fresh human head, a cut of breast meat (a slice of heart would do in a pinch) and one or two fingers. No outsiders are known to have stuck around to see what she did with these divine tokens of affection.

***Hogmany in auld reekie** is simply New Year's Eve in Edinburgh!*

A FINE FINN YOU WOULD HAVE MADE!

It was once the custom for young Finnish men, after becoming engaged, to bring gifts whenever they visited the girl's house. Shrewd Finnish fathers would permit their daughters to become engaged long before they would permit them to marry. They also let the young man know their favorite brandy and tobacco.

It wasn't totally one-sided, however. The boy could purchase the girl's favor with an extra gift or two. Either way, the fathers kept them coming back with loot for as long as possible.

The month of June is named for the Roman Goddess Juno...patroness of happy marriages.

YOU CAN'T PLEASE 'EM ALL!

The price of brides got so outrageous in 1901 in the Solomon Islands that they had to call a special session of the *Vaukolo* (their law-making body). A local teacher, and a Christian besides, had brought the problem to a head by peddling one of his daughters for a thousand porpoise teeth (really big money) plus 150 strings of shell money.

After the usual legislative bickering, the Vaukolo decreed that,

RIDDLE: In 19th Century Scotland, what was meant by *booking* the marriage?

ANSWER: When Scotch couples decided to marry, relatives from each family met to draw up the contract. That part wasn't any particular fun, but custom called for them to knock down a quart or two of fine Scotch whisky while working out the details. In no time, the Irish adopted the custom.

from then on, brides would go for *30* strings of shell money...tops, unless bride and groom were of a Chief's family — then it could go to *50* strings.

You would think that action would have made the Vaukolo members very popular. Wrong! The ladies of the islands, so incensed at being priced downward, cut off all favors and wouldn't speak to the men for months!

*Cro-Magnons left **graffiti** on the cave walls of their enemies!*

GOING ONCE, GOING TWICE!

In ancient Assyria, the big annual event was the public auction of girls for marriage. And they had a clever wrinkle. Naturally, the beauties brought out the big spenders, so they were auctioned off first. Whatever the bid price, it was given as a dowry to the less attractive girls. So the beauty-lovers got what they wanted, and the more practical fellows were willing to put up with a bit of ugliness for the dowry. Best of all, the auction was a total sell out each year!

Lord Chesterfield smoked a camel at his wedding. Everyone enjoyed it!

BOUGHT ANY GOOD BRIDES RECENTLY?

Ibo fathers in Nigeria used to get as much as $200 for a good-looking daughter, but an ugly one was lucky to bring three goats.

Zambales parents of northern Luzon in the Philippines were crafty where a dollar was concerned. They'd buy their son a very young girl for his future wife. The price was so much lower than for a girl of marriageable age.

But on the island of Mindanao, the price of *Subanu* brides got so high, two young men often pooled their funds and bought *one wife for the two of them.*

Things were even worse at one time on Sumatra where few men could come up with the price of a halfway decent wife. So, they put themselves into bonded servitude with their in-laws. If a husband still hadn't paid off the bridal price by his death, his children were put into bondage to pay for their own mother.

Change reels to Russia: Go-betweens for *Ostjake* men with marriage in mind sometimes haggled with the girl's father or his representative for months. This was part of a game, since most brides brought the same price: forty rubles in cash, a large iron casserole, two small iron casseroles, four beaver skins and two fox skins, three dresses and six yards of red material.

The *Ostjake* were fond of a tale of bride-selling between two poor families, too. The girl's father secretly arranged with the boy's father to steal a cow and a horse...*in payment for the bride.* The boy's father agreed readily...since the horse had died the day before, and because he was certain he could steal his cow back at a later time.

There was a subtle ceremonial way of jacking up the price of brides in olden Ethiopia. The man was required to go to the public square and, before official witnesses and a priest, list all the money and merchandise he was willing to pay. Not wishing to look like a piker, he invariably promised much more than he would have in a private negotiation. There were a few bankrupt show-offs in Ethiopia at that time.

So it shouldn't have been a total loss, the Aleut Indians of Alaska traded a wife they had tired of for food or a new parka.

HARD DAYS IN SICILY!

The time was when *Sicilian* mothers selected a son's bride for him. From such a bad start, things could and often did get worse. The morning after the wedding, the groom was required to hang the bed linen out the window so the whole town could see he had married a virgin. Male pride in Sicily was such that if a man's bride had not been

RIDDLE: Is there a Moslem counterpart to carrying a bride over the threshold?

ANSWER: Oh, yes! In Arabia they formerly sprinkled blood from a sacrificed sheep before the entry and the bride stepped over it. In Tunis, it wasn't unusual for the groom to enter the new home walking backwards with a dagger held out before him. His bride followed, keeping her finger on the dagger point.

a virgin, he cut his wrist and stained the linen; then, after hanging the sheets out the window, he went back inside and finished the job on his wrists. Looks to us as if a Sicilian girl of those times could have played a fatal trick on some boy from whom she sought vengeance.

All Sicilian men were ***matic*** *at one time — a few* ***charis,*** *the rest* ***asth!***

NEVER MARRY INTO THE YAM FAMILY!

It was taboo for a South African native woman to use the name of her father, her husband or the head of her husband's family. In fact, she couldn't utter a word that even sounded like their names. If any one of those names were similar to the word for *food* in their language, she had to devise a new word to indicate *food.* Since there were three different names to be avoided, the language problem often got sticky.

Freedom of choice applies to almost everything except relatives.

THERE'LL ALWAYS BE A MOTHER-IN-LAW!

Zulu men once had such a thing about their mothers-in-law that they never looked at them, even pretending not to see them if they met by accident. If circumstance forced a Zulu to communicate with his mother-in-law, he did so at a distance and often through a third person.

In the Belgian Congo, a man wasn't permitted to look at his mother-in-law. Should he have seen her coming from a distance, he had to run into the jungle to avoid her.

Celebes Islanders always spat after contact with a mother-in-law to remove the bad omen of seeing her.

The special place of the mother-in-law in bygone days was a part of the *Karelian* wedding ritual in Russia. After the ceremony, the wedding party went to the groom's home to celebrate...all but the bride's mother. Traditionally, she moped around and did some plain and fancy weeping until the groom's family returned and paid her a bribe to join the festivities.

So, it looks as if the groom's mother-in-law didn't get much respect. How about the bride's mother-in-law? In old China, at least, that lady held the big stick! Just three days after the wedding, the young bride had to go through a ceremonial washing of the mother-in-law's feet which signified two things: the mother-in-law was washed free of all household problems from then on; the bride had now embarked on a life of servitude to her mother-in-law. The Chinese bride sometimes paid her mother-in-law back by committing suicide. Barring that subtle way of getting even, the bride had but one thing to look forward to — becoming a domineering mother-in-law herself one day.

Zulu hunters hated indigestion! To prevent it, they tied a knot in the tail of all game they killed.

ALL YOURS, AND CLEAN, TOO!

A groom of yesteryear among the Mamprusi tribe of the African Gold Coast was assured of having a clean bride. At noon on the wedding day, the bride was taken to the center of the village and publicly bathed in hot water (filled with herbs) for five solid hours. Clean but wrinkled, she was led off to meet the groom.

No Manchu Tartar could marry a person with a different family name from his own.

BED THE BRIDE AND BACK THE WEDDING!

The doings the Scotch used to have following a wedding could put a person in a hospital. First, everyone went to a relative's house for a wee drappie. Then, it was off to the bridegroom's place, complete with pistol-firing and shouting. The bride and groom were parked at the head of a banquet table. The dancing and drinking went on far into the night. Finally, it came time to *bed the bride*.

The whole gang, except for the groom, marched her off to the bedroom. While she was disrobing, she threw her left stocking. The person it landed on was the next to be married. Then it was into bed with her. Now they got the groom, and tucked him in beside his bride. While everyone stood around sniggering, he drank the company's health.

Lest the wedded couple feel their friends thought little of them, the gang stuck around for another full day of carousing...called *backing the wedding*.

Maybe the Scotch came to be thought of as *dour* by outsiders, when all along they were simply trying to recover from *backing* too many weddings.

RIDDLE: Is the so-called *lovelock* a product of civilized society?

ANSWER: Not sure. Originally, the *lovelock* in England was reserved for men of fashion in Queen Elizabeth's time. We do know that, in the 1800's, the unmarried girls on the Friendly Islands of the South Pacific wore a *maiden lock* over the shoulder. It was one of their wedding rituals to cut off the *maiden lock*.

Robert Burns drank Bushmill's...on the sly!

UYA! UYA! WHO HAS THE BETEL NUT?

Some of the natives of the Philippine Islands used to have a wedding ceremony which a deranged historian described as, "Short and simple." We ask you, does any of the following make sense to you?

The groom snatched the veil from the bride's head, stuffed it into his loincloth and went panting off into the forest howling "Uya! Uya!" in imitation of a bird. Meanwhile the bride's mother settled down to a session of betel nut chewing, adding a touch of lime for flavor. When she got bored with this, she passed the half-masticated betel nut to her daughter, who continued mangling the stuff. About this time, the groom comes staggering back out of the wood, all uyaed out. Spying the badly chewed-up betel nut, he takes it and chomps on it a while. Then he and the bride stand and touch one another on the head. Wedding over. Uya! Uya!

If you don't like making sacrifices, you'd have hated Druid weddings!

DON'T CARRY US BACK TO JAVA!

Javanese brides of yesteryear were a bit weak by the time of the wedding. In the three-day feast preceding the wedding, she was allowed only three teaspoons of rice and a cup of hot water a day. On her wedding night, she shared a bowl of rice with her new husband. But the next night! When the couple retired to bed, right there by the head of the bed was a nice buffalo head someone had cooked for them.

Mayans thought ants made excellent wedding cakes. (And we didn't even know the little beggars had an oven.)

MY GOD, IS THAT THE BRIDE?

In Tunisia, a bride was not considered properly dressed until she had put on seventeen silk and muslin garments, one on top of another. Then she stained her toenails and fingernails with henna; and, to complete the picture, she pencilled her eyebrows together above her nose. At least you always knew which one was the bride!

Tamils of old Ceylon didn't require a wedding as an excuse to put jewelry in their hair, ears, around their necks, draped over their foreheads, around arms, wrists, legs and toes plus a couple of jewels stuck in the side of the nose.

THREE ANTELOPE BELLIES AND A WALL-EYED HORSE!

The Blackfoot Indians of Montana weren't above showing off to their neighbors when they had the wherewithal. A wedding was a great time for impressing the rest of the tribe. For instance, the bride's family might give a completely furnished tepee and a string of ponies. Their daughter received a pip of a buckskin dress with elk-teeth trimming. And, so the groom shouldn't look like a slumph, he got a bang-up suit trimmed in ermine tails. Once all this gift-giving started, it was hard to stop. Now, the groom gave a few nice horses to his father-in-law. More important, he made a promise to share any spoils of war and meat from hunting with his in-laws. As to the meat, he was expected to give the father-in-law the choicest cuts. No piker, the father-in-law then gave the couple some of his property.

Eric the Red was married in a boat with forty brightly-painted oars!

A NIGHT SUCH AS NO OTHER, THANK GOD!

A peasant practice in 19th Century Poland was enough to destroy romance. On the wedding night, friends of the bride cut all her hair off (who needs such friends?) and wrapped her shaven head in white linen. (She was expected to keep this cloth on her head until she bore a son.) Then they carried poor baldy over to the groom.

But the worst was still to come. The groom, propped up in bed, was given a special dish of bear testicles to eat; if they were fresh out of bear testicles, goat testicles would do. As soon as he managed to get this lovely repast down, the assembled crowd cheered and then sprinkled the wedding bed with water before leaving.

Very few Poles married a second time in those days!

Russian men used to frown on marriage...right after it happened to them!

SLIPPERIEST GIRL IN THE VILLAGE!

In the last century, the *Batoros*, who lived near Lake Albert in East Africa, had their own way of preparing a bride for the great day of her life. First, they shaved every single hair from her head and body.

RIDDLE: What were the West African *fattening huts?*

ANSWER: At one time in parts of West Africa, *fat* and *beautiful* were interchangeable. Girls were taken to special huts where they did nothing but eat, stuffing themselves with all manner of starchy foods and drinking gallons of milk. The crowning achievement was to get so fat *you had to be carried* to your own wedding.

Then they smeared her whole body with a mixture of butter and castor oil. Evidently the *Batoros* put great store in aroma and elusiveness!

Marriage was attributed to the altitude in Nepal!

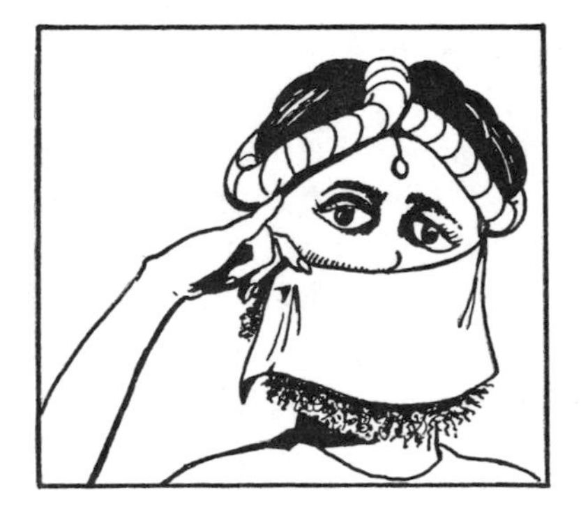

ACHMED SUE!

Around Fez in the mid-1800's, a husband-to-be thought it was perfectly swell to get dressed up as a bride to celebrate his engagement. Once in drag, his servant girls carry him on a cushion and set him down on a mattress facing his front door. He blushes a bit and closes his eyes in bridal yearning.

As soon as his buddies arrive, the servants give him a little milk to drink, to purify his life; then they put a date in his mouth, signifying wealth. Then each of his friends get the milk and date treatment.

By this time, the group is so a-twitter with the excitement of it all, each friend spits on a coin and sticks it on the future bridegroom's forehead.

This poor yokel was bound to find the wedding a big letdown!

The Moroccans used to give the mother-in-law the privilege of rushing into the couple's bedroom on the wedding night to congratulate them. That had to have made her very popular!

QUICK, CATCH ME! I'M A GROOM!

The *Bruneis* of Borneo were romantics at heart. Before a wedding, old women went to the bride's hut, washed her and dressed her. Then they went to the groom's hut and did the same for him.

The groom was a resplendent fellow, too...all decked out in orange silk and gold cloth and bedizened with jewelry. Traditionally, he was supposed to be so dazed with joy at the upcoming event that he staggered along as if about to swoon any second.

Grooms needn't wear watches at their weddings. It's already too late!

THROW HIM A GOOSE, THE WEDDING'S OVER!

In parts of Russia, the bride got a pretty good notion of what marriage was going to be like right after the wedding ceremony. The couple sat down to a supper where the main dish was a roasted fowl. The newly wedded husband promptly tore the fowl into shreds with his bare hands, tossed part of it over his shoulder and wolfed the remaining parts by himself. That gave her a fair idea of where she was going to be eating from then on...the floor, most likely.

On the east coast of Sumatra they held interesting wedding feasts, too. As soon as it was over, they smeared the groom behind the ears with a glutinous paste of fat and rice. That scared off evil spirits. Didn't do much for the bride either.

People who are ripe for marriage may only be spoiling for a fight!

THE OLD RAW EGG FERTILITY RITE!

Someone unfamiliar with superstitions in 19th Century Morocco, would have been taken aback to find a young bride squatting over a bowl containing a newly laid egg and some rainwater. It wasn't just any rainwater, by the way, since it had to have fallen on the 27th of April (actually its Mohammedan calendar equivalent). This was part of a ritual that would enhance her chances of getting pregnant. The rest went like this: she drank the rainwater, and placed the egg under a setting hen. If the egg produced a rooster, she would have a boy; a hen indicated a girl child.

Now, it wasn't always easy for her to find an egg to use for the rite. You see, her husband, somewhat concerned over his reproductive capabilities, had a raw egg yolk every morning, which he topped off by drinking oil from the eggshell.

A barren couple ran up a hell of an egg bill in those days!

And as long as we're in an eggy mood, we might as well tell you

RIDDLE: Are strangers welcome in the *Patagonian* region of Argentina?

ANSWER: With a bang, you might say! Patagonian husbands had a fixation about how to insure good fortune in the year ahead. They dispatched their wives to the woods with strict instructions to give themselves freely to the *first* person passing by. And loiterers? The Patagonian woods were full of them in those days!

how they conducted a wedding in Amboina, Indonesia at one time. The nuptial couple wore garments with wide sleeves. The person marrying them stood with his back to them and tossed eggs over his shoulder until he got one in the bride's sleeve and one in the groom's. A couple could be badly messed up before the ceremony was completed.

Orange blossoms at weddings was a Moorish custom symbolic of chastity and fertility.

*Should you get very chummy with a **pie-billed grebe**, call him a **dabchick!***

THREE NIGHTS IN A DITHER!

In many parts of Germany and Switzerland, it was once considered very dangerous for a wedded couple to have intercourse on the first three nights of their marriage. They believed that if they remained continent through these so-called *tobias nights*, the devil could do them no harm. It may have been these three nights of fearful anticipation which led to the old expression, "The Devil with it!" (And how did Tobias get in the act?)

Eloise Zinger had an exciting honeymoon. She and her husband caught a peeping tom at their window... sound asleep!

OH, NO YOU DON'T, SLEEPYHEAD!

You would have thought the Nufors of Dutch New Guinea would have killed off the custom of marriage the way they used to treat a bride and groom.

The first four nights of a marriage, bride and groom were forced to sit with their backs to one another without falling asleep. If one of them began to nod, an accommodating friend walked them around until the sleepiness left them. (And on the fifth night, all they did was sleep!)

*We don't know whether the missionaries confused them or what, but the **Trobriand Islanders** had intercourse the night **before** the wedding but not again until several nights after.*

ALONE AT LAST!

The French had a custom in olden times which required exquisite timing. Four nights after a wedding, all the friends of the newlyweds popped in with bowls of milk soup. The idea was to catch them in bed, and make them take one spoonful of soup from each bowl. This charming custom may have been responsible for honeymoons away from home. It certainly has killed the market for milk soup!

Ancient Scots kidnapped their brides...known as compounding a felony!

CROWDED HONEYMOON IN THE CELEBES!

In the old days in the Celebes, a wealthy family could afford to have a marriage ceremony run for a month or more. Throughout this time, the bride and groom slept in the same bed...along with eight old women who were highly trained in anti-hanky-panky techniques.

It was wise to stand in the rear of the crowd at a ***Kayan*** *wedding ceremony in Borneo. The priest, or* ***dayong****, closed the affair by sprinkling pig blood on those nearby.*

WHERE'S UBI? IT'S PAST FIVE DAYS!

The *Bavuma* of Uganda in bygone days, liked to have more than one wife if they could afford them. But, there were rules to observe. He was supposed to rotate his attentions from wife to wife on a four-day basis. If he overstayed his allotted time with one wife, the others ran around the village calling him all manner of quaint obscenities for his bad manners.

Most brides over-prepare. There's something old, borrowed and blue standing right beside them at the altar.

HIMALAYAN CONFUSION!

In the past it was not uncommon for a Tibetan woman to marry an entire band of brothers. Under such an arrangement, it was well-nigh impossible to determine exact paternity of children. So, the Tibetans decreed that the *oldest* brother of the family be considered the father of all the children, while the rest of them were referred to as uncles.

And to prove they weren't prudish, a Tibetan wife with half a dozen brothers for husbands was also allowed to have a lover. (Otherwise she'd get bored!)

The most tiresome of all tribes has always been the ***diatribe!***

BIG OPTIONS IN SUMATRA!

Time was when a Sumatran too short on funds to buy a first-class wife could exchange his sister for the girl he desired. Those without sisters to barter with often borrowed a cousin or even a friend's sister, promising to repay when his ship came in.

After marriage, should the Sumatran husband have grown disenchanted, he could often work an exchange, an outright sale or even pawn his wife.

The Sumatran term for *married love* in those days was...uh...

The price one pays for accepting a good turn is hearing about it over and over again.

LOVE AMONG THE HORSEY SET!

One of the Russian peoples, the *Kalmucks*, were such dedicated horsemen, the wedding used to begin on horseback and it went like a western movie.

First, the bride-to-be swung herself up onto a *Kalmuck* pony and rode off. The chap who hoped to be the groom took out after her on his horse. Now, the story has it that *Kalmuck* women were finer riders than the men; if the girl didn't care for her pursuer, she simply outrode him. However, if she said to herself, "Hell, for a man, he isn't too bad," she'd let him catch her.

Then, they got off their horses and consummated the marriage right then and there! (We know, you thought being such great horsemen and all...)

Many baseball players never make it to first base.

SUPERSTITION OK, BUT THAT WAS RIDICULOUS!

If there were *voyeurs* among the old Germans, they must have loved weddings. It was a strict custom that no marriage ceremony was considered finalized until the consummation had been witnessed. Even a German king and his new queen had to put up with this peeping-tomfoolery.

Dictionaries say 'to make perfect' is an obsolete definition of to consummate.

WHAT DO YOU HEAR FROM THE LIZARDS?

It wasn't bad enough being some of the poorest people on earth, the Hindus had to be racked with superstition, too. For instance, if a Hindu father was on his way to arrange for a son's bride and he met an animal...that spelled bad luck, so he went back home pronto.

If he happened to make it to the house of the desired girl's father, there's no telling how long he may have had to stand around tugging at his loincloth. You see, the girl's father had his routine to go through. He faced south and waited for the weird cry of a lizard. Indian lizards were on to the game, and they were known to be perverse as hell.

The 'dik-dik' antelope is only 12 inches high and mad as hell about it.

A LITTLE KINDLY BEATING!

The Yugoslavians had a custom which required a groom to beat his wife gently three times. It served a dual purpose, at least for them: it was a warning to the wife to forget any previous lovers, while reminding her to be obedient to her husband.

The ancient Welsh condoned a husband's giving a misbehaving wife three knocks with a stick. However, they built in some protection: the stick couldn't be any longer than his forearm or any thicker than his middle finger. The poor girl who married a long-armed Welshman with thick fingers was best off to behave herself!

The White Russians had a very different ritual beating. The groom's best man came to the marriage bed and gave the groom three whacks and then shouted, "Look at each other! Kiss! Embrace fast!" (Who asked him in the bedroom?)

Marasca cherries from Zara, Yugoslavia make good Maraschino cherries. (We knew.)

EITHER WE HAVE IT BACKWARD, OR...

There was a tribe that lived on the several small islands at the mouth of French Guinea's Rio Nunez which had a most peculiar approach to marriage. A young woman wasn't considered eligible for marriage until she had *at least two children old enough to walk*. Who wanted a bride in this state? The smart boys did! She had living proof that she could bear children. Second, the children were worth money. (Maybe we're the ones who have it backward?)

Serbians knew how to make sure a bride's first child would be a boy — they just tied a man's belt around her hand. (Wish we'd thought of that!)

MORE ABJECT WOMEN — MOROCCAN STYLE!

Not too long ago, when a Moroccan husband was away for a single night, his wife had to put on mourning clothes. She was allowed to wash her hands, (great privilege) but never allowed to take a bath during her marriage (now, that serves him right). Oh, and she could never eat in his presence either. She did have one special right: if her husband physically abused her, all she had to do was shout, ''Nifrex,'' three times. That meant *your nose*, and her saying it three times constituted a divorce...and she got her dowry back.

Bigamous women borrow from Peter to keep Paul!

THEY KNEW HOW HE FELT!

All *Masai* men traveled about a lot on their own. It was considered polite for a man to offer a visiting Masai of his own approximate age the overnight services of his wife. After all, the poor chap was away from home and wife. Inasmuch as this was a revered custom, some of the wandering *Masai* didn't wait for the offer. They simply stuck their spear into the earth outside a certain hut. The owner, like it or not, had to spend the night elsewhere.

Mate-swapping is a four-way act of hostility!

GETTING SANDALED!

Until some meddling Britishers of the mid 1800's put a stop to it, the *Malabar* women of India could have several husbands. To indicate the degree to which the wife ruled the roost, on the porch of every *Malabar's* house were wooden seats called *husbands' benches.* When a *Malabar* man arrived home, he made a great deal of racket as a courtesy to his wife, who may have been occupied with a lover or someone else's husband. Then he plunked himself down on the *husbands' bench* and waited for her to call him into the house.

Oh, one minor detail: when a *Malabar* husband came home and found his sandals sitting outside the door, he realized he had just been divorced!

His fourth marriage proved his unquenchable masochism!

BETTER THAN WHAT, THE SECOND TIME AROUND?

The Prussians became perfect crazies when a woman who had been married before became a bride again. First, she and her latest husband couldn't enter the house until the musicians had all clambered up onto the roof and blown music down the chimney.

If it happened to be her third marriage, bridegroom number three had to make an ass of himself by coming in through the window and then march through the house three times.

Meanwhile, two fiddlers and a bassoonist had fallen off their roof and a saxophonist was stuck headfirst in the chimney!

They each had a **vision** *of marriage: hers was* **re***; his,* **tele***!*

ADULTERY, WHERE IS THY STING?

Considering the severity of punishment for infidelity by women in Africa, a 19th Century woman must have had a most powerful yearning to commit the act. The *Bangala* cut off a wayward wife's ears and pierced her calves with hot lances. *Azandes* killed adulteresses and lopped off the hands and ears of the man responsible. The *Kwilu* were a bit kinder, just beating the unfaithful wife; the man became the slave of the wronged husband.

The *Ethiopians* were severe but not violent with adulteresses. She had her head shaved, was given one ragged dress, a single needle and was sent packing. She was expected to make her living with that one needle. But, let's say the husband became unfaithful. They gave the man's wife a mild beating on the grounds that she must have been partly responsible for his straying from the straight and narrow.

Lest you are led to believe these practices only existed in primitive Africa, the betrayed husbands of Afghanistan cut off the nose of a faithless wife and her illicit lover, if he could be found. In ancient Denmark, infidelity was a capital offence, whereas a murderer got off with paying a fine. And in the South Pacific, *Trobriand Islanders* had the right to kill an unfaithful wife, but they seldom did...sometimes merely going off to sulk for a week or so.

We get the feeling adultery was fascinating to some because of the high risk.

Once Saudi Arabians could divorce a garlic-eating wife. Good thinking!

NO FISH, NO MARRIAGE!

Among the *Ainus* of northern Japan, wives were permitted to seek a divorce, too. If her husband were an adulterer, she could tell him good-bye. A lazy husband was in jeopardy, as well as one so inept he couldn't catch enough fish or game to keep the family in food. Finally, if she plain disliked him, she could divorce him. Kept *Ainu* men on their best behavior!

RIDDLE: If adultery was not grounds for divorce with the *Todas* of India, what was?

ANSWER: Toda wives who acted foolishly all the time or who would not work were apt to find themselves single. But adultery? Perfectly natural event to a *Toda!*

Wedding cakes used to be baked. Now they're made by injection-molding.

SEEING IS UNBELIEVABLE!

19th Century custom in Lower Congo: Don't take any young man's boasts of his virility seriously. You went with the couple on their wedding night and watched for yourself. If the kid was a flop, the bride screamed, "Foul" and called off the marriage. Conveniently, she had witnesses to prove her point.

Tigris River watermelons grow to 275 pounds. (With eleven-pound seeds.)

AN OX IN TIME!

The nomadic *Masai* of East Africa never did care for divorce. For instance, a wife may have done something bad enough to put her in line for a beating, but, to avoid divorce, she would have gone to her father and requested an ox. Then she would have hurried back to her husband, apologized and given him the ox. Being a practical fellow, he would have accepted the peace offering and the marriage would have gone on.

The male horse does not divorce. Would you, if your wife carried a colt?

HINDU DIVORCE TIMETABLE!

The Hindus weren't known to be big divorcers but, if certain conditions persisted, a husband could end the marriage. If, after eight years, a wife were still sterile, that was grounds; ten years of nothing but stillborn children would do it, too; and if all the children had been daughters over eleven years, good-bye.

Himalayans do not marry on yakback...and they never have!

SEVEN CHINESE NO-NO'S!

A Chinese wife could be told to hit the road for any of seven reasons in the old days: if she disobeyed her in-laws; if she produced no male children after a few years; if she were promiscuous; if she exhibited jealousy; if she talked too much; if she stole; and if she contracted leprosy. Even letting too much smoke in the house was sure to bring divorce.

Matchmakers turn a profit from promises they have no way of keeping!

PITTER-PATTER OF TINY FEET!

A lot of romantic notions have been attached to the old Chinese custom of binding a woman's feet so they wouldn't grow normally. We're inclined to believe the story that it was originally a device for preventing runaways.

By the way, the Chinese didn't stop the practice by making it unlawful. They simply levied a three-dollar tax on the head of a house for every woman with bound feet. That knocked the thing into a cocked hat in no time!

The last line above is vivid: imagine a cocked hat filled with bound feet!

ETHIOPIA FOREVER!

Since the Ethiopians had four distinct types of marriage, adequate grounds for divorce varied from the extremely serious to dissolve the strictest marriage to almost frivolous grounds for ending a somewhat casual marriage. In the latter category, a husband could shed a wife who was a consistently lousy cook, and a wife could gain freedom from a husband who didn't give her enough cash to indulge in her greatest vanity — her coiffure.

Lepers, imbeciles, those afflicted with elephantiasis and women over sixty could not marry at all. A divorcee had to do special penance before remarrying; and a widow must have been in mourning at least ten months. But an Ethiopian prostitute could marry any old time she pleased.

Tinkerbell had a bent clapper!

HOW ABOUT A NICE, SIMPLE DIVORCE?

What with the so-called civilized practice of lawyers, judges, property settlements, dishing up of intimate disagreements and the like, there's much to be said for the way many primitive peoples used to call a marriage to a halt.

An aggrieved *Sumatran* husband took three chunks of betel nut

RIDDLE: In Burma did a man have to marry an older brother's widow at one time?

ANSWER: The *Kachins* of Burma had such a rule, even if the poor guy was already married. He did have one out: he could try to talk one of his younger brothers into relieving him of the responsibility. (Not your brother's keeper, hah!)

and passed them to his wife one at a time, pronouncing, "One divorce, two divorces, three divorces."

Samoans didn't say anything. One or the other simply went back to a parent. Afterwards, they referred to the marriage as having *passed away*.

A *Siamese* husband who wanted out had to give up the dowry and wedding presents, but a wife had to pay double to dissolve the union. Algerian *Arabs* also had to give back the dowry, if they sent a wife back to her parents.

Courts in Norway once automatically declared a couple divorced, if they had lived apart for three years. As recently as 1927, the Russians granted a divorce on request with the showing of identification papers; there was no need for consent by the other party, either.

Divorce was once so easy in Egypt — a husband simply said, "Thou are divorced," three times — some husbands acted too hastily. According to Mohammedan law, he was not permitted to remarry his divorced wife, unless she had been married to another in between. So, old fast-fuse had to get a friend to marry his newly divorced wife. Then the friend said the magic three-word phrase and the original husband was technically free to remarry his former wife. So, hold your temper, Ibn!

Women who marry for money usually get divorced for the same reason!

A CAPITAL TIME IN OLD TIBET!

There was a time when a Tibetan who *killed* his wife got off with a fine. If he *failed to pay the fine,* however, he was in for it. Then he was treated as a common murderer and punished with vigor.

You see, wife-killing was not a capital offence in Tibet in those days. But skipping out on a fine was serious business.

Who is the cry of the female owl. The male owl's cry is no one you know!

WIDOWS HAVE NEVER HAD IT EASY, BUT REALLY...

Long ago, a Chinese widow was truly between a rock and a hard place. She could commit suicide, thereby showing her devotion to her departed husband; or, if she decided to stick around, she and her children were sold.

Finally, the Chinese lawmakers relented a bit, outlawing the sale of widows...until the mourning period was over. At that point, she got a choice: be sold or become a nun.

If somehow or another a widow managed to survive all this and was in a position to remarry, it was okay. But first she had to suffer a beating of eighty blows.

Come to think of it, the suicide angle may have been the best way out.

Greenland Eskimos had nothing against widows remarrying. However, widows had to refrain from cleaning themselves, so they weren't in great demand.

WHO SAID YOU CAN'T?

Twenty or even one hundred wives were not uncommon for a *Fiji Island* chief to own. Back in those days, the chiefs weren't too well versed in such Christian aphorisms as *you can't take it with you.* They not only believed you could, but *they did* — all the wives got buried with him and later he lived very happily, they say.

***A Hottentot** woman, when widowed, cut off the tip of her little finger and then went on to other matters.*

SURE CURE!

It's not too hard to grasp why the Sioux Indians had very few children who were habitual bed-wetters. After the first incident, the kid's parents told him to stop or his next meal would be boiled mice! Try it...you'll see!

What with all the spoiled children one sees about these days, we expect a spare rod clearance sale any day now!

GET CRACKING, YOU FOUR-YEAR-OLDS!

The Sioux Indians were practical people. As soon as a child could walk, his or her ears were pierced for later ornaments. And when the children were four, they were given their own bedding, clothing, tools and eating utensils. They were expected to take care of them, too. The Sioux had no word for *juvenile delinquent.*

Chief Crazy Horse liked all Indians...without reservations!

AT LAST! A PRACTICAL CUSTOM!

When a male child was born, his Japanese parents planted a tree near the house. At the time of his betrothal years later, the tree was cut down and the wood was fashioned into a chest to hold his clothing and that of his bride. Right on!

CHAPTER TEN

The Inside Story

Who can forget the ringing journalistic credo of Mithron Mimby Twiggs — crusading editor of the *Hydraulic Lift Operators Quarterly* — when he said, "If the muck's there, rake it!" America, you have the right to know that *Lilli Putian* is not a jazz singer from Toledo! Take note that the *spleen* is on its way out as a popular internal organ, probably to be replaced on the most desirable list by the parathyroid glands. While we're at it: clean up your vocabulary by ditching the word *upstanding* — if there's no *downstanding,* what's the point?

Look for that marvelous old card game, *loo,* to make a smashing comeback under its original and much more dignified name — *lanterloo!*

You'll probably pat your forelock with joy to know the difference between *winch* and *wench*. A *winch* is a crank! Unwinding is done with a *wench!*

The National Enquirer will no doubt hop right on this one: Robert Louis Stevenson, British by birth, quit a perfectly good reporting job on a Monterey, California newspaper, (paying him two dollars every single week), just so he could go off and write trash such as *Treasure Island.*

We stand four-square for the ultimate wisdom of Calvin Coolidge and his thought-provoking analysis: "When a great many people are unable to find work, unemployment results." We need more straight talk like that there.

You can expect the feminist movement to be dealt a staggering blow when it discovers that way back in 1862 Salmon Chase (Abraham's Secretary of the Treasury), when told the federal government had no female employees, went right out and hired one!

The Department of Agriculture is sitting on a controversial research report which states that today's *Darjeeling* tea contains less than 10 percent *dar* and not a speck of *jeeling.*

It's predicted the birthrate will increase in *Nursery,* Texas...and they're prepared for it. On the other hand, *Fact,* Kansas has been rocked with rumors.

Don't be too surprised to learn that an Australian sheepherder has trained a wild dog to participate in local church functions. He's said to be the only bingo-playing *dingo* in the Outback.

We can all thank Mabel Abandricath of Smouldering Wharf, Louisiana for her courageous battle to have the *speedwells* and other members of the *figwort* family reclassified as something other than *scrophulariaceous.* It's about time!

The National Whipping Bee has been postponed due to a shortage of black leather.

Our movietown spies report that Tidworth Nimble has hired two coaches to teach him how to eat roast beef with his bare hands, which indicates he'll probably land the title role in the forthcoming film *King Henry VIII Visits Ashtabula, Ohio.*

You can give short shrift to this scary quote: "The World's population is growing faster than the ability to feed mankind." British economist, Thomas Malthus, said the very same thing over 150 years ago and nothing's happened yet.

When the new cereal, *Weevil,* comes to your market, buy some! If you can't wait, just hang on to your old cereal long enough and you'll have your own box of *Weevil.*

Giddyup, the best-selling manual on horsewhipping has run into a legal snag. Seems the Goat Floggers Society is crying,

"Discrimination!" Offers to have a photograph of a thoroughly beaten nanny in the next edition has not softened the Society's stand. So why don't they just butt out!

Dutch automotive engineers are predicting instant acceptance of their new wheel-less car. The vehicle rides along on a two-inch layer of Edam cheese. When it reaches decrepitude, it needn't be junked. Just pop a piece of rye bread underneath and grill until golden brown.

Requests have been pouring into our offices from the Far East for advance copies of our new instruction booklet on *scrutability*. Watch for it!

Nero turned thumbs down on a fiddling gig in downtown Plains. Something about not wanting to play for peanuts. Tune up, Billy!

The expression *knock your block off* has become a literal reality in New York.

America has five cities bearing the name *Ivanhoe.* There's nary a one in all of Scotland or England. We also have eight *Edinburgs* to Scotland's one *Edinburgh* (note how thrifty we are, too...not wasting a final *h* on any of ours).

Look for shark-riding to continue to wane in popularity!

CULTURE CONTEST FALLS ON PRAT!

In our rustic, uncivilized days we Americans engaged in such ludicrous competitions as spelling bees, quilting bees and husking bees. What made them doubly dull was the fact that they had a purpose, even accomplished needed work.

Therefore, it's rewarding to see the progress we've made. We salute the annual Camel and Ostrich Races, the World Heavyweight Ski Meet, the World's Wristwrestling Tournament, the Watermelon Seed Spitting Contests (all three of them), the International Chicken Flying Meet, the Annual Turkey Trot (for trotting turkeys...not a dance contest), the Annual Rattlesnake Rodeo and the World's Cow-chip Throwing Contest. We are enriched indeed.

To prove that America is bursting with invention, here's a preview of some of the spirited competitions now in planning stages:

The Annual Gum-chewing and Walking Derby to promote ability to do two worthwhile things at the same time.

The Grand National Frisbee-eating Contest, sponsored by the

RIDDLE: The greatest number of former presidents who were living at the time of a new president's inauguration was five, when Lincoln took office. Was there ever an occasion when no former president was living while a new president was inaugurated?

ANSWER: Tricky, tricky! No *former* president was around for either of Washington's two inaugurations.

Frisbee Manufacturer's Cultural Committee to enhance the replacement market.

The International Porno Fair, a gratifying opportunity for Americans to examine what the lascivious of other nations are up to. It is hoped it will bolster this country's waning eroticism by promoting the values of lewdness.

The Western Regional Squirming Jamboree, restricted to teenagers of the west.

The World Junk-food Eating Contest, with merit awards to those eating the packages *and* the food.

We may have to wait another year for the National Pot-smokers Festival. The federal grant they need to finance the event has been delayed.

It's with no regret that we announce the demise of the National Book Reading Competition. Its sponsors — apparently a radical group — made the limp excuse that their failure was due to an outbreak of illiteracy. Come on, guys! America wants contests with bite!

A century ago, the British essayist Charles Lamb wrote, "Boys are capital fellows in their own way, among their mates; but they are unwholesome company for grown people."

DELIVERING THE MESSAGE!

When Lincoln came to Gettysburg on November 19, 1863 to help dedicate the national cemetery on the site of the Battle of Gettysburg, he was in against a heavyweight. The other speaker that day was a distinguished orator named Edward Everett.

Lincoln's now famous *Gettysburg Address* took him five minutes to deliver. When he had finished, the audience did not react.

Orator Everett, on the other hand, harangued the audience for two full hours. At the close, they applauded and cheered him wildly.

Legislators, please note: one who breaks a young mare to the saddle is a fillybuster!

LET'S GET ORGANIZED!

A veteran Washington-watcher was once asked when Congress first began functioning, and he replied, "I wasn't aware that they ever had."

But seriousness aside, on March 4, 1789 a few of the members of the House of Representatives meandered into the House. After a solemn head-count, they realized they had no quorum, sighed as a body and adjourned. Each succeeding day the same thing occurred. However, the word began to get out that the House was a great place to get away from the cares of being a legislator. The daily gathering grew until, a mere twenty-two working days after their first meeting, they had a quorum. The fact that the first quorum took place on April Fool's Day was not lost on critics.

Of course, attaining their first quorum was such heady stuff, they adjourned. After four days of *getting organized*, the House of Representatives officially opened for business on April 6, 1789. It has been said that since then the august body has lost some of its efficiency. Oh, yes, Congressmen got $6 a day for each actual day they were in session. Some of them were worth it.

To 'convent' is the obsolete of 'convene.' So, why doesn't Congress convent?

WARFARE!

The use of poison gas in World War I was not an innovation. The Spartan warriors of the Fifth Century B.C. cooked up a batch of pitch and sulphur under the walls of cities they were besieging, then set fire to the concoction and suffocated the people inside.

The victors in modern warfare go broke making the losers strong enough to be winners!

THE OLIVE BRANCH!

Wars have always resulted in the need to communicate secretly. In World War I, invisible ink was used on the skin of spies. And there have been secret codes for centuries. The ancient Greeks had a unique way of transmitting secret messages. They would select a trusted slave, shave his head, tattoo a message on his bare scalp, then sit back until his hair grew in. Finally, he was dispatched. At the other end, his head was shaved and the message read. Of course, this had some considerable disadvantages. First, if the message was urgent, think how nervous they were as they stood around and watched the slave's hair grow. Second, if they employed this technique very often, they must have run out of heads to tattoo.

RIDDLE: How many U.S. Presidents suffered wounds in our armed forces?

ANSWER: Four: James Madison and Andrew Jackson in the Revolutionary War; Rutherford B. Hayes, four times in the Civil War; and John F. Kennedy in World War II.

If a battle was won, they had a speedier method of sending the news. They released a dove, often with an olive twig in its beak. That goes back to the biblical tale of Noah and the Ark, and both the dove and the olive branch still stand for peace.

If Dr. Spooner didn't say it, he should have: "The outbreak of World War I was precipitated by the assassination of Austrian nobleman, Archfuke Derdinand."

Following World War I, the United States paid more relief funds to veterans than the governments of Germany, Italy, Canada, France and England combined. It's even more dramatic when one considers those five countries combined had eight times as many men under arms as we did.

Origin And End Of Species: "To those who fully admit the immortality of the soul," said Charles Darwin, "the destruction of our world will not appear so dreadful."

Valley Forge immediately brings into one's mind the brutal winter of American forces under George Washington. The highest hill, and one used by Washington's men as a lookout point was Mount Joy...certainly one of the more inappropriate names in our history.

Russia took no sides in our Revolutionary War. They didn't hear about it until 1844.

It's said that the famous battle between the two ironclad vessels the *Monitor* and the *Merrimac* revolutionized naval warfare. Fortunately, it was not too bloody an affair. None of the participants were killed.

Cuba has been secretly mounted on pontoons. Fidel Castro plans to have the whole island safely beached north of Miami in time for the Hialeah meeting in 1980.

For many years flogging was a common punishment in our armed services. The United States Navy and the merchant marine gave it up in 1850. The Army, either because they couldn't think of a substitute or because they enjoyed it, didn't get around to abolishing it until 1861.

Most soldiers cherish freedom. In fact, the stockades are full of them.

HEY, SOMEONE END THE WAR!

You would think that when General Robert E. Lee surrendered to General Grant at Appomatox Court House on April 9, 1865 that the Civil War was over. Actually, it didn't even end the fighting. Union and Confederate forces were still going at it in Mississippi until May 31 that year.

Officially, the Civil War didn't end for more than a year after Lincoln's assassination, when the Union troops were demobilized August 20, 1866.

Union General, Pitius Mott, attacked South Dakota in 1863, but no one was there!

PRICKLY NIGHT IN THE HIGHLANDS!

You'd let out a yell if you stepped on some *Onopordon acanthium* in your bare feet. It's *Scotch thistle*, and that's exactly what happened some twelve hundred years ago. It seems a band of Danes were planning a sneaky night attack on the Scot's Stirling Castle. Approaching stealthily in their bare feet, the Danes discovered the joys of *Scotch thistle*. The Scots, hearing the Danes cursing their bleeding feet, spoiled the surprise. And that, children, is why the thistle is Scotland's national emblem. Perhaps it accounts for the fact most Danes wear shoes now.

*If Caesar's troops had eaten **K-rations**, France would still be Gaul.*

BANG-BANG AWARDS GO A-BEGGING!

A spokesman for the Greater New York Pistol and Rifle Clubs complained that their efforts to promote the use of firearms to repel intruders is meeting resistance. Although winners of the *Courageous Citizens Award* receive a handsome plaque and a check for $200, some eligibles have turned down the honor. The spokesman said his organization was going to screen recipients more carefully with an eye to their willingness to "accept media attention."

Obviously the club is unschooled in modern promotional methods. What they should do is declare a national *Shoot-A-People Week*.

RIDDLE: Did the United States ever imprison debtors!

ANSWER: Regularly! Kentucky was the first state to abolish prison terms for debtors...and that wasn't until 1821.

We've even got a bumper sticker for you: *I Shot Mine! Have You?* Effective and good clean fun, as well!

Samuel Colt was a pistol!

FORT BLUNDER!

The United States Army began building a very strategic fort in 1816 at Rouses Point, New York. The work went on for two years, and then someone discovered that the fort was on British soil, not American. The fort was ceded back to us in 1842. However, its name — Fort Montgomery — always ran second to its nickname: Fort Blunder.

Daddy Warbucks was a sniper in World War I, until his eyes fell out!

Speaker of the House of Representatives is one of the most prestigious posts an American politician can attain. However, Henry Clay was made Speaker in 1811, at the start of his very first term in the House. With that start, one would think Clay was destined for the presidency, but he was defeated in his two tries — 1832 and 1844.

*How come politicians **run** for office and, if successful, slow down to a crawl?*

F.D.R.!

There were cries of "Dynasty" when Franklin Delano Roosevelt was elected to a third and then a fourth term. So now we have a law limiting a president to two terms. Some critics of F.D.R. became so incensed they claimed he was the only man in our history to seek a third term. They simply didn't remember that Ulysses S. Grant, after two four-year stints in the White House, tried for a third. The fact that he was unsuccessful led to forgetfulness.

For some reason the Congressional Record had never been translated into Estonian.

URBAN RENEWAL ISN'T NEW!

We heard a politician recently praising himself and politicians of this day and age in general for the concept of urban renewal...

Well, praiseworthy as some urban renewal projects may be, Pericles, the Greek statesman of the 5th Century B.C. got there way ahead of you fellows. He and the architect Ictinus developed a master plan for beautifying Athens. With the help of such superb artists as the sculptor Phidias, they did a fair country job. The Parthenon was one of the results of the project.

The very best liars have the very best memories.

Bolsheviks have often been depicted with a bomb in hand. In the late 1920's, the Russians put this explosive penchant to practical use, dynamiting old buildings to make way for new structures rather than using old-fashioned demolition techniques.

Convicted criminal to Judge Sir Norman Biskett: "As God is my judge, I am innocent." Biskett: "He isn't; I am. And you're not."

WHAT KIND OF CHOICE IS THAT?

If you had a violent antipathy for New York State, you'd have been mad as a wet Ohioan in two presidential elections: In 1904, both candidates — Teddy Roosevelt and Alton Parker — were Empire Staters; and the same thing again in 1944 when F.D.R. ran against Tom Dewey. Anti-Ohio folks had no choice in 1920, when Warren Harding and James Cox faced off — both were from the Buckeye state. Then, clear back in 1860, Abe Lincoln and Stephen Douglas both came from Illinois. Of course, there have been innumerable elections in which both candidates were in a state of frenzy.

RIDDLE: Here are three oddities concerning one of our presidents: he was the oldest vice-president to assume the presidency; he was the only president to have but one child (six were childless); and he was the only president whose middle initial did not stand for a name. Who was he?

ANSWER: Harry S. Truman. He was also the only president to have been a haberdasher; only he and Lincoln had been postmasters; only he and Eisenhower served in World War I.

Truman said, "The buck stops here." A later administration went him one better — they laundered it first!

HEY, LIBBERS!

Abe Lincoln spoke out for women's rights, as much as twenty-four years before he became president, saying, "I go for all sharing the privilege of the government who assist in bearing its burdens. Consequently, I go for admitting all whites to the rights of suffrage who pay taxes or bear arms, by no means excluding females." Apparently, he did exclude blacks at that time in his thinking.

Always do right; this will gratify some people and astonish the rest.
Mark Twain

It took a special act of Congress to get Ida Lewis the job of keeper of Light Rock Lighthouse off Newport, Rhode Island in 1867. They made no mistake in selecting the twenty-six year old. She was so skilled with a boat and as a swimmer that she saved the lives of twenty-two persons between 1867 and 1904. She was awarded medals for bravery by Massachusetts, New York and the United States government. Apparently Ida Lewis didn't realize it was supposed to have been a man's world.

We knew a lifeguard who had such a heavy tan he sank!

Hetty Howland Robinson Green (1835-1916) may never have heard the cry of *Equal pay for equal work*, but she more than held her own in that bastion of masculinity, Wall Street. She dared to invest the fortune she had inherited, and she multiplied it again and again. In that all-male jungle, she earned the simple description — *American financier.*

The corset industry, feeling the pinch, has a new slogan: ***Down With Pantyhose!***

So you think the union label came about as a designation of superior workmanship? Back in 1896, white San Francisco cigar manufacturers couldn't compete with the low costs of Chinese labor. In a bit of racist fervor, they began labeling their cigars to differentiate them from the lower priced product.

Men who smoke cigars in bed have one thing in common — they're all bachelors!

WIN A FEW, LOSE A FEW!

If A and B are arguing, and A has all the facts on his side, the disagreement will end when B hits A a good one right in the snoot.

A Democrat once said Herbert Hoover's only known ad lib was 'Good Morning.'

WILL THE REAL PH. D. STAND UP!

Becoming President of the United States has its advantages. For one thing, every university with an unused sheepskin hanging around seems eager to present a president with an honorary doctorate. But only one U.S. President actually earned his doctorate. That was Woodrow Wilson who obtained a real Ph.D. from Johns Hopkins University.

I think this is the most extraordinary collection of talent, of human knowledge, that has ever been gathered together at the White House...with the possible exception of when Thomas Jefferson dined alone. *J.F.K.* (*at a dinner honoring Nobel Prize Winners 4/62*)

RING DEM BELLS!

It's rather nice to know that four U.S. Presidents and their wives celebrated golden wedding anniversaries. The first pair was John and Abigail Adams. Then John Adams' son, John Quincy Adams and his wife Louisa. It was a long wait for the next golden wedding anniversary — that of Herbert and Lou Hoover. And the last one was the fiftieth wedding anniversary of Harry and Bess Truman.

They say the Prohibition Party's national conventions are dry as hell!

IT'S A LONG JUMP!

Being a mayor isn't the most effective stepping-stone to the presidency, seeing that only Grover Cleveland (Mayor of Buffalo, N.Y.) and Calvin Coolidge (Mayor of Northampton, Mass.) ever made the jump successfully. Only two vice-presidents had been mayors, too: James Sherman (Taft's VP and Mayor of Utica, N.Y.) and Hubert Humphrey (Mayor of Minneapolis, Minn.).

RIDDLE: Has any U.S. President applied to become an F.B.I. special agent?

ANSWER: Nixon did. That was before his presidency, of course.

Most politicians wear waterproof shoes. Wouldn't you, if you had your feet in the trough?

Can you think of a U.S. President who instigated peace negotiations which ended a major war between two world powers? If you can't, try Theodore Roosevelt. It was through his efforts that the Russians and Japanese negotiated the end of the Russo-Japanese War. Teddy got the 1906 Nobel Peace Prize for his work, too.

On Bigotry: We send missionaries to China so the Chinese can get to heaven, but we won't let them into our country.

Pearl Buck

LET GEORGE DO IT!

Today, the expression *let George do it* implies passing the buck. It was first used by France's Louis XII in the 16th Century and in a differing sense.

The King was both blessed and cursed with having a First Minister of State who did everything well. You know the type — today, he's the fellow who corrects your speech, scoffs at your mode of attire, can answer any question put to him and does all this while beating you 6-love in tennis. Louis' burden, George d'Amboise, being First Minister, an army general, a wow with the ladies, a swordsman of great skill and a Cardinal, often caused the King to doubt his divine right to rule. Finally, when some minor problem arose which required an obscure skill to solve, Louis said, sarcastically, "Let George do it!" Maddeningly, George did...and well, as usual.

Al Capone liked Chicago politicians so well he always carried two in his hip pocket.

NAMES TO FIT CIRCUMSTANCES, OPUS 512!

Military historians say the reason Napoleon met his waterloo at the place of the same name was because one of his generals who was supposed to chase the Prussians, lost them. The Prussians hooked up with the British, exit Napoleon. The Frenchman who got the blame was Marshal Emmanuel Grouchy. Who wouldn't be grouchy, if people went around saying you'd blown the whole war?

Napoleon was exited to an island on his elbows.

BUFFALO BILL!

There he was, galloping across the plains in 1872, long hair flowing out from under his hat. And as he passed a band of Indians, one yelled out at him, "Hiya, Pahaska."

Of course, it was Buffalo Bill Cody. The Indians called him Pahaska, because that meant *long hair* in their tongue. If the Americans had known a bit more about zoology, Cody would have been correctly nicknamed Bison Bill.

General Custer tricked the Indians into a massacre.

MAYFLOWER CHILDREN!

One of the pilgrim families who came to America aboard the Mayflower in 1620 was named Brewster. Nothing particularly odd about that. But the Brewsters had four children...*Fear, Wrestling, Love and Patience*. Such names must have been infectious, because the only child born on that historic voyage was dubbed *Peregrine White.*

I am afraid we must make the world honest before we can honestly say to our children that honesty is the best policy.

G.B. Shaw

BUREAUCRACY FOREVER!

Considering that passports didn't become compulsory until 1914, we wonder if it was a Twentieth Century plot to support inept photographers or was it another way our federal government had of reminding us that life should not be simple. How inane to suppose that spies or criminals can't forge passports.

Originally, a passport was simply a king's ring with his seal. He pressed the signet into wax for sealing documents, so another country would know his emissary was genuine. A couple of centuries before Christ, *a letter of confidence* performed the same service. But poor common folk, such as we, didn't need any of those things to wander about...until the bureaucracy ran low on *make-work* tasks.

The way the federal government grows, it must be well-fertilized!

IT'S A LAW!

A Pennsylvania law of 1794 really clamped down on profanity. Anyone over 16 caught taking the name of the Lord in vain could be

RIDDLE: Has there ever been a royal title called *Dauphin?*

ANSWER: Oui! Until the Revolution of 1830, a French king's oldest son was titled *The Dauphin*, equivalent to Great Britain's Prince of Wales.

thrown in the House of Correction (jail) for a full day and night, unless he could come up with the fine — 67 cents. Presumably, blasphemy for those under 16 was all right. Ah, the freedom of youth!

Most sins are partially enjoyed; many can be rationalized. Neither applies to envy.

A LADY OF PARTS!

If you think our *Statue of Liberty* is all one piece, forget it! The head was the first completed part and the French exhibited it at the 1878 Paris Exposition. Then the French cast one forearm and sent it to America in 1883. Next came the construction of the mammoth pedestal for the statue. The cornerstone for that was laid on Bedloe's Island in New York Harbor in 1884. In the middle of 1885, the remaining 210 parts of the statue arrived by boat from France. Beginning in May of 1886, assembly continued almost to the day of unveiling...October 28, 1886.

So, if you feel guilty because you've been trying to get yourself together for a couple of years, relax! It took the *Statue of Liberty* eight years!

The U.S. didn't have to pay for the *Statue of Liberty* — it was given to our nation by the Franco-American Union to commemorate the alliance of France and America in the Revolutionary War. Even if we had paid for the statue, it would have cost less than the mammoth pedestal on which it stands.

If it wasn't for money, being broke wouldn't be half bad!

COXEY'S ARMY!

Stories being bandied about to the effect that our federal government is callous need straightening out, too. We recall very well that after the *Panic of 1893*, a fellow named Coxey put together an army of protesters. It's a fact that Coxey's Army, 500 strong, marched into the nation's Capitol with the full intention of forcing congressional action on a brief spate of massive unemployment. Now, did the authorities jail Mr. Coxey and his radical followers for sedition? No. In the kindly tradition of federal troops, they arrested the lot for ignoring the signs on the capitol lawn reading, "Please Keep Off the Grass."

George Ade said, "Early to bed and early to rise will make you miss all the regular guys."

SIGN OF THE PANHANDLER!

Lots of unemployed men took to the road in the 1930's. Many of these *new* hobos would not stoop to chicken-stealing or other larcenous means of getting food. They asked for odd jobs in return for which they received food or money. The professional tramp, on the other hand, simply went to the back door, knocked and asked for money. If he was refused, he asked for food. If he had been successful, as he left, he chalked a mark on the fence or on the sidewalk. A cross would indicate to other tramps that there was a good chance of getting money from that housewife. A circle signified a handout of food was possible.

In the Depression, so many bankrupt brokers sold apples, the apple growers prospered.

PUTTING ON THE PANTS!

When those bloodthirsty hordes of central Asian horsemen came slaughtering their way westward, it wasn't all bad. They brought with them a new type of male apparel — trousers. Seems they were more comfortable and a hell of a lot more efficient than full-length robes.

Speaking of trousers, sailors wore the bell-bottomed variety because they were easier to roll up when swabbing a deck or wading to shore from a long boat.

Fashion experts say women will be wearing the same things in brassieres this year.

RIDDLE: President John F. Kennedy's wife, Jacqueline, remarried after his death. Did any other president's widow remarry?

ANSWER: Yes, Grover Cleveland's widow, Frances, did.

Also, let's put an end to tales of woe about poor Dr. Mary Walker, that assistant-surgeon in the Union Army during the Civil War. It wasn't enough they allowed her in the surgical tent. Oh, no, she had to claim women's clothing was too voluminous, dragged in the blood and all that. She wanted to wear men's clothing while operating. Well, the men in our government were gallant chaps. As soon as Congress passed a special act, she got her wish. Imagine her raising all that fuss?

Johnny Carson would be alive today if he'd listened to Young Doctor Malone!

TURKEYFEED!

It's fair to say that John D. Rockefeller had a special talent for making money. And he didn't waste any time getting started. At age seven, he began a turkey-raising venture. He fattened them on curds his mother graciously donated from the family's milk cows. Unlike most seven-year-olds, Rockefeller entered every transaction in a ledger.

A man builds a fine house; now he has a master and a task for life: he is to furnish, watch, show it and keep it in repair, the rest of his days.
Emerson

THE PRICE WAS RIGHT!

In the 1820's, when steamships such as the *Royal William* plied the Atlantic from New York to London, the passage was just $140...and that included wine and food. Steamships also carried transoceanic mail, but it was a bit expensive — 25 cents for one-sheet letters, on the basis of $1 an ounce.

We doubt Dixie Cupp's claim that she flew to Paris on an American Express card.

HOW MUCH FOR YOUR MOTHER, JIMMY?

Today, the American painter, James McNeill Whistler, is known to most for one single work — the portrait of his mother. French government agents, out bargain-hunting for the Louvre, picked up Whistler's masterpiece for a paltry $650.

Old colleges never die. They just lose their faculties!

HONEST GEORGE!

The government wanted to give George Washington a salary for serving as President, but George said he wanted no more than expenses. His first year in office he kept detailed records of his expenditures. They came to 5,000 pounds, or $25,000. That's how the presidential salary was first fixed at that amount.

If you tell the truth, you don't have to remember anything.
Mark Twain

THE DANES FIGHT BACK!

The fact that America had paid the Russians $7.2 million for a chunk of frozen real estate called Alaska in 1867 was not lost on the Danes. Fifty years later, they peddled the Virgin Islands to us for $25 million. Figure a little and you'll discover we paid a measly $12.61 per square mile for Alaska, but $187,969.91 per square mile for the Virgin Islands. Of course, the climate's milder in the Virgin Islands, but 14,907 times milder?

Don't send money to "The Old Lady of Threadneedle Street!" That's the Bank of England.

BORN TOO LATE!

If you possessed the foresight to be born in 1650, you could have picked up Vermeer's *Lady Writing* on your forty-sixth birthday for $6.00...saving yourself a couple of hundred thou. Then, when you were just a shade over 200, you could have grabbed off Millet's *The Angelus* for $360. Next time you'll know better!

Finally someone asked how much New York's Grand Central Station cost to build: $1.62 for the men's-room sign and $75 million for the rest of the building.

MONEY, MONEY, MONEY!

When Victor D. Brenner designed the Lincoln penny issued in 1909, he put his initials on the back. Then someone decided that was a bit ostentatious, so the V.D.B. was deleted from the later mintings.

When was the last time a bank called to say you had ***sufficient*** *funds?*

RIDDLE: What did P.T Barnum pay Jenny Lind for her first American singing tour?

ANSWER: The *Swedish Nightingale's* take was $150,000. But, before you scream, "Highway robbery," that was for 150 concerts. Miss Lind spent about 400 nights in drafty trains, some 300 nights in strange hotels and put on a concert about every fifth night for a two-year period from 1850 to 1852. Barnum, being a sport, picked up the tab for the orchestra!

John Philip Sousa earned his title as "The March King" with such resounding compositions as *Stars and Stripes Forever,* which brought him over $300,000 in royalties, and the *Washington Post March,* which he sold outright for $35. When Sousa was asked to name his own favorite among his compositions, he said, "*Stars and Stripes Forever.*" Shrewd, eh?

We can think of one time when Sousa's 'The Washington Post March' wasn't popular.

Don't be taken in by wily Scots who have pointed to Andrew Carnegie's donations of three hundred million dollars as refutation of their infernal thrift. We happen to know that Mr. Carnegie held back over eleven dollars which he squandered on inane trifles such as shoes and shirts.

*Take the **irk** out of **shirk** and be quiet!*

Ever hear about the two million dollar comma? It happened in 1874 in Washington, D.C. Where else? It seems Congress was preparing a new tariff bill. One section covering duty-free items included *all foreign fruit-plants*. When the bill was copied in its final form, a clerk inadvertently substituted a comma for the hyphen so that the bill, as enacted, included in the duty-free category *all foreign fruit, plants, etc.* It took Congress a year to correct the language, and in that time all those growers of European and Asiatic fruit had a duty-free ball. Cost the federal treasury an estimated two million bucks in lost tariff revenue.

Percy Nutt and Meg Simmons have sucessfully crossed a nutmeg with a persimmon; now they're squabbling over what to call it.

There were five Secretaries of Departments forming the President's Cabinet under George Washington. Secretary of State, Thomas Jefferson, received $2,500; the other Secretaries received $2,000.

The Secretary of the Treasury is paid a dollar a year and all the money he can eat.

DEMOCRACY AND DEUCES WILD!

This is a true tale — we swear!

A certain attorney played poker one night a week for many years, usually getting home after his wife had gone to bed. The following morning she invariably asked, "Well, how did the game go?"

And every week for all those years, he said, "Oh, everyone won a little."

A pain in the ass is neither a symptom nor a disease. It's a species!

Trivia buff Fitzhugh Green had a ball back in the thirties. He set out to calculate what King Ferdinand and Queen Isabella coughed up in dollars to bankroll Christopher Columbus's 1492 jaunt. He came up with a bottom line figure of $2,115. Luckily for him, Columbus wasn't starting out today. He'd have to make the trip alone in an eight-year old stripped-down Volkswagen beetle.

Christopher Columbus received the equivalent of $320 for discovering America. It is not known whether or not he immediately went on welfare.

You think books, like almost everything else, are expensive today. And you long for the good old days. Well, harken: in 1492 in Venice, they were selling printed Bibles for as little as $30 a copy and as much as $60. 1492 was a good year for several people.

Anyone who has any doubts about the ingenuity or the resourcefulness of a plumber never got a bill from one. (So said labor leader George Meany, a former plumber.)

OUR FORGETFUL AUTHORS!

Harriet Beecher Stowe (1811-1896) busied herself in the movement to abolish slavery, in temperance work and in women's suffrage as well as in writing. Perhaps all these other activities accounted for one costly oversight: when she had written *Uncle Tom's Cabin*, she neglected to reserve the dramatic rights. She did receive $300 for the serial rights to the classic but, over the many years it was a dramatic smash, she got nary a cent.

RIDDLE: Since Queen Isabella bankrolled his voyage, on what day do they celebrate Columbus Day in Spain?

ANSWER: They don't! But, on March first, the Spanish pay honor to Martin Pinzon with Arrival Day. Pinzon was the Captain of the La Pinta, and he sneaked back home to give the first word of the discovery...proving again that he who *does* is often outshone by he who *tells* about it first.

Movie producers are bidding up the price on rights to Leonard Pucker's best-seller, 'How To Dial a Wrong Number When It's Busy.'

Everyone, aware of how the value of money dwindles annually, even daily, can commiserate with Ethiopians of another time.

Their money was in the form of blocks of crystalline salt. When an Ethiopian met a friend, he invited him to take a lick of his salt block. The more friends he had, the faster his money disappeared.

The Duchess of Simper owns a clamshell inscribed, 'Welcome to Pismo Beach.'

WELL, BUST OUR BOWSTRINGS!

The ancient Celts who inhabited Ireland and Wales bowed an early version of the violin. Their contraption had three strings sometimes; sometimes, six. The Irish called it a *crowd*. In Welsh it was known as the *crwth*. If you could pronounce it, there was a good chance you could play it.

Music lovers mourn the absence of the clavicle from today's symphony orchestras!

AWESOME MUSIC!

We've never heard anyone question the stirring qualities of the *Star Spangled Banner*, but we've seldom heard anyone sing it properly. Although Francis Scott Key composed it in 1814, it didn't become our official National Anthem until 1931...and still no lay vocalist seems able to get through it without embarrassment.

On a different side of music, there has always been a tendency to stand in awe of any music by a recognized composer. George Bernard Shaw, not easily awestruck, didn't let Gounod's reputation stop him from warning people about the composer's *Redemption*, saying, "Take the precaution to go in long enough after it commences and to come out long enough before it is over, you will not find it wearisome."

If you feel the 'Star Spangled Banner' is hard to sing, try dancing to it.

GOVERNMENT WITH A HEART!

When the poet John Keats died at age twenty-six in 1821, England was Catholic. The law decreed non-Catholics had to be buried at night. But in a fit of contrition, the government allowed friends to bury Keats in the morning.

Artie Fletcher has taught a wombat how to play the piccolo.

MARCHING THROUGH KARNAK!

Ancient Egyptians knew a musical note or two. They had hornpipes and harps. But the musicians who struck fear into the feet of Egyptian GIs were the trumpeters and drummers. When these guys showed up in the bivouac area, every Egyptian soldier knew he was about to take a twenty-mile hike...or more.

You want somber? Gustav Mahler knocked out a couple of sombers you won't forget.

WHERE THE CREDIT IS DUE!

If you've been digging around trying to unearth the name of the marine who composed the melody of the Marine Hymn *From the Halls of Montezuma,* stop right now. That stirring tune came straight out of Offenbach's comic opera *Genevieve de Brabant.*

If the sources for some of America's most popular songs were given, Handel would get some of the credit for the melody of *Yes, We Have No Bananas*, Chopin for *Alice Blue Gown*, Puccini for *Avalon* and Tschaikowsky for *I'm Forever Blowing Bubbles.*

And if there had been a musician's union in Austria in the 1820's, composer Franz Schubert would have been its hero. In one two-year stretch, he knocked out two hundred and thirty-nine compositions.

Taking something from one man and making it worse is plagiarism.
Geo. Moore

JUST STRINGING ALONG!

Going through the *yellow pages* under *violin-makers,* we notice very few entries...like none. Wonder why? All it takes is some maple or sycamore for the back, a little fir for the belly, some maple for the neck and a small quantity of ebony for the fingerboard and tailpiece. Maybe seventy individual pieces to put together. Any kid named Stradivarius could probably do it on his lunch hour.

RIDDLE: What are *Cremonas*?

ANSWER: Violins made in the Italian village of Cremona. Some fair violin-makers worked out of Cremona — Stradivarius, Amati, Bergonzi and Guarnerius for example.

Madeline Squeak plays the cello for all it's worth. Hers is worth a buck-75, tops!

CHILD PRODIGIES!

Many concert violinists started early. Jascha Heifetz, for one, took up the violin at age three, graduated from the Royal Music School at Vilna in his native Poland, studied in Russia and was pronounced a full-fledged, mature violinist at the doddering old age of ten.

"Child prodigies burn themselves out and you never hear of them again."

The fellow who made that statement overlooked a few gems. Felix Mendelssohn was knocking out serious compositions at age 12 and he didn't do badly after that. Franz Schubert began composing at 11. Frederic Chopin gave piano concerts at 10. Beethoven was performing in public at 8 and had compositions published at 10. But the most prodigious had to be Mozart. He was composing minuets at the ripe old age of 4.

We like the ***Half-Fast Waltz*** *— not too slow, not too fast, just half-fast!*

COMPOSE YOURSELVES!

A philosophy professor posed a problem in ethics for his class:

Imagine a syphilitic woman married to an alcoholic. They have brought into the world two blind and feeble-minded children, a deaf child and several others with severe handicaps of one sort or another. Now the woman is pregnant again. Should she have an abortion?

The class voted overwhelmingly for the abortion. The professor then informed them that they had just killed Ludwig von Beethoven.

If you're hard put to describe today's music, try ***Glarph!***

GET IN THE SPIRIT, WILLARD!

Almost every American recognizes the painting *The Spirit of '76* — the one with the fife-player, the drummer and the flag-bearer. But not just any old American knows the artist's name. Keep it to yourself, but it was A.M. Willard.

The woman who painted ***Seven Nudes On a Tricycle*** *was Gloria Mundi.*

PABLO THE PROLIFIC!

Even though Pablo Picasso lived ninety-two years, it's difficult to comprehend the enormity of his productive output. He did a few tapestries, illustrated some books, turned out close to 2,900 ceramic pieces, knocked out a mere 30,000 engravings, sculpted 1,355 pieces and still had time left over to do 12,000 drawings and 1,876 paintings. Small wonder his estate was valued at $300 million.

How did the great man feel about art? He termed it "a lie that lets us see the truth."

Picasso's works were first shown in America at photographer Alfred Steiglitz's 291 Gallery in New York around 1905.

*Iris Mulveylerp, after completing **Aardvarks In Limbo** for the south wall of the bus depot in Chilled Nostril, Wyoming, has hung up her brushes for good.*

WHICH SISTINE DO YOU MEAN?

The private chapel of the Popes in the Vatican is known as the *Sistine Chapel*. Michelangelo's frescoes are its major attractions.

The *Sistine Madonna* is totally unrelated. That painting — by Raphael, one of Michelangelo's contemporaries — was executed for the Black Monks of Sisto in the village of Piacenza in north central Italy. Got it straight?

Historians now claim the Renaissance was all part of a giant scheme to sell paint.

Giovanni Cimabue, a 13th Century Florentine painter, is remembered for being Giotto's teacher as well as for his frescoes in the Church of St. Francis of Assisi. In his own time he was easy to remember because the family name meant Bullhead.

Ludwig Orp's etching, 'Here Come the Doldrums' is a copy of Raphael's 'Kissing Mildred Goodnight!'

The great classical Greek sculptor, Phidias, gained fame in the 5th Century B.C. for his creation of the Parthenon sculptures. But who remembers the men who designed the Parthenon itself? The master builder was Callicrates and the chief architect was Ictinus.

RIDDLE: In their day, was Raphael thought to be greater than Michelangelo?

ANSWER: Our Renaissance reporter says, yes! Although Michelangelo was eight years older than Raphael, he didn't get the recognition. Raphael, by the way, had a unique calling card: when he found no one at home, he drew an almost perfect circle on a slip of paper and left it at the door. Everyone knew who had been there.

Ancient Greek physicians confined their profanity to Hippocratic oaths!

HOW ABOUT WESTERN GREEN AND SOUTHERN RED?

You've probably admired the lovely colors of Chinese rugs without realizing that each has a symbolic significance. Yellow stands for the Earth. Red can indicate fire or the direction south, while black represents water or north. East is indicated by white, but it may also be symbolic of metal or of mist. Greens and blues signify wood or west. Watch it! You're stepping on east mist!

Alexander the Great's father made him give up teacup painting, snarling at the kid, "Go conquer the known world...more, if you can find it!"

COLOR IT RED, WHITE AND BLUE!

Sure, the colors of the American flag mean something. The red is for valor; the blue symbolizes vigilance, perserverance and justice; and the white stands for purity and innocence.

The first flag was made six years after the first flagpole...filling a needless void.

WELCOME HOME, BEN!

Once upon a time Ben Franklin had a portrait of himself hanging in his home in Philadelphia. A Major Andre carried it away. Then Andre gave his booty to General Grey. General Grey went all the way to England with it. There it did stay until a later Grey, sensing things had gone astray because of Andre's foul play, did pay to have it returned to the U.S.A. to stay. Which it has to this day...in the White House, hey!

If someone were to claim Ben Franklin was five years old before he had a bath, we'd believe it. After all, he was the 15th of 17 Franklin children.

THE NAME WEIGHED MORE THAN THE PRODUCT!

Can't blame the folks at the *Fabrica Italiana Automobile Torino for* calling their car a *F.I.A.T.*, otherwise it wouldn't have had enough power to pull its nameplate. Since customers put the initials together into the word *Fiat* anyway, they added a wee bit more power by eliminating the periods.

Benjamin Franklin, ranked as the greatest inventive genius of his age, never asked for nor received a patent for any of his inventions or discoveries.

Don't get all upset when someone pilfers one of your hubcaps. Think of E.J. Pontifex of Norfolk, Virginia. Back in 1957, thieves began waltzing off with his hubcaps. In one year's time, he had to replace twenty-one of them.

We wonder what the zip code is for Zipp, Indiana?

ENCORE!

There are several things we all remember about Uncle Gerald. He was very old. He was partially deaf. And he could always be counted upon for a story of his youth told in language and construction of a bygone era.

One Sunday the family had gathered at Uncle Gerald and Aunt Mary's home. At a precise moment Uncle Gerald cleared his throat, waited a moment and then launched into one of his tales. Inasmuch as we all knew the story by heart, we gave him our attention for what we felt was the polite period of time and then we began talking quietly among ourselves.

At last Aunt Mary came to his side, and, in an appropriately audible stage whisper, said, "Gerald, I think everyone has heard that story of yours."

Without looking up at her, he nodded and replied, "I know, my dear, but I tell it so well I thought *I'd* like to hear it again."

Hunting for our **nom de plume,** *we found it on the bureau of our aunt.*

LET 'ER RIP, VAN WINKLE!

Fortunately for the literary world, Washington Irving botched up the English branch of his family's hardware business. So he came home and began writing full-time. His inventive mind didn't confine itself to the stories he wrote. He also came up with such pen names as

RIDDLE: How can you tell women from men in ancient Egyptian paintings?

ANSWER: They're color-coded. Egyptian painters used red for men and women, but the brighter red were the men. If a person was a prisoner, he was painted in yellow. Birds were traditionally blue and green. That answer your question, Red?

Diedrich Knickerbocker, Geoffrey Crayon, Launcelot Langstaff and Jonathan Oldstyle.

The term 'good old boys' defies factual definition as only the middle word is true.

SHAME ON YOU, HENRIK!

All these years you've been crediting Norwegian dramatist, Henrik Ibsen, with having a vivid imagination when he named a leading character *Peer Gynt*. Sly old Henrik simply borrowed the name of a trapper who had become famous around Norway for being idiotically reckless. Stop sulking, Henrik! It was bound to come out.

Twenty-one percent of all the cowboys nicknamed ***Tex*** *have never been to Texas. And, about half of that group has never been anywhere else either.*

SATISFIED?

If you've become satisfied with your children's educational accomplishments — such as being able to construct a simple declarative sentence while only a high-school senior — we've got bad news for you. Helen Keller, although deaf and blind, mastered French and German as well as English!

Have our pockets shrunk, or are ***pocket books*** *getting bigger?*

SENSE OF VALUE!

Which does one put first — material value or esthetic worth? Going back to another era, when both America and Great Britain began to be flooded with a rather low-grade literary efforts, we called the output *dime novels*. The British were more candid, referring to them as *penny dreadfuls*. At least the American publishers charged more! But, then what's new?

Did people really drag secrets from others with wild horses?

OSCAR, ARE YOU AT IT AGAIN?

The English satirist, Max Beerbohm, came in for a little acid, himself, at the hands of Oscar Wilde. Wilde characterized him as follows: "The Gods have bestowed on Max the gift of perpetual old age."

As long as he was feeling complimentary, O.W. said that Henry James "writes fiction as if it were a painful duty."

Littleton Freeby wrote an eleven-volume work on the left knee of the dragonfly.

S.O.B.!

We think it was Robert Benchley, when he was a drama critic, who wrote, "It was one of those plays in which all the actors unfortunately enunciated very clearly."

And we know it was Benchley who was shocked to learn that when people referred to him as that S.O.B.,they hadn't meant *sweet old Bob.*

If your father patronizes one certain cafe, that makes you a son of an habitue.

A LITERARY REPORT!

The serialized story is making a comeback in newspapers today. Almost fifty years ago, a newspaper in Parker, South Dakota began a serial. It took 1,178 consecutive editions of the paper to complete the story — twenty-two years and about eight months. The book they serialized was the Bible, which would require a long serial. The fact that the newspaper came out only once a week extended the time, too.

The old radio soap operas warped time. Bill, the barber in 'Just Plain Bill,' cut an attorney's hair for four and a half weeks. Imagine the excitement!

Liberty, Collier's, The New Yorker, Time, Literary Digest and the Saturday Evening Post were some of the country's popular magazines in 1932. The only ones that are still around from that group are Time and The New Yorker. Of course, some of the graybeard editors of this book were around in 1932 and are still around...just not all here.

Do you like magazines whose first bit of non-advertising material is on page 76?

RIDDLE: Who was the most famous author at the court of Frederick the Great of Prussia?

ANSWER: Not a German. It was a Frenchman named Francois Marie Arouet. You might recognize him more easily by his pen name — Voltaire.

ERIC'S REALTY, VIEW LOTS!

Just before Eric the Red got back to Iceland after discovering the island of Greenland, he took a couple of smart pills. He knew he'd have a devil of a time pushing Greenland acreage if he told prospective buyers that it was the world's largest snow pile. So he just said it was *Greenland* and let their imaginations do the rest. Had to sound good to an Icelander.

The last time you read the "Flateyjarbok" did it convince you that Norse explorers found America long before Columbus? Oh, you haven't read it. Well, the "Flateyjarbok" is a group of Icelandic sagas of the Fourteenth Century which were found on the island of Flatey, Iceland.

Who said the best thing to come out of Texas was Route 66?

If at first you don't see any connection between a well-known celestial phenomenon and the Caribbean island of Trinidad, don't fret. Very few know, or care, that English astronomer Halley (of comet fame), while on a scientific visit to the Caribbean in 1700, found that no one had bothered to claim the island of Trinidad. So he up and hoisted the British flag.

Achtung ichthyologists! Western Australia has a town called Salmon Gums.

The port city of Tarifa in Spain was ideally situated near the Rock of Gibraltar. Ships passing through the Straits of Gibraltar got smacked with duties for the privilege. That's one explanation of the origin of the word *tariff*. It has not been verified that ship captains of that day bragged, "Hey, I got a piece of the Rock."

Travel agents are people who wish you were there!

SPECIFY!

Before you go calling Benedict Arnold a traitor, make sure you specify *which* Benedict Arnold you mean. The first governor of Rhode Island Colony, established by royal English charter in 1663, was a gent named Benedict Arnold. The villainous Benedict didn't arrive on the American scene until more than a hundred years later.

Seaboard** is the side facing the sea. We guess the other is the **landboard.

HIKING TRIP!

Even though it's been over two hundred years since Lewis and Clark made their remarkable expedition across America's hitherto unknown wilderness, it still ranks as one hell of a feat. And the entire company totaled but 30 men. Nowadays, it takes almost that many to pack a station wagon for a weekend outing.

Did you know Marietta, Ohio was named after Marie Antoinette? It's a fact!

BRUSH, DAMMIT, BRUSH!

In the good old days, when we had Ceylon (now it's Sri Lanka or somesuch), that island had a city named Candy (now, they've made it Kandy). The big item in Candy was a tooth they kept in the temple. It was said to be one of Buddha's. Of course, with all that Candy, no wonder!

*In pre-smog days, the average **dervish** whirled 612 times per day!*

ROVER IS A NICE NAME FOR A SONGBIRD!

When the Canary Islands were discovered in the 1st Century B.C., packs of large wild dogs had the run of the place. From *canis* — Latin for dog — the islands got their name. It wasn't until seventeen centuries later that some enterprising Spaniards domesticated the small yellow songbirds which also inhabited those islands. But dog-birds?

*Man The Nets! Duck hunters, skulking in their blinds on Piddwinkle Island off the coast of Nebraska, were astounded yesterday when school after school of **skartles** swam right out of the water and headed for Omaha.*

FLOATING P.O.!

Now that upstanding citizens are conscious of such environmental eyesores as litter, why isn't anyone doing something about Tin Can Island? Well, Tin Can Island, one of the Friendly Islands between Fiji and Samoa, got its name because, for many years, the natives placed their mail in tin cans and left them floating offshore. Passing steamers would pick up the cans and deliver the contents.

RIDDLE: What ever became of Apollos Rivoire's third child?

ANSWER: He did very well for himself, thank you, what with his dentistry, his silversmithing and his riding around at night awakening patriots. His father, after arriving in Boston from Germany, changed the family name to Revere. Paul was the third child.

Wouldn't a scarlet tanager blush if he knew he was called an 'oscine Thraupidae?'

SVALA!

In Scandinavian countries, there's an old legend of a small bird hovering over the Cross on which Jesus was nailed. The bird was said to have cried, "Console, console." The Scandinavian word for 'console' is *svala*, thus the bird we call the swallow.

We pity a bird called the 'gallinule.' When he begins tracing his family tree, he's going to discover he's one of the 'precocial Rallidae' but also part of the ***rail*** *family...and you recall what bad news that lot was.*

Every year, one reads about families being swarmed under with starlings, barns filled, clothes lines, what have you. Blame it all on some bird nuts who turned fifty pairs of starlings loose in Central Park, New York City in the 1890's.

Kiwis *walk hunched over, pondering why their blessed wings won't work!*

NICE BIRD LADY!

Some 150 miles west of New Orleans there's a spot ideal for many birds native to the Gulf of Mexico. Margaret Olivia Slocum Sage bought the place — 72,000-acre Marsh Island — and gave it to the state of Louisiana as a bird and game sanctuary. And that was before World War I. Thanks, Margaret!

Bonny Bray's painting 'Emus Having Lunch' was torn to shreds by an affronted ostrich!

THE FAMILY ORGANIZATION!

A lady we know inherited an old house recently, complete with a basement full of magazines from 1927 through 1930. She passed along this article from one of them:

"The rewards of familyhood can be multiplied by forming a family organization. For those so inclined it can be entered as a regular incorporated body.

"Whether you organize your family in the incorporated or unincorporated fashion, your first order of business should be the election of officers and the scheduling of regular business meetings.

"One of the suggested officers is a family genealogist. This person can then compile the family lineage. A further duty should be the preparation of pamphlets on prominent members of the family as well as minor papers on events of note with which the family has been connected.

"Family gatherings of a social nature are acceptable, too. A family reunion is one such function."

Madame Mother, I rise to a point of order!

Rasputin gave his mother a peasant for Christmas every single year!

THE TZARINA!

The next time you receive a doctor's bill, it may soften the blow to remember that Russian Tzarina Catherine the Great once paid a doctor $50,000 to innoculate her and her son against smallpox, plus $10,000 travel expenses and a lifetime pension equivalent to $2,500 a year.

Doctors pour drugs of which they know little, to cure diseases of which they know less, into human beings of whom they know nothing.

Voltaire

THE MEDICS!

The official symbol physicians use is called the *caduceus* — a staff with two snakes twined about it and wings at the top. In reality, this was the staff of the office of Hermes, the Greek messenger god (*caduceus* means messenger in Greek). The snakes, by the way, are symbols of wisdom.

Hermes didn't make the caduceus himself. It was given to him by fellow-god Apollo, and it purportedly had the power to turn just about anything into gold. Perhaps that's the reason doctors adopted it as their symbol.

The red-striped barber pole has been in use for centuries. In days gone by, barbers moonlighted to supplement their income. The big item was 'letting' blood (thought to be helpful in treating many diseases). To advertise their services, they put out a white pole (representing a human arm) with red stripes (representing bloody bandages). Gruesome, but people got the message.

In the late 1700's, a Philadelphia physician, Dr. Phillip Physick,

RIDDLE: Why was the Bank of England founded?

ANSWER: William III, who ruled England with his wife Mary II as a co-regent until 1702, was a veritable nut about war. He couldn't keep out of one. So, he was constantly involving England in continental battles. It proved so costly, they had to start the Bank of England to finance him. That was also the start of a permanent policy of national debt. Thanks a lot, William III!

asked a druggist friend, Townsend Speakman, to develop equipment for making carbonated water. Speakman succeeded, and gave America its first carbonated beverage. Speakman was also known as medical supplier to General Washington's Continental Army. Dr. Physick may or may not be the source of what you're thinking.

Wallet's disease can be cured by attaching a medical leech to your bank account!

IT'S RELATIVE!

A downtrodden husband told a friend that his day at the beach had been both a calamity and a disaster. The friend asked, "What was the calamity?"

"My wife got caught in a riptide," the husband replied.

"Oh, I am so sorry," the friend commiserated. "Now I know what the disaster was."

"How did you know they saved her?" the downtrodden one asked.

Radio blooper we wish had occurred: "Now that comic pair — Boopnagle and Studd!"

Don't blame Queen Victoria for the acts of her grandchildren. One of them, Kaiser Wilhelm II, an overbearing militarist, got the whole world in a spot of trouble in 1914-1918. Instead of having a strong hand in causing World War I, he could have occupied himself more constructively. For instance, he could have created a great basketball team — his Prussian Guards were reputed to be seven feet tall in their stocking feet.

*Fascination with one's own name: Adolphe Sax invented the **saxhorn, saxotromba** and **saxophone.***

SIR WALTER-WHO?

Besides trivial trivia there are trivia errata. The editors ran across a source which stated that Sir Walter Raleigh sent five expeditions to

North America, but that Queen Elizabeth never allowed him to go along...*so he never got to North America.* Fifty-six pages further on, the author credits Sir Walter with the first discovery of iron ore in America at North Carolina in 1585. Oh well, what Queen Elizabeth didn't know couldn't have hurt her.

You didn't know that Queen Elizabeth owned 3,000 dresses when she died in 1603?

THE CLASSY CLASSIFIEDS!

There was a time when your family newspaper might contain a spicy item or two in the *Personals* column of the classified ad section. Innuendo was as far as they went, however. Now you can read the damnedest things under such ad headings as *Introductions, Escort Services* and *Massage.*

But is there anything titillating about the blatant statement we read the other day: *Rent a Girl. Use Your Credit Card*? Any tingle of sexual anticipation has to evaporate when faced with this invitation — *Cheap thrills...no frills.* Are they offering a quickie in an alley?

We wonder who answers a classified that proposes you involve yourself in a *Nude Rap Session.*

The baldness of claims and promises in the *Massage* column leave pitifully little to the imagination. Apparently *massage* has become a euphemism. Otherwise, why would one advertiser feel it necessary to offer *Non-sexual massage*?

PERSONAL: Little b. Blue, come home; cow/meadow; sheep/corn; blow/horn.

TWO GREAT MINDS WITH A SIMILAR THOUGHT!

Author Anne Morrow Lindbergh wrote, "I believe that what a woman resents is not so much giving herself in pieces as giving herself purposelessly."

Couturier Coco Chanel said, "How many cares one loses when one decides not to be something, but to be someone."

Jimmy Cunningham says he has put up with his last **versity:** *he suffered through* **uni,** *followed by* **ad;** *but* **per** *is simply too much.*

IT WAS A HOT TIME IN THE OLD BOILER ROOM!

Specialists perfected the art of telephone solicitation in the 1920's, but the heyday of the *boiler room* was during the depression of the 1930's.

Knowing how to sell over the phone made millions for several clever guys in those dark days. One of them told us how he went about it.

"We put on rodeos, donkey-baseball, motorcycle races...anything we thought the hicks would go for...just so there were tickets and program ads to sell. But our best all-around money-maker was the newspaper special edition.

"But first we had our advance man. He'd size up the next town for us...decide what they'd shell out for. Then he'd find us a place to set up in. Most of the time, the cheapest spot to rent was somebody's boiler room because it was something he never expected to get money for. That's how come it got to be called a *boiler-room operation.* Hell, all we needed was two sawhorses with boards to make a table, fifteen apple crates for the guys to sit on, fifteen telephones and one copy of the local telephone directory.

"Let's stick with the *special edition* bit...it being the best. Our advance man would waltz into some one-horse paper, flashing a big wad. He'd offer to put up the dough for a special edition...say, to celebrate the burg's sixty-ninth anniversary. All the newspaper had to do was get hold of some old photographs and write a bunch of stories from past history...and make up the ads we sold. We got all the advertising bucks most of the time.

"Then we were set to go. I'd have my fifteen guys on their apple crates and I'd start tearing pages out of the phone book's ad section and pass them around. The pitch was nice and simple: we started them out by getting them to say how much civic pride they had; then we'd explain this was a once-in-a-lifetime opportunity. Now, say the guy ran a hardware store, and he's trying to wriggle off the hook. Wham! We let him know his competitor is going for a big ad. If that didn't nail him, we'd remind him the whole town would know he hadn't supported the big sixty-ninth birthday fandango. I had this firm rule — *you can't close him in three minutes, hang up and go on to the next yokel.*

"I had one other rule — *you don't pass up any business*...no matter how small it was. Hell, I remember one time a barber with a two-chair shop got so hopped up he almost busted a leg buying a full page. See, I found out the owner of the newspaper got his hair cut there. You also had to remember that, for a lot of these little guys, this was the only chance they'd ever get to act like a big shot.

"Nowadays, you got a bunch of jerks selling funeral plots and roofing and hell, you name it...all nice and memorized...no idea of how to insult a guy into buying. One guy had me on the horn forty minutes last week trying to sell me color photographs of my family. In forty minutes, my boys could have sold half a town."

Like everything else, the *boiler room* ain't what it used to be. And those newspaper special editions? Many are cherished mementoes today.

Billy, in one of his nice new sashes,
Fell in the fire and was burned to ashes;
Now, although the room grows chilly,
I haven't the heart to poke poor Billy.

WHO KNOWS? THE SHADOW DO!

In the early days of radio, the combination of sound effects and a listener's imagination created many a dramatic illusion. In fact, the illusion was so forceful that many radio fans assumed the action emanated from the station they had tuned in and not from a New York studio.

Well, the owner of a small radio station which broadcast network programs was called one day by an acquaintance. The man was excited about something he had to show the radio man. When he arrived at the caller's house, he was shown a mammoth sound-effects table, complete with buzzers, horns, car doors, house-doors and dozens of other sound-producing devices.

Both impressed and mystified, the radio station owner said, "It's ...great...but what's it for?"

"For you! I built it for you," the ingenious man announced. "And I'm going to let you have it for just what I have in it — 900 bucks."

When the radio man recovered, he explained how radio networks fed their programs to their affiliates. Then he said, "George, before

RIDDLE: If a doctor says *errare humanum est*, what should one do?

ANSWER: Change doctors! That Latin expression means *to err is human*.

you went to all this work, why didn't you ask me if I needed a sound-effects table?"

"I would have," the other replied, "but I was afraid you'd say no."

Help us find a rock 'n roll group to hang this name on: 'The Lingering Doubt!'

RADIO BLOOPER!

In March 1933, listeners to a Southern California radio station were startled to hear the announcer say, "And now we'll hear...my God, it's an *earthquake!*" And they did and it was.

The French enjoy listening to the T.S.F., or they once did. T.S.F. stood for ***telegraphie sans fil*** *or telegraphy without wire — radio!*

TV EXPECTATIONS!

Back in the experimental days of television, it was envisioned that TV would flash on-the-spot coverage of news events to motion-picture theaters. They hadn't conceived of the millions of home sets which would come.

Color TV had some interesting experimentation, too. One of the systems involved a rotating disc which was to be placed in front of the TV screen in your home. Unfortunately, if your screen was a 24-inch size, the color disc would have been some ten feet in diameter. You don't see too many of those.

Who says ***sadism*** *is dead? 'The Gong Show' ended that rumor... among other things!*

THIRTY YEARS IN A DRAFT!

The zipper was patented in 1893, but it didn't replace the fly buttons on men's trousers until the 1930's...ushering in the era of the hasty recovery.

Another item women borrowed from men — ***the petticoat!*** *Thanks, ladies!*

The practice of having a shower for a bride-to-be has a romantic background. It seems that a father in the Netherlands thought he could break up a romance between his daughter and her impoverished boy friend by refusing to give her a dowry. So her friends got together and showered her with gifts. Exit irate father! Enter the shower!

Sure signs of affluence: buying your own paper clips; discarding used gift paper!

THE STRIP ACT!

In Turin, Italy in late 1977, a television station offered a live striptease quiz show from midnight until dawn. It was an instant success.

It seems contestants were teachers, clerks, housewives, etc. The emcee made a telephone call. If a man was reached and answered a question correctly, the contestant had to remove one item of clothing; an incorrect answer called for her to add clothing. The rules reversed when telephone contact was made with a woman.

Apparently, nudity, or the prospect of it, was not the program's primary attraction. For example, one amateur stripper, down to her bra, panties and stockings, then was required to take off one of the three remaining items.

The camera zoomed in as she began fumbling with her stockings. Between jigging about to avoid the blank stare of the camera and trying to unhinge her hose, her bra strap broke. With a wild clutch, she caught the bra at half-mast only to have her panties and hose slither slowly to the floor.

A Turin business executive described the program as "of tremendous social and cultural importance."

Describe the cultural aspects of TV in one word or less and win a trip to Vile, Idaho!

APPLAUSE, APPLAUSE!

When the Romans wished to show their approval of a performance, they had several options. To indicate mild approval, they snapped their fingers. Applauding was a sign they liked it even more. And the acme of approval was a wild flapping of the end of one's toga. Then there were the emperors and their succinct gestures to gladiators in the Colosseum — thumbs up, good show; thumbs down, good-bye!

In Ireland, the magazine ***Rogue***
Was once, begorrah, in vogue;
For, it's to Eire apparent
That costumes transparent
Hide not even a Rogue-girls' brogue.

OF BISHOPS AND BABIES!

Back in the days when it took a lot of yardage to make robes for the wealthy, one of the boys in the clothing game came up with a pure white silk. Going to Greek for a good hard-sell name, he came up with *diaper* (pure white). Then they added gold threads and made it into the most expensive clerical robes. Around the 14th Century, the English use *diaper cloth* for tablecloths. Because of its softness and absorbency it came to its present use, but we don't know quite how.

If we're to believe TV commercials, most infants must be badly neglected — after all, their mothers spend most of their waking hours discussing diaper absorbency!

KILLING TWO BARRELS WITH ONE BOAT!

Warehousing bourbon while it aged was an expensive proposition. Some clever Kentuckian offered barrels of whisky to an Ohio riverboat-line as ballast. The rocking motion of the boat speeded the aging so he didn't charge the boatmen a dime.

Rye whisky is a perverse drink!

BELIEVE IT IF YOU WANT!

On the pretext that the British forces might capture Philadelphia in 1776, the Continental Congress held its regular meetings in a Baltimore Tavern. Apparently, the surroundings were congenial, since they continued to meet there in 1777. Between deliberations and libations it was a very good time!

Before knocking beer, remember that Vassar College was founded and endowed by brewer, Mathew Vassar.

FATHER PIETRO'S FRISKY AS A KID!

History may say otherwise, but we like the old tale about the discovery of coffee better than dull accounts with facts and dates.

Picture a monastery on the coast of the Arabian Peninsula. The monks began to notice that when their goats fed on the berries of a certain bush, they became lively as all get-out.

The Arabian Peninsula being a trifle boring in those pre-gusher days, the monks decided to find out if their goats knew something they didn't. So they chewed on some of the berries. Ptooi — awful! Then they boiled the berries. Worse yet!

By this time, determined to pursue the matter through perdition or high water, they fricasseed the berries, sauteed them in camel butter and even marinated them in date wine. They roasted a few. Not too bad, but still they weren't getting the same kicks their goats were.

Work at the monastery had come to a halt. *The berry problem had to be solved.* Finally, Father Yuban, idly toying with his mortar and pestle, started pulverizing the roasted berries. Smelled nice. So he boiled some water and added the powder.

Things almost got back to normal after the great discovery. In fact, there was a frantic pace to their work. They tried coffee breaks, but still there was a certain nerve-jangling after-effect. Just about then is when Father Sanka had a brainstorm, but perhaps you've heard enough...

Don't knock drinking! How do you think we got the upside-down cake?

THE POLITICS OF PORT WINE!

In the early 18th Century, during the reign of Great Britain's Queen Anne, the English were on the outs with the French, again.

RIDDLE: Do the Japanese have a proverb about drunkenness?

ANSWER: You bet your sake cup they do: First the man takes a drink; then the drink takes a drink; then the drink takes the man.

They even took the desperate step of boycotting French wines. To save a thirsting nation, the Queen's Minister in Lisbon arranged to trade British woolens for the wine named after the Portuguese city from which it was shipped, *Oporto*. In order to assure a pleasing reception for their product, the Portuguese vintners spiked the *Port* with brandy. No one has been able to touch the British Port consumption rate ever since.

Tiny Dollop says he won't come out against sobriety until he's tried it.

A VOTRE SANTE!

In spite of the fact that to be a gladiator in ancient Rome was great sport, those to be opponents that day in the arena often drank a glass of wine together...before. There was always the chance the other chap might somehow slip a mickey into one's wine, so they poured the wine back and forth between the two glasses until it was completely mixed.

It caught on, and the custom was taken up by non-gladiators as a polite way of showing friendship. They continued to mix the wine, just in case.

Finally, when poisoning one's associates went out of vogue, there was no need for the mixing precaution. People then simply clinked their glasses together.

The poisoning craze also led to the custom we still practice: having the host pour a bit from the bottle into his own glass first, then drinking it to prove to guests they had a good chance of making it through the evening alive.

In later days, but prior to *the cork*, the Italians topped the wine with oil to preserve its flavor. It was a pretty lousy host who would let his guests get a wine with oil, so he poured it off.

If it weren't for winos, we'd be up to our lavalieres in muscatel.

THAT OLD PEARL IN THE VINEGAR STUNT!

Aesop — not the fable writer, but another venerable Greek — was dying to have the most expensive drink in the world. He waltzed off with the record, in a breeze, when he dissolved a $40,000 pearl in vinegar and tossed it off.

Queen Cleopatra must have read about it in Cholly Thebe's column. Quick as you can bite an asp, she bet Marc Antony she could put on a banquet costing $2 million (and remember, the dollar hadn't depreciated much in those days). She never would have made her quota if she hadn't ripped off an earring containing the world's largest pearl and dropped it into the vinegar. When she drank up, she topped the magic $2 million mark.

The puzzling part to us is why there was so much vinegar-drinking going on in those days. Are we missing something?

The word **alcohol** *comes from an Arabic word for a powder used to paint the eyelids. Let's just have a little glass of* **mascara** *and forget the whole thing!*

WHOOPEE IN THE ARCTIC!

One of the tribes of the Aleut Indians of Alaska called themselves *Hoocheno*. Having little else to do on one of those three-month nights, they dabbled with *spiritus frumenti* and came up with a product that would scald the hide off a full-grown polar bear.

An adventurous American, wandering through the *Hoocheno's* territory, was treated to the tribe's cocktail. During his recovery three months later in a Seattle hospital, he told doctors he had drunk with the *Hoocheno*. Soon strong spirits had a new nickname — *hooch*. The adventurous American's petrified innards were displayed in a Seattle real-estate office, until the jar exploded and flattened the building.

It's not polite to drink champagne from ladies' slippers. Unsanitary, too!

GET YOUR FORK OUT OF THAT OLIVE!

Don't you love the stuffy condescension of etiquette experts. We presume it's their intention to instruct the louts of the world, but their tone is enough to drive a man to vulgarity. To make the point, we've culled some high-class trivia from a book on etiquette.

"Never pick up a napkin which has slipped from your lap to the floor." *Death by firing squad is the suitable manner that comes to mind for punishing violators.*

"Bid good-evening to departing guests from your drawing-room. Accompanying one's guests to the front door is permissible, if one is living informally." *Living informally is that boorish state in which one removes his clothing before bathing.*

"When ill-bred persons persist in conversation while you are endeavoring to enjoy a talking picture, summon the usher. Instruct him to inform the manager, who, in turn, will request the disturbers to

RIDDLE: In royalty, is an Earl ranked above a Count?

ANSWER: The jolly English at it again. They have *Viscounts*, but instead of calling the next rank a *Count*, they make him an *Earl*. An *Earl's* wife is a *Countess*. (Shame, isn't it, we like the sound of *Earless*...but where would she wear her earrings?)

discontinue their conversation or leave the premises." *In dreadful contrition, of course.*

"While to address one's male parent as Dad was at one time considered extremely bad form, it is now *de rigueur* and will not connote inferior breeding." *Father, or in your case, Dad, wasn't that a striped ass ape I saw running through the foyer?*

"When meeting the first member in a receiving line, one must say, "I am Mrs.____." *This makes most men feel silly.*

"The olive is not to be eaten with a fork. One is to secure the olive between the thumb and forefinger." *Is it permitted to shake the gin from the olive first?*

"Should one discover a bone in one's mouth while dining, grasp it in the same fashion as the olive, remove it unobtrusively and lay it on the left side of your plate." *We wish Aunt Hazel had known that. A stickler for table manners, she simply choked to death.*

"The cultured procedure for eating a sandwich is to use a fork." *When was the last time you were out to the ball-park, sister?*

"When men and women are seated alternately at a dinner table, they should be served in sequence, regardless of sex." *Gee, at our place sex isn't allowed at the dinner table.*

"We were asked recently, perhaps with some jocularity, the proper manner in which to spread jelly upon bread at the table. Of course, it is definitely incorrect to spread jelly upon bread at the table. One should consume a small portion of bread, then transport a lesser portion of jelly to the mouth on the tip of one's fork." *Pardon me, Madam, I fear I have gulped the whole mess.*

"Upon completion of a meal, lay your napkin beside your plate, preferably at the right, although the left is somewhat acceptable. One's fork and knife are to be placed slightly to the right of the center on the plate. The tines of the fork must be in the upward position. The cutting edge of the knife must face the center of the plate." *Then place your wine goblet on your head, and as the wine trickles down your forehead, bray like a donkey!*

Throwing a meal on the floor and inviting your guests to root in it, is a matter of questionable taste.

If Cardinal Richelieu were among us today, he'd grow apoplectic at the sight of a toothpick dispenser near the cash register of many restaurants.

In the Cardinal's day, table knives had pointed tips. After watching his guests pick their teeth with their knives after countless dinners, he put his foot down. He had his servants file the knife tips to a round end. The standard table knife still bears the stamp of the Cardinal's sensitivity.

Al Fresco makes his own horseradish...using one of each.

THE AMERICAN COLONIAL LEGAL MIND AT PLAY!

A Massachusetts Colony edict stated, "Anybody who is found observing by abstinence from labor, feasting, or any other way, any such day as Christmas day, shall for every such offense be fined five shillings." Translation: you'd better work hard, avoid big meals and all other folderol on Christmas and any other day that faintly resembles Christmas, or you pay up. Or did they mean it was a crime to abstain from labor *and* feasting?

All things require skill but an appetite.
G.H. Hebert

COD FISH A LA NEW ORLEANS!

How can we expect people from other countries to understand us? For example, January 8 is set aside for celebrating New Orleans Day...but only in Massachusetts. Of course, it has to do with the Battle of New Orleans in the War of 1812, but wouldn't you think Louisiana might get into the act, too?

Presidents John Adams, Thomas Jefferson and James Monroe all died on July 4th.

TRICK OR TULLAMORE DEW!

The Irish go about in costumes and masks and muck up the area as we do on Hallowe'en. Only they do it on December 27 and it's called the Day of the Wren. The sensible ones stay at home with a drop of Tullamore Dew or similar beverage.

The shamrock isn't a pagan Irish emblem, me bucko! St. Patrick used the three-leafed shamrock to get across the idea of the Holy Trinity!

RIDDLE: Where do the largest crowds gather for the Fourth of July?

ANSWER: You wouldn't have believed Denmark, so we checked and our man on Denmark said, "Absolutely!" The Danes call it the *Rebild Festival*. No explanation of why they find our holiday so intriguing.

THREE BELLS AND WHAT THE HELL!

Londoners never look at *Big Ben* to tell the time when they are near the Parliament Tower of the Westminster Palace. Quite simply, old dear, *Big Ben* is the bell in the clock.

St. Swithin's Day is July 15. Make sure your **swith** *is cleaned and pressed.*

HAPPY PERSHIAN NOO EAR!

In Iran, they celebrate the New Year in March. The big day is called *Nourouz*. At our last New Year's Eve party we swear we heard several over-served guests crowing "Happy Nourouz," yet we had no idea there were Iranians present.

November is the month of Canada's Remembrance Day. We talked to thirty-one Canadians and not a one could remember what day in November!

HOLY CATS!

Every May the Belgian city of Ieper holds a *Feast of the Cats*. We've been too squeamish to inquire whether this is in honor of cats or is an indication of the menu.

The Icelandic version of Mardi Gras or Shrove Tuesday is called ***Bursting Day****...all because of the mammoth portions of pea soup and salt mutton they consume.*

ANOTHER DAY, ANOTHER DRACHMA!

The Egyptians and the Romans, good little chaps that they were, sensibly began the day at midnight as we do. The ancient Babylonians, for reasons known only to ancient Babylonians, insisted on saying the day started at sunrise. Not to be outdone, the Jews and ancient Greeks say the day begins at sunset. Frankly, we start our day when the newspaper boy bangs the paper against the front door.

Mimi Thrust owes the best two hours of her life to a faulty alarm-clock.

BE MY VALENTINE!

We're not going to let you maunder about with the sentimental notion that Valentine's Day began in honor of the Christian martyr, St. Valentine. We're going to tell it like it was.

The Romans, in pagan days, had a God for just about every contingency. For example, Lupercus was the deity they counted on to protect shepherds and their animals from wolves (shepherds carried heavy crooks, in case Lupercus was occupied elsewhere). In the middle of February each year, the Romans honored Lupercus with a gigantic bash called the *Lupercalia.*

The highlight of the festival was when the names of young women were dropped into a helmet. Then the Roman soldiers, one by one, drew out the names. The girl was then that soldier's sweetheart for a year...lock, stock and toga. Being someone's *valentine* in those days was no half-way measure.

NONSENSE
I love she,
I love she,
I wish her were die!
Her tell I
Her love I
But damn she, her lie!

RUN IT UP YOUR OWN DAMNED FLAGPOLE!

Even if you're a fly inspector in a trousers factory, you'll be surprised at your sudden sense of social contribution after you've spent some enchanted evening with Marketing People! We had this

RIDDLE: What two questions are the most difficult to answer?

ANSWER: For us they are: What do you send a sick florist? and *how* do mothers learn about all those things they tell their daughters not to do?

shattering experience recently, and now we can scarcely contain our self-esteem.

Despite this Marketing Person's pronouncement to the contrary, we refuse to accept, as a life-or-death matter, the fact that more senior citizens in Woonsocket, Rhode Island keep their bridgework from clattering with *Fang Cement* then there are teen-age marmoset breeders in Salem, Oregon.

When our rejection of his stimulating data became apparent, Marketing Person cried, "But look at the demographics, man. They're skewing out of control," to which we wished to applaud. "Don't you realize the nature of the problem," he continued, mustering his last ounce of pomposity. "We have a huge array of couples — married and otherwise — out there, simply defying classification."

We missed the next batch of statistical declarations, fuzzily contemplating the various possibilities of couples he listed as *otherwise* then married. Up until then, we had been content with but one possibility other than married.

"Picture, if you will," he intoned majestically, waving a chubby fist toward the window, (as if to imply his demographic sample stood at mute attention some thirty-eight stories above the street), "a giant consumer pool averaging thirty-five thousand dollars per annum — that's per year — and we can't figure out how to get at them."

We repressed a "Bully for them!"

"To fathom the extent of our dilemma," which wasn't at all what we had in mind for his dilemma, "these newly affluent couples may go to a fine French restaurant in frayed blue jeans, demand hominy grits with syrup and then order six liters of Mouton Rothschild. I mean, really...where do we place them?"

Devil's Island would have been our suggestion, but we'd dropped off to sleep by then.

Why is it that the time you need a vacation most is when it is just ending?

TRANSLATION OF STATE MOTTOES!

All our states have mottoes...mostly in Latin or French (Hawaii's is in Hawaiian). Quite a few aren't much clearer after they're translated. *It grows as it goes* happens to be the motto of New Mexico, and it leaves us with the thought of a casual, unplanned way of life.

There's an antiquated majesty to Massachusetts' *With the sword she seeks calm repose under liberty*, but we still need an interpreter. Connecticut, not to be outdone in the battle of confusion by its sister state, adopted a motto that reads *He who transplanted sustains.* When you've unraveled its meaning, let us know.

Oklahoma, on the other hand, comes right out in support of the virtue of honest work with *Labor conquers all.* Kansas evidently had a similar thought in mind — *To the stars by hard ways.*

Is it safe to assume that Oregon was praising self-reliance with these words: *She flies with her own wings*?

Now, Maryland had the foresight to adopt two mottoes. One of them is a mind-boggler of the first water — *Deeds masculine, words feminine!*

You probably would not have read any of this had you known what *our* motto is: *ex nihilo nihil fit*...which means *From nothing, nothing comes!*

To make apples turn over, speak in a low, firm voice. When they do as you command, reward them with a flaky crust.

THE FIRST WHITE MEN!

There once lived a man who is said to have been good for nothing.

But one day he metamorphosed himself into an Eagle. He went and lived upon a high, steep mountain and, coming down, killed people every day.

One day a little man who had decided to kill him went up the mountain; finally, he came to the place where the Eagle lived...the Eagle was away, but his wife was at home.

The woman told him that he must hide himself, for it was about time for the coming of the Eagle.

The little man at once transformed himself into a fly and hid himself near a pile of dead bodies.

In a few hours came the Eagle with more dead bodies. After eating his dinner, being weary from his long journey, he lay down and went to sleep.

The little man came out from his hiding place, cut off the Eagle's head, and poured warm water over the dead bodies, and they came back to life again. But some had been there so long that they turned white; and when the little man tried to talk to them, they talked different language. So he separated them from the *Indians* and called them *white men.*

A Yakima Indian woman, upon being complimented for the fineness with which her beef patties were ground, replied, "No grind. Chaw.

HEARTLESS ARTICHOKE AND OTHER BLOCKBUSTERS!

Hang on to your underwear, we're about to defy the establishment and let you in on the good stuff they've been keeping from you.

The Internal Revenue Service is thinking of going *external*, too. Start nailing down your shrubbery and outdoor pets!

A circuit-court judge in Willowmush, Arizona said it is unlawful for amnesia victims to lead the life of Riley without Mrs. Riley's express permission.

Ditmus Oiter has perfected a heartless artichoke, so you can stop ripping away all those leaves — it will lead you nowhere.

A Japanese electronics wizard has developed a pliable television picture-tube. Now, viewers can squeeze up to eight hours of continuous entertainment onto their living room rugs, where they may watch it or walk on it barefooted.

The National Society for the Prevention of Wealth was evicted from its headquarters last week.

Due to some rather sloppy predictions over the past two years, you can expect weather forecasters to be downgraded to *threecasters* in the near future.

Nieman-Marcus has yet to announce if they will include, in their next Christmas catalog, a sable-lined compression chamber which will enable the sickeningly affluent to enjoy *the bends* in the comfort of their own homes.

Unless the new amphitheater at Barnstable, Mass. is finished by August 11, you can count on the Annual Cod-Kicking Contest being held elsewhere.

Don Rickles secretly blamed the failure of one of his early television failures on the Law of Gravity.

Englishman James Gibb amassed such a fortune from his

invention of Table Tennis, he was able to build a summer home in Ping and a winter abode in Pong.

Botanists will soon be shocking you with a new willow genus which will not only weep, but will also roll over and play dead. This will follow on the heels of the already announced fruit tree that bears *figs* in the summer and *newtons* in the winter.

Expect Anita Bryant to turn thumbs down on the lead in the upcoming musical adaptation of Edmund Spenser's *The Faerie Queene*, if the offer should be made.

Madison Avenue insiders predict a revolution in air travel as soon as Mid-Iowa Airlines takes the wraps off its new plan — *Fly On the Outside for Half Fare!*

Automotive experts have long held that a car consumes excessive quantities of fuel when decelerating. If governmental objections can be overcome, look forward to far better mileage from the brakeless car of the future.

The new 14-pound *natural* ballet slipper is being tested by the Texarkana Chili Parlor Ballet Troupe.

The zoo in East Ningus, Wyoming is holding back all announcements on their experimental mating of a bear and a jackass, but an enterprising photographer on the local newspaper reports he has graphic proof of two healthy *bear-asses*.

Dimples Tremayne, until recently a powerful member of the Fright Committee in the Pure Food and Drug Administration, says that agency may soon reveal its findings that breathing is hazardous to one's health. She claimed the announcement has been delayed pending evaluation of a recent finding that bald eagles, when fed a strict diet of hominy grits in sorghum, have suddenly sprouted long strands of auburn hair.

Cabbage leaves, tightly rolled in the Wall Street Journal, can be extremely effective in swatting flies.

Due to pollution of Australian streams, the *duck-billed platypus* now quacks plaintively.

In an exclusive interview with economist Cicatrix Plasma, author of *How I Achieved Poverty on Less Than a Dollar a Week*, we learned there is a well-conceived plot among radicals to deny many Americans their God-given right to squalor. He added, that the finely-honed machinery of the FHA should foil the plan.

John, the new magazine for hookers, debuts with an hilarious spoof on VD.

Dak Seneila's new hit ballad — *I'm Up to My Ass in Hogwash Over You* — is headed for the top of the charts.

British horticulturists have developed a new walnut species with the shell on the inside.

A nationally known television newscaster recently protested that he doesn't have enough time to give the news if he must be constantly annoyed with facts.

THE ANNUAL TRIVIA AWARDS

Many enormously insignificant events go unnoticed. Our folly is we notice! Now we share our folly with you, whether you wish it or not. So, we salute the people and events which have made us all realize it is never late enough!

— Lusty Bumfender: for memorizing Paradise Lost in the vulgar edition.

— Standish Off: for crossing the squid with the herring to produce the *squipper* — an eight-armed kipper.

— Doc Severinson: for out-sparkling Liberace...in wardrobe.

— The Panama Canal: for raising such a fuss about landlords.

— Charles O. Finley: on general principles.

— Tom Watson: for failing to win the Madagascar Open, even if he didn't enter.

— Charlie's Angels: for raising insipidity to an art form.

— CHiPS: for bringing the buffalo back from oblivion.

— Billy Martin: for making tantrum out of old epithets.

— Bella Abzug: for proving that milliners are underpaid.

— Kissy Henrigger: for crossing a Buff Orpington hen with a White Leghorn rooster to give us white-horned chicks with buff leg-orps.

— MacDonalds: for doing it all for you instead of us.

— Hayes J. Wood: for gathering his wits about him...or at least half of them.

— Premier Kosygin: for keeping his mitts off the internal affairs of Disneyland.

— Ferngrowers: for turning the whole damned world into a hothouse

— Jug Wines: for proving the French have no monopoly on *vin ordinaire.*

— Reading Teachers: for beating their walls against stone heads.

— Idi Amin: for sticking around Uganda most of the time.

— Frozen Foods Mfgs.: for printing on the package so it can be distinguished from the contents.

— Hang-gliders: for demonstrating that intelligence is not soaring out of control.

— Kuwait: for their offer to buy Cleveland and haul it off to the Persian Gulf.

— Brewers: for dietetic beer. Next to go: the foam. Then the fluid. Finally, we'll have a hop-impregnated cardboard square painted with yeast.

— Pete Rozelle: for his charitable attitude toward the blind in striped shirts.

— Telly Savalas: for general lollipoppery.

— Rock Music: for lowering the threshold of patience.

— The Price of Gold: for keeping pace with international idiocy.

— Plop, Plop, Fizz, Fizz: for giving America a tune it can hum again.

— TV: for thrift. Now we can have a whole week of viewing one 60-minutes show.

— U.S. Army: for painting the entire government olive drab.

— OPEC: for doing unto others what they're dying to do unto you.

— The National Debt: for maintaining vigorous growth in the face of poverty.

— Jerry Brown: for a sideways glimpse of yestermorrow.

— Newspapers: for abandoning the archaic task of proofreading.

— Bisty Wumpers: for his drain-opening story of a sick plumber, *The Elbow Joint's Connected to the Pocketbook.*

— Ronald Reagan: for keeping pace with Marshall Tito in the Hair War.

— CIA: for telling it like it should have wasn't.

— Weather Forecasters: for giving us all hope that we can rise above the floodtide of our mistakes.

— IRS: for standing behind its motto: *Leave a little if you have to.*

— Super-Jocks: for using a dollar to pry the *w* loose from wretch.

— Chris Henkel and Burt Rowdy: for...er...where are we?

— Toothpaste Mfgs.: for grabbing the flouride between its teeth and running amok.

— Dolphins: for keeping secret their language and thereby their opinion of man.

— TV Award Shows: for the ability to combine a handful of envelopes, any old accounting firm, some sparsely gowned ladies and some uncomfortable men with a ceaseless string of banal acceptance speeches. Spectacular...zzzz!

— Liberal politicians: for turning left at every corner, thereby going about in circles.

— Conservative politicians: for doing the same to the right and avoiding headlong collisions with the Liberals.

SEND US YOUR NOMINATIONS FOR NEXT YEAR'S TRIVIA AWARDS!

If we don't like your submissions sufficiently, we will send you money for the privilege of printing them and thereby distributing the misery more equitably. Send all entries, along with a self-addressed, stamped envelope, to Doneve Designs, Inc., P.O. Box 1072, Saratoga, California 95070.

ABOUT THE AUTHORS...

Donner and Eve Paige Spencer, husband and wife, draw upon their dual talents of writing and editing. Donner Spencer gave the broadcasting and recording industries a twenty-year shot before plunging into writing full time. Eve Paige Spencer began her book career on the editorial side as one of the founders of the now famous *Galaxy* science fiction magazine. She, too, put in several hitches in radio and television.

The Spencers have co-authored several mystery short stories. They will soon be publishing another co-authorship work — a novel — along with their son, E.J. Gold, a well-known writer.

Spare time being at a premium, the Spencers confine their other activities to preparation of textbooks in large print for the visually handicapped and a host of art projects (Eve is an internationally exhibited artist in copper enameling and silver cloisonne).

The irreverent style of *A Treasury of Trivia* stems from the Spencers' belief that trivia is to be enjoyed.